# STANLEY
# CLASSIC
# CAR
# YEARBOOK

# STANLEY
# CLASSIC
# CAR
# YEARBOOK

## THE ENTHUSIAST'S COMPENDIUM VOL. 2

## JOHN STANLEY

**OSPREY**
AUTOMOTIVE

**DEDICATION**
To my first Mini. She gave me freedom – and I gave her a hard time.

Published in Great Britain in 1998 by Osprey,
a division of Reed Consumer Books Ltd,
Michelin House, 81 Fulham Road, London SW3 6RB
and Auckland, Melbourne

© 1998 John Stanley/Reed Books

ISBN 185532 704 8

Editor: Shaun Barrington
Sub-editor: Judith Millidge
Index: Janet Dudley
Design Manager: Mike Moule
Design: the Black Spot
Stanley Yearbook logo: Pete Mays

Printed in Spain.

# CONTENTS

## AUTHOR ACKNOWLEDGEMENTS

My sincere thanks are due to Jonathan Parker, Shaun Barrington and the Osprey team for supporting and realising my ideas, to Paul Kime for his designs, again to Mike Kettlewell for research assistance, to Reflections Colour Laboratories of Norwich, to Symon Biles for his Porsche model constructions and to Mario Vignali of Graypaul for extensive cooperation.

I am personally indebted to Peter Garnier for both his kind foreword and enthusiasm, to my distinguished panel of judges and the invaluable input from a large number of experts, archivists and manufacturers.

For the enormous task of creating and maintaining the Price Guide, my sincere thanks to Shaun Biles and Barry Sample for computer programming, to Tom Dean for specialist currency data and finally to Janis for her huge contribution to the administration of this book and unfailing personal support.

## PICTURE ACKNOWLEDGEMENTS

Andrew Barrington: 157(br).
Tony Beadle: 83(t).
Beaulieu Motor Museum: 79, 82, 126, 130, 148(t), 155, 164, 168, 169, 178, 179, 180(t), 181(b).
Chris Bennett: 128, 129, 210.
Peter Burn: 196, 197(b).
Andrew Dee: 1, 3, 115, 146, 170, 190.
Demon Tweeks: 231.
Guy Griffiths: 85(t).
Manufacturers: 17, 19(b), 24(t), 29(t), 31(t), 37, 44, 49, 55, 56, 61, 68(t), 70(l), 75(b), 76(t), 83(b), 97-104, 106-110, 112-114, 118-121, 123, 138, 142, 143, 149, 151(t), 159, 162, 163, 176, 177, 193, 208, 209, 216, 217,220-223, 243, 245.
David McLavin: 13, 14.
Men & Motors: 9(b), 10.
Andrew Morland: 28(tr), 33(t), 65(t), 105, 127, 131, 132, 160, 167, 172, 174, 188, 189, 198, 204(t).
Mike Moule: 136(t), 137(b).
Richard Newton: 181(t), 207(t).
Andrew Orr: 77(b), 86-94. 171, 218, 219.
Quadrant Picture Library: 53(t), 78, 80, 81, 136(b), 137(t), 144, 154, 206.
RAC: 11.
Reed Consumer Books: 8, 20(t), 36(b), 41, 57; 117, 122, 125 (Nicky Wright), 133, 134(t), 135(t), 141(t) (Ian Dawson), 145, 147 (Dawson), 148(b) (Wright), 156(t), 158 (Dawson), 160, 173 (John Lamm), 180(b), 184, 191 (Wright), 194(t), 199, 200(t), 205 (Dawson), 207(b) (Wright), 212, 213.
David Sparrow: 45(t), 152(t), 204(b).
Janis Stanley: front jacket, main image.
John Stanley: 4, 9(t), 18-77, unless otherwise indicated – (portraits of the author by Janis Stanley), 96, 111(m), 124, 135(b), 150, 151(b), 165, 166, 175, 182, 183, 185, 186, 187, 192, 194(b), 195, 200(b), 201, 202, 203, 211, 214, 215, 224-230, 232-239.
Duncan Wherrett: 240-242, 244, 246(bl), 247(t).

# FOREWORD
## by Peter Garnier

Many books have been written about Classic cars, each of them helping to increase the appreciation – and the preservation – of a way of motoring long past. But it has taken the discerning nature of John Stanley, with his accomplishments as a best selling author to approach the subject in his own informed and enthusiastic way, discussing not only today's Classics but also those of future years.

It is said, given of course an in-born love of cars – that we turn instinctively to the models of our youth in search of bygone joys. One might expect, therefore, that John, who was born during the war, should look to the Classic era … which he does in a new and original manner. A member of the Guild of Motoring Writers, he is well qualified to assess the merits – and otherwise – of the cars he has driven. In this capacity for the 1998 edition he has driven and put into perspective over half a millon pound's worth of today's outstanding sporting cars – all aspiring to become tomorrow's Classics. These include the mid-engine MGF, the Porsche Boxster, Lotus Elise, the new V8 Jaguar XK8, Alfas, BMWs, Mercedes, the Aston Martin DB7; and clearly love at first sight between the author and the 155mph Fiat Coupé Turbo, with its Pininfarina styling, generous accommodation and modest price of just £21,000.

Inevitably, he has a considerable, and a growing, following because Classics, cared for responsibly, can not only recapture one's youth but provide everyday transport too; whilst the numbers qualifying for this classification – those over 20 years old – are on the increase year by year.

If you already own a Classic you may well learn something new about it, and its forebears; and, perhaps more particularly, of the variations in value since the day of its announcement. As a Classic owner I found several bits to be profoundly interesting – not least the very intelligent price/value tables which must have taken ages to calculate. If you are contemplating buying one, then you will be helped greatly in your choice. Either way, you cannot fail to be charmed by the contemporary advertising artwork that was used to advertise – and to flatter unrestrainedly – a few of his subjects when they were first announced.

*Peter Garnier*

# WHO CARES?

## *Expanding our horizons*

Some people would have us consider cars classics only after they have passed the arbitrary threshold of 20 years – and some demand far more on the clock – yet they will grudgingly accept that the occasional younger supercar might have a fast track to this status. You will, however, have to agree with their choice to remain friends. The truth is like food, music, art – it's a matter of personal choice. As before, I make no apology for the fact that this book is filled with my classic car landscape but trust that my comments sharpen your own opinions and understanding. This may be a Classic Car Yearbook, but we certainly have no intention of sticking to any arbitrary rulings.

This year's edition boasts probably the most exhaustive look at contemporary sports cars ever undertaken by a single writer. Not one of them formally qualifies as an authentic classic car – yet. The chapter on the Works Alfa race car doesn't qualify on the twenty-year ruling either, and nor does the feature on the current incarnation of the Mini Cooper S.

True motoring enthusiasts just love cars, admire their performance, appearance, and it is their adoption of particular cars that is the real hallmark of a classic. I have driven over one million pound's worth of models for this edition and it's just the most brilliant job in the world. If you love the excitement of driving in fine machines, the seduction of expressive bodywork, then you too will not care if it happens to be 20 days or 20 years old. 'Classic' denotes cars which succeed, be it the practical loyalty of a Minor Traveller or the gut wrenching intentions of a 200mph Italian supercar.

That's not to suggest this book ignores the intake of new Stanley Hundred candidates, nor the strange story of misadventure which created the successful Triumph Herald range. No post-war engine can match the sheer scale of success achieved by the fabulous XK engine; nor is there a better rally school-master than World Champion Roger Clark, two more featured. Exploring the forgotten world of past motoring magazines brought back waves of memories – and indeed old friends – whilst the chapter on considering a Ferrari purchase attempts to be more factual than the usual offering, which tends to leave the reader aside whilst the journalist plays.

At last year's British Grand Prix I was fortunate enough to be the guest of the RAC Motor Sports Association who were the organisers. Apart from enviable parking arrangements and good food it meant penthouse hospitality from which to view events. Inevitably it was a room full of the auto-motive great and good: and whilst the world's fastest race cars circulated, conversations kept returning to classic cars. A young woman in her twenties recounted her nearly completed Morris Minor restoration whilst the RAC MSA Executive Chairman Sir John Rogers chronicled an enviable list of his cars past and present. There was something rather reas-suring about his reminiscences. There we were looking out over Silverstone with the RAC airship above us, the circuit festooned in his organisation's logo, 20,000,000 watching the build-up to his event on television, and yet there he was detailing the restoration and tunning repairs on his MGC GT. Whilst we talked, a cavalcade of 27 RAC historic vehicles moved slowly round the circuit, A35, A40, Ford Anglia, Morris J Type, Bedford and Mini vans, Land Rovers, Escorts, Marinas, Metros – right back to Austin Chummys. All these had been bought or restored over just 18 months by Norman Winchester, RAC Special Events Manager, as part of their Centenary celebrations.

Ginny Buckley and Mike Rutherford are two of the regular Granada television presenters bringing their individual motoring opinions to the screen.

Sir John clearly feels passionately about both motor sport and classic cars. The RAC he feels has played a major part in the growth of classics with the introduction of their Classic car events such as the Norwich Union, the Haynes event and the Chrysler Euro Classic. Every one becomes fully subscribed. The Norwich Run has had over 13,000 entrants in its eleven years of staging.

However fancy your invitation, leaving a Grand Prix by road requires patience and for the next two hours we simply sat, occasionally crept, through the improvised one-way system of tiny back lanes in rural

Working on Men and Motors provides some dream drives. Here are two.

Another contributor to Granada's new onslaught on motoring programmes has been the famed racing driver Stirling Moss. His views on motoring topics never fail to interest.

Satellite programmes often suffer from limited production funds, but what they can offer is a chance for subjects to be covered in depth. This report on the Aston Martin DB7 and Jaguar XK8 could therefore be far longer than possible on terrestrial channels.

Northamptonshire. It snaked through small communities peppered with resigned locals and occasional kids hustling race day souvenirs. Briefly I caught sight of a lone man standing at a low white paling gate between the hedges. I could not see his face but he was holding a goblet and dressed in a smart open necked shirt on which was sewn a small Union Jack and a breast badge of the Reliant Scimitar Car Club. Clearly, he had watched the televised race and then settled at his gate to catch the passing spectators, and to quietly express his very own motoring involvement through his club. From the race organiser's Chairman to this garden gate enthusiast, the passion for cars has a wide constituency.

This love affair has been well catered for through decades of motoring magazines – as our chapter 'Cover Stories' underlines, but on television (in the UK at least) the coverage has been less even. Left field series such as the recent BBC *Driving School* are great fun and do record public feelings pin sharp. Motor sport itself receives clinically successful

Norman's work. Some of the fabulous collection of 27 RAC service vehicles which Norman Winchester acquired and restored for the RAC to illustrate its century of service to the British motorist. The earliest is the 1912 Phelon & Moore motorcycle, the 1990s are represented by Isuzu Citations. In between are lots of small Austins, Morris, Bedfords and even Bubble cars.

coverage but general motoring and more especially enthusiast's interests suffer from tussles for control between backroom power and presenters hellbent on personal fame. There are certainly moments of distinction such as Tiff Needell's unrehearsed excitement as he track tested the F1 McLaren, but by and large we are subjected to over-rehearsed scripts and manicured jibes designed to highlight the personality rather than the car in question. Even the *Car is the Star* series, though enjoyable to watch, failed to embrace real owners, real advice, owners clubs.

I have recently become involved again with television, this time as a presenter for Granada/Sky's *Men & Motors* channel. As with any satellite channel they are working on small budgets, which inevitably shows from time to time, but there is an authenticity which is rare, and which prompted my interest. Unlike rivals, they enjoy the privilege of more time for classic programming, which producer Peter Baker uses to the full. When they look at a motor show the camera walks around the event, stops and talks with

those on stands. It might bore you, just as the show itself could, but it will let you 'see' the show and feel you have been there. Talking to enthusiasts at motoring events offers stories script writers could never dream up and, if you are assessing a car, there is enough time to provide its background story. Granada wanted a piece on the Jaguar XK8 and the Aston Martin DB7 I was testing for the Yearbook and the film lasted a full 15 minutes – because the cars' backgrounds warranted the time. I hope this doesn't read too much like a plug for a TV show: it is in fact a puff for books! Any books, perhaps this one, because they provide space for analysis and reflection, as I hope the test drive of sporting cars/sports cars included here demonstrates.

If there is some topic you strongly feel has not been covered sufficiently in books such as this, then let us know. We hope there is something here for the genuine enthusiast, for those who care. That man proudly wearing his club badge at his garden gate – now he really does.

# CLASSIC CAR OF THE YEAR
## *Conventional Wisdoms Shine*

RAY HUTTON
*European Editor of Car & Driver, contributor to Sunday Times, Company Car and Motor Trader, former Editor of Autocar, Vice–President of International Car of the Year Jury.*
*First Car – Morris Minor*

GEOFF BROWNE
*Editor of Classic Car Weekly, formerly Daily Telegraph Birmingham Post.*
*First Car – 1928 20hp Rolls-Royce*

GINNY BUCKLEY
*Television motoring presenter for Granada/Sky "Men & Motors" and ITV's "The Road Show".*
*First Car – VW Beetle 1600*

Placing cars in order of performance or value for money is a familiar sight in all the motoring journals – naturally reflecting the tastes of the journalist involved. It is true that the leading motoring journalists are the most knowledgable, but every day their work is focused on the latest models or a specific historic theme – no one asks them to stop and provide a non-technical vote from the heart. Our twelve judges are significant figures in the motoring world and span differing generations, different interests; together they represent an impressive repository of independent knowledge.

The chosen cars were all 1960s British open sports cars sold for under £1,000 (exc. purchase tax) and guidance on their personal ballot paper explained "Period styling and affection are as important as performance or innovation in Classic Cars". Unless a car endears itself to you, it will never survive to the 20-year classic qualification: maintaining a middle-aged car is far too expensive if you haven't made friends.

In a significant display of conformity this distinguished panel of judges has nominated the Austin Healey 3000 as the Classic Car of The Year. It is a runaway victory for the familiar big BMC Healey which so covered itself in motor sport glory. Ironically, many blame British Leyland for ending the Healey but in truth BMC themselves swung the axe before their absorption into BL. The message to car makers from such a personal vote of experts is that true drivers' cars build strong reputations, that quality will out. Hundreds of thousands of Spitfires were sold in its day, yet it languishes in last place now because of poor handling, whilst the basic Lotus Seven rests comfortably in second place through memories of its pin-sharp handling, its driving pleasures. Of course the car wasn't everbody's number one: if it were there would be no Classic Car movement! The MGB, MGA and TR3A had their

| THE FULL VOTE | | | | | | | | | | | | | |
|---|---|---|---|---|---|---|---|---|---|---|---|---|---|
| AUSTIN HEALY FROGEYE | 4 | 11 | 8 | 2 | 6 | 5 | 6 | 5 | 12 | 10 | 3 | 7 | 79 |
| AUSTIN HEALEY 3000 | 1 | 2 | 3 | 7 | 1 | 1 | 2 | 2 | 4 | 1 | 1 | 1 | 26 |
| DAIMLER SP250 | 7 | 8 | 6 | 12 | 10 | 12 | 1 | 11 | 6 | 2 | 6 | 2 | 84 |
| LOTUS SUPER 7 | 5 | 1 | 1 | 11 | 3 | 9 | 3 | 3 | 5 | 5 | 2 | 4 | 57 |
| MG MIDGET MKI-III | 6 | 4 | 11 | 3 | 11 | 5 | 7 | 4 | 11 | 6 | 8 | 10 | 86 |
| MGA 1600 MKII | 9 | 7 | 7 | 1 | 5 | 7 | 5 | 8 | 10 | 3 | 5 | 8 | 75 |
| MGB MKI | 3 | 6 | 9 | 4 | 7 | 2 | 11 | 1 | 3 | 9 | 9 | 11 | 75 |
| MORGAN 4/4 SER III-V | 12 | 9 | 5 | 10 | 2 | 11 | 12 | 7 | 7 | 8 | 12 | 12 | 107 |
| SUNBEAM ALPINE MK I-V | 11 | 10 | 2 | 8 | 4 | 10 | 4 | 9 | 8 | 4 | 11 | 6 | 87 |
| TRIUMPH SPITFIRE MKI-II | 10 | 12 | 12 | 9 | 9 | 8 | 10 | 6 | 9 | 7 | 7 | 9 | 108 |
| TRIUMPH TR3A | 8 | 3 | 10 | 5 | 8 | 3 | 9 | 10 | 1 | 12 | 4 | 5 | 78 |
| TRIUMPH TR4 | 2 | 5 | 42 | 6 | 12 | 3 | 8 | 12 | 2 | 11 | 10 | 3 | 78 |

fervent supporters. But as *Practical Classic's* Nick Larkin points out, the Healey is really easy driving – the "last of the hairy sports cars" reputation refers, extremely accurately, to the Works rally cars such as the one I featured in last year's edition.

## AUSTIN HEALEY 3000

Looks and Power – A Gentleman Adventurer's car.
**John Blauth**

The "Big Healey" must of necessity come first because of my two years–plus as a member of the BMC Works team, co–driving with Jack Sears.
**Peter Garnier**

A Supercar of its day with bags of character to match its strong performance.
**Sue Baker**

Back then it was the sports car that we all ached to own — eventually I did!
**Anthony Peagam**

Styling approaching perfection, power galore from wonderful BMC straight six and not the hairy unyielding brute legend would have you believe.
**Nick Larkin**

Sums up the 60s – it's a real stunner with plenty of raw power – British style at its best.
**Ginny Buckley**

## LOTUS SUPER 7

Its brilliant handling, its total involvement for the driver, its instant response. The wonderful concept of pure driving pleasure.
**Liz Turner**

Advanced sports car. Light, fast, responsive: Dedicated to the driver.
**Robert Coucher**

## MGA 1600 Mk II

Fifties style and fine handling.
**Geoff Browne**

## MGB Mk I

I've owned several of the nominated cars and when I think back, the memories of the MGB were all good. It was the only one never to let me down!
Jonathan Ashman

## DAIMLER SP250

Gem of an engine and styling with a great sense of humour.
Gavin Conway

## TRIUMPH TR3A

Sentimental – TR3 was my first sports car in the 1960s and you were either a TR person or an MG/Healey/Morgan person!
Ray Hutton

**ANTHONY PEAGAM**
*Group Public Relations Director –*
*AA, Ford Times, Drive Magazine,*
*TV Times editorship.*
*First Car – 1935 BSA Scout*

**SUE BAKER**
*Contributor to The Times, Daily*
*Telegraph, BBC Radio. Former Top*
*Gear presenter, Observer motoring*
*correspondent and past Chairman of*
*Guild of Motoring Writers.*
*First Car – 1958 Ford Popular*

**JOHN BLAUTH**
*Motoring Editor of ITV's The Road*
*Show, contributor to Daily Express,*
*The Independent and formerly*
*director of Complete Car.*
*First Car – Austin Healey Sprite*

**GAVIN CONWAY**
*Editor of Classic and Sportscar,*
*formerly senior staff writer for*
*Autocar.*
First Car – Ford Galaxie

**NICK LARKIN**
*Features Editor Popular Classic and*
*Practical Classics. Editor of GT-Eye.*
First Car – Ford Anglia 105E

**JONATHAN ASHMAN**
*Director of Major Events –*
*RAC MSA.*
First Car – Sunbeam Imp Sport

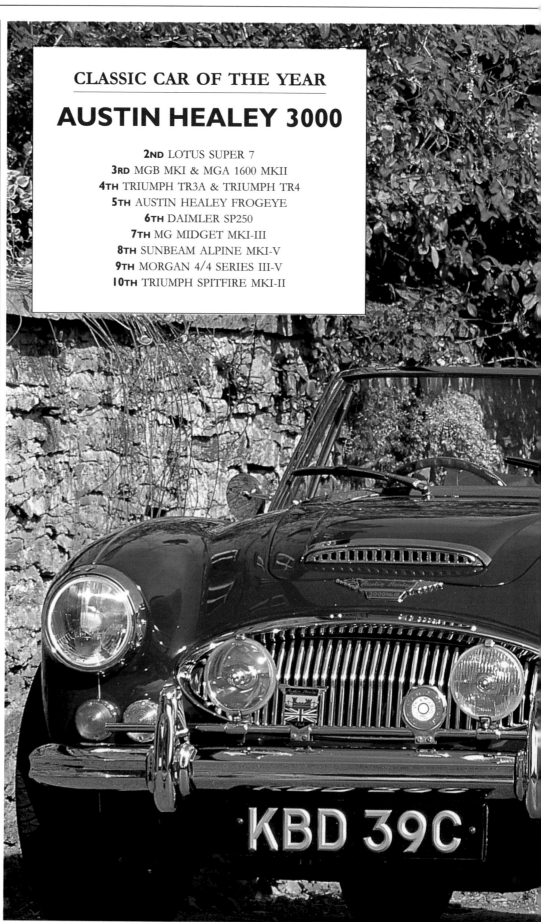

## CLASSIC CAR OF THE YEAR

# AUSTIN HEALEY 3000

**2ND** LOTUS SUPER 7
**3RD** MGB MKI & MGA 1600 MKII
**4TH** TRIUMPH TR3A & TRIUMPH TR4
**5TH** AUSTIN HEALEY FROGEYE
**6TH** DAIMLER SP250
**7TH** MG MIDGET MKI-III
**8TH** SUNBEAM ALPINE MKI-V
**9TH** MORGAN 4/4 SERIES III-V
**10TH** TRIUMPH SPITFIRE MKI-II

**PETER GARNIER**
*Sports, Deputy and then Editor of Autocar for 25 years. Motoring Author & former Guild of Motoring Writers Chairman.*
First Car – 1925 Jap-engined Morgan 3-wheeler

**ROBERT COUCHER**
*Editor of Classic Cars, Your Classic.*
First Car – Lancia Aurelia B20 GT

**LIZ TURNER**
*Editor of Ford magazine, formerly Chief Reporter for Autocar, contributor to BBC Radio 4, The Guardian, Classic Car.*
First Car – Nash Metropolitan convertible

# THE CLASS OF '98

## *How many of the world's best sporting cars are truly future classics?*

2 0,000 words of assessment on the very best sporting cars is far beyond any magazine's scope – such are editorial and advertising pressures. Most of the following models have been splashed across half a dozen pages, frequently in a head-to-head with another photogenic but ill-matched car. Designers and manufacturers battle for years to tailor a model for a precise niche in the market, only to be damned in a magazine comparison with another car costing 40 per cent more and aimed at different customers: It helps no one.

We are in danger of losing our motoring perspective under the weight of circulation wars and over scripted television reports. A nod, a wink and some line referring to 'the most fun with your trousers on', does not mean the rejected alternative hasn't been engineered and perfectly built to suit your motoring needs. Good one-liners have sold tabloid newspapers for years without the need to resort to balanced news coverage. Our personal judgement is easily influenced, and there is a similar danger that before long manufacturers will slip from serious investment to producing cosmetically-pleasing cars for such casual commentators.

The specialist sports section of the motor industry is small but hugely influential, for successful models attract substantial growth for manufacturers' mainstream products. Equally significant is the expansion of public interest in sports cars. Between 1987 and 1994 the European sports car sales figures quadrupled and the UK growth alone between 1994 and 1996 was 55%. In an industry that is increasingly fragmenting into niche markets, this is clearly a significant battlefield, and not surprisingly the showrooms are heaving with seductive offerings, all hoping to become classics.

The following pages contain probably the most comprehensive assessment of the leading contenders yet published. I have not been restricted on space, or influenced by potential advertisers, nor are the judgements the merger of anonymous editorial members' thoughts. They are my own undiluted impressions drawn from driving these cars on both public and private roads. I took the diminutive Elise into central London for meetings, I drove the Boxster across the UK into headwinds that were making the national news, even the Ferrari 355 endured a rush hour as well as open roads. It's fun to watch a model negotiate a race circuit chicane on full opposite lock, but it has, or should have, negligible significance on public roads. Track development is an important part of automotive progress, but the resultant models should be expected to suit our daily needs. The only aspect neglected in my appraisals was experience in slippery conditions, which the Almighty failed to deliver.

Each of these cars has been chosen and judged on its own merits. Naturally, comparative elements come into play, but the assessments have taken six months and over such a period there is time to view each one individually. The most satisfying cars may vary wildly in performance, accommodation and certainly cost, but each succeeds in offering specific values. There are deliberately no comparative tables matching all their acceleration figures, fuel consumption, and top speed – each is viewed on its own and from my findings I hope you can form your own opinions.

To create some editorial order I have tried to at least group the cars into types – though not necessarily the one the manufacturers' marketing teams would wish. Cars such as the Fiat Barchetta fall honourably into Sporting Cars, as does the BMW Z3 and the flawed Mercedes SLK which makes efforts to masquerade as a Sports Car. In that category the Lotus Elise and Porsche Boxster are pure sports car classics. The MGF in lower-tuned form straddled the borders, but its mid-engined configuration edged it across. The Alfa GTV probably ought to remain a Sporting Car, but the heady mix of glorious engine, gearbox and steering moved it on. The Grand Tourers are a mighty and glamorous breed in their own right.

The one maverick in the pack is the astonishing Fiat Coupé Turbo. It's unquestionably the freshest and most exciting car I have driven in some years, and its combination of qualities defies clarification. A £21,000 Fiat ought to sit alongside the BMW Z3 as a Sporting Car, but the machine can travel at 155mph and covers 0-60 in around 6.0 seconds – a match for every car except the £100,000 Ferrari. So logically it's a sports car – until you consider it has a greater passenger and luggage capacity that the Aston Martin or the Ferrari 355. So I have placed it as a GT. It shames virtually every car in one way or another, and Fiat must be congratulated on returning to powerful sports models after so many years.

As to which of these cars will be considered significant classics in 20 years, only time and public affection will tell. Certain are the superb Porsche and the stunning Ferrari, while the Jaguar's all round qualities ought to ensure its future. The Aston's looks and status buys insurance which I cannot extend to the flawed SLK or the MGF. The little Mazda that single-handedly launched the current sports car craze is now so much part of our motoring landscape that I fear it could endure a mid-life crisis. Like MGBs before them, they may cease to be special and suffer neglect, but those that survive to be 20 years old will be deservedly cherished.

This has taken a long time to prepare and has been a fabulous opportunity to drive everyone's dream cars. You would think 30 years of driving, competing and testing cars would reduce the excitement – it doesn't. There is nothing to compare with the deep satisfaction of matching your skills to a finely balanced sports car. Five months into these tests – and virtually every car experienced would make anyone blasé – when I approached the magnificent Ferrari and turned the key ... it was magic. As long as sports cars exist which have that 'tingle factor', future classics are guaranteed.

# MAZDA MX-5

PRESENCE ★★★★ Still very satisfying
GRUNT ★★★ Dated, but entertaining
CRUISING ★★★ Adequate
HANDLING ★★★★ Quintessential sports car
COMFORT ★★ All the basics
SPACE ★★★ Decent, if shallow boot
DASHBOARD ★★★ Ageing, yet functional
NIGGLES - Driving distraction of raised lights
BUYING - Still without real equal
RIVAL Fiat Barchetta – more style
         MGF – less practical

## OVERVIEW

There are so many cars in our lives: models that were going to change history, the way we drove, even the way we live. If every landmark launch had proved as important as the company hoped, we'd have been overwhelmed by it all. The fact is, like record producers, they bombard us with all the latest hype and then hold their breath to see if the public imagination can be captured. Real milestones are actually rare. The Jaguar XK120 and the Mini are genuine examples and, in the fullness of time, this little Mazda will be too. Alec Issigonis' 1959 ideas spread like wildfire around the manufacturing world, and in 1989 the emergence of the MX-5 generated a similar impact. The majority of the cars in this section of the book owe their place in the 90s market to the global impact of this trail-blazing two-seater. The pureness of its inspiration and the thoroughness of research and development paved the way for almost unprecedented sales success.

## HORIZONS

Mazda alone pressed on with the development of the Wankel rotary engine after the 1973 international oil crisis. Whether because they had already committed such huge sums of money, or indeed just retained unshakeable enthusiasm, the result was two generations of rotary engined MX-7 coupés, convertibles and turbos. – a credible total of around 750,000 sales. Such technical perseverance brought Mazda many new friends in the motoring media.

One such visitor to their Hiroshima headquarters was Bob Hall, the American West Coast editor of *Automotive News*. His informal meeting with Managing

*As you can just see in the leading picture, the rear of the Mazda holds its head up even in the company of the Jaguar XK8 seen behind. So much care went into design research that the MX-5 still remains pleasing to the eye after nearly 15 years.*

Director Kenichi Yamamoto developed into a discussion over what Mazda should next build. A further generation of MX-7 would inevitably move further up-market, and so they debated the possibilities of a simpler model. Hall had been brought up in a family hooked on open two-seaters, and in his enthusiasm for the topic he got up and drew his ideas on a blackboard in the Mazda meeting room. Talented teams in two continents and fortunes would follow, but the 'LWS' – Lightweight Sports Car – was born of such simple passions. Yamamoto was given a Mazda-owned Triumph Spitfire to drive through the beautiful Hakone mountains, and gradually a comprehensive appreciation of 1960s roadsters was born. Others, such as the Austin Healey Frogeye, the Lotus Elan, and MGs, were all scrutinized, and design teams in Japan and in California (where by now Bob Hall worked) competed for the LWS prize. The Japanese team were impressed by the excellent Honda CRX, and thus concentrated on a mid-engined rival, while the American team stayed with the more conventional front-engined rear-wheel drive configuration. So MANA (Mazda Research & Development of America) were to provide the concept which a multi- national team refined with an awesome understanding of the real essence of 1960s motor cars – culminating in the April 1989 Japanese launch of the MX-5 Roadster. It would be easy to say the 'rest was history', but Mazda's marketing contribution was just as significant, for at that time we loved our hot hatchbacks and occasional coupés – definitely not economy open two-seaters. The combination of near-perfect design concepts and unshakeable vision, backed by real resources, quite literally generated the present day affordable sports car market.

Privately, every manufacturer out there plugging their two-seaters owes a great deal to what Mazda alone set out to achieved. This is a car every bit as significant as the Mini or Jaguar

## THE CAR

### DESIGN

There were front-engined, mid-engined and rear-engined 'LWS' development versions of this car as well as coupés, but in the end the production model was a design of unalloyed brilliance. So many competitors have clumsily 'borrowed' period styling, or launched nostalgia marketing campaigns to stimulate our affection. Mazda openly admitted to looking at

*An important and rare picture of the original inspiration for the MX-5, drawn on the factory blackboard for the Managing Director by the American motoring journalist Bob Hall.*

ABOVE *So much care was taken to embrace the spirit of the affordable 60s sports car that Mazda's Managing Director was given a Triumph Spitfire to take into the beautiful Hakone mountains just to appreciate the joys of such simple motoring.*

ABOVE RIGHT *The engines and 5 speed gearboxes are beautifully balanced and although on paper represent only modest performers, the fact is, once behind the wheel, the package is so much more appealing than the cold specifications would indicate.*

cars such as the Elan and the Spitfire, but in this case the results are extraordinarily sophisticated for a mass production manufacturer. They have somehow encapsulated the spirit, the feel, even the fun, of the best 60s soft-topped motoring, without resorting to any excesses; reputedly, they even spent two years tuning the exhaust note. The MX-5 is, by present standards, already a dated design, yet still it turns heads. From literally every angle it is still a gem, with gentle flowing curves and detail wherever you look. It is the epitome of the affordable sporting design and ought to be a compulsory case study for everyone involved with the soulless Ford Probe. The nose section – which is manufactured in plastic to resist stone chipping – was not just conventionally tuned for aerodynamics, but also for its 'expression'. Mazda wanted the car to be loved, and so endearing frontals such as the famed Frogeye Sprite were studied before the MX-5 shape was achieved. The pop-up headlights are perhaps the single aspect of the body design which is beginning to look old.

## MECHANICAL

The excellence of the mix extends to all mechanical areas of these little cars. The 1.6 and 1.8 litre alloy engines enjoy race bred injection systems with distributor-less ignition and lightweight flywheels generating rapid throttle responses. Both engines use four valves per cylinder to reinforce low and mid range torque, with the 1.6i reaching 0-62 in 10.6 seconds and a top speed of 109mph, while the 1.8i delivers 123mph and 0-62 in 8.6seconds. It's easy to pass over these figures, but once behind the wheel you will understand that the package is skilfully supplemented by a five-speed close ratio gearbox, rack-and-pinion steering (power assisted on the 1.8i), classic, all-independent suspension of double wishbone and anti-roll bars, and all-round disc brakes. There is a clever aluminium power plant frame which locks the engine, transmission and differential into one rigid unit, and on the 1.8i they also fit a brace bar and performance

rods which further enhance body rigidity. The result is the kind of chassis and body strength that would be the envy of every Alfa Spider & GTV owner! With the known core buyers stretching from 25- to 54-year-olds, the simple, proven mechanical package holds great attractions, is supported by a three-year warranty and fuel economy to please everyone. The 1.6i betters 42.9mpg at 56mph, while the larger 1.8i returns slightly over 40mpg.

## INTERIOR

Mazda deliberately set out to offer the simple uncluttered trim of a classic sports car without any of the modern gimmicks. Everything is in its place and functions well. The folding hood operates with the greatest of ease, although the cover for the retracted hood requires a certain dexterity. The interior, however, is now beginning to underline the number of years since

*The cockpit design stuck very closely to original thinking. The simplicity of the detailing has helped keep its appeal despite aan increasinfly dated feel. The short gearchange is light, direct and very satisfying.*

In 1984 the fierce internal design competition for the new MX-5 came to a sudden end when Mazda's America Studio unveiled this stunning hard top model in Hiroshima's viewing hall.

its design. The starkness remains quite appealing and is certainly practical but it has a slab-like quality which is now beginning to look dated in comparison with the current design obsession with curves.

## PERFORMANCE

With a mere 90bhp from the 1.6i and 131bhp for the 1.8i, the models have always been considered slightly under-powered yet, like the Mini, its ability to corner well presents drivers with faster journey times and a huge amount of motoring enjoyment. It will under-steer a touch, and the rear end can eventually become restless, but under dry conditions this will only be the result of coming off the accelerator during the corner. In slippery conditions it's a bit more lively, but with such well balanced steering and a tiny ultra rapid gear change, these moments are instinctively dealt with and part of the driving fun. That, in the end, is the MX-5's triumph, for it makes you feel like a good driver, makes you smile and makes other heads turn – for an incredibly reasonable price.

## PERSPECTIVES

With 400,000 sold in seven-and-a-half years, the car's popularity speaks for itself. It is currently on sale in 50 countries, and in the UK, annual sales figures, far from declining, are doubling year on year. It has won over 70 awards from around the world, proving that this car is an object lesson in manufacturer's skills. If more companies would spend time assessing public mood and taste, rather than recycling permutations of

cars none of us find interesting, then the car market would be far more rewarding for everyone. According to Mazda, there is an equal appeal for men and women, with the 1.6i favoured by younger women, and of those who take up the 1.8 specification, around 60 per cent are men. The car will out-live most contemporary rivals because it's genuinely loved and offers both performance and sensible economy – the very formula for the best of those original 1960s classics. It is no surprise that the MX-5 is now the world's second highest-selling convertible sports car behind the equally trusted MGB.

## SPECIFICATIONS
Price as tested (1.6i): £14,410

No. of cylinders and arrangement: 4 in line
Position: front
Displacement: 1598cc
Max. power: 90bhp
Transmission: 5 gears – rear-wheel drive
Braking system: all disc
Suspension: Independent double wishbones and
    anti-roll bars all round
Steering: rack-and-pinion.
Fuel capacity: 10.5 gallons (48litres)
Fuel consumption: 33.2mpg ( 8.5mpl)
Top speed: 109mph (175kmh)
Acceleration 0-62 = 10.6 seconds.

Length: 3975mm
Width: 1675mm
Height: 1230mm
Wheelbase: 2265mm
Luggage capacity: 3.9cu. ft. (110 litres)

# FIAT BARCHETTA

PRESENCE ★★★★ A pretty car from every angle
GRUNT ★★★ Willing once up and going
CRUISING ★★★ Useful once at speed
HANDLING ★★★ Undistinguished
COMFORT ★★ Nothing special
SPACE ★★★ Average: no behind seat space
DASHBOARD ★★★★ Basic, but very well styled
NIGGLES - Over-clever handles, finger-damaging gearshift,
                    suspect boot support
BUYING - LHD destroys its chances
                    Lost in its own time warp

## OVERVIEW

Fiat first opened a British showroom in 1903, and by the late 1920s were collaborating with a young coach-builder called William Lyons on a Fiat-Swallow based around their Fiat 509A chassis. Both Lyons (with Jaguar) and Fiat's array of models went on to flourish. The Italian factory's association with open cars stretches back to their 1922 model 510 S, and through the decades they have produced many affordable two-seaters. While most of the world's motor industry is busy trying to standardize models and create 'world' cars, Fiat have made deliberate statements committing themselves to make more and more specialist cars catering for individual tastes. The Barchetta is the latest demonstration of this philosophy, and reinforces the tradition which was last served by the Fiat X1/9 and the 124 Sport Spider. It has used so many styling cues from the past to underline their tradition, that it's virtually a mobile 'Spot the Source' parlour game. Is it all just a bit too contrived? Do the sum total of all these nostalgic parts actual amount to a desirable car?

## HORIZONS

The fact this car is available in Britain signals an extraordinary attitude from Fiat. The model was never intended for this country and there is no provision made to manufacture a right-hand drive version. After the initial Italian launch the glowing press reports generated interest from the UK, and so Fiat's inspirational boss, Paolo Cantarella, pledged to fulfil this UK interest by agreeing to officially import the still LHD car. All too often such foreign delights creep in unofficially with no factory back-up and leave the proud owner unsupported. Fiat sell between 100 and 150 Barchettas a year in Britain which is hardly significant to an organisation with an annual turn over of 1.9 billion pounds. Yet to their credit they sell these little sports cars officially, and therefore provide the full factory after-sales back-up for these few owners. These actions provide further image enhancement for Fiat, and a chance to show both the media and the public that they are the ones in tune with the ever more fragmented market place. Much of the promotional material surrounding this car focuses upon nostalgia – 'Bridging the gap between past and present', proclaims the first page of

a celebratory book, and indeed Fiat's claim to an historical pre-eminence when it comes to affordable open two-seaters is entirely justified. The 1957-60 1200 Convertible offered open-air style and comfort for two, as did the later 1963-65 1500-1600 S, which had bodywork by Pininfarina and five all-synchromesh gears. They appeared to be able to provide the spirit of sporting travel without excessive costs, and no car illustrated this better than their 1965-68 850 Spider. This Bertone model, with a 52bhp engine, sold over 140,000 to potential MG Midget owners seeking more style and individuality. (A further 350,000 Coupé versions were also sold.). The 124 Sports Spider from Pininfarina joined the list between 1966 and 1969, while the familiar mid-engined X1/9 flew the flag until 1978, by which time Fiat's build quality had undermined trading.

Next up was the Barchetta, with a name reminiscent of classic 1950s Ferraris and a concentration of ideas and details designed to trigger nostalgia for happier motoring times. Their own promotion declares 'The sight of this car is bound to stir up countless jumbled memories of other famous sports cars … it could be fun, an exciting challenge, to isolate these visual clues, extract them from the jumble and pinpoint their exact historical location.' Does this make us feel catered for or just plain targeted?

## THE CAR

### DESIGN

Having been told it was designed to push our memory lane buttons, one feels reluctant to play into their hands. However, there is no doubt that it's an extremely pretty car from every angle. Essentially the body is a one-piece section, but all the detail adds interest. The nose is distinctive, the light cowling retro (yes, Fiat, that rings bells) and I find the tail sections particularly successful, with those recessed lamps and the detailed undertray wing. The boot lid is free of catches or solid stays, and the door handles are a frustrating two-handed push button and then 'catch the emerging handle' device (Yes, that one's straight off the Mercedes 300 SL). The original plans, we are told, were for a more angular model with thus a more economic build cost, but passion beat off logic in Fiat's design house and the agreed shape was 'Focused on surface rhythm and the plasticity of volumes and materials'. The intention was to offer a car more 'in touch' with its workings, its form and the

*A truly elegant rear section would still be at home on a sports car many thousands of pounds more than the humble Fiat. Creating models for niche markets such as their Turbo Coupé and this Barchetta has given Fiat designers much more freedom.*

*Reasonable storage can at least be fully utilized, thanks to the uncluttered access, though it is a bit disconcerting in a wind with no boot stay to keep it in check.*

*Italian style versus the British dumpling. The much applauded MGF is generally considered to look at its best from the front, yet besides the Barchetta it looks distinctly overweight and ill considered.*

*Quite comprehensive instru-mentation includes some splendid retro ventilation flaps and a centre console which rises sharply into the dash panel, causing you to knock the back of your fingers during some gear changes.*

*Designed specifically for low maintenance, this 1747cc engine offers simple flexibil-ity and economy with a power output of 130bhp. Once into the mid-power range it offers reasonable fun in the vein of the MGB.*

joy of motoring. Certainly the low doors, the absence of quarter lights, and the hidden soft top, all defi-nitely contributed to a very real sense of being out-side rather than tucked up in a motoring cocoon.

## MECHANICAL

The heart of this model is Fiat's new four cylinder 1,747cc 16 valve power plant which employs variable valve timing gear to generate 130bhp. A new produc-tion line is creating these engines to a specification which already meets EC Phase 2 emission control reg-ulations. The plan has been to provide a unit which is simple, flexible and very low on maintenance – all aspects highly desirable in a busy life. The five-speed box, the rack-and-pinion steering and all-round disc brakes do build up a credible specification, while the independent suspension apparently incorporates addi-tional tricks at the rear to smooth out the bumps. On the road that bit of kit wasn't very obvious – indeed the handling generally was fairly easy to catch out. Sitting behind the wheel of a nostalgia-ridden machine is all very well, but it is disappointing to turn the key

and discover that the engine kicks in sounding more like a diesel. Indeed, I found initial getaways belonged in the same league: 0-62 actually comes up in under 9 seconds. But just as you are resigning yourself to a poor performance, the elements fall together in the mid-power range and suddenly it all begins to feel and sound something like fun.

Find reasonably surfaced B roads, a sunny day and the package begins to fulfil the Fiat brochure dream of carefree days. Unfortunately, most of us in a hurry would actually choose a responsive hatchback rather than a fairly long, under-powered two-seater with a name that means 'Little Boat' - even if Ferrari did once use it.

## INTERIOR

Inside, the general effect is really rather good. There is strong use of the outside body colour – a trick used to perfection in the bigger Fiat Coupé – while the great sweep of the central console up into the main dash generates a sense of considerable space. The dri-ver's position is good and there are delightful old-fashioned flapped air vents (yes, another memory trig-ger). Unfortunately, it all feels as if it might fall apart before too long. Clearly style minimalism and striving to keep the car affordable have a bearing on con-struction. The declared aim is a car you fall in love with, that will need minimum maintenance and thus serve you long and true – but surely you are going to want it to stay in one piece for the duration. The short gear lever is capped with a large pistol grip han-dle, so changing gear means you effectively grasp the shaft. Such is the gradient of the rising central con-sole, that what is actually quite a long-shafted gear stick is largely submerged in a deep cavity around the

Between 1966 and 1985, 198,000 enthusiasts bought this Pininfarina-styled Fiat 124 Spider, which was based on a reduced 124 saloon and was offered with four different engine sizes. Like the Barchetta, it offered opentop motoring without any drama.

gearshift apron. Rapid changes into third or fifth ensure that you smack your knuckles between the stick and the forward edge of the centre console: There must be an appropriate Italian expression for the associated pain!

## PERFORMANCE

Is it a car that will become your friend? Will it ease you home after a rough day at work, and help you celebrate the freedom of your weekends? Well, maybe. It all depends on what you expect of a car. The sales brochure conspicuously refrains from showing any 'Lifestyle' settings, activities or indeed defining role model owners. The truth is it's a pretty car that the big boss has declared is to be made available on demand, and I don't get a sense from Fiat or the dealers that they really know what to do with it other than service the individuals that discover its charms. It is a hard car to pin down. It does not have jaw-dropping performance or handling, but it is economical at 36mpg. Nor is it blessed with excessive storage space, but it does transport you with a degree of Italian style and distinction.

## PERSPECTIVES

So where does this estranged motor car belong? The easy benchmark is the Mazda MX-5, but whereas that world-beater was inspired by 1960s two-seaters, its road manners and performance are very much of our time. The Barchetta, on the other hand, enjoys very creative retro styling, but strangely it's also easier to find a match for the car in those earlier times. It is, give or take a few delicious curves and touches, a variation on the theme once played by the trusted MGB. Not spectacular, but trusted; brisk, but not threatening. Despite Fiat's proclamations, neither it, nor indeed the MGB, were outright sports cars, but sporting cars. That category existed for the most part in the past, and

one suspects that Fiat have become so embroiled in pushing all our memory buttons, that perhaps they've missed the current market by trying to exploit one which was probably at its height a decade or so ago.

### SPECIFICATIONS
Price as tested £15,516.33

No. of cylinders and arrangement: 4 in line
Position: front transverse
Displacement: 1747cc
Max. power: 130bhp
Transmission: 5 gears - front-wheel drive
Braking System: all disc; ABS
Suspension:
Front – Independent. MacPherson struts with lower swing arms anchored to a subframe, offset coils + anti-roll bar
Rear – Independent. With trailing arms anchored to a subframe, coils springs + anti-roll bar.
Steering: rack-and-pinion, power-assisted.
Fuel capacity: 10.9 gallons (50 litres)
Fuel consumption: 36.6mpg
Top speed: 124mph (199.5kmh)
Acceleration: 0-62 = 8.9 seconds.

Length: 3916mm
Width: 1640mm
Height 1265mm
Wheelbase: 2275mm
Luggage capacity: 5.83cu. ft. (165 litres)

# BMW Z3

PRESENCE ★★★★★ Unrivalled street admiration
GRUNT ★★★ Not as bad as critics suggest
CRUISING ★★★★ Enjoys best-selling Series 3 experience
HANDLING ★★★★ Traditional rwd excellence
COMFORT ★★★★ Reasonable for the keen price
SPACE ★★★★ Intelligent use of what's available
DASHBOARD ★★ Dull — lacks style
NIGGLES - Vulnerable rear window
BUYING - Affordable – practical & pretty
RIVALS Toyota Celica – less glamour/more space
Alfa Spider – best engine/poor space
MGF — fun/cramped

## OVERVIEW

The 1980s visited a social stigma upon this illustrious Germany manufacturer. As for Golf GTis and fish-tailed Porsche 911s, it was the drivers and their attitudes which tarnished their naturally desirable road machines. That frenzied era of excessive ambition has passed and BMW now prospers supplying discreet up-market saloons to the professional classes. Although they maintained a tasteful presence with appealing coupés, their sports cars have been few and far between – until the announcement of the BMW Z3. Headline-seeking experts almost immediately started baying for the larger six cylinder 2.8 engined version, followed predictably by the same individuals pressing for the 155mph M version. While these cars naturally cater for those in a real hurry, the 1.9 litre Z3 is in fact, a real gem eminently capably of getting you quickly from A to B in great style, safety and without breaking the bank.

## HORIZONS

Bayerische Motoren Werke's famous blue logo may now represent solid predictability, but their background is rather more chequered. Initially producing aircraft and motorcycle engines, they bought the Dixi plant in 1928 and produced their first automobile – a model based on the British Austin 7. Others followed, and during the 1930s they earned an excellent reputation for well mannered sporting cars, best personified by their 1937 open 328. Following the devastation of the war, BMW struggled on the edge of bankruptcy, producing cars as diverse as big V8 saloons, (and unsuccessfully trying to poach Mercedes owners) and the 1953 Italian Iso bubble car which BMW manufactured as the Isetta. Cheap parts and an international fuel crisis helped sell this baby, and by the 1960s BMW could stabilize with new ranges of saloons. These matured in the 1970s, reached high fashion in the 1980s and became the Series 3, 5, 6 and 7 ranges with coupé versions to further massage their image.

Back in the commercial haze of their V8 confusions they shortened the chassis of a 503 V8 saloon and clad it in a fine open two-seater body to create the now highly desirable 507 classic – just 253 were manufactured. Much later in 1988 they announced another open two-seater, the Z1, and although they sold 8,000 of these, it was initially just a test bed for Series 3 saloon technical developments.. Carbon fibre, steel and glass fibre were employed in its construction, a 140mph 2.5 litre engine was used, along with bizarre doors which slid down and away.

However, with just two models and total sales of 8,253 sports cars since the 1930s the importance of the unveiling of the Z3's full-scale production cannot be underestimated.

Manufacturing began in BMW's American plant in South Carolina in 1996, but the sheer volume of orders delayed right-hand drive versions, requiring the UK company to pledge 'Thanks for your Patience' gestures to over 3,000 early British orders. Greater engines and differing bodies are in the pipeline (the 135-mph 2.8 already here, from August 1997) and BMW finally appear to be on course to generate their first true sports car best-seller. The UK's managing director, Kevin Gaskell, certainly has a very clear vision of its initial position, with 25% of the market being female, 40% married with children and over 50% business owners. Unlike Mercedes, a huge 80% will be privately purchased, and most sig-

nificantly 67% prioritize 'style' as their main reason for purchase. Like the original 507, the Z3 might be based on a BMW saloon and in basic form may not burn rubber, but it's a charismatic leader.

## THE CAR

### DESIGN

Like most aspects of this car, its appearance has been the subject of much debate. Many critics have decried the model for not pushing forwards contemporary sports car design. However, BMW wants to employ nostalgic style codings – hardly a matter of concern while Aston return to DB prefixes and MG to the next appropriate alphabetic suffice 'F'. Fiat nick 1950s Mercedes door handles, the Merc SLK clones the same era's dashboards, Alfa rejuvenate their Spider, and Mazda openly take inspiration from the Lotus Elan. The public enjoy period features providing their new model remains mechanically contemporary and reliable and that's something BMW know lots about. The Z3 looks like a proper sports car even stationary, and the design treatment ahead of the passenger section is filled with the classic 'Architecture of Performance'. The convergence of

*ABOVE A successful union of conventional modern design and nostalgia, the Z3 projects power and style. Of the 12 models under assessment the Z3 was amongst the most crowd-pulling, despite its relatively modest power output.*

*ABOVE LEFT German design at its best. The exquisite Porsche Boxster looks taut and simple compared to the more extravagant lines of the BMW.*

*The wide wheel arches blend beautifully with the retro styling vents unashamedly borrowed from the 1950s BMW 507. Integrating such period features does not mar the overall package.*

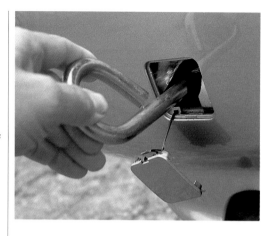

RIGHT *Discreet - even the tow hook attachment point is nicely concealed behind a cover and when not in use the hook lives within a neat tool kit.*

FAR RIGHT *The BMW 507, from which the Z3 air vents were copied, is a much sought-after classic both because of its style and its V8 power plant. Just 253 examples were built in the late 50s, making them extremely hard to find.*

*One of the side-effects for sports cars born out of an existing saloon platform is that sports seating tends to get forgotten. The Z3 is no exception, with little lateral support when motoring hard. The cockpit generally isn't as interesting as the exterior.*

raised bonnet lines and the plastic covered headlamp clusters towards the chrome-edged BMW grille works well. The borrowed 1950s side vent embellishments from their 507, and the discreetly macho front wheel arches flatter the graceful, dipping waistline. Somehow, from above the front wheel arches appear the width of a DTM race car, yet they smoothly disappear into the front bumper moulding and lower side aprons. Parked in the street it caused more attention than either the Porsche Boxster or the Mercedes SLK – both over £10,000 more expensive.

## MECHANICAL
Here we divide the fans and the foes, for essentially the Z3 is an open touring version of the hugely successful Series 3 saloon. This inevitably means the suspension isn't outright high performance stuff, nor is the familiar 1.9 four cylinder engine earth shattering. It's all a matter of what you want from your car. On paper the Z3 isn't going to catch the tiny mid-engined MGF nor growl like the awesome Alfa Twin Spark engine, but it is going to get you around without drama, without grief and in huge style. It's based on a shortened version of the Series 3 saloon chassis with wide track, wheels pushed into the very corners of the bodywork and the saloon's suspension, though the lower centre of gravity actually improves on the saloon's traditional handling. Much attention has gone into using smooth body panels for safety and 'soft' bumpers ensure slow speed accidents don't cause expensive damage. Indeed, the body panels themselves are now bolt-on, rather than welded to reduce repair costs and time. The 1.9 litre model which I tested developed 140bhp, while the 2.8 offers 193bhp, and the mighty M version is promising a serious 321bhp The test car's five-speed box again comes from the well-proven saloon, and the use of all these tried-and-tested elements does generate a genuine feeling of confidence and trust in the car.

## INTERIOR
Given that the body styling is among the most eye-catching on the market, the interior is a great disappointment. The seating is adequate, though lateral support is minimal. Strangely, manufacturers such as BMW and Mercedes, with their SLK, appear to forget that saloon-based sports cars actually need body supporting seats just as much as exotic sports cars, for compromise suspension generates greater body roll. The steering wheel was on the large size, and the bleak dashboard layout suggests a part bin raid on existing saloon parts. That said, everything functioned well and the slightly lowered doors offered a great sense of airiness and were the right height for resting an elbow! Immediately behind the seating are two very practical stowage bins with central locking, and beyond that a useful well area when the hood is erected. Available manual or electrically operated, the roof functions well, but does create distinct blind spots while raised and screen creasing suggests a limited lifespan for the rear window.

## PERFORMANCE
0-60 in 4.9 seconds is promised from the Z5, which is serious motoring, but such extrovert members of the model family should not detract from what the

basic Z3 offers. True, the 1.9 only turns in 0-62 in 9.5 seconds, but not everyone wants to break the speed limit in the lower gears. The engine is known to be excellent, and from around 4,500 revs onwards a good deal of fun can be generated while it still delivers around 35 mpg. It is a pity BMW hasn't followed Mazda's example with the MX-5 and taken a little while to tune up a decent exhaust note, but even without that satisfaction the Z3 still enjoys hard driving. The delights of a well-balanced front engine/rear wheel drive package provides communicative steering and predictable handling. There is some scuttle shake, but nothing on the Alfa's scale, though if driven in anger, the suspension begins to show its saloon origins. However, cars are rarely driven that hard, and the compromise set-up achieved really excellent levels of comfort and control

## PERSPECTIVES

Has BMW chopped the top off a Series 3 saloon to join the party, or is the Z3 about to become their very first high selling open two-seater? I have absolutely no doubt it's the latter, and that it will give birth to a family of successful models. Critics should remember that the all-time best-selling open two-seater in the world was the MGB, with the Mazda MX-5 now second, Neither ripped the treads off

their tyres, but both offered the joys of open motoring along with reliability and style. In many ways, the Z3 is a more sophisticated version of the MX-5, and like that car, the Z3 will still be running, and still loved and admired by enthusiasts long after more sensational rivals have rusted away.

---

### SPECIFICATIONS
**Price as tested £22,045**

No. of cylinders and arrangement: 4 in line: 16 valve
Position: front
Displacement: 1895cc
Max. power: 140bhp
Transmission: 5 gears — rear-wheel drive
Braking system: all disc: ABS
Suspension:
Front – Independent. MacPherson struts, coils, lower
    wishbone + anti-roll bar
Rear – Independent. Semi-trailing arms with coil + anti-roll bar
Steering: rack-and-pinion, power-assisted
Fuel capacity: 11.2 gallons (51 litres)
Fuel consumption: 35.2.mpg (met 8.7mpl)
Top speed: 127mph (204kmh)
Acceleration: 0-62 = 9.5 seconds.

Length: 4025mm
Width: 1692mm
Height: 1288mm
Wheelbase: 2446mm
Luggage capacity: 6.35cu. ft. (180 litres)

---

*From 1988 8000 Z1's were sold, complete with tricky little doors that slipped away underneath. However, it was really the development platform for the future 3-Series saloon range, making it a direct relation to the present Z3.*

# MERCEDES-BENZ SLK

PRESENCE ★★★★ Crisp and assertive
GRUNT ★★★★ When supercharger dominates box
CRUISING ★★★★★ C Class saloon qualities
HANDLING ★★★★ Reassuring until pushed
COMFORT ★★★ Traditionally poor Benz seating
SPACE ★★ Room for your roof + incidentals
DASHBOARD ★★★★ Nostalgic and handsome
NIGGLES - Auto box and engine often in conflict
BUYING - For serious minded drivers
RIVALS Alfa Romeo Spider – lacking strength
BMW Z3 – similar saloon basis

## OVERVIEW

Despite all the road test headlines, this is NOT a sports car – it is a Sporting Car. Forget the Mercedes-Benz tradition as supplier to the ageing and the staid, this is a car for those just entering their 40s. These words are not merely obvious opening lines, but actually the view of Mercedes themselves, who consider the new SLK to be an important strategic move to consolidate wider markets. I approached this car with some curiosity. Mercedes have their own unique qualities, and in order to enjoy them to the full you have to actually adjust your driving approach. The SLK may look like a modern sports car, but it treats you to high quality saloon qualities unless, or until, you have the courage to take it by the scruff of the neck and push it. Only then do the engineering treats and 'sports car' shortcomings truly come into view.

## HORIZONS

So much mystique surrounds Mercedes-Benz that it's quite hard to place their products into the motoring landscape. Customer loyalty is simply huge, and the industry respect for their engineering prowess is equally substantial. However, the bare truth is that since the post-war rebirth of Germany, the majority of their products have been substantially-built variations of saloons which made Volvo styling look exciting. Before World War II they had enjoyed an excellent sporting tradition, with big-engined models, but even their famous 1950s gull-winged 300SL was actually built up around existing materials from their 300 Series saloons. Now there is absolutely nothing wrong with such a tradition, but brand loyalty, keeping prices high and sophisticated marketing does not necessarily produce cutting-edge sports cars. Low depreciation, safety, reliability – these have been the hallmarks of a line of SL models often tagged as 'boulevard cruisers'. While the famed 300SL was a competition car needing limited road production for accreditation, Mercedes-Benz simultaneously launched a rather more modest 190SL based around the humble 190 saloon. This car was instantly belittled by critics as 'too small' and 'not a real sports car', but they sold thousands of them to first-time Mercedes owners, building up the very hard core of their present-day repeat customers.

Given the 1990s climate of high spending Baby Boomers reaching mid-life, and the frenzy of manufacturers offering them sports car freedom, it is hardly a surprise that Mercedes have carefully placed their own offering into the market. They know 90% of existing Mercedes owners are professionals in their late 40s/early 50s, who buy through companies. Such a solid customer base with those extra few years is a serious turn-off for those stepping from their 30s into their 40s, and so Stuttgart set about creating a brand new sporting model which deliberately didn't overlap with the sweeping glories of the expensive SL flagships. Not surprisingly, the factory returned to form by basing the new model on an existing saloon range – this time the C Class cars. They have set about acquiring the next decade's new loyal customers with the SLK using the very same tactics employed with the 190SL all those years ago.

## THE CAR

### DESIGN

I've walked round and around this car trying to decide if I like it. Certainly it has a real presence. A

*Even on these factory design studio sketches the lines were already there. Unlike for so many initial concepts, the requirements were already clearly defined and road going SLK's don't look that different.*

kind of Tonka toy simplicity of line and form which at the front works well with the polycarbonate headlamps, the lookalike SL190 twin bonnet bulges, the flared wheel arches and the steeply raked windscreen. The stark, unsculptured sides, however, make no attempt to disguise the rising slabs born of the fashion in wedged bodies. The snub rear helps project the agility of a 'wheel at each corner' school of design and the illusion of a generous boot. From certain angles it is indeed a pretty car, though never as sensuous as the best of the Italian design houses. Mercedes appear to have made a fetish out of being different with SL rooflines. The Gullwing certainly provided that car's trademark, and with the SLK they have designed an intriguing retractable metal hard top. It works very well, and in just 25 seconds converts a roadster into a genuine coupé – and both guises look at home with the basic body styling. The cost of this special feature is loss of boot space. Over 60 per cent of the large boot area has to be kept empty for the stowed roof, and the remaining area

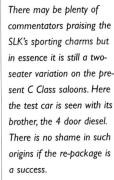

*There may be plenty of commentators praising the SLK's sporting charms but in essence it is still a two-seater variation on the present C Class saloons. Here the test car is seen with its brother, the 4 door diesel. There is no shame in such origins if the re-package is a success.*

*An engineering lesson. The 2295cc 4 cylinder engine benefits from enormous attention to detail, with special attention paid to gas flows; the supercharger enjoying compression from the intake side to produce fine boost pressure. The complexities of the new gearbox are not always quite as rewarding.*

*Despite fake carbon fibre material the interior is a huge success, blending colours and differing materials to produce a cockpit of great style. The seating itself is supposed to have new suspension but remains poor in comparison to rivals'. It's good to know they are wired to tell you if someone is seated beside you!*

has three irregular floor levels, despite a slimline inflatable spare wheel. Nothing must even press into the plastic curtain divider and the maximum real boot height is about the same as a packet of Corn Flakes! If you want to go touring and use the retractable roof, then pack very lightly indeed.

## MECHANICAL

Drive the car normally and you are taken care of in the same style as a C Class saloon. The suspension is firm but friendly, the steering is positive, despite an enormous, uncompromising steering wheel, and the braking always delivers. As with most Mercedes, it's a reassuring package of finely engineered elements. The 2295cc engine is combined with a supercharger to deliver high torque, low emissions and good fuel consumption figures – six cylinder performance from a four cylinder power plant. The four valve per cylinder configuration greatly improves gas cycling, and with the supercharger set up on the intake system, the incoming air is compressed before reaching the cylinders; this boost pressure is at the heart of the

SLK performance. The brand-new gearbox is a five-speed automatic transmission which uses a mini-computer meant to adapt the gear changes to individual driving situations and styles. Sampling situations and making instant database comparisons is most worthy, but calculations on how often and how hard you step on a pedal aren't really what I want a car to do half way around a demanding corner.

Essentially the conversion of an excellent saloon into an appealing sporting model is a logical and commercially prudent decision. However, to then expect the handling finesse of a pedigree sports car is grossly unfair on the manufacturer. Fair or not, *you* wait two years for your new SLK, sit behind the wheel, know it's supercharged and then try to rationalize away any shortcomings!

## INTERIOR

Now here, Mercedes have triumphed. Seating apart, the design detail is a joy, with a well planned dashboard offering most functions. Switch gear is simple and where you expect it, and there are plenty of small storage areas and great use of colour. The test car featured the red leather trim option which wasn't overpowering, but relieved the conventional mass of black surfaces. The centre console was dressed with fake carbon fibre, while stainless steel pedals, sills and door pockets add contrast. The actual instrumentation is stunning, particularly at night, with backlit, ivory faced dials, using red needles and framed in chrome. Strangely, among all the inevitable electronics there were no warnings if a door was not properly closed, a belt not fitted or a boot lid still ajar. However, there were plenty of electronics in the seating with sensors to tell if a passenger is there or indeed if a child's seat is fitted – valuable diagnoses if the car is deciding on whether to fire the second air bag. Unfortunately, the company's long-standing tradition of hard seating continues, despite claims that the SLK enjoys 'suspension' rather than steel springs. Comfortable seating with degrees of lateral support remains anathema to Mercedes.

## PERFORMANCE

Succumb to the general flow of traffic and the car becomes unremarkable apart from the passing admirers. It gets on with the task without any flair or excitement, but see a brief gap and its efforts to simulate a real sports car are really rather poor. Enjoy a moment's fling around a corner and it remains deeply unimpressive. However, if you have the courage to take it by the scruff of the neck and override that mini computer trying to analyse every move you've ever performed, then the car does become lots of fun. Keep the supercharger on song and the strength of Mercedes engineering becomes a reassuring asset as the pace rapidly quickens. Eventually, you do expose the saloon heritage with body roll, slow suspension, the big heavy steering wheel and the most complex of technical arguments around fast corners. You approach a fast open double bend, ease back on approach, boot the throttle and drive through. Wrong. The mini computer is busy considering the gear options you might have previously used so you dive deep into the first turn with just lots of selection whirring and no instant power to temper the growing body roll; by the time you have a suitable gear, instant power is really rather critical. Not there. You have to wait while the supercharger picks up. By the exit to the second bend there is certainly plenty of power surging, but the passenger, the suspension and hopefully that mini computer are all thoroughly shaken up. It's all a huge compromise which only shows up if you try to treat the car as it is dressed.

## PERSPECTIVES

As you may have gathered, the car represents dilemmas. It's beautifully built, turns plenty of heads in the street, has a two-year waiting list, and is a total success for Mercedes now and, perhaps more importantly, in the future as these new owners purchase again and again. Is it fun? Well that depends on your travel companion, and the number of shop window reflections you encounter of yourself and the SLK – certainly other SL drivers don't wave or smile as you pass. As a sporting car it's just fine; as a sports car it's a bit of a fraud, but then Mercedes themselves admit it's 'Civilized and Sporting', so perhaps the only deception is self-delivered. Succumbing to the fantasy that an SLK is a high-performance sports car

ABOVE *The 1950s Mercedes 190SL was considered an underperformer but went on to become a successful entry level sports model. The SLK is treading the same path, hoping to build up new generations of Mercedes owners.*

LEFT *Backlit ivory, red and discreet chrome - a very sophisticated and successful dashboard console.*

is simply seduction via clever market profiling and good advertising. However, as a dual roadster/coupé with a great badge, good build qualities and street presence the Mercedes SLK stands almost alone for £30,000.

## SPECIFICATIONS
Price as tested £31,741.20

No. of cylinders and arrangement: 4 in line
Position: front in line
Displacement: 2295cc
Max. power: 193bhp
Transmission: 5 speed automatic – rear-wheel drive
Braking system: all ventilated discs; dual circuits, ABS
Suspension:
Front – Independent. Wishbones,, coil + anti roll bar
Rear – Independent. Multi-link, coil springs,
Steering: rack-and-pinion, power-assisted
Fuel capacity: 11.7 gallons (53litres)
Fuel consumption: 31mpg
Top speed: 142mph (228km)
Acceleration: 0-62 = 7.5 seconds

Length: 3995mm
Width: 1715mm
Height: 1270mm
Wheelbase: 2400mm
Luggage capacity: 12.3 cu. ft./348 litres (hood up);
    5.12 cu. ft./145 litres (hood down)

# ALFA ROMEO GTV

PRESENCE ★★★★ True film star qualities
GRUNT ★★★★ Best 4 cylinders available
CRUISING ★★★ Average
HANDLING ★★★★ Well balanced
COMFORT ★★★ Harsh ride
SPACE ★★ In the Lotus Esprit zone
DASHBOARD ★★★ Self-conscious retro
NIGGLES - Frustrating door handles
BUYING - **Alfisti** passion vs more practical rivals
RIVALS Toyota Celica GT, Vauxhall Calibra 2.0
16v Audi & BMW Coupés

## OVERVIEW

I own an Alfa so I approached this car with maximum enthusiasm. and indeed even a thought to purchase. Now I am confused, torn between a craving to get back into one and the pinpricks of logic pointing to other more practical rivals. Matters of the heart are never easy.

The open Spider is simply a beautiful fun car with the expected range of pros and cons. However, the GTV – selling two to one over the Spider in the UK – is a more complex entity. A Toyota Celica beats it hands down for accommodation, luggage capacity, comfortable journeys and even fractionally on top speed. Yet drive the GTV with its near perfect four cylinder Twin Spark engine oozing mid-range power, the precision steering, the swift five-speed box, and suddenly you will find your head turned. It's like an unaccompanied supermodel at a suburban cocktail party: hard as you try - you cannot walk away.

## HORIZONS

Founded in 1910 and active in motor sport just a year later, ALFA (Anonima Lombardo Fabbrica Automobili) was taken over by industrialist Nicola Romeo in 1915, creating the familiar Alfa Romeo name. In the 1920s engineer Vittorio Jano and team manager Enzo Ferrari were brought in, and Alfa dominated motor sport. They won the very first Grand Prix World Championship in 1925, then with drivers like Nuvolari and Ascari they scored 11 first and 11 second places in the punishing Mille Miglia road races, while in 1933 every car in the top ten was an Alfa. Much later, in 1950, they went on to win the very first post-war Grand Prix World Championship with Farina driving. They did the same the following year, while in World GT and Sports Prototype Championships they won the 1975 World Makes Championship, repeating this victory in 1977. In 1987 Fiat took control, and entered Alfas in Touring Car events, immediately winning the Italian Championship in 1992, the German DTM in 1993, the British Touring Championship in 1994 and the Spanish in both 1994 and 1995. 86 Grand Prix wins, 11 Mille Miglias, nine Targa Florios, five Le Mans, two Formula One Championships and three World Sports Car Championships create a tradition, and a

A complex mixture of resin and carbon fibre is used to manufacture the huge one-piece bonnet. The powerful convergence of lines toward the classic Alfa grille is amongst the most successful of sporting designs.

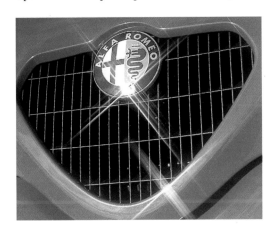

pedigree so pure that enthusiasts grieved at the marque's sad efforts in the 1970s. They tried entering the mass production domestic vehicle market creating cars unworthy of their heritage – fortunately many have rusted away.

Now under vibrant Fiat leadership, Alfa are buoyant again, with a shimmering range of new models, 100 per cent sales increases and, in the Twin Spark engine, they have one of the most beautiful four cylinder engines ever produced.

The marketing men have now moved in, using expanded dealerships and slick advertising to lure customers. Alfa views its target GTV customer as likely to be a 35-50-year-old male, with a comfortable income and buying privately, while the Spider is considered a more even male/female divide with the age bracket extending further towards the mid-50s. Given its high styling, limited space and significant acceleration, I suspect there are many 25-35s who may well be moved to own one, while the fractionally more practical GTV will certainly suit young female executives just as much as their male equivalents. Whatever the marketing, it is glimpses of the car – and more dangerous still, a ride in one – that makes the impact. Until that moment it's easy to admire and step away.

## THE CAR

### DESIGN

After such a long period in the design hinterland, the elegant 164 celebrated a brand-new Alfa confidence. It was a collaboration between their styling department in Milan and Pininfarina. At the Geneva Motor Show Alfa displayed the Proteo Project which was a wedged Spider/Coupé two-seater based around the 164 V6 – a possible replacement for the famous Duetto/Spider first launched in 1966. That car was in production for nearly 30 years and again was the product of Alfa and Pininfarina. Wisely, the new Spider/GTV acknowedges that tradition, with similar convergence of all front styling on the badge/grille, while long, gouged flank lines echo the old Spider. Behind the A pillar the new Spider conforms to the old, tapering-off style, but with the GTV (Gran Turismo Veloce) everything stops dead with a dramatic cut-off wedge. The front end design is probably the most impressive of any current production

LEFT The dramatic cut-off wedge shape generates a powerful rear section but Alfa's gesture for luggage is utterly unacceptable. Such space is largely taken up with a centrally mounted spare wheel leaving virtually no useful storage.

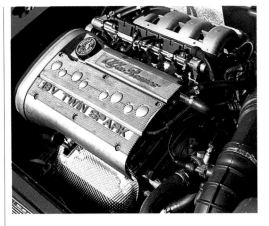

*Perhaps the very best 4 cylinder power plant in the world, using main and secondary spark plugs for each pot. The result is a joy to drive and has helped resurrect the reputation of this famous Italian marque.*

*For a car with such a stunning exterior the cockpit lacks any flair. Yes, there are some cute retro sunhoods over the dials but generally the cockpit feel is akin to a mediocre Japanese model. Such a pity.*

*Alfa's tradition with 2 door coupés is long and distinguished; and always the styling has been as important as the performance. This 1954 Giulietta Sprint is a fine example. The 1300cc twin cam four cylinder gem gradually became more potent, until the introduction of the larger Giulia in 1962.*

car, though the rear is more controversial. The sheer complexity of curves on the one-piece bonnet made steel construction impossible, so they have used the latest composite technology in manufacturing. The entire bonnet, radiator and half wings are in a hi-tech mix of polyester resin and carbon fibre called KMC. It's very tough, resists all corrosion and even absorbs minor bumps.

## MECHANICAL

This same advanced thinking has been applied to some of the mechanicals, in particular the rear suspension. They have created a new multi-link system with all the parts mounted onto a light alloy subframe which itself is attached to the body via rubberised fixings. The suspension parts themselves are also buffered with slightly flexible connections. The overall concept is that rapid cornering generates transverse loadings which lead to body roll. This new system is designed to flex and absorb some of this tension keeping tyres that much nearer the perpendicular, and thus more effective. Interesting yes …

but one wonders how much future trouble lurks in these 'soft' linkages. Meanwhile, it certainly combines with beautifully balanced steering to provide dreamlike control. Unfortunately, the main body is prone to some flexing, (particularly the Spider) and when combined with this rear suspension, you are subjected to a fairly constant chattering and bumping.

This, however, is really the extent of the mechanical criticisms. Except for the occasional harsh jolt, the ride gets forgotten once you have fired up the Twin Spark engine. Using a main and secondary spark per cylinder, combined with four valves for each pot, it is super-efficient, offers a wonderful exhaust note and

provides instant smooth power. There simply isn't another four-cylinder engine with the same qualities. You floor the pedal, and it truly delivers speed which, combined with the quick gears, great steering and that low hungry nose ahead, all adds up to a connoisseur's sports car.

The 90s GTV is a confident and forceful design, but during the 50s and 60s Alfa produced a number of exotic coupés such as the Giulietta SS by Bertone (1963-65) some of which boasted twin carbs, 5 speeds, disc brakes, and 120mph.

## INTERIOR

The interior, sadly, is rather dull. Purists may applaud the all-black appearance and the token retro feel with individually cowled dials, but with such styling outside, one might have hoped for something more original. The rear 'space' in the GTV isn't even that much use for luggage, but you will be glad of it when you open the boot and discover the area is virtually filled with the spare wheel. Logically some fold-down rear seats might have been the answer, but one suspects their body flexing tendencies prevented them cutting away the metalwork.

## PERFORMANCE

Once on the road all reticence deserts you. The sound of the engine, the fact it responds to your right foot the very instant you press, the finely weighted steering, all becomes a heady perfume. Actually a relatively heavy car, it's been road-tested to death against all manner of faster and/or lighter machines, but what those findings don't tell you is that this car works beautifully. Yes, the first Italian cars fitted with the 24v 3.0 V6 engine are finally a match for their rivals – on paper. But this Twin Spark engine is lighter, and the balance within the GTV is magnificent: greater power and greater weight may or may not offer the same delicacy.

## PERSPECTIVES

The GTV's sporting pedigree runs directly back to 1910. Has the factory just cashed in on a past best selling model's name to make profits, or is this new car a genuine extension of a great tradition? The '60s Duetto/Spider too was criticised for being underpowered and for its appearance. 'Alfa's best-selling Spider: the Return' – perhaps. It's certainly good business, but much more importantly the new models are not just badged nostalgia, but breathtakingly beautiful, rapid and relatively affordable sporting machines in true Alfa style. Bold coupés are nothing new to them – look at the Bertone Giulietta SS and Zagato SZ which made much the same statements in the late 1950s and early 1960s. And another two-seater coupé with outstanding looks was shown to the public for the first time at Geneva in 1997, the Nuvola concept car. This could be one to watch, with an adaptable spaceframe chassis which might just mean it makes it into production

## SPECIFICATIONS
Price as tested £21,351.38

No. of cylinders and arrangement: 4 in line
Position: front transverse
Displacement: 1970cc
Max. power: 150bhp
Transmission: 5 gears – front-wheel drive
Braking system: all disc; diagonal circuits, ABS
Suspension:
Front – Independent. MacPherson struts and lower wishbone + anti-roll bar
Rear – Independent. Multi-link with upper wishbone, double lower arms, coil springs, dampers, anti-roll bar and passive rear wheel steering
Steering: rack-and-pinion, power-assisted
Fuel capacity: 15.4 gallons (70 litres)
Fuel consumption: 29.7mpg (9.5mpl)
Top speed: GTV, 133mph (214kmh); Spider, 130mph (209kmh)
Acceleration: 0-62 = 8.4 seconds.

Length: 4285mm
Width: 1780mm
Height: 1318mm
Wheelbase: 2540mm
Luggage capacity: 3.9cu. ft. (110 litres)

# MGF

PRESENCE ★★★ Cute nose, shame about the rest
GRUNT ★★★ Better than expected
CRUISING ★★★★ No problems
HANDLING ★★★★ All the joys of a mid engine
COMFORT ★★★ Unsuccessful seating
SPACE ★★ Restricted by engine position
DASHBOARD ★★ Uninspired
NIGGLES - Hood storage; build qualities;
                sun visors from Airfix; ground clearance
BUYING - Badge & handling vs rivals' refinement
RIVALS Caterham 21 - same engine, more style
           Mazda MX-5 - the complete package

## OVERVIEW

Most enthusiasts cringed at the last British Leyland MGs and shrugged at the more recent Heritage bodied effort. However, world-wide affection for this once-famous marque was rewarded in the spring of 1995 when they unveiled the brand new MGF. Rover contributed the excellent K Series power plant, a mid-engined layout offered fine handling; and the eternal British lack of imagination produced a body style resembling a builder's brick. With such a wonderful MG tradition, and so many rivals offering imaginative styling, why do we sometimes continue to present our motoring gems with the same drabness as post-war British dress sense? This is a wonderful little car simply spoilt by a lack of courage. The Fiat Coupé looked fast while stationary; almost anything you could unbolt from the Barchetta could be exhibited in a design gallery; the GTV bonnet is inspirational, and the Aston and Jaguar slice through the air. The MG just looks like a doorstop.

## HORIZONS

This marque has always been synonymous with sporting cars. Right back at the beginning, when they were just Morris Garages, MG re-bodied saloons, offering the Morris Bullnose and Flatnose, and then went on to create the 1929 M type model. Two-seater after two-seater followed until the last few pre-war models, such as the VA and the WA, which concentrated on four seats. After the war they resumed their fine tradition of approachable two-seaters with the charismatic TC, TD and TF models, before the merger with BMC tilted the emphasis back towards four-seater sporting saloons. The first modern MG sports car arrived in 1955. The MGA was followed by the best-selling MGB in the early 1960s. The little MG Midget also appeared at this time, and the various Midgets and B incarnations held the 'sporting' image together, although following the 1968 formation of British Leyland, the marque was starved of investment and support. The models crept on until they were nothing more than Austins with an MG badge hunting for a loyalty vote.

Slab sides and a colossal rear end spoil a promising front treatment. Perhaps Rover should have spent more money on styling the car and less on titivating the photographs of it in brochures.

LEFT, ABOVE AND BELOW Roof catches have for some reason led MG to use very limited sun visors, with thin plastic fold-out extensions which are like vulnerable parts from an Airfix kit.

life is far more competitive and the ever-present desire to drive something open and nippy has been thoroughly fulfilled by the hot hatchbacks and subsequently the cabriolet versions.

Open-air fun motoring now embraces creature comforts as well as the vital styling cues and, rather like some ageing pop star's latest release, Rover have relied initially on hard-core support for commercial success. The question is whether its qualities will continue to spread the word beyond that central cluster of buyers, while its body styling so completely lacks either seductive or nostalgic signals.

## THE CAR

### DESIGN

If you pick up a sales brochure you will be treated to many glamorous pictures of this little car, all boasting pronounced and flattering waistline reflections. A great deal of money and skill has gone into such picture enhancement simply to try and inject some kind of excitement and movement into what is actually a car with slab sides terminating in a colossal rear end. Why didn't they spend the money on body styling which might help create more 1990s MG fans? The nose section looks good, but there has been a complete failure to manage the aesthetics involved in the

Now under the new BMW/Rover era the MGF has appeared with a bold new claim as the best affordable sports car – the F, we are told, stands for FUN. Over a hundred development cars were explored with front and rear wheel drive before this mid-engine layout was selected. Unlike the Barchetta which trawls the past for stimuli, Rover have deliberately designed and engineered a modern car, but have placed it in exactly the same market-place as their past products. It's a bold move and they deserve to succeed. The danger with this route concerns the car's style. A bright red MG T series was perfect transport for the young, untroubled youth of its era, who were often without undue pressures of work or hard-nosed ambition: Like many Morris Minors in the 1960s, the little MG was a comfortable social match and statement. Now

The actual rear boot storage behind the engine is very limited whilst the nose section is largely taken up with spare wheel and ancillaries. A fine sports car is trying to survive some muddled design work.

*The seating leaves you sitting high and poorly supported but the controls and particularly the dials work very well. The steering wheel too feels right, but the general build quality is pretty marginal.*

*The tradition of small sporting MGs stretches back into motoring history and has provided whole generations of fun in club competition. Here a post-war MG holds off younger blood at the old Woodcote Corner during a late 1960s Silverstone race.*

mid-engine position. The Lancia Monte Carlo looked good in its day, the Fiat X1/9 managed a then-fashionable approach to mid-engines, while Zagato produced some devastatingly beautiful rear-engined small Abarth coupés. A certain litheness and the accumulation of curves and angles are the universal visual language for sporting cars, and it is sad that Rover have displayed such style illiteracy in presenting to us what is essentially a brilliant little car. There are some nice touches such as the macho-looking filler cap, the good looking light clusters, and the door handles, as well as the underplayed engine intake ducts behind the doors. It all grows on you, but do we always have to bow to continental styling skills when it comes to great bodies?

## MECHANICAL

This is all a great success. The choice of the mid-engine position provides a 45% front/55% rear balance, creating excellent handling characteristics. Combining this with the tried and proven double wishbone suspension on each wheel, and linking it all up to Rover's Hydragas units means excellent road manners at speed, while the Hydragas system irons out much of the tiring buffeting. This set-up gives very exciting and positive cornering capabilities and light and responsive steering. These ingredients are the fun aspect of this little car, along with Rover's fine K series engine. The up-market 1.8i VVC model includes Variable Valve Control which greatly enhances the performance yielding 145bhp, 0-60 in 7.0 seconds and a top speed of around 130. However, the standard 1.8i model which I tested still generates 120bhp and 0-60 in 8.5 seconds, and these statistics conceal the fact that a mid-engine layout, and the lightness of the package, gives you the acceleration edge over most other cars. Despite being

transverse-mounted just behind you, the engine noise levels are remarkably low and the fuel consumption is simply outstanding. Sadly the PG1 five speed manual gears are still notchy, but the new 1.8 multi point injection engine offers wonderful levels of mid-range torque, so you can drive for hours calling on acceleration without constantly having to wind up the gearbox. Like the past BMC A Series engine, this K Series power plant is the mainstay of the company and its reliability is reassuring for the owner. This is just as well, as it is virtually impossible even to glimpse the unit tucked away behind grilles beyond the boot storage area. They do however provide a remote oil filler and dip tube for owner convenience.

## INTERIOR

On the drawing board it must have all looked great, but actually it's a bit of a muddle – a bit unfinished. The actual dash is quite pleasing, providing you don't mind meeting those universal black twist controls yet again. The dials are clear and well placed, and the steering wheel is just right. Build qualities in the dash are rather poor – you can literally rock the back panels to the switch gear. The sun visors interfere with the hood catches, and thin plastic wings are provided to click out when required (these are like something from an Airfix kit). The electric windows trundle up and down with disconcerting noises, while the driver's non-slip rubber carpet insert is ribbed from front to back creating an ice rink for your heels even with dry feet. Heating is good, the seating nothing special and rather too high for tall drivers, while the the windscreen pillars – designed 'for maximum safety' – are so fat they quite concealed a Ford Escort waiting at a side junction: so much for safety! Forward storage is really limited to the car's own ancillaries, while the boot behind the engine is reasonable and didn't get excessively hot.

## PERFORMANCE

Much of the lack of design and construction finesse falls away once you get to drive the little thing. The car's willingness to accelerate, the pin sharp steering and the excellent suspension, balancing performance needs and passenger comfort, all these assets add up to genuine driving pleasure. There are no rude awakenings when cornering, and it offers an unusual level of driver satisfaction. Of all the road tests in this book the MG was also unique in being the only car to bottom on certain roads in my town – the ground clearance is poor. There was no opportunity to explore traction and handling in wet or slippery conditions, and mid-engined cars do behave differently under those circumstances. That's not an indictment of the layout, but perhaps just a reminder that changing life-long driving habits with a front- or rear-

*The 1960s MG Midget was the last hugely successful affordable two seater and now the MGF hopes it too can earn a similar place in the enthusiast's heart.*

engined car does call on you to rediscover your driving – something the MGF truly invites.

## PERSPECTIVES

This is a wonderful little car flawed by a lack of finish in its styling and construction. The hard top option is a great idea, the soft top reasonable to operate, yet the cover when lowered is unwieldy. However, there is so much promise that one can only look forward to even greater things based upon this model. It is a joy to see MGs on the road again, to be driving one and to be exchanging waves with fellow owners. It may be lacking in many areas of detail, but it is a genuine sports car, not just a sporting car, and that actually places the MGF in quite a small and distinguished list of MG models.

---

## SPECIFICATIONS
**Price as tested £18,640**

No. of cylinders and arrangement: 4 in line
Position: mid-engine: rear-wheel drive
Displacement: 17960cc
Max.power: 120bhp
Transmission: 5 gears
Braking system: all disc
Suspension: Independent All round double wishbone and
    Hydragas springs interconnected front to rear. Front &
    rear anti-roll bar
Steering: rack-and-pinion
Fuel capacity: 15.4 gallons (70 litres)
Fuel consumption: 39.8mpg (7.1 mpl)
Top speed: 120mph (193kmh)
Acceleration: 0-60 = 8.5 seconds.

Length: 3913mm
Width: 1628mm
Height: 1264mm
Wheelbase: 2375mm
Luggage capacity: 7.4cu. ft. (209 litres)

# PORSCHE BOXSTER

PRESENCE ★★★★ Understated beauty:
GRUNT ★★★★★ Seamless power curve
CRUISING ★★★★ Firm ride for performance' sake
HANDLING ★★★★★ Absolute joy to drive
COMFORT ★★★ Mixed offerings
SPACE ★★★★★ Seriously impressive
DASHBOARD ★★★★ Crisp, discreet
NIGGLES Skimpy seating
BUYING A sports car with GT capabilities
RIVALS Mercedes SLK – Less composed
BMW 2.8 Z3 – more body glamour

## OVERVIEW

"Great car, you've done your best, what's next ... should have been cried a decade or more ago" reads a line in the Stanley Hundred Porsche 911 entry which goes on to bemoan the decades without truly new Porsche models. Such a backdrop makes the Boxster's arrival all the more important. According to Porsche this model is designed to appeal to a much younger, more independent driver, with higher proportions of females and quite heavy dependence on finance house loans. True, there are more financially independent women and certainly aiming younger will raise HP dependence, but the appeal of this sparkling new car ranges much wider than their expected 35-40-year-old. It's for all true enthusiasts who are tired of such a great marque being associated with just one model – and one tiresome breed of owner. The Boxster is gloriously understated, brilliantly engineered and a delight to drive.

## HORIZONS

The first real Porsche to carry the good Doctor's name appeared in 1947 and it was designed by his son Ferry and long standing friend Karl Rabe working from the Austrian town of Gmünd. Drawing number 356.00.105 was dated June 17th 1947 and showed a two seater sports car with a mid engine boxer engine – still largely resembling their previous

project, the Volkswagen. It boasted a lightweight tubular space frame chassis helping the modest 40bhp model to reach 87mph and to corner impressively well. Ironically, the prototype was sold off to a Swiss customer and all the subsequent production cars used monocoque steel plate construction with the engine perched precariously behind the rear wheels. However, Boxster PRs can justifiably claim that the principle of a mid-engined two seater with luggage stowage at both ends has been on a Porsche drawing board for a long time. Indeed, in 1953 Porsche returned to this concept for a competition car. The Spyder used a 1.5 litre air cooled four cylinder, four overhead camshaft boxer unit generating 110bhp at 7800rpm mounted in a lightweight body – race versions were just 550kg (1212lbs). Just 78 road going examples were produced costing twice as much as a 1300 Porsche and just DM2,400 less than the fabled Mercedes 300SL.

Why on earth did such a world-class engineering company sit on the idea they first thought of, and which in 550 Spyder form, won them class victories at Le Mans, Mille Miglia, Reims 12 hour, Carrera Pan American, etc? Perhaps like other large organisations their attention was distracted by the 80s City customers, who lusted only after the social status of the ageing 911. Whatever the reasons, after a few decades Porsche have now delivered the car they first thought of – and it's worth the wait. Naturally there are critics who feel that after so long the car is something of an anti-climax but to the factory's credit they have resisted all the temptations to attach dramatic fins and spoilers – the statement is consistently an understatement, that of a useable car with an impeccable engineering pedigree. It's priced and presented with a new realism which guarantees considerable success and makes direct comparisons with rivals hard to

establish. A Mercedes SLK is roughly the same price, and another German two seater, but there – despite numerous magazine attempts to the contrary – the comparison should cease. One is a well-built 2 seater conversion of an excellent saloon whilst the other is a custom-built, outright sports car that just happens to offer greater luggage storage.

## THE CAR

### DESIGN
According to Harm Lagaay, the Director of Porsche Design Studio, the Boxster body is supposed to evoke 50 years of sports car heritage – whatever that feeling is. Certainly the famous image of James Dean sitting in his 1950s Spyder isn't hard to muster looking at the Boxster, but the overall impression is closer to a modern, almost minimalist form than a nostalgic design exercise. Just wash this car and watch

the escaping waters to appreciate how perfectly formed is the body style. Lamps, indicators, door handles flow smoothly with the body and even a flat underneath is designed to reduce the drag factor by 6%. I drove for five hours in a crosswind so fierce the damage was making the national news and not once did the nose go light. It's a simple, undramatic and a highly efficient body, though surprisingly it's 75mm longer than its 911 sister. An enormous amount of race knowledge has gone into the fabrication of the body, down to varying panel thickness to gain strength where needed and lose weight where possible. Being mid-engined there is a greater degree of calculable passenger protection because both ends boast controllable crush zones whilst race-proven individual roll-over bars combine with steel tubes in the windscreen frame to provide extra protection.

## MECHANICAL

Naturally the focal point of this Porsche is its 2.5 litre 204bhp six cylinder boxer engine which may not have the back wrenching thrust of turbos or superchargers but delivers a magnificent stream of continuous power. Perfectionists might question the strength in the early stages of the power curve but reach around 4,500 revs and the power, plus the glorious sounds, really make the grade. Porsche have now selected a water cooled power plant and have adopted the race car design of two separate radiators nestling in the front wings whilst the engine airflow is via an intake on the left side cowling, hot air dispersed from the right hand side. The short stroke engine naturally offers a wonderfully free revving unit which thanks to water cooling can fully enjoy the latest four valve technology. The crankshaft is set with seven bearings using new composite shell materials, and the six steel

connecting rods are individually forged. Porsche have reduced the number of hoses and pipes by using a new integrated dry sump lubrication system.

The braking system too reflects change, with four pot aluminium brake callipers cast from a single monoblock – used by Porsche in their awesome Group C 956s and now adopted by F1 teams. These more or less dismiss brake fade and can for instance take you from 62 - 0mph in just 2.7 seconds. My test car used the 5 speed manual gearbox but there is also the option of their Tiptronic S system which provides a 5 speed automatic gearbox with controls and overrides on the steering wheel, directly drawn from F1 race technology. It offers lots of nice touches, if slightly less performance; any lift off approaching a corner doesn't spiral the box into unwanted changes – as with the SLK – but holds the gear you are currently in. There is also a traction control option, featuring the ABD automatic brake differential used on 911 Carreras.

## INTERIOR

Here the judgement is less absolute. The immediate cluster of dash instruments – dominated by a rev counter not speedo, are crisply overlapped and set under an open backed trimming. This and the central cluster look elegant and complement the door panel styling. There are a couple of useful small storage areas and a general feeling of tasteful modernity. The hood requires just one manual release and around 10 seconds with a finger on the button for it all to store away delightfully over the engine itself – thus not consuming otherwise useful space. This feature won a major design award even before the car was launched. The luggage storage in the conventional boot area is about average but can get a little warm

*The brilliance of the Boxster is under the skin, the fine sense of balance, the glorious gearbox and that sweet revving flat six engine amidships all contribute to one of this decade's great driving experiences.*

*During the 50s their 1.5 litre Spyder was used as a lightweight race car and under 100 road going versions followed. Their 550 Spyder enjoyed class victories in many international races, including Le Mans, proving a mid-engine concept that would wait until the 90s to be fully realized as a road going sports car. This is a 1957 550A, 1500cc, 135bhp, enough horses to beat more powerful rivals simply through agility and outstanding reliability.*

whilst under the front bonnet there is an enormous, deep cavern providing a combined Boxster capacity of 260 litres (9.1 cu ft). However, rather less successful are the seats which feel a little small and as a result only give partial side support. They look fine in pictures and, being scaled down, they add to the impression of space.

## PERFORMANCE

Whether you feel the Boxster is glamorous or under-styled is relatively unimportant once you turn the key and the real delights unfold. It doesn't thunder like some heavyweight V8, it doesn't lurch away as though impatient and uncontrollable, it simply builds up that famous Porsche whirring until around 4,500 revs it bursts into full song. It is the anthem of true sports cars, conducted through a gearbox as fast and sweet as you can imagine. It takes corners flat, as though on some hidden rail, calling all the time for the very best of your driving skills in order for you to share the privileges of such supreme handling. Mid engined poise, finely weighted steering and skilfully set suspension create a heady driver confidence. Drive it badly and there are hints of over- and under-steer and certain road surfaces generate a degree of discomfort, but such criticisms amount to very little. Incidently, it is good to find that the headlights are powerful enough to service its speeds.

## PERSPECTIVE

So much praise from a confirmed Porsche critic speaks for itself. They have finally produced a con-noisseur's sports car which doesn't need an excess of styling or top speed to satisfy the driver. It honours its company's traditions without indulging in nostalgic marketing and provides cutting edge engineering. The luggage follies of the Alfa GTV, the MGF and even the Mercedes SLK remind us that even Sporting Cars have trouble offering a touring prospect. Though it might not be as outrageously fast as the 1998 GT1, with its scary Le Mans-born technology, the Boxster is a leading example of the most restrictive variation defined here – the outright Sports Car – yet its storage is virtually identical to Europe's best selling Supermini, the Fiat Punto. It's as practical as it is satisfying – a rare achievement.

---

## SPECIFICATIONS

Price as tested £33,950

No. of Cylinders & arrangement: 6 flat six configuration
Position Mid engined
Displacement 2480cc
Max. Power 204bhp
Transmission 5 gears – Rear wheel drive
Braking System: All ventilated disc; twin circuits, ABS
Suspension:
Front/Rear Independent. MacPherson struts, longitudinal
   & transverse arms, coils + anti roll bar
Steering Rack & pinion, power assisted
Fuel capacity: 12.5 gallons (57 litres)
Fuel consumption: 30mpg
Top Speed: 149mph
Acceleration: 0–62 = 6.9 seconds.


Length 4,315mm
Width 1,780mm
Height 1,290mm
Wheelbase 2,415mm
Luggage Capacity 9.1 cu feet

# LOTUS ELISE

PRESENCE ★★★★★ Can't be ignored:
GRUNT ★★★★ K Series excels in light body
CRUISING ★★ Dependent on road surfaces
HANDLING ★★★★ Exciting and challenging
COMFORT ★ No pretensions
SPACE ★ Virtually no practical storage
DASHBOARD ★★ Minimalist but pleasing
NIGGLES - Desperate fuel gauge. Soft top from hell
BUYING - Pure fun car
RIVALS Caterham 7 - same power, period looks
MGF VVC - same power, compromises

## OVERVIEW

By what standards does one judge such a car? With an ageing population and ever-increasing ecological consciousness, is such a plaything, a third car, really a wise item to manufacturer, even to own? *What Car* magazine clearly think so, for it won the 1997 Roadster of the Year against the Porsche Boxster. Yet for the same price as a BMW Z3 or an Alfa Romeo Spider the Lotus delivers engineering design brilliance and little else – not even a set of sun visors. Against a truly desperate background of financial crisis, Lotus have managed to deliver the Elise and, with it, a great many of the company's traditional values. The prayer now from all enthusiasts is that the car, and the company's fortunes, will grow from strength to strength. There is no pleasure in criticising such endeavours, and yet bald facts are useful when parting with thousands of pounds for a motor car.

## HORIZONS

The Lotus story is well known to most enthusiasts. Colin Chapman's modest start was in a North London lock-up, building Austin Seven trial cars. His passion for performance led to such gilt-edged Classics as the famed Lotus 7 (now the Caterham 7), the beautiful late '50s Coventry Climax-engined Elite and the inspiring 1960s Elan range – a crucial role model for Mazda's world-beating MX-5. Concealed behind that single fact rests perhaps the greatest flaw in the Lotus story. Chapman and his team were brimming with ideas, with ways to squeeze greater speeds and performance from both their road and race cars.

Converting these thoughts into practice took time, and funds, and neither were ever really in full supply. Conversely, when the giant Mazda Corporation decided to invent a fashion for 1960s two-seater motoring, they spent mountains of time and money developing the little MX-5, devoting two years to tuning the exhaust note. Lotus could not afford to be that methodical, and so a string of brilliant road-going Lotus sports cars were born, each nursing poor reputations for build quality and reliability. Their race cars didn't have to last long, and enough finished to win them world-wide acclaim on the track. I had many adventures with an Elan, not all enjoyable but you forgave it because it was such a joy when it worked. I even had a very special factory-test Europa expire on me right in the middle of London. That car, too, was an exciting drive, with an Elan-based backbone chassis united to a mid-engine power plant. That mid-engine experience helped pave the way for the Italian designed Esprit which has served the company over many years and proved that mid-engined cars could look positively sleek.

The constant search for cash was helped by Lotus' growing reputation as an engineering company,

*Lotus Engineering is much admired but the complexity of the soft top calls for much patience. Fiddling with works of art such as the SLK's is fun. The secret to the Elise is the oversized Allen key pushed into the interior bodywork. Once discovered you can begin the process of detaching the various separate elements.*

*Deep sculptured side panels terminate in air intakes which combine with spoilers and fins to underline the value of many long hours of wind tunnel testing. The result is a bodystyle full of interest.*

including work on the infamous De Lorean cars. Lotus Cortinas added to the pot, but the pressures increased following Chapman's death in 1982. Toyota became involved the following year, and the entire organisation was bought by General Motors in 1986. They struggled to produce the new Lotus Elan in 1989, suffered still further pressures, were bought out by Bugatti, tried again with the same new Elan, went bankrupt and eventually found Proton's backers as a new owner. Against this backdrop, the pretty Elise was born. A true triumph of spirit over adversity.

## THE CAR

### DESIGN
This is Lotus at its best. All the car's true qualities stem from the skilful concentration on saving weight

without loss of strength. The central spaceframe chassis is built from extruded anodised aluminium, and then bonded together with a special epoxy with the front and rear body clamshell sections constructed in composite. This epoxy bonded technique is a first for a production car, and the extrusion process is extended to the smallest of details such as the pedals which are anodized to save on paint and stripped of rubber cappings. The rear sub-frame is in galvanised steel and the net result of all this attention is an overall weight of just 690kg and a brilliant power-to-weight ratio.

The body styling is spectacular. It looks like a concept vehicle, but is actually the result of detailed wind tunnel testing – evidenced by the chin and tail elements working with an underbody defuser, a combination familiar in motor sport. From any angle, the bodywork screams excitement with its complex curves and intakes, and it commands public attention wherever you travel. Normally the type of person recognising your car tends to reflect the market it's aimed at, but with the Elise you catch everyone: school children adore it, the young aspire, the middle-aged are envious, while the elderly, witnessing a fast approaching orange blob, are not entirely sure what to make of it!

### MECHANICAL
It may appear to be an ultra-modern motor car, but mechanically it's disarmingly straightforward. The

*Bare aluminium and minimalist fittings have been combined with considerable skill to create an interior that looks crisp and modern. A lack of sun visors doesn't aid safety and the minor display information is ill conceived; but generally the cockpit is great.*

*The engine which started life in the 1.4 Rover saloon, and is now shared with the MGF, is a 16 valve, 118bhp 1.8 unit. Transverse-mounted just behind the seating, it is linked to a five speed gearbox.*

*Excellent, large rev counter and speedo give instant information whilst the tiny variable backlit incidental panel can easily deny you key information about fuel – it depends on the light conditions!*

heart of the machine is the Rover K Series engine which first appeared in 1989 under the bonnet of a 1.4 Rover saloon. As any owner knows, this engine is remarkably willing and in this 16 valve 1.8 form it delivers 118bhp and a top speed of 126mph. It's mounted transversely just behind the driver, and is married to a five-speed gearbox – an identical set up to the rival MGF. Comparisons between these two cars on price and specifications are seriously tempting, but their characters are just so different. Both are double wishbone suspended, with ventilated disc brakes, five speeds, less than 1mpg between them,

less than £100, just 4mph, yet one car has arrived at these figures by trying to be a club racing car and the other dreams of one day being a Porsche Boxster. One mechanical advancement from the Elise is the use of aluminium metal matrix composite brake discs, which is a technology previously only seriously used on competition cars.

## INTERIOR

If you suffer from a bad back, if you aspire to a set of sun visors, a practical fuel gauge, a range of seat adjustment, the odd piece of carpet, somewhere to place your mobile phone, don't even think about this car. The Elise concept is to use a standard but willing power plant in a super lightweight body to up the performance without incurring costs. The crunch comes in trying to offer a cockpit environment which alleviates weight, but remains appealing.

Generally speaking, Lotus have succeeded by using bare aluminium and minimalist fittings to emulate race car allure. The seating is actually quite supportive, with only the drivers enjoying any adjustments – including a pump-up lumbar support. The driver's position is good, visibility commendable for such a car, and the key tachometer and speedo straight ahead. The tiny backlit digital display underneath provides the rest of the information, including fuel levels, and this is a disaster. Like an early digital watch it adjusts its back light to accommodate general light levels, but in such a thoroughly open car fitted with no sun visors when you are very often wearing sun glasses – which the little display cannot compensate for – you can see nothing at all. Sitting low in the aluminium tub means negotiating wide and tricky door sills, but this immediately deteriorates into a

*The body styling is a real triumph – one of the best from Lotus, and its crowd appeal is obvious. In a world where models look more and more alike, the Elise is such an optimistic and satisfying break from the norm. Should anyone need convincing that Lotus Engineering is still at the forefront of technology, it is the Elise and the eco-friendly E-Auto project developed in 1996 which have probably convinced the British government that Lotus should help produce the 150 mpg high-tech car planned for the millenium.*

tunnelling exercise if the soft top is fitted. The hood actually functions quite well, but it requires an engineering degree and much patience to remove the various separate elements. The secret is to discover a large rubber grommet behind the driver's seat into which is thrust a large Allen key!

## PERFORMANCE

I had to take it through central London and it never boiled. I crossed England and nothing fell off, I drove motorways and by-roads and loved every minute. It has a punishingly hard ride and cat's eyes literally wobble your cheeks, but the rapid acceleration time (0–62 in 6.3 seconds) and the responsive non power-assisted steering provide great satisfactions. It's very much a car that lets you find your own level of driving skill. Even if you really push the Elise hard the resultant oversteer is easy to read and offset; though at those moments, it would have been useful if Lotus had provided a rev counter with some kind of red line.

## PERSPECTIVES

In many ways the Elise perfectly mirrors all the traditional pros and cons of their former sports cars: exciting, imperfect, pretty. The well-proven running gear improves the reliability factor, and its appearance supports Lotus' boast of having the 'most fun on four wheels'. At the risk of sounding disgruntled, the trouble is, ordinary driving with this car isn't 'fun': and 'foot to the floor' kind of 'fun' really isn't responsible on public roads. They are selling a road car with nowhere realistic to play, and this may well reduce its sales and its status over the years – as it did with the Europa. Producing such cars is fine, but they need to capture the public imagination – and work as transport – in order to have some kind of purpose in life. If the car had arrived with a cheap liveried kit bag, a set of Lotus race overalls and an RACMSA motor sport introduction pack, I'd be praising them for identifying both youth and middle-aged markets of aspiring amateur competitors. Building such cars isn't enough. Lotus need to focus more closely on niche markets to really progress.

### SPECIFICATIONS
Price as tested £22,490

No. of cylinders & arrangement: 4 in line
Position: mid engine – transverse mounting
Displacement: 1796cc
Max. power: 118bhp
Transmission: 5 gears – rear wheel drive
Braking system: all disc; non- servo
Suspension:
Front/Rear– Independent. Double wishbone with single coils
    over monotube dampers - all round
Steering: rack-and-pinion.
Fuel capacity: 8.8 gallons (40 litres)
Fuel consumption: 32.0 mpg
Top speed: 126mph (202kmh)
Acceleration 0-62 = 6.3 seconds.

Length: 3726mm
Width: 1701mm
Height: 1202mm
Wheelbase: 2300mm
Luggage capacity: 3.35 cu. ft. (95 litres)

# FIAT COUPÉ 20V TURBO

PRESENCE ★★★★ A car with real 'attitude':

GRUNT ★★★★★ Just magnificent

CRUISING ★★★★ No problems

HANDLING ★★★★ Faultless at normal road speeds

COMFORT ★★★ Good seats

SPACE ★★★★ Surprisingly useful

DASHBOARD ★★★★★ A work of art

NIGGLES - It has a clinical name

BUYING - Nothing matches it for the price

RIVALS Toyota Celica GT – slower and pricier

Vauxhall Calibra – much slower

Jaguar XK8 – twice the price and slower

Mercedes SLK – £10,000 more and slower

## OVERVIEW

This machine is an absolute joy. Driving different cars all the time tends to numb the senses and one tends to judge them simply as better or worse than one another. This one is just spectacular: it is not directly comparable with any other car within £10,000 of it in value, not even some evolutionary jump of an existing model range. It completely redefines a whole category of motor car.

Fiat and Pininfarina have created a true masterpiece, with acceleration to match that of a Tiptronic Porsche 911 Carrera costing £42,280 more than the Fiat. It has genuinely useful interior space, a powerful styling attitude, braking so good it becomes a talking point, plus a turbo punch that creates an involuntary grin every time you floor the pedal. For years

now, most of us have had to be content judging the merits of an extra 'i' or 'T' or some such item on the boot of the same old cars. The industry has lost its imagination. Every inch of this car is new, exciting, and actually revives the joy of motoring.

## HORIZONS

Founded in 1899 by the Agnelli family, Fiat has grown over the decades into a vast and powerful industrial empire encompassing robots and railways, aero industry and motor cars. They own Abarth, Ferrari, Alfa Romeo, Maserati, Lancia and Autobianchi, and as such have produced millions of motor cars, the bulk of the Fiat models inevitably targeting the mid- and economy ranges.

Now, the sudden appearance in the market of this

high performance Fiat must raise a complex situation within the corporate family. The V8 355 Ferrari is only 1.5 seconds faster through 0-60, and costs £97,300 in its cheapest form. The fastest available Alfa is the old five-seater 164 Cloverleaf, which is over 1.5 seconds slower than the Fiat and still costs an extra £10,000. If the coupé is truly the beginning of a new dynasty of fast, sporting Fiats, then the gauntlet has really been thrown down within Fiat Group's empire. Pininfarina collaborated on the design of the Fiat coupé as they did with Ferrari on most of their classic models. Can you imagine the excitement, the global sales avalanche, if this genuine high styled, 155mph 2+2 coupé had been unveiled as a brand-new entry-level Ferrari? With nothing changed except a few badges, there would have been an instant waiting list – even with a price hike to £31,000. Just contemplate the stampede had it occurred at the actual coupé price tag of £21,000.

I'm full of admiration for Fiat for having decided to redevelop its own sporting tradition and one can only guess what further developments are in train. The only real error seems to have been the car's name. Time and again during my test period I would exude enthusiasm for the car to friends, or to those who stopped to talk. Its performance and appearance all reinforced the Supercar status until they asked its name. Fiat may have the income and the industrial might virtually to represent Italy, but as a brand name there are no high visibility milestones in competition, no Supercars that are easily remembered – just a crop of poorly produced, cheap saloons that began rusting before you could finish paying for them. If only they had given it a punchy name, or a purposeful numeric code, something, anything, that would separate this

*The powerful rear quarters from Fiat's Design Studios are strong and aggressive, yet concealed beneath the Pininfarina bodywork is a very practical boot. Hingeing arrangements lift the lid well away from the opening to ease loading and one of the rear seats folds down to allow over-sized items.*

glorious machine from the associated gloom of past Fiat products. Every colleague has praised this car: *What Car* voted it 'Coupé of the Year' in 1996 and again in 1997 in turbo form, so all the endorsements are there and massive colour advertising is doing its best to generate excitement. It just seems they haven't so much given the model a name as a job description: the Fiat Coupé 20v Turbo. It's bizarre that imagination and flair should have deserted Fiat at the very point they had completed quite the most stunning and original motor car on the market.

## THE CAR

### DESIGN

With so many manufacturers increasingly unwilling to risk their model looking too different from its predecessor, or indeed, its close rivals, we have become grateful for small design cues of individuality. 'My car includes a built-in sunglass case' (the Laguna) hardly makes a compelling claim for your machine's uniqueness. The Fiat Design Studio and master coachbuilders Pininfarina have started with a clean sheet of paper and designed a coupé you simply cannot ignore. You may or may not like the highly individual lines, but you will never mistake it for any other car. Somehow they have managed to produce a coupé with decent accommodation, visibility and engine access, which can match an Aston Martin DB7 to 60mph yet still look like it means business

*The detail is just a delight, yet the overall shape still meets the airflow requirements of a 155mph supercar. All too often, manufacturers of high performance cars cannot resist over-embellishment: not so with Fiat.*

*The vast bonnet exposes the compact transverse-mounted 2.0 litre power-plant linked to a turbo jointly developed by Fiat and Garrett. The output creates astonishing acceleration figures, embarrasing rivals costing tens of thousands more.*

*Interior details include body colour across the dash panels - a Pininfarina styling touch reminiscent of the 1960s.*

when stationary. Almost uniquely in production cars, the desire for styling excellence has overridden the exigencies of manufacturing. There are actually welds on this stunning body for which the computerized robots have to give way to the skills of factory craftsmen. Most people are likely to view the powerful rear section (complete with wonderful racing filler cap) as it disappears into the distance, but actually from every angle there is interest and signs of hand-crafting. This car isn't just another 'designed in association with …' some famous coachbuilder: they actually construct the cars themselves at the famous coach-building works. The very firm that build Supercar Ferraris work on these wonderful coupés. What other car in the price listings can offer you Italian coach-built status for the price of an upmarket Mondeo?

## MECHANICAL

Cars with this performance are almost always the result of years of development, sometimes generations of models – as in the case of the Porsche 911. Somehow Fiat have come straight out of the box with this highly creditable mechanical package. The model first appeared in the UK at the 1994 Motor Show in a four cylinder 16v form, and progressed to the current 20v five cylinder status in 1996, with the turbo versions launching simultaneously.

The actual engine is remarkably compact, allowing transverse mounting. Even the turbocompressor finds a home. The huge one-piece, wing-embracing bonnet is derived from race car practice, but even

with this huge access, working in the engine bay is definitely for those with skill and patience. The turbo has been a development between the specialists Garrett and Fiat Autos, and the result is really the jewel in this car's crown. They have managed to generate a really high rate of air flow, while limiting exhaust back pressure, to provide excellent fuel consumption along with great performance. An idling turbo ticks over at 20,000 revs and jumps to 150,000 revs when you put your boot down (the time taken to gather up that momentum is the infamous turbo lag). Through an extraordinary refinement of air flows, valve timings and exhaust manifold tuning, Fiat have managed to reduce this lag significantly and to offer the enormous thrust of the turbocharger virtually as though this were a much larger, normally aspirated engine. The resulting acceleration is simply electrifying. Being front-wheel drive, this much power could be a severe embarrassment and there is certainly wheel spin if you try. However, they have fitted a Viscodrive viscous coupling to the differential unit, so when you travel over slippery surfaces or corner fast, this equipment detects deteriorating traction and pushes more of the power over to the less affected drive wheel. Oddly, in many ways the biggest surprise was the brakes. Once you'd come to terms with the enormous bursts of acceleration you take instant overtaking and very high cornering speeds almost for granted. However, for the first time in years I found myself actually talking about brake performance. They are fabulous. Fiat looked to the experts, Brembo, to develop a one-piece cast aluminium brake calliper which uses four piston action onto the ventilated discs. This extra pressure and surface area makes a significant difference.

## INTERIOR

As if this car isn't satisfying enough externally and mechanically, the interior is a gem. Excellent, supportive and yet comfortable seating sets the tone, with relatively usable rear seats, one of which folds forward providing limited access through to the spacious boot. I was going to use a set of golf clubs to underline this extra long facility in a photograph, but found the clubs would fit comfortably in the boot itself. The dashboard is a touch of genius from Pininfarina's studios, with decent-sized controls and dials, and to top it all, a stunning upper dashboard painted in the exterior body colour. Only the Italians seem to have this kind of design flair.

## PERFORMANCE

Trying to describe this car on the road without calling on every cliché in the book is almost impossible. The first time I got behind the wheel of a genuine Cooper S, it gave me a huge rush of excitement, and

made me feel great as a driver. In the intervening years I have been able to drive most available cars – including many desperately valuable and exotic machines – but none have brought back that sense of euphoria – until this coupé.

I read a report by one television expert criticizing its handling at race speeds on a circuit, but surely those are not the conditions this car is set up for, or even pertinent to road journeys. Another colleague pitted it against the awesome BMW M3 Evolution Coupé, which is 101bhp more powerful and approaching twice the price. They managed identical top speeds, but far more relevant to us road users, the Fiat was faster to 30, 40 and 50mph and just 0.1 seconds slower to 60 – overtaking performance we have all dreamed of. This car has the speed, the charisma and the price tag to make it king of the road – if only they could give it a name worthy of its presence and abilities! What's in a name? Absurdly perhaps, thousands of sales. Ask Mr Iacocca about the Mustang.

## PERSPECTIVES

Fiat has in the past occasionally produced powerful coupés. The late 1960s Dinos were the last coachbuilt examples, with 2.0 and 2.4 Ferrari engines shared with the mid-engine Ferrari of the time. On that occasion Bertone crafted the coupé and Pininfarina the Spider version. Before that, there was the beautiful and rare early 1950s 8V. Just 114 were built on lightweight, all independent, tubular chassis, and with, obviously, V8 power, but the car was poorly promoted and slipped into history. In many ways, this new Turbo Coupé is more of a competitor to the over-priced Porsche 911s than it is to its paper rivals such as the Toyota Celica.

### SPECIFICATIONS
Price as tested £21,720.33

No. of cylinders and arrangement: 5 in line: turbo-charged
Position: front transverse
Displacement: 1998cc
Max. power: 220bhp
Transmission: 5 gears – front-wheel drive
Braking system: all disc; diagonal circuits, ABS
Suspension:
Front – Independent. MacPherson struts with transverse lower
    wishbone onto auxiliary crossbeam, offset coils, telescopic
    struts & anti-roll bar
Rear – Independent. Trailing arms onto auxiliary cross beam,
    hydraulic dampers separated from springs & anti-roll bar
Steering: rack-and-pinion, power-assisted
Fuel capacity: 14 gallons (63 litres)
Fuel consumption: 28mpg
Top speed: 155mph (249kmh)
Acceleration 0-60 = 6.0 seconds.

Length: 4250mm
Width: 1766mm
Height: 1340mm
Wheelbase: 2540mm
Luggage capacity: 10.4cu. ft. (294 litres)

# JAGUAR XK8

PRESENCE ★★★★ Undeniable star
GRUNT ★★★★ Plenty once stirred
CRUISING ★★★★★ First class
HANDLING ★★★★ Surprisingly nimble
COMFORT ★★★★★ Excellent
SPACE ★★★ Poor secondary seats – good luggage
DASHBOARD ★★★★ Restful and efficient
NIGGLES - half-hearted low fuel warning
BUYING - Coupé offers more practical package
RIVALS Mercedes SL - Ageing elegance
BMW 840 - Overlooked

## OVERVIEW

This is one of those rare cars that's complete: new engine, bodystyling, a return to quality trimming, status, pedigree. It would be churlish to start picking holes just to sound knowledgeable, and equally silly to heap praise simply because it is a new Jaguar and they haven't been swallowed up by the great Ford industrial maw. The fact is the combined resources of Jaguar and Ford have created a new generation of 'Grand Tourer', and Jaguar tradition is the richer for their efforts. Whether, as we head towards the year 2000, there is a place for such machines on our roads, remains to be seen. Certainly there are dangers in just replicating a type of machine which was fashionable when roads were less congested and fuel more affordable. The principles and benefits of offer-

ing up a 1990s two-seater MG package are still much the same as in the 1960s, but 4.8 metres of personal transport using a gallon every 20 miles is a gamble. Does it work?

## HORIZONS

As everyone knows, enthusiast or no, Jaguar boasts a proud reputation with sporting cars. Virtually all their models have managed to achieve some kind of cult status. Fine models such as the SS 100, the XK120 and its developments, the E-Type and even saloons such as the 3.8 Mk 2 are all recognized classics. However, their history is not without its dramas, and in recent years, they have been in rather a sorry state. An inability to bring new products through research and development on time or budget has seriously affected business. In addition, for a number of years poor build quality wounded Jaguar's once proud reputation. The early 1990s were a low point, but Ford executive Nick Scheele became the new Jaguar boss and gradually he rebuilt team confidence. His greatest struggles were actually with the parent company Ford, who, not surprisingly, were uncomfortable underwriting further investments. Jaguar managed to create fresh variants on the XK6 saloon on budget and to schedule, so Scheele used this evidence to press for a chance to create an XJS replacement. Although it was Jaguar's best-selling sports car, the XJS numbers were not seductive to Ford. Jaguar's battles continued, but their campaign for a new V8 engine was countered by political moves to use an existing American Ford power plant. Even after initial acceptance that a new high profile flagship Jaguar sports car was needed, there were serious pressures to have it constructed in Portugal. Finally, the British Department of Trade and Industry helped commit production to the UK, and Nick Scheele's team designed, constructed and then evaluated four different development cars. One million testing miles and four hundred million pounds later, the new XK8 was unleashed at the 1996 Geneva Motor Show.

The resultant worldwide record-breaking sales are a rich reward for victory in the huge internal battles to steer Jaguar back into good health. In many ways the centrepiece of this new factory prosperity is actually not the seductive new sporting car, but the arrival of the new AJ-V8 4.0 litre engine which will in time power a whole new generation of Jaguar models. However, the car is wreathing itself in global success – sports car sales in the first three months of its existence provided the best sales figures ever in Jaguar history, and were, not surprisingly, a huge 257 per cent up on the equivalent three months for the same quarter the previous year.

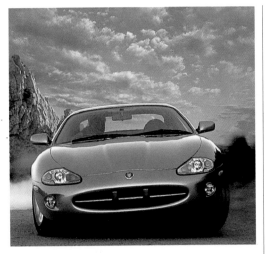

*It was a tall order to unite the romance and glamour of the original E-Type with all the modern technology available to Jaguar. Although elegant, the bold lines have managed to project something of the muscle car.*

traditionally moulds a classic Jaguar. The number of body panels have been reduced by 30 per cent over the XJS to minimize potential problems, and 80 per cent of the XK8's parts are new, with just 10 per cent carried over from the present XJ Series saloon. The actual floorpan is a substantially modified development of the XJS, with new front and rear understructures. The convertible version was deliberately launched at the New York show a month after the coupé, because approximately 60 per cent of XK8 production is likely to go to America, and 70 per cent of those cars are going to be the open version.

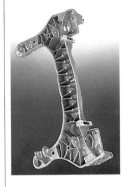

*A work of art; conventional cross members would be made up of mild steel and welded. For the XK8 they has been cast in aluminium and then machined finished to provide greater integrity.*

## MECHANICAL

This is Jaguar's very first V8, and development alone has cost over two hundred million pounds. It's remarkably compact and lightweight, delivering 290bhp from the 32 valve, quad cam, all aluminium unit which is coupled with another Jaguar first, a five-speed automatic gearbox. Based on the ZF transmission, it includes a 32-bit Intelligent Electronic Transmission Control Module, which works out the right gear change points based on a series of criteria.

## THE CAR

### DESIGN

Bob Dover, the Project Director, laid down that they wanted 'the refinement of the XJS and the excitement of the old E-Type'. The car had to be genuinely new, yet echo the design hallmarks of a traditional Jaguar. A task Fergus Pollock, the Design Manager, described as 'incredibly intimidating' given the legendary inspirations such as the C-Type, D- and E-Types. There had been a Jaguar-commissioned F-Type which became desperately overweight and expensive, and which Ford buried once they were in control. The four trial XK8 designs were from Ghia, Ford and two from Jaguar – one of which became the final choice. It's big, beautiful and it sits there oozing power and authority – the very criteria which

joke in the convertible: The Coupé is rather more practical. Boot storage was very good, while the electrically operated hood requires nothing from you except to press a single button and wait 20 seconds. In fact, it's even possible to operate this function while travelling at up to 10mph.

When closed, you simply forget it's a soft top, for wind noise is negligible and the depth of insulation is wonderful. The complex air conditioning/climate control system only requires the press of a button to dial the desired temperature, which was commendable, though a small driver's side button called Valet repeatedly failed to produce any man servant or drinks. (It is, I believe, a device to isolate and protect your personal items in the boot when you hand over the ignition key to the valet parking staff at smart establishments).

*Two hundred million pounds worth of development has resulted in Jaguar's first V8 – a triumph of lightweight engineering, offering 290bhp, 32 valve, quad cam excitement delivered seamlessly through Jaguar's first 5 speed automatic gearbox.*

*ABOVE RIGHT Gone are Jaguar's days of poor quality control. This left hand drive coupé interior for instance, offers beautifully finished seating and interior trim which has helped turn this model into Jaguar's all-time best selling sports car.*

Actually, in real life it means a box so smooth you really are not fully aware it's busy shuffling gears. A 'sports' mode button helps optimize performance, and I found I used it most of the time. The car is heavily dependent on high technology, and there are even chilling warnings in the car manual that in the event of electrical crisis, a limp home gear ratio is provided. The suspension is particularly successful considering the size of the car and the high-performance engine. The twin wishbone set-up is greatly helped by an electrically controlled Variable Ratio, Speed Proportional power steering. The electronics and engine management systems are worthy of a scientific paper; it's even possible to diagnosis faults via a version of a flight recorder which stores all relevant data from five minutes before the trouble extending to five minutes afterwards. With such hi-tech dependencies, it is indeed reassuring to know that under Ford, Jaguar's old failures with electronic build quality are all a thing of the past!

## INTERIOR

The design and trim qualities in the test convertible were quite faultless. Everything fell to hand: the switch gear was uncluttered, even the audio with steering wheel controls were never a distraction, and it was a joy to sit in. Late-night driving in what is designed to be a long-distance cruiser, however, becomes a bit nerve-racking when the low fuel light comes on: it gives you just 2.2 gallons and not many miles. The main seating was comfortable yet supportive, with plenty of electrically controlled settings, though the occasional rear seats are something of a

## PERFORMANCE

The roar of a Jaguar V8 at work is a new experience for everyone, and the results don't disappoint. However, the engine is silky-smooth, and with the seamless gear changes, expensive suspension, and high levels of sound proofing, you forget the aggressive potential of the car. As a comfortable long-distance road car it is very hard to beat. If, on the other hand, you floor the accelerator, there is a sudden reminder of the immense power. The engine tone tells you there is action, and the landscape passes a great deal quicker, but the edge of the seat performance experience isn't going to be yours unless you approach racing conditions and speeds. It's assured, fast, comfortable, and surprisingly, doesn't call on great deeds of heroism to negotiate double bends and back roads – assuming there's enough width. Perhaps the most alarming aspect is the speed the fuel gauge descends when you do choose to drive it hard.

## PERSPECTIVES

Well, is this a glamorous motoring dinosaur destined for some future motor museum? Probably. Has it succeeded in extending the famous Jaguar values? Most certainly.

It is a truly beautiful car, particularly in the coupé form, and the qualities of the new engine and gearbox deserve the highest of praise. In truth, this is really a celebration of the best of the 'Grand Touring' tradition, and Nick Scheele's tenacity, his battles to justify the existence of a new Jaguar sports car have been totally vindicated. I suffered a congested day in central London with the convertible, watching out for every corner of the bodywork and the hyperactive fuel gauge – and I dreamt of a compact Jaguar coupé with luxury and rapid acceleration figures through a manual box. Then, towards midnight we hurtled over the Sussex Downs with the hood down, waves of heat from the climate control, a satisfying array of glowing dials before me, the CD playing Miles Davis and, believe it or not, a full moon. Such motoring joy is virtually extinct nowadays, and that drive will long remain a reminder of a particular kind of motoring heaven ... and an XK8 was responsible.

## SPECIFICATIONS
Price as tested (Convertible) £56,625

No. of cylinders and arrangement V8
Position: front
Displacement: 3997cc
Max. power: 290bhp
Transmission: 5 gears electric auto – rear-wheel drive
Braking system: all disc; anti-lock & split circuits
Suspension:
Front – Independent unequal wishbones with isolated crossbeam, coils and anti-roll bar
Rear – Independent anti-squat, anti-lift double wishbones, coils and anti-roll bar
Steering: rack-and-pinion, variable ratio power-assisted
Fuel capacity: 16.5 gallons (75 litres)
Fuel consumption: 23.3mpg (met 12.1 kml)
Top speed: 154mph (248kmh)
Acceleration 0-60 =6.7 seconds

Length: 4760mm
Width: 1829mm
Height: 1306mm
Wheelbase: 2588mm
Luggage capacity: 10.8cu.ft. (307 litres)

*Along with Rolls-Royce and the Morris Minor, the E-Type has become one of Britain's great motoring icons. That car had set extraordinarily high standards in style and performance which the new XK8 had to follow. And it had to be, somehow, 'British', despite being, indirectly, the product of one of the American giants.*

# ASTON MARTIN DB7

PRESENCE ★★★★ Stunningly elegant

GRUNT ★★★★★ UK speed limit in 2nd gear

CRUISING ★★★★ Surprisingly refined

HANDLING ★★★★★ Assured, effective

COMFORT ★★★ Adequate

SPACE ★★ Disappointing for its dimensions

DASHBOARD ★★★★ Classic traditional Aston Martin

NIGGLES Pedals – dreadful alignment; audio - no cassettes
in 1st or 5th gear

BUYING - High badge premium and satisfaction

RIVALS Mercedes 500SL – dull & ageing
Ferrari 355 – high passion

## OVERVIEW

Once into this price bracket you begin opening up a moral debate on values: 'it's the same price as a decent house' ... 'you can buy a brand new car for a tenth of its value'. You cannot refute such statements – only remember that automobiles are a business, and such cars are intended for those who are wealthy. Aston Martin director Harry Carlton points out that their massive Vantage costs around £190,000, is infrequently used by owners, and is viewed rather as one might a fine piece of jewellery. The DB7 is the company's cheapest car and appeals particularly to the younger 35+ market who are actually using it as their main (if not only) motor car. Like Lotus, Aston Martin has been through lean financial times, but now under Ford Motor Company ownership, minds

are more focused, and the DB7 is re-writing their history books by becoming the marque's best-selling model of all time. Is this Big Brother flexing his muscles, or have Aston Martin given birth to yet another masterpiece?

## HORIZONS

Conventional wisdom would suggest that a company with this many financial crises is probably following the wrong path. However, Aston Martin have managed to lace their chequered trading history with some of the industry's landmark sporting cars. Robert Bamford and Lional Martin produced their first car in 1922, just two years before their first cash drama. Actually founded in 1913, the company began developing Singer Specials as hill-climb cars, and the company name refers to their success on the Aston Clinton hill-climb. Three more owners and the Second World War brought Aston and its popular 1.5 litre cars into the hands of Yorkshire industrialist David Brown during 1947. The famous DB models followed, including the much-publicized fantasy DB5 for the James Bond movie *Goldfinger*. Then in 1972 Brown decided to divest himself of Aston Martin and it was sold on to Company Developments, only to be taken on by an American and a Canadian in 1975. Five years later, CH Industries sold their interests to Automotive Investments and Pace Petroleum. In

The finely sculptured rear presents both a sleek and powerful image but it does reduce the boot capacity in comparision to the cheaper Jaguar XK8.

were slow and costly, so the Bloxham factory was turned into the hand-assembly point for bodies made in Coventry by Mayflower Vehicle Systems. The engines come from TWR, and Rolls-Royce undertakes most of the paint work. A cocktail of high class sub-contractors thus leaves Aston Martin to use its skilled labour force to build many more cars than would otherwise be possible. This takes place along a 28 bay assembly line with a two to four hour build session by craftsmen at each of the stations. By contrast, the Virage built in-house took 56 staff hours to paint, used ten hides to trim and the engine alone cost over £20,000 to construct. Ford's management expertise has dovetailed with Aston's strengths.

LEFT *A DB4 rested in Ian Cullam's Design studio as he worked on designs for the new DB7 and shadows of that former classic are evident - this side vent straight from that era.*

## THE CAR

### DESIGN

Much has been made of the similarities between the Jaguar XK8 and the DB7, and indeed of the common Ford Motor Company parentage. Walter Hayes had been shown the secret F Type Jaguar, but neither the shape nor the four-wheel drive were close to his vision for a new Aston Martin. However, to speed the development process up, and save funds, Hayes did look to the then best-selling Jaguar sports car, the XJS. The well-proven chassis platform was used by both the DB7 and the XK8 as a starting point, but

1988 the Ford Motor Company took a 75 per cent interest, extending later to total ownership.

Throughout its troubled history, competition success and then the DB road cars have been Aston Martin's key advantages, and naturally Ford were keen to capitalize on this. A convergence of various executive enthusiasms and events created the seedbed for the DB7. Ford owned Jaguar and their faltering 220 Supercar was leaving empty an excellent specialist factory. F1 Arrow boss Tom Walkinshaw, who had brought the XJ220 into production, was a JaguarSport partner who had recruited British designer Ian Callum from Ghia. Aston Chairman Walter Hayes fired up Walkinshaw to build the DB7 engines, Ian Callum was given a free hand, an actual DB4 and loads of past DB designs. The brief was to design a modern sports car with a clear lineage back to the company's past glories. Aston production methods

The door handle above left belongs to a £14,000 Japanese motor car, the lower one is from the £80,000 Aston Martin – one wonders if replacement parts for each are the same price.

*Though the basic block does belong to the Jaguar XJS, Aston are quick to point out that 70% of the DB7 engine is exclusively Aston's. Supercharged and built by TWR, it punches out a massive 335bhp.*

*Most of the interior sticks closely to tradition, though rear passengers require not only children's legs but also children's hips to enter the deeply sunk seating.*

*Totally different nose treatment to the Jaguar with almost delicate styling obediently mirroring the former Aston tradition lines of intake and lamp clusters.*

was minutely examined in and outdoors to see how light fell across its glorious lines. The final car looks suitably pretty in pictures, but doesn't reveal its true beauty until you walk round one, and see the interplay of every sculptured section. Park it among other cars, and its sleek lines and crouching beauty make conventional executive cars look like Ladas.

## MECHANICAL

If you read that an 'expert' views the Aston as merely an over-expensive version of the XK8, be sure they have never driven the DB7. Certainly, there are common elements between them, but not from the engine room. Ironically, while the Jaguar boasts the silky-smooth manners of their very first V8, the DB7's engine actually began its development with the XJS block. However, 70 per cent of the finished unit is unique to Aston Martin, and united to an Eaton Supercharger, it delivers a shattering 335bhp from the 3.2 litres, 24 valves. Just 15 TWR craftsmen build all the DB7 engines, and every one is tested for 30 minutes; every 60th engine is then stripped down again, closely inspected, rebuilt and then retested. There is even a unique database for each engine's construction right down to torque settings for every nut and stud. Such quality control is one of the many invisible luxuries which contribute to the car's high price tag. Married to this powerful unit is either a four-speed automatic or a five-speed manual box. My test car was manual and it was a great disappointment. It was long throw, notchy, slow; it reminded me of an upmarket MGC box and frequently spoiled the thrills of the engine. One can only assume it is the best available to cope with the engine power and is not an issue for the main, automatic-loving, US market.

## INTERIOR

The cockpit is a splendid balance of modern functions and traditional trimmings. The immediate set of dials was classically Aston Martin, while the central panel conceals the vast transmission tunnel well. The rear +2 accommodation is so deeply sculpted that only species with modest backsides need apply for a seat. Yet such space saving somehow leaves the DB7's boot wanting compared to that of the near identically wheelbased Jaguar. With such expensive cars there is a right to be prickly about small items. If I were buying a car for over £80,000 I would not expect to see plastic door handles identical to those on a £15,000 Japanese motor car. I would also expect to enjoy cruising motorways playing my favourite tapes. In the DB7 no cassette could be inserted unless I changed down into fourth gear. Again, I guess it works fine for the American auto models, but surely my £80,000 counts too. Sometimes I just want to change the music, not the gear.

only between the A and B pillars. Aston's search was for a model instantly identifiable as a return to the classic DB series, while embracing modern attitudes and increased crash safety legislation. The passenger section was deliberately kept towards the rear, behind an unfashionably flat windscreen and there was a subtle pinching of the cabin at the back – a fingerprint of former DBs. A traditional grille, light covers and side vents added to the package, and the vehicle

A unique picture of Walter Hayes, then Aston Martin's Chairman, with Sir David Brown and the latest car to carry those famous DB initials.

## PERFORMANCE

The thing is Jekyll and Hyde. Unobtrusive in town and when cruising, but clamber down through that disappointing gearbox, and the power plant erupts. There is none of that sudden jolting from a turbo, just continuous supercharged glory: 45mph in first, 65mph in second, 90mph in third, 130mph in fourth and 165 in top. It takes corners like a well tuned race car, and stops on command. Well … if you can get a foot to the brake. I tested this point with eleven pairs of feet, and everyone found the same troubling problem. Such is the bulk of the gearbox housing that the right-hand drive models have the accelerator so far into the side wall that it's been shaped to make space. Unfortunately, the clutch and brake pedals have long travel, while the accelerator is much lower and almost tucked under the brake. It isn't possible to 'heel and toe', and any rapid switch from power to brake pedal is tricky, frequently catching the shoe edge on the underside of the brake pedal. One factory manager passed it off saying he hadn't read of such a criticism, while back on the factory floor gearboxes were mentioned. Certainly the lower right part of the brake pedal is shaved off in the hope your foot gets by – hardly bespoke engineering.

## PERSPECTIVES

So we have the glories of the DB4, 5 and 6 incarnate in this car. The power and the beauty are certainly there in abundance with Ian Callum's brilliantly subtle bodylines. The general interior does not disappoint, but the car is flawed by the strangest of items. Aston addicts will put up with the gearbox, but the disappointing action is there for all to witness. The pedal issue may also get brushed aside by the adrenaline rush of brute acceleration, but there are avoidable accidents lurking in those ill-positioned pedals.

However, the general package is a thing of great beauty and Ford's £65,000,000 investment is suitably rewarded, for the DB7 is already the best-selling Aston Martin of all time.

## SPECIFICATIONS
Price as tested £82,500

No. of cylinders and arrangement: 6 in line, supercharged
Position: front
Displacement: 3239cc
Max. power: 335bhp
Transmission: 5 gears – rear-wheel drive
Braking system: all disc; four pot callipers, ABS
Suspension:
Front – Independent. Double wishbone, coils & anti- dive geometry + anti-roll bar
Rear – Independent. Double wishbone, coils, longitudinal control arms and anti-roll bar
Steering: rack-and-pinion, power-assisted
Fuel capacity: 19.5 gallons (89 litres)
Fuel consumption: 19.5mpg
Top speed: 165mph (265kmh)
Acceleration: 0-62 = 6.0 seconds

Length: 4631mm
Width: 1820mm
Height: 1268mm
Wheelbase: 2591mm
Luggage capacity: 6.14cu. ft. (173 litres)

# FERRARI 355

PRESENCE ★★★★★ Ferrari rarely falter
GRUNT ★★★★★ Searing performance
CRUISING ★★★★ Sets high standards
HANDLING ★★★★★ Astonishing
COMFORT ★★★★ Bespoke, understated
SPACE ★★★ Best use of what's available
DASHBOARD ★★★★ Understated, functional
NIGGLES - Off-set pedals
BUYING - A pilgrimage
RIVALS Porsche 911 Turbo – brute beauty
Mercedes 600SL– slower and ageing
Aston Martin DB7- less glamour

## OVERVIEW

A Jaguar XK8 for around £50,000 appears to be value for money, a flawed Aston Martin DB7 at £80,000 starts to raise questions. So can one even begin to rationalise £100,000 for a Ferrari sports car? For me the answer is clear, but the reasons are hugely complex. To stand near, sit in, let alone drive a Ferrari is extremely seductive, and so to honour the other eleven cars I have tried hard to off-set this powerful magnetism. Moving to the top end of any price list, you rightly expect everything to look and feel just right. Forget for a moment that this is a Ferrari, and clinically tick off the assets: devastating speed, sophisticated road holding, high style, comfort, and you are forced to acknowledge its high station, even without that powerful talisman, the Ferrari badge. There are a handful of motor cars in this price bracket, but nothing which honestly competes with this machine, except perhaps the ageing Porsche 911 Turbo. Just what makes this new 355 just so special?

## HORIZONS

Enzo Ferrari was born 1898 in Modena, and during his 90 years he created, not just a motoring legend, but *the* motoring legend. Passionate about competition, he joined Alfa Romeo and was their Competition Team Manager until 1938, when he began developing his own racing car ideas. Initially, cars such as his Tipo 815 were based on Fiat parts, but soon he had become associated with V12s – soon a Ferrari trademark. In 1947 a 1500cc V12, the 125 Sport, led its first race until the last lap, and just two weeks later was victorious in the Rome Grand Prix. Under 40 of the Ferrari 166 were built between 1947 and 1953, yet one went on to win the 1949 Le Mans race. Model after model followed, each one enhancing and improving Ferrari's status. While competition cars blossomed, so too did the road cars which basked in the reflected circuit glories. Road versions of his track machines have become motoring icons: cars such as the fabulous and mighty 275 GTB/4, the fabled 250GT and America's favourite, the Daytona, all propelled by great Ferrari V12 power plants. The smaller, transverse-mounted, mid-engined V6 Dino 206 and 246 opened up new markets in 1967, and led to the less exciting 1975 Bertone-designed 208 2+2 which used a mid-engined V8 layout. The 208 was eventually replaced by the 1980 Mondial, while the Dino flag was attached first to the V8 308 and then to the 328. These were a huge success and sold alongside the mighty V12 cars which had become mid-engined monsters such as the Boxer and the Testarossa.

The relentlessly growing need for investment capital led in 1969 to the Fiat Group taking a 50 per cent share of Ferrari, and following Enzo's death they took control of the organisation. Ferrari have managed to maintain their own identity, however, and after testing times are again a dominant force. The somewhat rushed replacement for the 328 Dino was the 348 which failed to present a totally convincing package, even with a fine Pininfarina bodystyle. However, afforded the luxury of time plus Fiat's facilities, Ferrari announced the arrival of the 348 replacement, the 355, in 1994. It virtually rewrote the rule book for performance in its class, and has already guaranteed itself a place in Ferrari's crowded Hall of Fame.

## THE CAR

### DESIGN

The stunning Pininfarina bodystyling had to meet highly technical requirements. 1300 hours of wind tunnel testing, and Ferrari's vast experience of the race track prioritized the air flow. Thus the 355's passage of air currents created channelled cooling to all the ventilated disc brakes, and a complex floorpan ducting system. Surprisingly, these specifications have been achieved without any compromise of body form. The car is available as the closed Berlinetta, the detachable targa-topped GTS and the Spider convertible. All are built of aluminium and steel, incorporating styling cues from the rare 1984 288 GTO

*The Pininfarina styling house has used all its experience to produce a masterpiece, every subtle curve accentuating the power and glamour of a Ferrari. Virtually every collaboration between these two organisations has been a triumph.*

*The 355 carries the requisite grilles, vents and Prancing Horse logo. Ferrari's badge is considered the world's third most recognised branding behind Rolex and Coca Cola.*

and the best-selling 1973-1989 Ferrari 308/328. Stand beside one and you get an extraordinary sense of compactness. There are no excessive overhangs or aerodynamic attachments, and it is actually six inches lower than Ferrari's flagship 456GT. It might appear pretentious to describe such a car as sculpture, but that art form conveys emotions and movement through a three-dimensional form: just as a stationary 355 manages with panels, angled vents and intakes to generate a forward thrusting energy, like a powerful arrow head.

### MECHANICAL

The strength of the chassis is inspiring, with an auxiliary spaceframe cradling the mighty powertrain. The V8 is practically a brand new engine using five valves per cylinder and generating 109bhp per litre, which is the most powerful output of any non-turbocharged

RIGHT *Simple, functional and probably your most likely view of this 180mph supercar; the tail light cluster of the GTS test car.*

FAR RIGHT *The boot is relatively small at 220 litres, but the space has no restrictions, spare wheels or limited access.*

ABOVE *Enzo Ferrari himself was always more concerned about engines than aesthetics and he would certainly have looked fondly on the 355's 375bhp, 4.3 litre V8 powerplant. Revving to 8,500 and controlled via the sweetest of 6 speed gearboxes, it can propel the Ferrari from 0 to 60 in just 4.6 seconds.*

ABOVE RIGHT *The test car featured dramatic trim, but whatever you select you are assured of a fabulous environment. F1 paddle type gearchanges are the thing of the future, but some may find it hard to give up the classic open gate.*

and adjust to maintain maximum stability. Directly employing F1 technology, Ferrari have forced the car to rest evenly on its suspension by creating an underbody ducting system capturing the rush of air via the nose and splitting it amidships, forcing air currents upward at the tail. The result both glues the body to the suspension, and in turn improves traction as airflows press the whole vehicle to the road. There is power assistance to the steering, a Bosch engine management system, and a delightful six-speed gearbox which is mounted transversely. Interestingly, extra bhp has been found by adopting two exhaust systems. The conventional one is augmented by a bypass branch which opens up at high speed to reduce the back pressures. The attention to every mechanical detail is astonishing – inspiring great confidence when your right foot falls to that inviting pedal.

## INTERIOR

Many modern sports cars use the black trim tradition as a loose excuse for cutting production costs. This particular Ferrari is finished in white/black with the interior crafted in Connolly leather. All the key gauges and switches are exactly where they need to be, the dials themselves traced with thin chrome and the cross-flagged emblems of Ferrari and Pininfarina. The cockpit feels airy, and visibility is remarkably good, while on my test GTS version, the colour-coded clip-out targa roof fits so well, I literally forgot that it wasn't the Berlinetta. There is full air-conditioning and, as you would expect, a considerable range of movements to find the perfect driving position. The seats themselves offer full support, and for the more flamboyant there are optional scarlet and black composite racing style bucket seats.

## PERFORMANCE

There really isn't a satisfactory way to convey the driving experience. To sit at the controls feels special, to hear the Ferrari engine just behind you, to ease the famed metal knobbed gear lever across the open plated gate is as nothing compared with what follows. The six-speed gearbox is filled with close ratios which

production engine in the world, including the McLaren F1. With four overhead camshafts, titanium connecting rods and massive 370bhp output, it ought to present plenty of handling problems, but the car is spectacularly stable. One of the many reasons for this is the sophisticated version of the classic wishbone and coil suspension incorporating electronic damping programmes. These read events and instantly adapt

Pininfarina and Ferrari have had a long and superbly effective relationship. This is a 1977 styling study on a 308GTB. One wonders just how many studies like this never see the light of day, or the photographer's lens.

means frequent use of the glorious short gearchange. The stunning V8 propels you so fast that you always appear to be taking a further gear. Using F1-strength con rods, the engine screams around the dial to 8,500 revs, daring you to feed in another cog, only to immediately push you there again. With 0-60 in just 4.6 seconds, the 355 has proved an unbelievable 4.0 seconds a lap faster than their awesome 5.0-litre V12 512TR on Ferrari's own test track. The handling is every bit a match for the performance, and while you are pushing hard, the driver involvement is total. Rapid travel just envelopes you in this magnificent motor car. Interestingly, the car's dominating nature simply disappears in rush hour traffic and really, if it were not for the mesmerized bystanders, you'd easily forget you are driving one of the world's fastest and finest.

## PERSPECTIVES

Even within Ferrari's own history, this is an exceptional vehicle. It rather had to be, in the wake of their somewhat disappointing 348, and in the presence of such an overwhelming wealth of new sporting opposition. What they have created isn't just a new and worthy addition to their legendary smaller-engined GTs, but a car that is so good it challenges even its own more expensive and powerful siblings. It's just 0.3 of a second slower to 60mph than the V12 550 Maranello, which costs another £50,000, and it approaches a full second quicker to 60mph than their 456GT, which is priced at an extra £70,000. Such sums of money are beyond the imagination and pocket of most people, particularly for a motor car likely to get only occasional use. In this respect, Ferrari have actually broken the mould with the 355 and indeed (though at an even higher price) the 456GT. These are Ferraris which are genuinely practical for regular use. That might appear unimportant, but to potential customers, a glorious 355 would save £9,000 over the cheapest Bentley for example – and put an enormous smile on his or her face. It's a genuine transport option for the well-heeled.

### SPECIFICATIONS
Price as tested £99,437.88

No. of cylinders and arrangement: V8
Position: mid rear in-line
Displacement: 4369cc
Max. power: 375bhp
Transmission: 6 gears - transverse, rear wheel drive
Braking system: all disc; ventilated, ABS
Suspension:
   Independent. Wishbones, coils, electronic dampers
   + anti-roll bar all round.
Steering: rack-and-pinion, power-assisted
Fuel capacity: 18 gallons (82 litres)
Fuel consumption: 16.7mpg
Top speed: 183mph (294kmh)
Acceleration 0-60 = 4.6 seconds

Length: 4250mm
Width: 1900mm
Height: 1170mm
Wheelbase: 2450mm
Luggage capacity: 7.78 cu. ft. (220 litres)

# CHANGE OF LIFE
*Window Dressing the Mini Cooper S*

Suddenly we appear to be surrounded again by the little Mini. For those of us around in its heyday it all feels quite normal, but a new generation of drivers are just discovering the endearing qualities that have kept Alex Issigonis' classic 1959 design in production ever since. To help publicise its hundred birthday *Autocar* announced the Mini as the "Car of The Century" and the razor sharp Rover organisation are trading all things Mini under the fashionable banner of retro. At the 1996 Birmingham NEC Motor Show Rover glass-boxed its latest Mini incarnation and staffed the stand with pseudo 60s mini skirted young girls – both looked extremely awkward. The very essence of the 60s girls (or the idea of the 60s girls) was their freedom – in stark contrast to Rover's self conscious NEC staff. Putting the latest Mini under glass and draping it with so many cosmetic extras was again contrary to the spirit of the minimalist joy of the original cars. For the first time in its distinguished life there is now an entire Rover-licensed catalogue of Mini merchandise to tempt the young urban enthusiast. Their advertising

campaign has edged the car Issigonis meant for district nurses into a strange netherworld somehow divorced from the driving experience.

There is nevertheless much to celebrate in Rover's new commercial interest in this wonderful little car, along with no small amount of irony. This attack of motoring trendiness actually has very little in common with how the cars were perceived during the 60s. Yes, they were highly fashionable motor cars to own in any form, but the cars themselves were nearly always standard – except for the Radford and

Wood & Pickett coachbuilt examples. I owned four, including two 1275 Cooper S's and enjoyed many miles in Minis belonging to friends: apart from audio gear I don't even remember anything distinctive in cars owned by Beatles. Flowered shirts, mini skirts, see-through clothing and some strange personal habits amongst the owners, yes, but the cars were just loved and used straight from the showroom. The Cooper S dominance in motor sport made the 1275 the Beautiful People's first choice, but the roads of Chelsea were not choked with rally lamps, sump guards and race numbers. The Mini was simply enjoyed, respected and used to the full by everyone from that district nurse to Works rally drivers.

The long standing and informal relationship between the factory and John Cooper ended when Lord Stokes felt the association had become redundant. The resultant 1275GT – without Cooper's name – proved Stokes wrong, but ties were broken. Now Rover and Cooper are back, with thousands of Mini Coopers helping to keep the Mini flame alive. The very first Coopers were really planned as a limited edition plaything for John Cooper's Grand Prix friends – his team won the World Championship the same year as the Mini Cooper launch. The concept was brilliant and its success universal. The Cooper S variations were really intended to be built just in sufficient numbers to qualify competition versions. Again, the success on road and track changed motoring history. The 1990 return of the Mini Cooper had, in the words of Rob Golding in

*Mini - 35 Years On* (Osprey) 'Something of a fairytale quality … One of motoring history's great good guy cars making an emotional return 19 years after the villains thought they had buried it.' With such happy memories I was of course keen to take up John Cooper's invitation to test the 1990s Cooper S.

In fact, there are two models which are exclusively available from his own headquarters in Worthing. One is the Touring, the other the Sport 5. Essentially both are the 1.3i Rover Mini but with a 30% increase in power through development of the top half of the engine – including twin point fuel injection raising power to 85bhp. Most of the substantial list of benefits and options are customizing refinements and trims, except for the one significant extra on the

*The trim may have changed but so too have the prices, with current Cooper S prices higher than many more spacious and rapid motor cars.*

*The new Cooper S is a strange hybrid attempting re-creations of former Radford and Wood and Pickett interiors whilst promoting its sporting heritage. The result is a kind of present-day Riley Elf.*

Sport 5. This boasts oversized 13-inch wheels and more significantly a road going version of the Jack Knight 5 speed gearbox used for so long in competition cars. At around £1,700 this is an expensive item, but does use the quieter helical gears rather than traditional competition straight cut versions. The Sports 5 model starts at around £13,000 whilst the Touring model is from £11,000 with 12-inch wheels and the conventional 4 speed Rover gearbox.

The test car proved to be a rather exotic purple example which John Cooper hovered around with the same care and enthusiasm he has always shown for motor cars. First impressions were unsurprisingly déjà vu and I set off into the depths of the West Sussex countryside complete with broad smile. Good leather seating, the same great visibility, other Mini owners waving at you and an eagerness to corner and overtake anything in sight. The ride was better than I had expected and the combination of engine tuning and that fifth gear ratio offered enjoyable main road progress. Parking was as simple as ever and the car instantly attracted onlookers of all ages. The wooden dashboard and door capping treatment was hardly traditional Cooper S but worked well, housing three white faced supplementary dials – all signed by John Cooper. In fact everything is signed by John Cooper, it's up the bonnet on racing strips, on the gear lever knob, the window winders, the door handles, pedals,

*The 1.3i Rover Mini engine gets a 30% power increase through John Cooper's reworking of the upper half of the engine - helped by incorporating the twin point fuel injection system. For the top of the range Sports 5 version there are also the benefits of a 5 speed Jack Knight gearbox – at a price.*

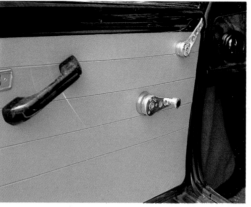

Something old, something new: a nice sporting retro filler cap (far left) for the rear and interior door panels (left) boasting modern lightweight handles inscripted with the Cooper name.

whilst the name is printed on each wheel, the bonnet, the boot, the steering wheel, the side transfers, the backs of certain seats, the chassis plate, oil dip stick. With Rover so actively selling the soul of Issigonis' creation it is perfectly just that John Cooper and his son Michael share in the spoils.

The victim in all this is the Mini itself, or maybe its reputation. The test car specification represented around £17,000 and enjoyed a top speed of 100mph. That's the price of a 2.0 litre 145 Cloverleaf Alfa Romeo complete with hatchback and a top speed of 130mph. So it's "not the same" because you are buying a piece of motoring history – that doesn't sit right either, for a mint condition, genuine 1960s 1275 Cooper S can be bought for around £6,500. I took the purple car onto the back roads just to savour once more the wondrous roadholding and fun of my last 60s S. The new gearbox, the progressive mid range torque, promised more than occurred, for the suspension was confused and you were forced to check speeds before any kind of uneven surface: No more could you hurl the nose into a corner and just pull it through under full power. I actually stopped and looked back at the road wondering if I ever had to wet nurse my Cooper S's over such lanes – but never did. It's as though changing the centre of gravity with 12-inch and now 13-inch wheels has upset the balance and then, as on this car, altering the suspension to compensate just confuses the whole set-up. Perhaps I was asking too much, and was not considering the car with a cold enough eye, free of prejudicial past experience.

I returned the eye-catching little machine to the works and have thought much about it, and my past Cooper S's, ever since. It seems to me that the present day commercial exercises around the Mini are evoking characteristics modern marketing men imagine were 60s style. The world beating engineering skills of John Cooper and Issigonis are now

buried in the original discreet connoisseur's semi-competition Cooper S's.

However, if you want a usable modern fun car with some real status, then a new Cooper or S is still a unique choice. The all-singing, all-dancing John Cooper Touring and Sports 5 are virtually mobile motoring catalogues of individual trimmings and extras you could add to your new or secondhand Mini. John and Michael have established a long list of tuning and accessory equipment which is being sold off the back of Cooper's spectacular tradition in motor sport. Like Abarth – consumed by Fiat – John Cooper's name is one to sport proudly on your car.

One of the most significant changes appears to to have been made for looks rather than handling: the 13-inch wheels. Unfortunately, raising the Mini Cooper S those extra few inches in comparison with the original's 10-inch wheels seriously affects its centre of balance. It would be a brave driver who attempted to throw a new Cooper S around with the same abandonment as was possible with the earlier incarnation.

# HIGH RENAISSANCE
## *Alfa Romeo's Return To Glory*

Motor sport's history makes a mighty tome. A global fascination with heroes and victims, setbacks and excitement seducing the industry to spend millions in an effort to claim public affection. The progress of competition falls into discrete chapters, with single manufacturers enjoying periods of invincibility: the powerful 1960s grip of Jaguar's C- and D-Types, the winning qualities of Lotus and Jim Clark, the unstoppable Works Mini Coopers, Porsche at Le Mans in the 1980s, Lancia rally cars. Each era of glory engenders waves of nostalgia in those who remember. Certainly I recall standing by the then flimsy Silverstone barriers watching the lithe and glamorous 3.8 Mk 2 Jaguars dominating races. As the likes of Roy Salvadori screamed round Woodcote straining wire wheels and bodywork, it seemed nothing, not even the highly tuned American Galaxy challengers, could defeat a Jaguar saloon. Yet within a generation that marque was reduced to catering for business executives, the Mini Cooper reverted to humble shopping duties and Lotus was left fighting for its very existence.

In motor sport the adage every dog has his day is truly fitting. To any real enthusiast, the saddest of sights is not perhaps the death of marques but the tragic attempts to keep or resurrect them using loved names on lesser machinery – an MG 1100, a Porsche 924, a TR7, a Riley 4/68 or Spridget. Not necessarily bad cars, but shadows of former glories.

There is however a marvellous exception to this traditional decay and it is to be applauded by every real enthusiast, whether a fan of the marque or not. Under the visionary eye of Fiat supremo Paolo Cantarella, their Alfa operation is reaping the rewards of a brilliant five-year strategy and millions of pounds of investment to revivify the great tradition of this sporting name. A marque whose very first car, a 1910 24hp model, entered and won events, a marque which hired and worked with Enzo Ferrari, the marque to win the first Formula One Championship. Cantarella saw the credibility of not just badging and marketing past glories, but using successful competition profiles to help launch new models and enter new markets. Six back-to-back Lancia Rally

*This was to be the last test day before the British Championship-clinching race and the all conquering Works cars were to be tested to extremes ...*

*... After every few laps each would come back to the pits where the factory mechanics made those subtle changes in the hope of securing the critical winning edge ...*

*... The cockpit had little in common with the road going 155; every inch was filled with equipment and safety items.*

has been a commensurate investment in new model ranges and revitalized dealerships. As Larini crossed the line in Avus near Berlin securing Alfa's historic 1993 Germany Touring Car Championship, back in Italy secretive teams were developing a completely new stable of road cars. Important mass market models such as the new 145/6, the GTV and Spider, and the long awaited replacement for both the 155 and 164. Against this backdrop of unimaginable investment and continual new car launches, the pressure Fiat placed upon the racing teams for success was simply enormous.

Paolo Cantarella presented the plan as a personal challenge to every member of the team: "we embark", he declared, "on this new venture to prove to ourselves that we can succeed in an endeavour that many people consider risky and perhaps even too much for a newcomer to take on at all". To a team of proud Italian engineers, technicians, drivers this was a call to arms, to stand under the famous Alfa flag. In a single German DTM season they clashed head-on with the fully developed racing giants such as Opel and Mercedes. The first two 1993 rounds at Zolder saw Larini and Danner simply destroy the opposition, finishing first and second in both races. The stunned Germans were quite unready for such an onslaught and by mid-season at Nürburgring, the crowd attendance had reached an unheard of 120,000. These scarlet machines were to triumph in half of all the championship races with Larini earning eight more victories than his nearest rivals. 15 fastest laps from the 22 races, Larini as Champion and Alfa Corsa claiming the vital Manufacturers' prize. All this was achieved in front of vast, mesmerized crowds and huge TV audiences, all shocked at the triumphant return of this famous marque and thus primed for the planned arrival of new road models.

To reinstate such sporting dominance is no mean feat, given that the standard 155 was just a modest road car. However, Larini and Danner were both gifted crusaders, Giorgio Pianto the team manager a

Championships and the Schumacher/Ferrari marriage underline his corporate strategy, and for Alfa he set an ambitious target to the then Competition Chief Giorgio Pianta. The team and cars subsequently covered themselves in glory: less conspicuously, there

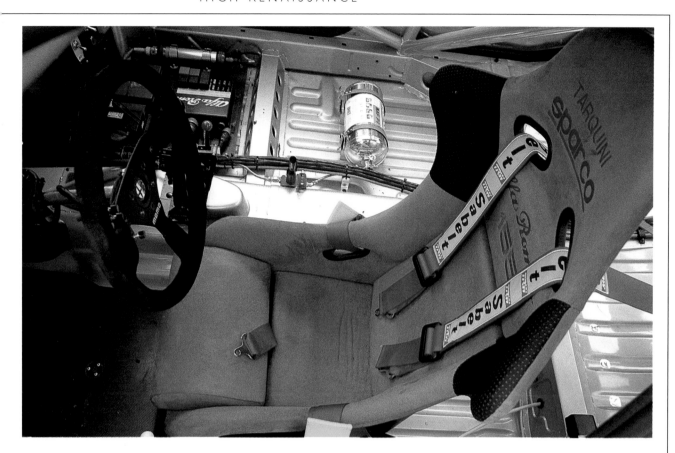

brilliant tactician and the army of highly skilled race team members were inspired by the challenge. Such a dramatic return to the competition world left competitors anxious to discover the Alfa secrets and a great deal of security surrounded their work.

For 1994, the might of Pianto and his team focused on the UK and the British Touring Car Championship. Their impact mirrored Alfa's German dominance with team drivers Gabriele Tarquini and Giampiero Simoni winning the first six times out. Mid-season protests from another team caused the removal of part of the Alfa front air dam and caused inevitable performance loss, but by Silverstone's September event it was possible for Tarquini to secure the BTTC Championship for himself and for Alfa. Immediately after Tarquini's championship-winning victory the team gathered at Donnington to practice and test for the final round. I was invited to join the team for the day and witness how they create their winning ways.

I approached the rendezvous past rows of rival team support trucks each reversed up towards the rear of their individual pits. The Alfa Corsa area was the exception, with the huge red trucks parked to create three protective sides. Alfa and Italian flags flew high over the encampment and one car rested under its shadow, carefully concealed beneath dust

covers. I was greeted by many pairs of brooding Mediterranean eyes, each mechanic in Alfa-badged overalls, uneasy at an outsider's presence. I was introduced to the brilliant and apparently impassive team manager Nini Russo and steered quickly away to the hospitality tent. The atmosphere slowly thawed, the wine, fruit and cheeses a reminder of the origins of the 25 team members. Eventually I was invited onto the pit lane as rival teams tore by, chasing extra power for the impending race against the all-conquering Alfas. Tarquini and Simoni scream in and out of the pit for adjustment, tyres and brief, animated discussions. It was business-like, contained,

ABOVE *The stark and lonely environment for a race driver is a thin solitary fixed seat and that small steering wheel. Once in the seat the emptiness all around you doesn't feel at all sporting – just clinical.*

LEFT *It's not just that these car were like bullets under acceleration but they also stop extremely rapidly. Not surprisin,g if you get a chance to see the massive 14-inch racing disc brakes. That's a full 4 inches larger than the actual road wheels on the original Monte Carlo winning Mini Cooper S. Alfa's very first Darracq-based cars from 1910 came in for particular praise for their brakes.*

*The 25-strong team of Italian racing mechanics travelled back to Italy with the cars after every race and cared for the two cars as though they personally owned them. It took some considerable time before they were comfortable with the author having access to their pride and joy.*

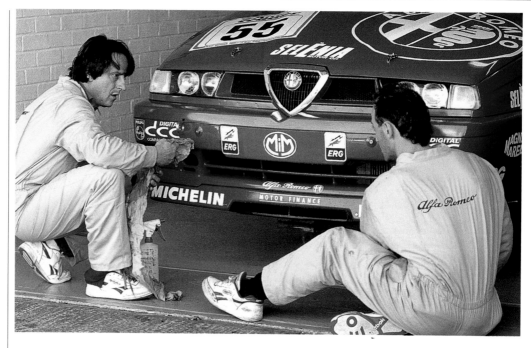

*Once you are strapped into this most special of racing Alfas, you are immediately struck with just how low you are seated, even in relation to the dashboard …*

each crew member alert in case their individual skills were required. As the day progressed I was even invited into the support trucks themselves, one carrying enough body parts to rebuild a complete Alfa, the other an awesome mobile spares department including an Italian coffee maker and eight complete V6 racing engines. So great was the concern for secrecy, so protected the £250,000 race cars, that they were driven back to the Italian factory after every race in that spares truck – requiring special dispensation to use a heavy vehicle on the French motorways during Sundays.

There was more Italian coffee, more waiting, before quiet words with Russo led to a reluctant mechanic lifting the dust sheets for my benefit. The

*… Once things get going it all becomes something of a blur!*

*In the privacy of the Alfa pits there is technical insight into the very heartbeats of both the Works race cars as their laps are scrutinized on the factory's telemetry.*

scarlet car had a tremendous presence. The huge heraldic logos, its ground hugging eagerness – like encounters with a Ferrari, it demanded respect. I was not allowed to approach until two mechanics had dusted the body panels, the screen had been sprayed and wiped and the telemetry aerial screwed into place. The pride of the two mechanics was obvious, it was as though they were grooming their own offspring for a visitor. Eventually I was presented with everyone's dream, a Works Alfa. Scarlet race harness locks you into the racing seat, the entire passenger floor filled with engine telemetry equipment. There were 30 sensors around the race car providing continuous data back to the pits, although such

*One of the major beneficiaries of this, the latest, of many decades of Alfa competition achievement, is the best-selling Alfa Romeo GTV. Once again, there is an additional, sporting frisson in owning and driving a car bearing the famous badge.*

*It is ironic that the 155 which was turned into such an international championship winner was actually a relatively medico road car, and probably had the weakest public image within the production car range. The 156 for 1998 is claimed to be 'the new Giulietta', that marvellous mid-size saloon of the the 1950s. Whilst still based upon the Fiat Tipo chassis platform, the 1.8 and 2-litre versions will certainly be less sporty than the GTV, but the planned 190bhp 2.5-litre V6 – with 'Selespeed' transmission as in the Ferrari F355 F1 – sounds interesting.*

transmissions were not permitted during races – hence the removal of the second aerial.

I sat there surrounded by unfamiliar items. The wing mirrors were covered in a black shroud with a clever forward air intake which scooped cool air to the driver. On the left of the wheel there was a small switch box with indicators on top, the wiper, lights, heated front screen and rear lights. The wheel itself boasted three small push buttons to operate the pits radio and directly ahead, above the rev counter, there were three warning lights set into the console. The left green for 8200 revs, the middle yellow for 8300 and the third, red, which represented maximum revs of 8450, above which an inhibitor kicked in. On the other side another control station with start button, battery switch, fuel pump and hazards. Down on the floor to the left were twin levers which effected limited changes to the front and rear anti-roll bars, on the right another black lever permitted a preset shift in the balance of the braking if racing conditions altered. The gear change was sequential through six forward gears, reverse separately controlled.

I was granted permission to photograph, though strictly under the searching scrutiny of the team. The bonnet was raised to reveal the mighty 2.5 litre V6 power plant. The front disc brakes concealed behind the distinctive black race wheels were 14 inch – the diameter of some car's wheels!

On the track, Simoni was still pushing the other race car to its limits. Twice he came in with bits out of the front air dam. Russo didn't raise an eyebrow and indeed, armed with a screwdriver, helped disconnect the offending bodywork. Out on the circuit the Alfa was in its element, its stability and power unquestioned, its exhaust note a clarion call. For some reason I was very aware of the sounds of small stones flying from the sticky slick tyres and striking the wheel arches. It wasn't however any individual aspect which caused the heart to flutter, it was the general attitude and appearance of the car; it simply hunts with all the purpose of a predator. The initial vision Cantarella had of an Alfa team instantly winning championships and thus capturing the public imagination must have seemed extremely far-fetched, but such deeds do reflect Alfa's age-old philosophy that it's hardly worth competing if the odds aren't stacked against you. I slowed into the pits lane and was then granted the final privilege of viewing their race telemetry, scrutinizing the differing heartbeats of this trailblazing car as it returned to screaming around the 2.5 mile circuit in pursuit of the perfect lap.

I drove from the circuit contemplating the sheer scale of Cantarella's plan – to awaken Alfa's competition reputation whilst simultaneously pinning so much new production investment upon its success. There is no doubt each of those men in the race team were aware of that responsibility and carried it, and their racing badges, with enormous pride; but gambling on passion in big business is risky. That vast investment, in money and people, has been a tremendous success, with cars such as the GTV and Spider offering 'classic' ownership for any enthusiast. The impact of that initial German race season instantly got Alfa voted the 'Top Marque' in the leading German motoring press; 1996 saw a 98% rise in Alfa's UK sales. It would appear that Signor Cantarella not only understands business but also the

power of loyalty to fine cars and traditions. It is to be hoped that BMW, with clusters of our motoring heritage, also choose to relaunch the great UK motoring names in their natural settings and with real commitment, and not repeat the tragic Leyland abuse.

As mentioned earlier, marque domination in any form of competition can be brutally short: fast forward to June 1995 to find Derek Warwick finishing in 13th place in the 155 at Donington: his eighth place on the grid their highest slot of the year thus far, after 13 rounds. But the gamble has already paid off for Alfa, as the lag between victory and road car sales winds up …

*Racing success didn't just bring glamour to production models, it also generated memorabilia such as this set of four collectors' 1/43rd scale models of the winning DTM race cars, produced by Minichamps. When they make the model, you know you've made it.*

# 1997/8 COLLECTION
## *New Eligibles*

The term 'classic' has long been abused and is usually more to do with automotive love affairs than it is with calender years. However, a specific qualification category is needed for competition and so the RAC Motor Sports Association ruling of twenty years or more continues to be the formal benchmark. Thus this year we see a further batch – the 1978 models – arriving at formal Classic status. Whatever your opinions are on individual models, the fact is that for someone, each will represent a classic. For many the mid 70s was a grim time with recessions and the global fuel crisis bringing uncertainty to households. The car industry too held its breadth and some of this year's classic first-formers were exercises in trying to rebuild market position.

This year a significant number of decent cars (not just those discussed here) indicate the globalisation of the marketplace and in particular we see the emerging Japanese influence on the Classic world. The Mazda RX-7 and the Datsun 280XZ were crafted for the West and both were best sellers. For a long time purists enjoyed decrying Japanese automotive styling but it's a foolish game today, and as the best early Japanese efforts slip into classic status, such critics will disappear even more quickly. Shrewdly, to ensure success Datsun simply used Western eyes to create the shape, just as in recent times Mazda studied 1960s European two seaters before producing the exceptional MX–5. Many design houses would do well to learn from such simple ground rules …

**OWNERS' CLUB**
*Datsun Z Club*
*Mark Bukowska*
*Tel: 0181 998 9616*

*Datsun Owners Club*
*Gullege*
*Imberhome Lane*
*East Grinstead*
*W. Sussex*
*RH19 1TX*
*Tel: 01342 324069*

**SPECIFICATIONS**
ENGINE: 2,753cc 6 Cylinder In–Line
GEARBOX: 5 Speed manual/ 3 Speed Automatic option
POWER: 140bhp
BRAKES: Discs
SUSPENSION: MacPherson struts/coils
  Semi trailing arms/coils
TOP SPEED: 114mph
FUEL: 19 mpg
LENGTH: 161.81in/411cm

CURRENT PRICE: £2,563 – £3,000

### NEW ELIGIBLES

#### DATSUN 280ZX
The Datsun Z range was designed by a German expressly for the American market using styling cues from the Porsche 911 and Jaguar E-Type – it worked, for after its 1969 Tokyo Motor Show launch there were 10 American fans for every car available. This was a very real rival for the big Healey and after its spectacular US launch the UK too enjoyed the powerful design and performance. The ever tightening US emission controls forced larger engines until the 1978 arrival of the 280ZX in 2 seat and 2+2 coupé forms which turned it into a comfortable Grand Tourer rather than an outright sports car. It was longer, heavier with full independent suspension, power steering, fuel injection, disc brakes all round and either 5 speed box or automatic gears. With its long, striking bonnet line and great strength this actually became the Datsun Z best seller in the UK, and it sold approximately 70,000 a year in the States. Like Jaguar E-Types, early 2 seater models are favoured over later big engines, whilst the then fashionable 2+2 versions are universally shunned. However as with the V12 E-Type, the later 280ZX's give you a great deal for your money. T-Bar Targas and Turbos followed later.

## SAAB 99 TURBO

Body design changes to a SAAB are rare, making the 99 model an important landmark when it was launched in October 1969. Larger than the 95 & 96, this front-wheel drive, independently sprung car was in time to be available in 2 door, fastback, hatchback and four door with fuel injection plus different engine sizes and transmission options. The powerplant was the result of collaboration between SAAB and Triumph with lineage back to Stag and Dolomite designs. An individual and very strong car, the 99 basked in the shadow of SAAB's former rally success. For a couple of years engineers had tried the actual Stag engine in their rally cars but felt the extra weight and fuel consumption outstripped the advantages. So turbocharging was explored and in January of 1978 the public was presented with the 99 Turbo. The safe and conventional SAAB instantly became the smartest car to own. The initial Turbos were all finished in black with spoilers, big alloy wheels and great sound systems. Practical daily transport with excitement just a floored pedal away, these currently remain excellent value for money. Watch for rust towards the rear and that you don't buy a Turbo enhanced "standard" 99 – true Turbos had strengthened gearboxes.

### SPECIFICATIONS
ENGINE: 1,985cc
GEARBOX: 4 Speed manual
POWER: 145bhp
BRAKES: Disc
SUSPENSION: Ind wishbone/coils fixed beam axle
TOP SPEED: 120mph
FUEL: 26mpg
LENGTH: 178.35 in/453cm

CURRENT PRICE: £2,600

### OWNERS' CLUB
SAAB Owners Club GB
K.Piper
16 Denewood Close
Watford
Herts WD1 3SZ
Tel: 01923 229945

SAAB Enthusiasts Club
Tom Noonan
P.O. Box 96
Harrow
Middlesex
HA3 7DW
Tel: 01923 672388

## FIAT 131 MIRAFIORI SPORT

This was Italy's "Cortina" of the time and approximately 1.5 million were produced from 1974 using a variety of engines from 1297cc to 2,445cc diesel. A high proportion of them succumbed to rust which plagued Italian cars during that period – a fitting end for many examples. The 131 range replaced the successful 124 but failed to generate the same passion from either press nor public. However in 1976 a homologation exercise to qualify for competition saw Bertone build Fiat just 400 131 Abarth Rallyes with fibreglass bodies, 16 valve twin cam engines and wonderful Colotti gearboxes. These were really something and a good example now is extremely valuable. In 1978 Fiat launched a road going version, a kind of Italian Lotus Cortina using the Twin Cam 2 litre powerplant, two door bodywork, egg box style grill and twin headlights. Low profile tyres, front spoiler, a touch of wheel arch flaring all tried to breed association with the Fiat rally team's three World Championship victories. The 131 Mirafiori Sport is well equipped, has a brilliant gear change and is a gem. Don't just take my word – last year in our price analyses this model posted a 33.20% rise in value over the past three years, stabilising in 1998. If it interests don't leave it too long.

### SPECIFICATIONS
ENGINE: 1,995cc
GEARBOX: 5 Speed manual
POWER: 115bhp
BRAKES: Discs
SUSPENSION: Ind McPherson/coil
    Ind MacPherson strut/coils/semi trailing arms
TOP SPEED: 110mph
FUEL 28mpg
LENGTH: 163.39 in/415cm

CURRENT PRICE: £1,475

### OWNERS' CLUB
Harry Collier
FIAT Motor Club of GB
Barnside
Glastonbury
Somerset
BA6 8DB
Tel: 01458 831443

FIAT Twin-Cam Register
19 Oakley Wood Road
Bishops Tachbrook,
Leamington Spa
Warwks
CV33 9RW
Tel: 01926 335097

## FORD CAPRI MK III

As detailed on page 120 (Stanley 100) the whole design ethos behind the Capri was of maximum choice for the mass market of the post-war Baby Boomers. This formula had been a resounding success for Ford in American with the multiple-optioned Mustang. The resultant 2,000,000 Capris have created sub cultures of their own, with the early Mk I's being revered for their simplicity and pseudo Mustang design whilst the later high performance 2.8i commands enthusiasts' respect. Inevitably the last incarnation, the Mk III, is still seen as too recent and not a true classic. However, as with Porsche or Volvo, long production runs naturally mean the last variations are usually the best sorted. The Mark III Capri boasted better aerodynamics, with a new grille, lamps and bumpers and all these late cars were built out of the German plant in Cologne. The 2+2 seating, the convenience of a hatchback, that seductive long nose, the ease of spares, all make these late cars attractive. With an excess of Capris around – and these late models only just coming of classic age – prices are still depressed. As no longer a "nearly new" car by any stretch, the 1978 Capri is actually a liability to traders and worth maybe just a few hundred pounds.

**OWNERS' CLUB**
*Ford Capri Enthusiasts*
 *Register*
*46 Manningtree Road*
*South Ruislip*
*Middlx*
*HA8 7BG*

**SPECIFICATIONS**
ENGINE: 1298cc, 1593cc, 1993cc, 2993cc (V8)
GEARBOX: 4 Speed
POWER: 72bhp–138bhp
BRAKES: Disc/Drum
SUSPENSION: Ind MacPherson struts/coils
        Rigid axle/Semi Elliptical
TOP SPEED: 87mph – 120mph
FUEL: 20–30mpg
LENGTH: 168 in/427cm

CURRENT PRICE – £750 to £1,500

## MAZDA RX-7

Mazda's sports car reputation is in orbit because of the wonderful little MX–5 but this isn't the first time the company has captured western hearts. For years they had been building nearly a million trucks and cars using a water cooled twin rotor Wankel engine until, that is, the international fuel crisis found its Achilles heel – fuel consumption. Not beaten, Mazda looked at the engine's assets such as weight saving, smooth power, silence, and decided to house it in a brand new coupé – result the 1978 RX-7. First launched in the USA (without rear seat squabs) this pretty, slim line 2+2 became an instant success selling 4,000 every month, generating waiting lists and even selling for up to $2,500 over book price. It was serious opposition for both the Porsche 924 and Datsun 240Z and, being easy to tune, in 1981 it received a power increase lifting the top speed to 125mph. With free revving engine, satisfying gearbox and good ride this became one of the world's best selling sports cars and allayed many people's fears of the revolutionary engine. Recently these Mark I RX-7's have started getting noticed. An Owners Club has been formed and last year's Price Data Base showed the start of its swing into profit. These are well made cars but you need to look for various engine signals when buying. Check with the club for a full briefing.

**OWNERS' CLUB**
*Mazda RX-7 Owners Club*
*Des Sullivan*
*44 Tower Close*
*Charlton*
*Andover*
*Hants*
*SP10 4RS*
*Tel: 01264 353625*

**SPECIFICATIONS**
ENGINE: 1146cc x 2 (twin rotor engine)
GEARBOX: 5 speed
POWER: 105 bhp
BRAKES: Disc/Drum
SUSPENSION: Ind wishbone/coil
        Watts linkage/trailing arms
TOP SPEED: 117mph
FUEL: 22mpg
LENGTH: 169in/431cm

CURRENT PRICE: £5,125

NEW ELIGIBLES

## OPEL MONZA

Like the SD1 Rover, the Opel Monza and its sister the Vauxhall Royale suffered from a middle age crisis. Last year's Data Base showed the SD1 depreciation at over 50%, the Monza fell by 25%. However, most of us have looked twice in our mirrors to identify a keen looking car approaching which proved to be a SD1 Vitesse. This whole genre of sleek four seater coupés will rise in classic status as we grow tired of vehicles looking like Tonka toys with every angle rounded off. The new GM large car range appeared in 1978 as the Opel Senator and Monza Coupé powered by the 2.8 or 3.0 litre six cylinder engines. Later in the same year Vauxhall versions appeared as Royale saloon and Coupé though initially without the larger engine option. All cars were built in Germany and enjoyed a good reputation for build quality including factory-applied rust prevention treatment. Virtually everything was standard on the Monza with air conditioning and manual gearbox as the only extras. Despite weighing 1.5 tons the cars performed well with smooth power all the way up to the 6400 red line, so naturally the much rarer manual versions offer considerable driver satisfaction. Such cars are presently "Sleepers" with good examples still cheap and eminently useable.

### SPECIFICATIONS
ENGINE: 2,784cc & 2,968cc
GEARBOX: Automatic, 4 & 5 speed options
POWER: 138bhp–180bhp
BRAKES: Discs
SUSPENSION: MacPherson Strut
    Semi trailing arms/coils
TOP SPEED: 125mph
FUEL: 20mpg
LENGTH: 185in/ 470cm

CURRENT PRICE: £2,375

### OWNERS' CLUB
*Opel Owners Club for*
*  Enthusiasts*
*123 Withersfield Road*
*Haver Hill*
*Suffolk*
*CB9 9HG*
*Tel: 01440 704681*

NEW ELIGIBLES

## PORSCHE 924 TURBO

Traditionalists hated this model range and decried its Audi engine, Golf/Scirocco front suspension/ steering and Beetle based rear suspension; which is strange as the reputations of each of these cars are individually admirable. It might have been planned as an Audi model but under Porsche parentage the 924 perfectly created an entry point model. The standard 924 qualified as a classic last year (page 59 of 1997 Yearbook) but it is a mistake to assume the Turbo is just a bolt-on extra. The team at Weissach went right through the entire car changing absolutely anything not suited to the 45bhp power hike that came with the KKK Turbocharger. Indeed the engine itself was not built at the old NSU Neckarsulm factory but at the actual Zuffenhausen Porsche centre before transportation back to Neckarsulm for installation. There were visual changes such as the additional air vents on the nose to assist cooling, discreet rear spoiler, wrap round rear window and inevitably, different wheels, but under the skin rear disc braking, enhanced suspension and a turbo tuned to kick in low down the rev range all turned this into a practical and pretty 140mph gem. Seals around rear window often leak which is nothing to repair but cracks on top of dash board are a real expense. Turbos last well if properly maintained but brakes always wear quickly.

### SPECIFICATIONS
ENGINE: 1,984cc
GEARBOX: 5 speed
POWER: 170bhp
BRAKES: Disc
SUSPENSION: Ind coil trailing arms/torsion bars
TOP SPEED: 142mph
FUEL: 28mpg
LENGTH: 166in/421cm

CURRENT PRICE: £5,667

### OWNERS' CLUB
*Porsche 924/944 Owners*
*  Club*
*Mr G Downs*
*P.O. Box 3000*
*Woodford*
*Salisbury*
*Wilts SP5 4UF*

*Porsche Club of Great Britain*
*Mr S Carr*
*Ayton House*
*West End*
*Northleach*
*Glos. GL54 3HG*
*Tel: 01451 860792*

## OWNERS' CLUB

*Aston Martin Owners Club*
*Mr J. Whyman*
*1a High Street*
*Sutton*
*Nr Ely*
*Cambs*
*CB6 2RB*
*Tel: 01353 777353*

## SPECIFICATIONS

ENGINE: 5,340cc (V8)
GEARBOX: 5 speed; 3 speed automatic
POWER: 304bhp
BRAKES: Disc
SUSPENSION: Ind wishbone/coil rigid axle, trailing arms/
watt linkage/ coils
TOP SPEED: 150mph
FUEL: 13mpg
LENGTH: 182in/462cm

CURRENT PRICE: £44,875

## ASTON MARTIN V8 VOLANTE

We judge our favourite movies by what we see on the scene not the years of fund raising and graft creating the picture. We look on cars like the Aston in the same manner: whilst the V8 turned heads the company battled for survival. Starved of funds David Brown finally sold the company in 1972 for £100. DBS V6 became the AM V8 but within a year the Arab-Israeli war and fuel crisis tore the heart from the supercar market. By January 1974 the company was insolvent, by 1975 it was in receivership, bought again in 1976. Whilst all this was happening rivals were stealing the market. Affordable facelifts and a switch back to carburettors helped and then in a brave move they launched a convertible version of essentially a standard Aston – no extra power or gimmicks, just an 11-year-old model with a serious price increase. The Volante had a power hood and air conditioning but none of the excitement of Vantage specifications. The gamble paid off with hundreds built over more than a decade, some eventually combining the open air pleasures with the blistering power of Vantage. The Prince of Wales' Aston led to an unofficial P of W specification. Incidentally, the new for '98 350bhp, 494 cm Vantage-based Volante will cost you £169,500.

## OWNERS' CLUB

*Fiat X1/9 Owners Club*
*S. Cant*
*25 Windmill Close*
*Ryde*
*Isle of Wight*
*PO33 3JB*

*Harry Collier*
*Fiat Motor Club of GB*
*Barnside*
*Glastonbury*
*Somerset*
*BA6 8DB*
*Tel: 01458 831443*

## SPECIFICATIONS

ENGINE: 1,498cc
GEARBOX: 5 speed
POWER: 85bhp
BRAKES: Disc
SUSPENSION: Ind MacPherson strut/coil Ind
MacPherson strut/coil
TOP SPEED: 112mph
FUEL: 27mpg
LENGTH: 150.79in/383cm

CURRENT PRICE: £3,500

## FIAT X1/9 1500

It wasn't just Aston Martin caught in the commercial downturn following the 1973/4 oil crisis. Fiat too held back on investment and developments until the situation stabilized. Eventually they focused on a modest hatchback design to replace the ageing best seller the 128. The result was the highly individual front wheel drive Strada with transverse mounted engines of 1.1, 1.3 and 1.5 capacities which were unveiled during 1978. For six years they had also been successfully selling their pretty little mid-engined sports car the X 1/9 using the modest 1290cc engine from the old 128. Like the original Frogeye Sprite the Fiat X1/9 looked a faster car than it actually was – struggling to 100mph via a four speed box. However the 1978 advent of the Strada package (1.1, 1.3 and 1.5 on offer) gave Fiat the opportunity to enhance the sports car's performance. The 1978 Mk II X1/9 offered a 5 speed all sync gearbox, 1489cc power plant, virtually 3 seconds off the 0-60 figures and a top speed of 112mph. There were new bumpers to accommodate their thriving US market requirements and some interior changes. Opinions remain split between Mk I and the Mk II but Bertone's styling is the epitome of that era's love affair with the wedge shape and it may be that the style's classic charms will seduce generations who didn't attend the birth.

NEW ELIGIBLES

## TRIUMPH TR7 V8

British Leyland tried to create a Triumph sports car integrating fashionable wedge styling, Stratos glamour and yet still meet the crippling new US safety regulations. It actually nearly succeeded but from Speke to Canley to Solihull, the project was was fraught with industrial unrest and poor build quality. However in 1978 BL Competition Dept at Abingdon unveiled the homologation TR7 V8 using a highly tuned Rover V8 engine generating up to 300bhp. Officially 400 were built and Tony Pond immediately led three TR team rally victories and a 4th in the RAC Rally. The promise was enormous but the usual problems meant delay till 1980 to launch a road going version (the TR8) by which time the American market had dried up: a year later TR production stopped. An unknown number of TR7 V8's exist whilst estimates place around 80 rhd UK TR8's among the 2,715 produced. All homologation specials were coupés, most production TR8's convertibles. The addition of V8 power to a spacious two seater makes for an interesting classic whilst an industry has sprung up converting TR7's into further examples of what might have been a best seller model. Thoroughly check any such conversion on a Speke manufactured car (mid 1974 to May 1978).

### SPECIFICATIONS
ENGINE: 3528cc
GEARBOX: 5 speed manual
POWER: 300bhp approx
BRAKES: Disc
SUSPENSION: Ind MacPherson/coil/Live axle/coils/radius arms/Panhard rod
TOP SPEED: 127mph (depending on gearing)
FUEL: Unknown
LENGTH: 164in/418cm

CURRENT PRICE: N/A

### OWNERS' CLUB
*Alun Jones*
*TR Drivers Club*
*40 Carr Lane*
*Hawley Hall*
*Wigan, Lancs*
*WN3 5ND*
*Tel: 01942 498001*

*TR Register*
*Mr R Good*
*1B Hawkesworth*
*Southmead Ind Park*
*Didcot*
*Oxon OX11 7HR*
*Tel: 01235 818866*

NEW ELIGIBLES

## VOLVO 262C

This car has a number of features ensuring its classic status. Firstly like all Volvos it's built to last and then only around 6000 were ever made – with substantial numbers sold to the USA. Its heritage is a little complex with the basic car a 264 saloon, though actually the prototype was constructed around a 164 model. The V6 power plant was the product of development between Peugeot, Renault and Volvo and was originally intended to be a V8. To save fuel and weight it was reduced to a six, always leaving this large Volvo a little short on performance, although the 1980 increase in power was a significant improvement. Another credibility plus was the use of the Italian coachbuilder Bertone who designed the interior and assembled these striking coupés from parts delivered by Volvo. These cars are capable of extraordinarily high mileages and offer greater standards of personal safety and comfort than other classic cars of the period. It may have been 20 years ago but interior treats included black leather, electric windows, air conditioning, electric mirrors and even heated seats. With the weight of these executive cruisers combining with only adequate reserves of power, beware of likely cars from the States – where meeting their regulations further reduced performance. Rare, highly individual, future classics.

### SPECIFICATIONS
ENGINE: 2,664cc (V6)  (2849cc after 1980)
GEARBOX: Automatic
POWER 125bhp (155bhp after 1980)
BRAKES: Disc
SUSPENSION: Ind McPherson strut/coil; Live axle/Panhard rod/coils/trailing arms
TOP SPEED: 110mph
FUEL: 18mpg – 27mpg
LENGTH: 192.91in/490cm

CURRENT PRICE: £2,875

### OWNERS' CLUB
*Volvo Enthusiasts Club*
*Kevin Price*
*4 Goonbell*
*St Agnes*
*Cornwall*
*TR5 0PH*
*Tel; 01872 553740*

*Volvo Owners Club*
*John Smith*
*18 Macauley Avenue*
*Portsmouth*
*Hants*
*PO6 4NY*
*Tel: 01705 381494*

# COVER STORIES

*Telling it like it was*

Almost all of us owe a debt of gratitude to the motoring press. Long before we could own the cars of our dreams we had studied them in every detail, digested their faults, become armchair experts through the pages of our favoured magazine. I vividly remember sitting on the floor at college stunned at the images on the pages of *Autocar* when the E-Type Jaguar was announced.

For periods in life our chosen motoring publication was an important part of our education for it fuelled us with enthusiasms and opinions we still air time and again. It is perhaps less obvious that the journals themselves journey through their own ups and downs. Though the central core of motoring experts may move around the titles, the publications themselves often struggle to survive. To gather together this collection I have spoken again to many colleagues last worked with 20 or 30 years ago. Long

removed from our former editor/contributor relationship I have been overwhelmed with private stories of just how tough survival was for the very journals I was then trying to impress. I've learned of not enough funds to put issues out, of complex private relationships, monumental mistakes, desperate battles with disenchanted proprietors and on occasion irrational closures.

The merger and rationalizing of the motoring giants killed a number of titles and panic measures during the oil crisis removed still more. But a central reason for some of the losses has been the increasing specialization of the magazines themselves – dividing the market into ever smaller sectors. Once *Autocar* and *Motor* fought it out from positions of huge power, but sporting magazines dented their pre-eminence whilst the eventual *What Car* launch wounded their circulations. I asked the distinguished former editor of *Autocar* Peter Garnier what was the perceived difference between these two rivals. He paused – "I can't think of one," he said "but we always considered ourselves the Times newspaper of motoring magazines. I suppose," he continued, "that on Wednesday we bought the *Autocar* to see who had won the race; on Fridays we bought *The Motor* to read about what he had won it in, and then at the end of the month bought *Motor Sport* to digest how he had gained the victory."

Gathering in the news: Simon Taylor, now a presenter for ITV's Grand Prix coverage and author of AC Heritage (Osprey), and the author climb the edges of Prescott Hill Climb in the course of their regular weekly work preparing material for Autosport. (Picture by Guy Griffiths)

## SPEEDWORLD INTERNATIONAL

### Born 1968–Died 1968

When Haymarket Publishing bought *Autosport*, its Managing Editor Gregor Grant left to create a rival magazine concentrating on international motor sport events at the expense of club news reportage. Launched in the April of 1968 and largely staffed by ex–*Autosport* experts it had considerable potential but was quickly hamstrung by a reluctant backer. They changed printers and staggered on only to close by Christmas. One wonders how often this has happened in the history of publshing. Copies are now of course rare.

Nearing the end of its short life, this is a rare copy of the breakaway international magazine inspired by Autosport and dated November 1968.

A typical early 50's "paid for" cover advertising Ferodo brake linings – providing extra income for this magazine which sometimes barely had the funds to publish, alongside a later edition with the famous white pin stripes over green motif. The striped covers were often thought as a constant feature of Motor Sport's long history, but surprisingly it only featured for roughly 12 years of its life

## MOTOR SPORT

### Born 1924–Current

Starting out in 1924 as the Brooklands Gazette it changed to *Motor Sport* in 1926 and staggered through various owners and cash crises, publishing as few as three or four issues in a year. Staunch Methodist Wesley J Tee took over in 1936 with Bill Boddy as a contributor. Through the war years Boddy effectively edited *Motor Sport* by telephone whilst writing aircraft manuals. Later he became editor proper. From near the end of the '50s the late Denis Jenkinson added his enthusiasm and expertise. Now owned by Haymarket it's just enjoyed a substantial facelift under Gordon Crookshank, incorporating many old styling cues and the same infectious celebration for motor sport in all its guises.

*Edging into the 60s with a cover picture of the rare saloon bodied Daimler 250 sports car, this Christmas issue boasted racing driver Roy Salvadori road testing the then new Ford Anglia 105E. Alongside is an example from near the end of its life. This June 1967 edition boasts "New Competition Chief tells all" – in fact an exclusive interview with Peter Browning by the author which talked of the uncertain future, Cooper S's and competition trials with an 1800.*

## SPORTING MOTORIST

### 1959 – 1967

This was a publishing venture by the owners of the famed Autocourse annuals. They initially issued quarterly, then bi–monthly and then monthly *Autocourse* magazines – later called *Autocourse and Sporting Motorist*. Then in 1959 it became *Sporting Motorist* with plans to steal, or share, some of *Motor Sport* magazine's market. It blended sport subjects with more general material including an extended series by the author on celebrated sporting motorists. For some time it was steered by an enthusiastic Philip Hutchinson before it was sold in 1965 to Harry Jackson of Bugle Press who also ran a nursing journal and the *Gas & Oil Pioneer*. *Autosport's* assistant editor Mike Kettlewell undertook editorship and this lasted until Bugle was sold to Haymarket in 1967 when the magazine ceased. Mike Kettlewell now runs the highly respected specialist car book suppliers Mill House.

## FORD TIMES

### 1912 – 1974

Actually started in the USA in 1908, it was first published in the UK shortly after the opening of the Manchester manufacturing plant and was initially used as a house magazine for the many visitors to the new plant. The switch to war vehicle production ended the need for printed promotion until in 1924 the firm W J Rand relaunched *Ford Times* under the colourful editorship of Mr Duffield – a friend of the founder. In 1947 he retired to followed by a spate of editors and designers who, along with use of colour, transformed the magazine. In the 60s first Bill Patton and then Tony Peagam mirrored Walter Hayes' vision of giving the customers what they wanted. *Ford Times* shone, it hired significant contributors and actually won awards. In 1970 management decided it ought to become a newspaper which was not a success, returning to a quarterly magazine in 1974 for a brief period. The oil crisis, with all its corporate cutbacks, saw the end.

## HIGH ROAD MAGAZINE

### 1969 – 1970

British Leyland boasted that with "the world's leading motoring writers" *High Road* – its new large format colour monthly, would be "aimed at the broadest section of the public" and be visible in embassies and airports around the world. Early on, it claimed it would gain a 100,000 readership, and did. It was to replace the long standing separate marque publications and unusually it also sold well on bookstalls, generated good income from adverts. Within a single year it broke even. Within months it shot to a 130,000 circulation but Lord Stokes axed it as part of his 'streamlining'. His henchman given that illogical task has in the last couple of years finally hunted out a complete set of copies for himself.

*The award winning Tony Peagam's 60s psychedelic motorway cover. Beneath lies a 1952 edition of Ford Times offering fur coats, Hollywood pin ups, roller skating forecourt attendants, west country monks and the Duke of Edinburgh. At the back, the very first edition of Ford Times in newspaper format – a long and distinguished publishing tradition begins to fade away.*

## HOT CAR

### 1968 – 1983

Magazines such as *Car and Car Conversions* and *Custom Car* were steady sellers for Mercury House publishers, but 60s flamboyance got to them and they launched *Hot Car* in 1968 under the editorship of Tony Bostock from *Popular Motoring*. It rapidly reached a circulation of 150,000 by combining Bostock's exuberance with technical editor Paul Davies' insight. Inevitably that success led to the editor being moved across to work the magic on a different magazine and Paul Davies was also poached by another title. In 1973 it was bought by AGB in Slough who injected more investment, then under the umbrella of Business Publications it became integrated into *Performance Car* in October of 1983, reflecting the increased interest in fast cars generally.

*"Lets Go – Be a Whizz–Skid" proclaims the editor over skid control whilst Paul Davies finds a "Real Mod Mini" – Hot Car entertaining those famed Swinging Sixties enthusiasts. Groovy.*

*A mid 1970's edition exclusively revealing the Vauxhall Viva HB as the "Mini Mangler" – ironically decrying the very car which gave birth to the magazine.*

## CAR

### 1965 – Current

Begat of *Mini Owner & Small Car / Small Car* it started life with a July issue investigating the truth about Rolls-Royce – emphatically shaking off the small car restrictions. It also unveiled it's CAR of the Year award to be judged every January. Under the editorship of Doug Blain it gathered in notable contributors such as Stirling Moss, LJK Setright and Nick Brittan and in September 1967 incorporated *Q-car* which was published upside down and bound with *Car* – creating two front covers per issue and no back cover! However *Q-car* would in time join *Small Car* as nothing more than a tiny publisher's acknowledgement. The magazine pressed on through the 70s creating a solid market catering for the middle ground in motor car ownership. Still growing – and still receiving material from Leonard Setright, *Car* has successfully blossomed from that 1962 Mini owners magazine.

## MINI OWNER & SMALL CAR / SMALL CAR

### 1962 – 1965 (Also see *Car* above)

Just a couple of years after the launch of the famed Mini a magazine catering for the revolution it caused was inevitable. Art editor Charles Pocklington – who had worked on the legendary Eagle comic, designed the first edition of *Mini Owner* but was then required to change it as first *Sporting Driver* and then *Small Car* was added to the title. It successfully catered for all smaller car interests as well as motor racing features and specific pieces under the heading *Woman Driver* – another title considered for a magazine. (Still seems like a pretty good idea.) It moved to the simplified title of *Small Car* and then in July 1965 became simply known as *Car*.

## MODERN MOTORING AND TRAVEL

### 1930 – 1965

In 1929 Billy Rootes bought Humber and Hillman (Rootes Brothers Ltd actually took over Humber management in 1932) and invited leading journalists to drive the still secret Wizard to Africa. They had to be back by January 20th so photographs and film records could be processed before the launch. The film was shown to 1000 invited lunch guests in the Albert Hall whilst the photographs launched the first regular issue of *Modern Motorist and Travel* – occasional issues had preceded it. Through all its years just two editors shaped the magazine which reached 90,000 circulation and offered a skilful mixture of Rootes news and general travel. From the mid 60s American Chrysler bought into the company – it was development work on the Imp that did the damage – Rootes increasingly regretted this, and one by one aspects of the UK operation, including *Modern Motoring and Travel,* disappeared.

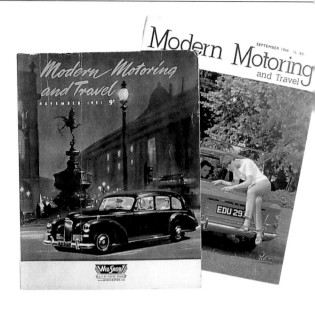

*The November 1951 edition under Tom Mulcaster's editorship offered Capetown to Livingston in a Minx, the 36th London Motor Show, Jamaican hurricanes, mechanical guidance for owner drivers, a Rank starlet in a white fur stole and an editorial demanding attention be given to the fact Princess Elizabeth had to travel to Canada in an American aircraft, as we didn't have one to cross the Atlantic. Later, and with a decorative model closely inspecting the paintwork, a 1966 example from the second editor Stanley Seeley extols the Imp, Bermuda, Jordan, more Imps and a decent pub in Surrey.*

## MOTOR RACING

### 1954 – 1970

This was published by Knightsbridge Publications every third Friday of the month primarily for the benefit of the British Racing and Sports Car Club. Based at Brands Hatch race circuit, for two guineas per annum BRSCC membership offered privileges at Brands and Mallory Park, club functions, free entry to the Racing Car Show and naturally a complimentary subscription to *Motor Racing* magazine. It provided detailed, uncluttered reportage of Grand Prix, Endurance and other major events along with BRSCC eventing. By 1970 the club could no long afford to give the magazine away free and without that guaranteed circulation the magazine rapidly disappeared. For a period from 1956 it incorporated *Motor Rally* and from 1968 incorporated *Sportscar* as a title.

*Summer of 1963 and* Motor Racing *reported the Dutch and French GPs, reviewed Le Mans, the Brands Hatch 6 hour saloon race and provided a close-up of the new BRM race car.*

## AUTOSPORT

### 1950 – Current

First reaching the news stands in the summer of 1950, this specialist sport and competition journal quickly built up a fine reputation under the inspiration of its editor Gregor Grant and technical boffin John Bolster. Its list of staff and contributors reads like a Who's Who of motoring experts, belying its once small and gloomy offices near Paddington Station. In 1967 it was bought by the hungry Haymarket Publishing – currently chaired by Simon Taylor, himself an ex–*Autosport* editor. With weekly readership of over 68,000, *Autosport's* status continues to grow.

*The early covers showcased a single photograph – a much sought-after prize by photographers. Above is an early 1964 season trials study by the author, in the centre is another, this time showing the revamped design and the move to colour photography. 26 years later, the single photo is replaced by a frenzy of pictures, type and information, indicative of the huge expansion of interest in motor sport.*

## STANDARD TRIUMPH REVIEW

### 1931 – 1969

Priced initially at just 2d this publication would run for 37 years in various guises with a very clear policy – 'This magazine is to create and foster interest amongst Standard and Triumph car owners and in Standard Motor Co Ltd. – we make no attempt to disguise it as a general motoring publication'. It ceased in September of 1939 and resumed as *The Standard Car Review* in January of 1947 until late 1959 when it changed title again to the *Standard Triumph Review*. It died at the close of 1969 to make way for BL's flagship *High Road* Magazine yet, by always remaining a Standard/Triumph mouthpiece, it left a thorough record of the marque's history.

*Two covers under the final title of* Standard Triumph Review. *Arnold Bolton would prove to be the last Editor but then he would move on to work on the launch of its replacement,* High Road. *Nowadays, editor Tony Beadle does a great job at* Triumph World.

# THE AUTOCAR

### 1895 – Current

This is the oldest of the motoring publications, launched many years before most of the automobile industry. Always published as a weekly, through the decades it built up a strong and loyal following by skilfully blending a wide variety of motoring topics alongside detailed news on each new model. Rivalry with the near identical *Motor* meant a bonanza for the enthusiast over many years. In 1963 it shed the prefix 'The' and under the confident control of Haymarket it finally absorbed its rival *Motor* in 1988, thus ensuring its survival in name at least. Despite a whole century of publishing to authenticate its claim to pre-eminence, ever more newcomers are emerging to challenge for this middle ground.

*It's the mid 50s and Autocar offers comprehensive road tests of the Peugeot 403 and the Wolseley 6/99 along with a classified list to make the mouth water. An unmarked low mileage Austin Healey 100 for £875, a nearly new 100M version for just another £120, whilst a virtually new Morris Minor costs around £500.*

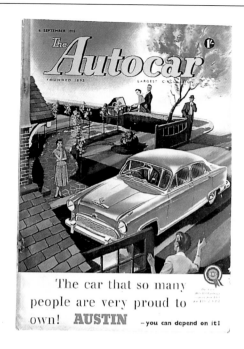

# THE MOTOR

### 1902 – 1988

Just those few tantalizing years younger than *Autocar* the initial issues were actually targeting two wheels under the title *Motor Cycle and Motoring* but before long its guiding light Edmund Dangerfield sensed the automobile gaining the upper hand and changed the title to *The Motor* incorporating *Motor Cycling*. Like its famed rival it built up an enormous weekly following, covering the widest range of motoring topics; but after the Second World War the upsurge in single marque publications and motor sport journals began to splinter circulations and by the eighties both *Autocar* and *Motor* were poor shadows of their former selves. Inevitably, one would fall and in 1988, despite having the larger circulation, it was *The Motor* – bought by the ever-expanding Haymarket and merged into a revitalized *Autocar*.

*A single London Motor Show could mean Preview and Report issues of 200 pages each and an actual show issue of 300 pages. Here, the October 1954 Show Report issues warnings of future congestion as post-war production grows – at that time in Britain just 1 in 18 owned a motor car.*

# SAFETY FAST

### 1959 – 1968

After the Austin/BMC merger and the expansion of the MG range a new dedicated magazine for MG owners and enthusiasts was created by editor Wilson McComb using leading contributors and selling to the public at the same price as *Motor Sport*. In 1964 Stuart Seager took over editorship joined by Peter Browning who was also secretary of the Austin Healey Club. It was flagged as 'The magazine for those who practise driving as an art' and became the mouthpiece of both the

*This much loved cover style is seen here in its final year. In this issue there was a detailed essay and itemized competition record of the fabulous Austin Healey 3000 by Les Needham – dream material for researchers!*

MG Car Club and the Austin–Healey Club. In fact the Works Cooper S also crept onto the pages, turning it into virtually a Competition Department journal. In 1967 Browning went on to became the last Competition Dept chief whilst *Safety Fast* was sacrificed at Lord Stoke's altar of modernization. The new multi-marque *High Road* magazine made no effort to reflect MG interests; but eventually the MG Club itself created a modest periodical of its own.

## MOTORING

### 1945 – 1968

In 1924 there was the Morris Owners magazine which turned into *Morris Owner* and *Nuffield Mail* during 1942. After the Second World War Nuffield launched the magazine as 'The New Outlook on Motoring – incorporating Morris Owner'. Designed as a general interest publication for owners of Morris, Wolseley, Riley and MG cars it gradually incorporated actual Riley and MG Owners Club sections. In March 1950 it simplified its title to *Motoring* and survived unscathed the following year's merger between Austin and BMC. With the birth in 1959 of *Safety Fast,* MG had its own dedicated mouthpiece. *Motoring* gently wandered on, offering Spring Accessory Reviews, Training Tomorrow's Motorists and Go Sell Thine Oil – a story of oil from Biblical times to the atomic age. The arrival of *High Road* meant (chintz) curtains.

*Freshly liberated from its more cumbersome earlier title this 1951 edition tries to unravel the new laws surrounding pedestrian crossings, debates the question of plain clothes police patrols and looks at a racing Special based on an MG. Underneath is a mid 60s issue, with Motoring slipping further and further into the quiet safety of Home Counties preoccupations.*

## DRIVE

### 1967 – 1985

Launched to reflect the then new Director General's vision of a modern AA it was a free distribution quarterly largely concentrating on motoring as opposed to motor cars – although its incisive testing paved the way for the later *What Car* approach. As the journal of the AA membership it instantly enjoyed a UK record-breaking print run of 3.7 million copies – rising to 4.8 by the mid 1970s when free distribution ceased. It soldiered on until the mid 80s as a conventional retail magazine but with diminishing readership. Produced by Readers Digest for the AA – hence its familiar Digest format – it boasted distinguished contributors, thanks to a series of impressive editors, including one of last year's Stanley Yearbook Car of the Year judges Tony Peagam, with whom the author worked on numerous features.

*Small in size but far and away the biggest circulation magazine in the UK, Drive magazine was for many years the most powerful motoring publication, creating the Square Wheel of the Year Award for the worst car and pioneering studies into the effects of drugs on driving.*

## AUTO NEWS

### Born 1966 – Died 1966

*Motoring News* had long held a healthy slice of the weekly motoring market with its rather subdued newspaper. It offered page space for many UK motor clubs to report their events as well as coverage of the more notable events in racing and rallies. The equivalent for the two wheel brigade was the famed *Motor Cycle News* published by East Midland Allied Press of Kettering. A decision was made to try and steal *Motoring News'* readership with the publication of *Auto News* – a rival newspaper format motor sport weekly with crisper layouts and more international coverage – in fact, virtually a newsprint version of *Autosport*. However, enthusiasts' loyalty to the existing publications meant that *Auto News'* circulation was slow, the publishers lost interest, and it was closed 31 issues later on 1st December.

*August Bank Holiday at Brands Hatch for the Guards International Trophy. This last big race for full Group 7 sports racers drew big crowds to enjoy these powerful cars. Auto News marked the event with an unusually large picture by the author of John Surtees in a 5.9 Lola Chevrolet leading Chris Amon in the works 5.4 McLaren Elva-Chevrolet, followed by the rest of the thundering pack: Surtees won.*

## VAUXHALL MOTORIST

### 1933 – 1975

Like rivals Ford, Rootes and Austin, Vauxhall owners had been treated to their very own journal from before the second World War. Sedately, it led you through the delights of camping, golf, the law, some servicing aspects and endless pootling. Once in a while a new model would revive its editorial purpose, as in the December 1961 issue when they concentrated on 'The Car For The Man Who Wants A Bit More,' the Vauxhall VX4/90. The publication was suspended between 1939 and 1945. Re-born in 1946 it survived into the 1970s, becoming bi–monthly, until its demise with the October/November issue of 1975. Although all house magazines were gradually fading away during the reign of its Firenza Sports owning editor Gwyn Hughes, *Vauxhall Motorist* did increase its editorial strength with extra competition reports … to say nothing of the photo spread of nine young production line girls under the headline "Thank Heavens for Little Girls"!

*The Christmas 1961 issue sees the launch of the VX4/90. In the letters page the Shrewsbury Weights and Measures Dept point out that 1 lb and 2 lb loaves of bread are now legally replaced by short weight versions. Beneath it rests a 1951 summer issue which celebrates the opening of the new Southampton Ocean Terminal whilst inside a single sentence from the RAC announces they will not be renewing the lease on Silverstone Circuit – not one of their better decisions!*

# THE STANLEY HUNDRED

## *History, specifications, advice*

As we said last year, it seems very strange that most classic car books, in the main, continue to be devoid of any personal voice. Naturally, this is explained in part by the fact that any author is unlikely to sweat out a manuscript about a model or marque which he actively dislikes; the mere fact of the book is evidence of his affections, which therefore do not have to be enunciated at every turn. That does not however apply in the case of the across-the-marques guide book such as this. So why are most commentaries so anodyne? Partiality is very much a part of the classic car world – more than half the fun in fact. So there *is* a personal voice to the Stanley Hundred. Agreeing with the following list of classic cars and the comments made about them – including some cars perceived as disasters – may not actually be as satisfying as disagreeing violently. The new additions to this year's 100 are not, however, solely the choice of the author. We have read the letters (some of them indignant about the absence of obvious classics that tower above any of the tawdry entries that *were* included) and have occasionally been swayed.

To repeat some good advice, one thing which all existing classic car owners do agree upon is the value of the Owners' Car Club. If you are even thinking of buying, talk to them, they will steer you, perhaps even help find a reliable car. They have no commercial axe to grind – just a common love for the car you are considering.

## VALUATION

As last year, basic information on the 100 is given about each model's evolution, its place in the production family tree and which particular examples have appeal. The Star System for valuations is drawn, quite simply, from our own price guide which, thanks to months of data imput represents the most balanced figures we could produce. We have studied all the valuations for these cars from four years ago and again as to current price, created the mean average and then adjusted for the change in the value of the pound – as provided by the Bank of England – to show a percentage swing. The point to bear in mind is that the star rating is a double-edged sword. The car which shows the most calamitous drop in price, it could be argued, is the best bargain around.

## SPARES

Consider the spares heading as really a shorthand for the level of problems that you might encounter if you own any specific model. Virtually no classic is trouble-free and ownership often provides a parable of the heart ruling the head. However, it is important to know what you are heading into and so hopefully through this gradation you will begin to assess the risks. It is not merely the *price* of spares which is being evaluated; which would be pointless. In this star system, a Ferrari can beat a Ford Consul.

## STANLEY RATING (SR)

The Stanley Rating (SR) is entirely personal. We all favour some cars over others and yet might well find it hard to explain why. Grading feelings for 100 models certainly proved extremely hard. Each of these cars was considered separately for looks, ideas and for personality, and then the accumulated scores converted into the five star segments. The cars you drove when young, or admired when young, will always score highly; but in addition this year, my reaction to the new Fiat 20V Turbo and, perhaps not quite so unreservedly appreciative, of the Jaguar XK8, were as enthusiastic as for the older 'domestic' models I remember with such affection.

# CITROËN DYANE

CHEAP, HIGHLY INDIVIDUAL AND ADDICTIVE

### MANUFACTURER
# CITROËN

Conceived in the 1930s to the design brief "transport passengers and eggs across a ploughed field", the aluminium and canvas-built prototypes with the single headlights, were concealed during the German occupation of France in World War II and emerged as the famous 2CV in 1948. French taxation on power favoured tiny engines, and the 375cc engine gave birth to the 2CV name – two being HP, CV or *cheval vapeur,* literally meaning steam horse. In 1968 engine power was increased to 602cc and 3hp and the name remained. Well over 7,000,000 cars were sold worldwide, seducing drivers with their simplicity, pure logic and extraordinary economy. A British Citroën Bijou was produced in 1960 with a fibreglass body. In its first 30 years there were over eleven models including the Dyane, which first entered the UK in 1968. The 435cc Dyane 4 model initially featured inboard front drum braking and lacked rear quarter lights, while the Dyane 6 enjoyed front discs and a heady 602cc engine. Essentially it was the 2CV with a slightly more conventional five-door body, full length sun roof, air cooled flat twin engine and minor refinements like integrated headlights, greater visibility, sliding windows. The 4 offered 58mpg, while the 6 returned 46mpg and a top speed of 70mph.

The Dyane offers incredible space. The back seat can be unclipped to provide space for an entire bath-

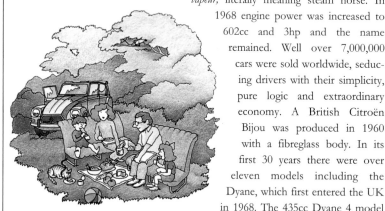

| SPECIFICATIONS | |
|---|---|
| **ENGINE:** 425cc; 602cc flat twin | **BRAKES:** Drum; front discs 61 onward |
| **BHP:** 21; 28.5 | **SUSPENSION:** Ind inter–connecting front/rear |
| **FUEL:** 58–46mpg | |
| **GEARBOX:** 4 speed manual | **YEARS:** 1967–1984 |
| **SPEED:** 60 – 70 mph | **PRODUCTION:** 1,443,583 |
| **BODIES:** 5 door | |

room suite, including the plumber. Brilliant gears are positioned directly on the dash, providing a large amount of leg space, and the soft, passenger-friendly suspension brings a sense of fun to cornering. I've owned four Dyanes, and while they all took their time going uphill, loved going flat-out. In an average working life, they can tot up over 200,000 miles and still perform with reliability.

## RELATIONS

In addition to the Ami 6 of the 1960s, there was a large 2CV-based family of commercial vans, special editions, multi-purpose pick-ups, and even a twin engined model, with production in 18 countries.

## BEST BUY

Front floor panels are prone to rust and king pins need regular greasing. The engine and gearbox survive high mileage. Body panels just unbolt: the entire 2CV body only requires 20 bolts and two sets of hands to lift it away from the chassis. With so little to go wrong choice is really down to condition.

| Cost | £1,050 |
|---|---|
| (Dyane 6) | |
| % swing | -4 |
| | |
| Spares | ★★★★★ |
| V.F.M. | ★★ |
| S.R. | ★★★ |

# MANUFACTURER
# ROOTES

Big Austin-Healeys, TRs, MGAs and MGBs all dominated the late 1950s and early 1960s. The image problems of the Rootes Alpine – it never quite matched the speed, elitism or, more importantly, the sales of its rivals – are its greatest assets as a classic car. It was over-engineered, heavy, and consequently slower than its competitors. However, the body offers more period style and grace than any of the others; the 7mph loss of speed to the contemporary MGB is hardly important now, and the Alpine's extra strength and passenger comfort are great advantages. The Rootes concept utilised existing elements from the Hillman Husky and Sunbeam Rapier. With a fashionable sporting body, the Sunbeam Alpine offered interior comfort with wind-up windows, overdrives, automatic options, detachable hardtops.

Essentially, the 1959 Mk I used the 1494cc engine with an improved cylinder head; the 1960 Mk II had the 1592cc; the Mk III in 1963 had changes to windscreen, doors and quarter lights, a refurbished interior, and a much larger boot. There was also a new detachable GT hardtop version. In 1964 the Mk IV brought slightly improved power to both the sports and GT, reduced rear fins, a changed grill and improved gearbox. The Mk V of 1965 offered 1725cc, five bearing cranks, and a power-plant shared with the Mk V Sunbeam Rapier. A limited number of fastback Alpines were also produced by the coachbuilders Harrington between 1961 and 1963.

## RELATIONS

Key elements, including the floor pan and rear suspension, were taken from the Hillman Husky estate, while the engine, gearbox and front suspension were from the Sunbeam Rapier. The beautiful body was an original design by Ken Howes.

The Sunbeam Tiger, a Ford V8-engined rival to the AC Cobra, was sold between 1964 and 1968.

## BEST BUY

Everything mechanical is fairly reliable, but uncontrolled body rust is a problem. Sunbeams are full of water-traps, so check the undersides, suspension points and sills, but better still, (as is always the case) get an expert to come with you. Regular servicing is advisable. Early cars, particularly the Mk III, are extremely collectable.

The spectacular new
**SUNBEAM** *Alpine*

*Nomenclature is confusing. Because of Lago-Talbots, Sunbeam-Talbots were sold in France as Sunbeams; the name was then adopted by the '53 Alpine sports car.*

## SPECIFICATIONS

**ENGINE:** 1494 / 1592 (II, III & IV) / 1725
**BHP:** 78 / 80 / 82 – (77 GT) / 92.5
**FUEL:** 26 / 22 / 25 / 22 auto/ 25mpg
**GEARBOX:** 4 speed – Automatic option post -64
**BRAKES:** Disc–drum
**SUSPENSION:** Coil/wishbone – semi-elliptic

**SPEED:** 98 / 97 / 98 / 92 auto / 98 mph
**BODIES:** 2 door open – Detachable GT hardtop – post-63
**YEARS:** 1959–1968
**PRODUCTION:** 11,904 / 19,956 / 5863 / 12,406 / 19,122

*N.B – 400 Harrington Alpines built 1961–63*

| | |
|---|---|
| Cost | £6,200 |
| % swing | 1 |
| Spares | ★★★ |
| V.F.M. | ★★★ |
| S.R. | ★★★ |

# BMC 1800
### A PRACTICAL MGB FOR HALF THE PRICE

MANUFACTURER
# BMC

'We have been given orders to go out and make it into a rally-winning machine', the newly appointed BMC competition manager Peter Browning said in 1967. His first Works car was a black development 1800, nicknamed the 'Mobile Coffin' by the Competitions Department. The car used full Group 5 modifications (equivalent to a full Group 6 competition works MGB) and driving it was exhilarating. The Landcrab rally car became a legend.

The strongest BMC car ever built, the 1800 was voted Car of the Year at the 1964 Motor Show, and *Autocar* declared it "undoubtedly one of the most important cars of the motoring world". What went wrong? Early Austin/Morris versions gained a poor reputation for clutches, driveshafts, bearings, pistons, and oil consumption. Issigonis, back from the still-born Hydrolastic Alvis project, expected a V4 and V6 for the new family car but both were cancelled and the faithful BMC B series used. The body was to be a beautiful Pininfarina design but BMC rejected it and Citroën took advantage of the design for their GS.

The 1798cc 5 bearing engine married to a new all synchromesh gearbox, Hyrdrolastic suspensions and truly incredible interior space eventually pushed it into the UK Best Sellers list. The Austin, Morris and Wolseley versions were launched, peaking with the 100mph 1800 S Sports versions. In 1972 all but the basic 1800 were replaced with the 6-cylinder 2200.

## RELATIONS

The body drew on the Mini and the Hydrolastic Alvis; the 1800 engines variation on the Series B unit within MGB. The 2200 version derived from the Maxi E series.

## BEST BUY

A strong sill structure and sub-frames that do not catch water reduces rust slightly. The 1800cc engines are much more reliable than the 2200s and the automatics; clutch replacements can be costly. Sparse interiors, a strange driving position and heavy non-power steering on some models. With spares plentiful, it is ideal for daily use. (Competition Chief Peter Browning is shown below, with the 'Mobile Coffin.').

| Cost | £1,500 |
|------|--------|
| % swing | 66 |
| Spares | ★★★ |
| V.F.M. | ★★★★★ |
| S.R. | ★★ |

### SPECIFICATIONS

| | |
|---|---|
| **ENGINE:** 1798cc, | **SUSPENSION:** All Ind |
| **BHP:** 80 – 96 | Hydrolastic |
| **FUEL:** 24 – 22 mpg | **BODIES:** 4 door |
| **GEARBOX:** 4 speed manual | **YEARS:** 1964–1975 |
| **BRAKES:** Disc/drum | **PRODUCTION:** 408,953 |
| **SPEED:** 90 –99 mph | |

# MANUFACTURER
# ROOTES

In the mid-1950s two men in their early twenties designed the excellent Hillman Imp, and Rootes bought adjacent factory land for a new production line. The plan was to counter Ford's 105E Anglia and BMC's FWD revolution, but at the time the governement was trying to encourage a wider dispersal of employment, and the planned factory site was declared a Green Belt area. Ten million pounds of governement loans encouraged the manufacturers to move to a new £22 million factory in Scotland. Having lost a certain degree of market initiative, the model finally appeared in 1963. Built rather hurriedly by a workforce of ex-ship builders, the early Imps suffered from niggling engineering problems, and inevitably lost ground to the growing band of Ford and BMC followers.

The Imp boasted a glorious engine pedigree based around the legendary Coventry Climax FWM 750 which in FWMV form was the F1 Grand Prix power plant. Initially 875cc, later 998cc, this alloy engine and gearbox weighed roughly half that of some of its rivals. It was slung behind the rear axle, but through skilful suspension and steering set–ups it created excellent handling characteristics – particularly in poor conditions. The homologation-seeking Rallye model enjoyed much competition success, and the Imp even claimed outright victory in the Tulip Rally. Rootes skilfully marketed saloon, estate, commercial and sports versions, along with coupés under Hillman, Sunbeam and Singer badges. The coupés were pretty, lowered models with reclining seats, folding rear squabs and lacked some of the marque's initial teething troubles. The three coupé

versions were the Hillman Californian (1968–70) and Chamois Coupé (1967–70), which were rebodied Imp saloons, while the Sunbeam Stiletto coupé (1967–72) boasted the fast 51bhp sports engine, suspension set-up, servo brakes and amazing quad headlights.

## RELATIONS

Uniquely original, it bears no direct lineage to former models. The designers, Mike Parkes and Tim Fry conceived a conventional three box body which concealed a space saving rear-mounted engine.

## BEST BUY

Early models have problems such as throttle linkage and the auto choke, but later coupés were less suspect. As cheap classics, expect to undertake some restoration on cylinder heads, for example. With a little care, and limited cash, they make brilliant miniature GTs, and the sports-based Sunbeam Stiletto is probably the best bet.

### SPECIFICATIONS

| | |
|---|---|
| **ENGINE:** 875cc; 998cc | **SPEED:** 87–92mph |
| **BHP:** 51; 65 | **BRAKES:** Drum |
| **FUEL:** 34–38 | **BODIES:** 2 door coupé |
| **GEARBOX:** 4 speed manual | **YEARS:** 1967–72 |
| **SUSPENSION:** Ind coil/wishbone / ind semi-trailing | **PRODUCTION:** 440,032 – all Imp variants |

| | |
|---|---|
| Cost | £1,575 |
| (Imp Stilleto) | |
| % swing | -3 |
| Spares | ★★★ |
| V.F.M. | ★★ |
| S.R. | ★★ |

## CITROEN GS
ACCOLADES & FEARS

**MANUFACTURER**
# CITROËN

This is a hard car to categorize. A very high number have been scrapped and in the eyes of many, their reputation is very grim indeed. Yet this was a major model in Citroën's history, which sold over 2,500,000 examples and was so widely applauded that in 1971 it was voted 'Car of the Year'.

Until recent times one of the true delights of Citroën has been their individualism: the raw simplicity of the 2CV, the sleek elegance of the DS, the mould breaking TA. Yet advanced design work not only leads to well earned accolades, but also to fear and confusion over maintaining cars as they grow older. The GS is a fine example of this situation. It was the first new Citroën in 15 years and filled a major gap between their DS range and the modest 2CVs and Dyanes. It appeared at the 1970 Paris Motor Show as a 1015cc four door fastback, but over the years it would become both a four and five door hatchback with a range of trim, and engines up to 1299cc, plus a brief trial period using a rotary piston engine. Now, however, most dealers view the car's technical originalities as trouble, and so prices are rock bottom. On the plus side, the car was fabulously comfortable, riding on Citroën's unique hydropneumatic self-levelling suspension. It had one of the most aerodynamically efficient bodies, and there was a perfect boot with all the internal surfaces flat panels and a boot lid incorporating the bumper – revealing a low loading platform with no obstructions. On the negative side, it was a relatively heavy car which was sadly under-powered. The all-new flat four air--cooled engine initially produced just 55.5bhp, a top speed of around 93mph and about

30mpg, though later GSAs reached 68bhp and 100mph. In certain ways these cars set standards still to be met by rivals but if you love them, you take the gamble of expensive repairs. If your worldview accepts the law that all commodities now have limited life spans, then the GS is indeed a true classic. If you want an indestructible and economic classic, this is not for you.

## RELATIONS

A highly original model which used aspects of the DS range including the self-levelling suspension, along with numerous secondary parts from the smaller Ami.

## BEST BUY

A wide choice, from 1015, 1129, 1222 & 1299cc engines, four and five door fastback and hatchbacks, plus trim levels from basic Comfort and G Special to deluxe Pallas. The complex suspension is not generally a problem, but camshafts are expensive. Buy the best you can find for some peace of mind.

---

### SPECIFICATIONS

**ENGINE:** 1015cc – 1299cc
**BHP:** 55–65
**FUEL:** 30–35mpg
**GEARBOX:** 4 & 5 speed; automatic
**BRAKES:** Disc
**SPEED:** 90–98mph
**SUSPENSION:** Hydropneumatic self-levelling
**BODIES:** 4 & 5 door fastback: hatchback
**YEARS:** 1970–1987
**PRODUCTION** 2,464,346
*(incl 847 rotary unit cars)*

---

| Cost | £750 |
|------|------|
| % swing | -31 |
| Spares | ★★★ |
| V.F.M. | ★ |
| S.R. | ★★★★ |

# MANUFACTURER
# AUSTIN

AUSTIN ALLEGRO

*EVERY CONCEIVABLE MISTAKE*

There is an Allegro Club which manfully pushes to preserve this car. We should all be grateful, for concours examples are the prime evidence of British Leyland's supreme incompetence. They had the funds and the time; they had a successful collaboration with a major Italian design house, and yet BL pressed ahead with a DIY replacement for their best-selling car, the BMC 1100/1300 range. They made every conceivable mistake. The 1100 was a decade old, but still represented a full quarter of BL sales. The replacement was to be bigger and better – bigger it was, but the eventual interior was marginally smaller! Twelve model versions would be offered employing the trusted BMC Series A engine and the larger E Series (under-used after their equally disastrous Austin Maxi exercise) all coupled with new independent Hydragas suspension. This car, designed by blind committees, managed to destroy the trust of over 1.5 million 1100/1300 customers who might have bought a replacement. The car was awful. BL thought differently and invited journalists for an early preview, but their doubts prompted BL to promise a review. It was finally launched in 1973 exactly as previewed, and thus alienated even the journalistic support British Leyland needed. It looked older than Pininfarina's classic 1100 and so the public kept buying that car. It boasted a truly modern Quartic square steering wheel that everyone warned them was a bad idea. Build qualities were dreadful, most things failed, or overheated, and the car construction was so feeble that if you did not follow exact jacking procedures, it would literally bend out of shape. (That's where those stories of windows popping out emanate from.) BL spent four years and over £21,000,000 creating this disgrace.

## RELATIONS

The two base model ranges use the trusted BMC Series A engine from the outgoing BMC 1100/1300 range, while the two other models used the Series E engine from the Maxi.

## BEST BUY

I can't personally recommend one. In 1973, I admitted 'It's not a car I would rush to buy', and that was before its inglorious history! From 1973 1100/1300 models were available as two or four doors, but only the 1300 as estates and automatics. The 1100 became the 1000 for its last three years, 1980-83. The 1500/1750 versions only had two doors for the first year. The Mk IIs, from 1976, and IIIs from 1980, with the various 1750cc cars, were badged up under Sports names. Vanden Plas models are now making some advances at auction.

---

## SPECIFICATIONS

**ENGINE:** 998cc; 1098cc; 1485cc; 1748cc
**BHP:** 48–76bhp
**FUEL:** 25–40mpg
**GEARBOX:** 4 & 5 speed: automatic
**BRAKES:** Disc/drum
**SUSPENSION:** Hydragas all independent system
**SPEED:** 80–95mph
**BODIES:** 2 & 4 door saloon: estate
**YEARS:** 1973–1983
**PRODUCTION** 642,350

# POPULAR 100E
## A 'WELL SORTED' BASIC CLASSIC

## MANUFACTURER
# FORD

While the old perpendicular Popular 103E continued to sell, the Prefect and Anglia were replaced in 1953 by the modern-bodied 100E. Borrowing design themes from the larger Fords, the two door (Anglia) and four door (Prefect) cars were powered by a reworked 1172cc unit. Big Ford thinking also introduced independent MacPherson strut front suspension and hydraulic brakes, among other mechanical improvements. The old three speed gearbox remained, but the improved engine and gear ratios brought steady 60mph cruising and a maximum speed of 70mph. My first rally was in a friend's 100E, and I vividly recall our climb up Porlock Hill in the pouring rain. Former owners will remember that these willing cars always got there in the end, but in their own time, and any pressure on the accelerator slows, or sometimes stops the quaint vacuum-driven windscreen wiper.

The De Luxe versions, introduced in 1955, were followed by the Escort/Squire estate bodies in 1957. However, in 1959, the brand new Ford Anglia 105E, complete with cut back rear window and brilliant Kent engine, caused the retirement of the Prefect/Anglia 100E and old Popular 103E. Intriguingly, Ford chose this moment to launch a 'New' Popular in the dropped 100E body. A De Luxe option was really a variant on the deceased 100E Anglia. Six years of production ironed out all the niggles before the late entry of the 100E Popular which remains a cheap and eminently usable classic.

## RELATIONS

With scaled down Consul body style and running gear from the previous Popular 103E, the cars had improved suspension, and braking mirrored the Zephyr. The same 1172cc side-valve engine was much improved. Anglia and Prefect 100Es, and Escort/Squire estates were in parallel production.

## BEST BUY

Despite their original cheapness, these cars have lasted well, and there are many examples of the Popular/Prefect/Anglia in existence. Watch for rust problems on sills and rear suspension points, otherwise be guided by the basic rules for buying. Any concerns over suspect engine symptoms can be checked with the Ford Side-valve Club.

| Cost | £1,600 |
| --- | --- |
| % swing | 83 |
| Spares | ★ |
| V.F.M. | ★★★★★ |
| S.R. | ★★ |

### SPECIFICATIONS

| | |
| --- | --- |
| **ENGINE:** 1172cc | **SUSPENSION:** Ind coil – semi |
| **BHP:** 36 | elliptical |
| **FUEL:** 32 mpg | **SPEED:** 70mph |
| **GEARBOX:** 3 speed manual – | **BODIES:** 2 door saloon |
| no 1st synchromesh | **YEARS:** 1959–1962 |
| **BRAKES:** Drum | **PRODUCTION:** 126,115 |

## MANUFACTURER
# FORD

### SPECIFICATIONS

**ENGINE:** 997cc; 1198cc
**BHP:** 39; 48.5
**FUEL:** 30–40mpg
**GEARBOX:** 4 speed manual
**BRAKES:** Drum
**SPEED:** 75–80mph

**SUSPENSION:** Ind MacPherson strut & semi elliptics, live axle
**BODIES:** Saloon, 2 door estate and commercial
**YEARS:** 1959–67
**PRODUCTION:** 1,083,960

Reliable, forgiving and full of individuality, the Anglia 105E was Ford Motor Company's counter- attack on the simultaneous launch of BMC's Mini and Triumph's Herald. They sold 1.2 million before the Escort took over, and both that model and the Capri continued to use the inspirational new Anglia engine, known as the Kent. This fabulous oversquare OHV 997cc power-plant remained a star of road and track for 25 years, making the Anglia utterly trustworthy. The body styling, though highly original, was far from a gimmick, with the reversed back window providing cleaner glass, improved passenger headroom and a wider arc for the boot lid.

The initial models, launched in 1959, were a Standard, on sale for £589, which had a small grille, scanty amount of chrome and basic interior trim, while for another £21, the De Luxe offered luxury items such as a passenger sun visor and locking glove locker. Two years later, commercial models and a family estate version were launched, followed in September 1962 by the Super - the 123E - which used the 48.5 bhp 1198cc version from the Mark I Cortina. This model offered additions such as dual paintwork and side stripes, as well as pleated pvc upholstery, and carpets.

Common to all models were features such as the first electrically operated windscreen wipers – previous Fords were powered by vacuum and tended to stop with hard acceleration. Then there was the first four speed gearbox, complete with high gearing to make for stress free motorway travel. The suspension was MacPherson strut with semi elliptic sprung live rear axle. The car could be driven hard for long periods without any repercussions - it actually thrived on hard work.

## RELATIONS

An original. The style of the 1959 Anglia 105E was completely new, with only the name and some of the running gear in common with the pre-war mechanics of the 1954 100E Anglia. This was the first car from Ford UK's new Research & Development centre in Birmingham, with some input from the American designer Elwood Engel.

## BEST BUY

Earlier engines are slightly more rugged, but all Anglias are mechanically reliable. Of the one million built, over 750,000 were De Luxe models, and 130,000 were Estates. The reason they are uncommon now is rust – examine the front apron and headlight moulding areas carefully. Previous repairs tend to reflect the car's relatively humble status. The basic Standards are rare, while the last 500 were 'Specials' finished in a vibrant metallic gold or blue. The Super 123E represents the best all-round model for the classic car collector.

| | |
|---|---|
| Cost | £1,780 |
| % swing | -6 |
| Spares | ★★★★ |
| V.F.M. | ★★ |
| S.R. | ★★★★ |

# MANUFACTURER
# STANDARD

STANDARD 8 & 10

A VERY BRITISH ANSWER TO THE 2CV

STANDARD **10**

In the commercial gloom of the early 1950s, austerity was still the watchword in Britain, and private transport was something of a dream. Standard launched the humble Standard Eight in 1953 to compete with the new wave of A30s and Morris Minors. They named it the Basic Eight; it had no chrome grille or trim, and access to the boot was via folding rear seats. However, then as now, it answered drivers' needs: it was a simple car with an economic and virtually unbreakable engine and gearbox. These features, and the independent suspension units, would remain a factory influence on other models for over 25 years. This four door model deliberately lacked any frills, but small refinements were added over the years to make driving a little more comfortable. Spring 1954 saw the Eight De luxe; 1955, the Family Eight and the Super Eight, then in 1956 the Family Eight Phase II and the ultimate version, the Eight Gold Star. New items such as sun visors, wipers, a heater and finally, a chrome grill appeared.

Born eight months after the Basic Eight, the Standard Ten had a larger engine at 948cc, and frills such as wind-up windows, an opening boot and chrome trimmings. Progressive minor upgrades largely echoed those of the Eight, while from 1954 there was also an estate version known as the Companion. A further reckless extravagance on later cars was the optional Standrive – a solenoid-triggered centrifugal clutch arrangement.

## RELATIONS

These cars brought new design to the company and passed engines and suspension down the design lines to the Herald, Spitfire and even the Dolomite.

## BEST BUY

Standards are inexpensive to buy and run, and, like the 2CV, are so fundamentally pure in their purpose in life, that trim levels and outright performance are almost superfluous. If you are tempted to own a genuine classic, try to find an early Basic Eight and boast of its spartan values. Standard engines are sound, although steering and gear levers can feel tired.

| Cost | £1,250 |
| --- | --- |
| % swing | 1 |
| Spares | ★★★ |
| V.F.M. | ★★★ |
| S.R. | ★★ |

## SPECIFICATIONS

| | |
| --- | --- |
| **ENGINE:** 803cc; 948cc | **SUSPENSION:** Ind coil – |
| **BHP:** 26; 33 | semi -elliptical |
| **FUEL:** 44; 40 mpg | **BODIES:** 4 door saloon, |
| **GEARBOX:** 4 speed manual– | estate, commercial |
| no 1st synchromesh | **YEARS:** 1953–60; 1954–60 |
| **BRAKES:** Drum | **PRODUCTION:** 308,817 |
| **SPEED:** 61–69mph | |

# MANUFACTURER
# STANDARD TRIUMPH

Introduced as a replacement to the Standard 8 and 10, the Triumph Herald (originally known as the Zobo project) had a new chassis with the old Standard engine, gearbox and final drive. Despite modern body styling by Giovanni Michelotti, the early cars inevitably suffered from teething troubles.

The initial 1959 models both used the old Standard 948cc engine; the two door saloon offered 70mph and 34.5bhp, while the pretty twin SU carburettored two door coupé enjoyed 45bhp. Raised gearing and compression ratios pushed this model's speed up to 80mph. Although the old gearbox lacked synchromesh on first, the independent suspension at least was a new design – albeit utilising a rather basic swing axle which could confuse handling. The Herald turning circle was an impressive 25ft, aided by excellent rack and pinion steering, while fuel economy for the Coupé was 40mpg. In 1961 Leyland took over the ailing company and injected fresh enthusiasm. That year an upgrade to 1147cc gave the saloon the Coupé carburetters, and both enjoyed power boosts, higher gear ratios and an option of front disc brakes.

## SPECIFICATIONS

**ENGINE:** 948cc; 1147cc
**BHP:** 45
**FUEL:** 40mpg+
**GEARBOX:** 4 speed, 3 syncromeshed
**BRAKES:** Drum; front disc – post 1961

**SUSPENSION:** Ind with transverse leaf/swing axle
**SPEED:** 80+
**BODIES:** 2 door fixed head coupé
**YEARS:** 1959–64
**PRODUCTION:** 20,472

The Herald concept of bolt-on panels and a forward-swung front body assembly suited an easy expansion of body styles, and now greatly helps modern DIY maintenance work. Slightly over 20,000 coupés were built (only 5319 of which were 1200s) before this body style was dropped in 1964.

## RELATIONS

The engine, gearbox and final drive were brought forward from the elderly but reliable Standard 8 and 10; the original body styling came from Turin. Everything else was essentially original Herald except the coupés' own roof sections.

## BEST BUY

Bolt-on bodywork means easy DIY, but consequently there are lots of badly fixed-up examples. A good chassis is essential, as are sound mountings, and, like the Frogeye Sprite, that one-piece front end is an expensive replacement. However, if you can find a disc-braked 1200 Coupé, it will provide a highly individual, yet practical, day-to-day classic without breaking the bank.

**HERALD 1200 SERIES**

| Cost | £1,880 |
|---|---|
| % swing | -1 |
| Spares | ★★★★★ |
| V.F.M. | ★★ |
| S.R. | ★★★ |

# AUSTIN A40 FARINA

SIMPLE, YET EMINENTLY PRACTICAL '60S DESIGN CLASSIC

## MANUFACTURER
# BMC

BMC launched this car in the teeth of unprecedented competition with the new Triumph Herald, Ford Anglia 105 and the Mini, rapidly followed by the 1100 series. The three previous post-war A40s had all been BMC series B-engined, but this new model boasted only the smaller A unit. Worse still, virtually everything mechanical was from the A35 with roots dating back to 1951. It ought to have sunk without trace, yet the very virtues which sustained public affection for the A35 gave the A40 creditability, while the totally new body styling set it apart from any other British post-war model. The A40 marked the beginning of a commercial link with the Turin design house of Pininfarina, and the resultant unique two box A40 design paved the way for generations of future 'Hot Hatchbacks'. The folding rear seats, the tailgate feature, excellent visibility, and fuel economy all transformed this off-beat car into a mainstream contender. The commercial implications of the impending BMC FWD cars reduced the A40's lifespan to eight years, leaving us to wonder how many subsequent BMC models might have been born of the Farina A40 stable without the radical period of white heat instigated by Alex Issigonis. A year after the launch in 1958, the Countryman version appeared, which incorporated both upper and lower tailgates. With flattened rear seating, it offered considerable storage for a 12ft long family car, and these two versions continued in production until 1961.

The A40 then profited from a wheelbase that was four inches longer, extra power from Morris Minor carburation, improved suspension, and upgraded interior trimmings – including proper wind-up windows. Just a year later the Morris 1100 was launched and the A40 was bequeathed the new 1098cc engine, an improved gearbox and additional interior improvements. FWD had become the BMC shibboleth and the Farina A40 was laid honourably to rest in November 1967.

## RELATIONS

Under the skin it is a trusted A35 with the BMC A 948cc engine, gearbox, basic suspension, braking and interior fittings; the Morris Minor 1098cc engine variant was used in late Mk II form.

## BEST BUY

Although sixties' tuning kits were common, the A40 is not a sporting car It is an excellent classic, simple to work on, and economic to run. The post-1961 longer wheel base Mk II offers better handling, while the post-1962 model – still termed Mk II - has the extra performance of the 1098cc engine.

| Cost | £1,860 |
|------|--------|
| % swing | 5 |
| Spares | ★★★★★ |
| V.F.M. | ★★★ |
| S.R. | ★★★★ |

### SPECIFICATIONS

**ENGINE:** 948cc; 1098cc
**BHP:** 34–48
**FUEL:** 38–32 mpg
**GEARBOX:** 4 speed manual– no 1st synrchromesh
**BRAKES:** Drum
**SUSPENSION:** Ind coil & wishbone – half ellipitic leaf
**SPEED:** 75–80 mph
**BODIES:** 3 door hatchback
**YEARS:** 1958–1961
**PRODUCTION:** 364,064

## MANUFACTURER
# BMC

BMC and British Leyland personified the mindless badge engineering which did so much to run down the reputations of once-proud marques. As they bought up factories, they stuck appropriate badges and radiators on the same car and pushed them upon a dealer structure which still bred rivalry – an Austin garage would regard a Morris set-up as the opposition. So two years after the simple Mini stunned the automobile world, it became the turn of the Riley and Wolseley marques. In fact these two probably represented the best of BMC's superficial marketing, with the Riley Elf being selected for the superior treatment. Launched in 1961, it was essentially a standard 848cc Mini with an additional 8.5 inches owing mainly to an extended boot. The interior trim was in leather and the dashboard was far from a standard Mini's, with a new central instrument panel, matched glove lockers on each side, all finished in burred walnut. Extra sound proofing was used, and even the gear lever was chromed.

From March 1963 the engine was enlarged to 988cc for the Mk II, which compensated for the slight weight increase over the Mini, and produced good cruising at 70mph and 80mph as a top speed; the Mini 1000 would not enjoy this engine until 1967. The Mk II Riley was given the brand new Hydrolastic suspension 18 months later, providing a softer ride. For the 1966 Motor Show a Mk III version was launched with wind-up windows and eyeball ventilation, while the Mini Cooper remote gear change was also installed. A full synchromesh gearbox appeared in mid-1968, and the following year an automatic

---

### SPECIFICATIONS

**ENGINE:** 848cc: 998cc
**BHP:** 34–38bhp
**FUEL:** 33–35mpg
**GEARBOX:** 4 speed: automatic
**SPEED:** 71–77mph
**BRAKES:** Drum

**SUSPENSION:** Ind rubber cone, coil / rubber cone, coil, trailing arms
**BODIES:** 2 door Saloon
**YEARS:** 1961–1969
**PRODUCTION** 30,912

---

option was available until not just the car, but the name Riley, was terminated by BL. If you fancy a Mini but like some comfort, if you want to be different, then a good Elf could be just the car.

## RELATIONS

Everything is pure BMC Mini, from the baulk ring synchromesh gearboxes, Hydrolastic suspension, enlarged engine, Mini Cooper remote gears, wind up windows and towards the end, an automatic gearbox option. The Wolseley Hornet mirrored this progression with slightly lower trim levels.

## BEST BUY

Most mechanical problems are easily solved and there are plenty of spares still available. Body work is the stumbling block, so check sills, wings and bulkheads, the sub-frames and the floor area, as problems here could be more costly. The scarcity of the Elf makes restoration work all the more worthwhile.

*The Riley 1.5/Wolseley 1500 is nudging into the frame on the right. A 1936 advert for Riley admitted cheerfully 'We make far too many models of course. But then we have a pretty fertile design department, and we like making nice interesting cars.' The receiver was in by February 1938.*

| | |
|---|---|
| Cost | £1,900 |
| % swing | -19 |
| Spares | ★★★★ |
| V.F.M. | ★ |
| S.R. | ★★★★★ |

# FIAT 850 COUPÉ
## A FUTURE VINTAGE

### MANUFACTURER
# FIAT

Few enthusiasts grieve as decades of family Fiats reach their rightful incarnation as mounds of rust. Inferior steel, questionable build qualities and little corrosion prevention all helped erase large numbers of indifferent models. However, Fiat had the knack of creating small cars that everyone loved and, as squadrons of Morris Minors illustrate, loved cars get preserved. The tiny Fiat 500s and 600s sold close to 6,000,000 in the 1950s, 1960s and 1970s, while giving birth in 1964 to the slightly larger Fiat 850. This model, too, used a three-bearing, water-cooled engine installed beyond the rear wheels, but with its sleek new body providing valued extra interior space. Motorists again voted with their feet, buying over 800,000 in the first couple of years' production. Coachbuilders, too, recognised the saloon's potential offering variations such as the Bertone Spyder, but it was the ideas of Fiat's own in-house design team which emerged in 1965 as the beautiful little 850 Coupé. Based upon the saloon underpan and running gear, it offered one of the very best proportioned miniature Grand Tourers with disc brakes, slim pillars, lots of glass and classic sporting good looks. The high revving 850cc engine enjoyed a revised head, with higher compression ratio, new cam shaft, valve gear, manifolds and twin choke Weber carburation – all prescribed by the Grand Master of Fiat tuning, Abarth. It was a brilliant sporting car, instantly adopted by press and public alike for its looks, performance and character.

Then, at the 1968 Geneva Motor Show, Fiat put the icing on the cake by increasing the power output to 52bhp raising acceleration, top speed and even fuel consumption figures. Although its name remained, the 850 Coupé, it was by then 903cc, and external changes included a second pair of headlights and even more side glass. These excellent cars handle well and are eminently usable in congested towns or speeding at 90mph on the open roads – still returning 30 to 40mpg.

## RELATIONS

Fiat's own body styling added to the 1964 850 Saloon, itself derived from the hugely successful Fiat 600 formula. Components such as disc brakes are from the Fiat 124.

## BEST BUY

The passage of time has simply made good examples scarce – and thus more collectable. Obviously, post-1968 models enjoy more power and refinement, but it's really more about condition. Buy the best and enjoy wonderful motoring.

### SPECIFICATIONS

| | |
|---|---|
| **ENGINE:** 843cc; 930cc | **BODIES:** 2 door coupe |
| **BHP:** 47 – 52 | **SUSPENSION:** Ind transverse |
| **FUEL:** 35 – 40mpg | leaf/wishbone – semi-trailing |
| **GEARBOX:** 4 speed | arm/coil |
| **BRAKES:** Disc – Drum | **YEARS:** 1965 – 72 |
| **SPEED:** 87mph – 94mph | **PRODUCTION:** 380,000 |

| | |
|---|---|
| Cost | £2,150 |
| % swing | 13 |
| Spares | ★★★ |
| V.F.M. | ★★★ |
| S.R. | ★★★ |

# MANUFACTURER
# ROVER

Somehow this car virtually escaped the appalling BL philosophies. Right from its launch during that 1976 heatwave, this Rover looked, and was, a winner. True, the early models still suffered from BL's tendency to use the public to iron out teething troubles, but as this sleek five door car developed, it grew in status. Initially it used the lightweight Buick-based V8 from the Rover 3.5 Coupé and 3500, which gave 120mph performance and up to 30mpg when driven carefully. An OHC 2300cc, a longer stroked 2600cc, a 2.4 Turbo Diesel and another with the ex-Morris Ital 2 litre O series engine, all added choice. The V8 was the best equipped, with power steering, electric windows and central locking, while the most humble was the 2300. All models were upgraded during 1979-80, with a new top of the range 3500SE and a Vanden Plas version dressed in real leather. One curious choice was the 1979 V8 S, which boasted gold wheels and shag-pile carpets. The undoubted classic was the Vitesse, unveiled in 1982. This was a 192bhp, 130mph five-seater hatchback on lowered suspension, complete with fuel injection and ventilated disc brakes. Few genuine family cars were ever made with domestic niceties such as folding rear seats and self levelling rear suspension with a V8 growling under the bonnet. The Vitesse and the Vanden Plas Efi, which lacked the lowered suspension, have increasingly been recognised as future classics.

In competition form these 300BHP racers were dominant until a technical disqualification caused the team to withdraw, leaving privateers to enjoy the victories. The SD1 even beat off the factory BMWs to win the 1986 European Touring Car Championship. To competition homologate certain specifications the factory sold a late Vitesse with 'Twin Plenum' chambers unofficially worth another 20bhp which has added mysticism and value to these rare examples.

## RELATIONS

A brand new Rover design reputedly inspired by Pininfarina's Ferrari Daytona using the Rover P5B and P6 Buick V8 engine. The smaller engines were designed by Triumph.

## BEST BUY

There are superficial rust problems and BL 'quality-control' means good and bad examples are available. Watch for occasional water damage under carpets and blocked sunroof channels causing rust. Some fuel injection can be troublesome, so can oil leaks, while early plastic trim deteriorates. A late Vitesse is a brilliant classic for the price of a second hand Escort.

### SPECIFICATIONS

**ENGINE:** 3.5 V8; 2.3; 2.4 Turbo D; 2.6; 2
**BHP:** 100–155
**FUEL:** 42–20 mpg
**GEARBOX:** 5 speed manual–3 speed auto
**BRAKES:** Disc/drum
**SUSPENSION:** Ind MacPherson strut – Live axle, coils
**SPEED:** 104–133 mph
**BODIES:** 5 door hatchback
**YEARS:** 1976–1987
**PRODUCTION:** 191,762

| Cost | £3,100 |
|---|---|
| (SD1 3500 Vitesse) | |
| % swing | -26 |

| Spares | ★★★ |
|---|---|
| V.F.M. | ★ |
| S.R. | ★★★ |

WOLSELEY 15/60 & 16/60

TRADITIONAL BRITISH COMFORTS

## MANUFACTURER
# BMC

## Extra power ... rock-steady roadholding ... the new Wolseley 16/60

The Wolseley name is one of the most respected in the history of British manufacturing, despite never having been an independent company. The 15/60 was the car which launched the Farina range in December 1958, replacing the old 15/50; it didn't let the side down. Critics may sometimes belittle the Farina cars, but the more traditional 15/50 sold a little over 12,000 cars in total, while the initial 15/60 Farina variant alone sold 24,579, and the collective Riley 15/60 & 16/60 sold an impressive 87,661 – despite ever diminishing interest from the soon to be defunct BMC. Just as the basic Austin/Morris were the workhorses of the company, so the better equipped Wolseley and Riley were the more civilised motor cars. Morris Minors have proved that being a classic car is as much about dependability and character, rather than glamour. Likewise, the Wolseley offered the all the advantages of a modern Italian five-seater saloon, along with practical features such as a 19 cubic capacity boot, which was increased by spare wheel stowage underneath the car. Driver visibility was a significant improvement on previous Wolseleys, with modern wrap-around front and rear windows. Overall, the Wolseley carried the kind of high trim levels associated with the later Riley, but without the twin carburettored power-plant. The traditional Wolseley grille treatment looked good on the Farina bodyshell and included a traditional integrated Wolseley badge, while the early 15/60 version boasted the more flamboyant tail fins.

Inside, there was English leather seating, carpets, polished wood door cappings and a splendid burr

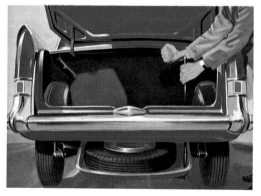

walnut veneered fascia with glove locker and semi-circular chrome horn bar. The sales brochures may have revelled in the association with a famous Italian designer by showing background drawings of Rome and Pisa, but climbing into the car instantly showed that it was both very British and traditionally Wolseley.

| Cost | £2,700 |
|---|---|
| % swing | 53 |
| Spares | ★★★ |
| V.F.M. | ★★★★ |
| S.R. | ★★ |

*Interior 'fashioned for the fastidious.' Despite having such an immediately recognisable and evocative name, Wolseley was never actually an independent manufacturer, owned by Vickers for the first 26 years and Morris thereafter.*

## SPECIFICATIONS

**ENGINE:** 1489cc; 1622cc
**BHP:** 52;61
**FUEL:** 28–26
**GEARBOX:** 4 speed,
   3 syncromeshed
**BRAKES:** Drum
**SPEED:** 77–81mph

**SUSPENSION:** Ind coil & wish-
   bone / Half elliptic
**BODIES:** 4 door saloon.
**YEARS:** 1958–71
**PRODUCTION:** 900,000 – all
   Farina family

## RELATIONS

The body style is purely Italian from Pininfarina although BMC personalised the cars of each marque with badge-engineering. The trusted BMC B series engine, gearbox and some of the running gear stemmed from former BMC models. 'Wolseley' evokes the spirits of three motor magnates: Herbert Austin, John Davenport Siddeley and William Morris.

## BEST BUY

They are well-built cars, with trustworthy engines while rusting tends to be in fairly obvious places. As the Wolseley enjoyed high levels of trim, it was not blessed with the more sporting engine; the earlier 15/60s are naturally slower than the later 16/60s. A late 16/60, along with the equivalent Riley, makes an excellent and economic classic car.

Like the others in the range, the initial model lacked qualities introduced with the upgrade to the Wolseley 16/60. Once it enjoyed the later benefits of a longer wheel base and the engine elevation to 1622cc, it became an excellent buy, although extravagant BMC claims that it enjoyed 'Faultless Performance', and was 'Fashioned for the fastidious' were bold ones to make for any mid-market family car … even today.

## MORRIS MINOR
### STILL THE BENCHMARK FOR A DAY-TO-DAY CLASSIC

**MANUFACTURER**
# BMC

*Morris 1000 convertible (above) with new full-width screen, 1957 model year.*

One legendary car with two distinct followings. So brilliant was it that there is still a present day, non-enthusiasts, market for models as daily transport. Aficionados hunt out the initial 1948 version, called the Minor MM, which incorporated low integrated headlights and a split screen along with the Morris 8's 918cc sidevalve engine. Issigonis's friendly yet spacious design favoured a strong unit construction, while advanced rack-and-pinion steering, and torsion bar independent front suspension won many new fans. The initial two-door saloon and convertible (called the 'Tourer' until 1951) were joined in 1953 by the Traveller van and pick-up, further widening the appeal. The only significant alteration was in 1951, when the headlights were moved up into a more conventional wing position, complying with North American requirements.

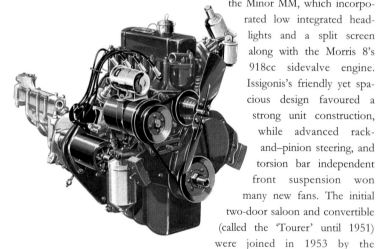

1952 had witnessed the merger of Austin and Morris, and within months BMC had replaced the ageing sidevalve engine with the Austin A30 BMC A 803cc engine and transmission. Then there were only

nominal changes to grille and dashboard before the Series II ended its run in the autumn of 1956.

The new Minor 1000 enjoyed greatly improved visibility with large wrap-around front and rear screens, upgraded interior trim and more significantly, the new 948cc version of the A series engine corresponding to the Austin move from A30 to A35. Adding improved performance to great handling simply iced the cake, and sales roared on past the 1,000,000 mark (350 commemorative two-door cars were built). The only further real change was the launch of the BMC 1100, which meant that 1098cc unit went into the Minor, thus becoming 1.1 litre. 1970 ended its distinguished career and the Traveller ran until 1971.

## RELATIONS

An original Issigonis design, with engines from the Morris 8, then briefly the Austin A30, the A35's

| SPECIFICATIONS | |
|---|---|
| **ENGINE:** 918cc (sv); 803cc; 948cc; 1098cc | **SUSPENSION:** Ind torsion bar – semi elliptical |
| **BHP:** 27.5; 30; 37 | **BODIES:** 2 &4 door saloon, |
| **FUEL:** 40;36;38mpg | estate, convertible, |
| **GEARBOX:** 4 speed | commercial pick up |
| **BRAKES:** Drum | **YEARS:** 1948–71 |
| **SPEED:** 61; 62;75mph | **PRODUCTION:** 1,303,331 |

| Cost (1000) | £2,350 |
|---|---|
| % swing | -14 |
| Spares | ★★★★★ |
| V.F.M. | ★★ |
| S.R. | ★★★★★ |

948cc, and ultimately in 1956, the 1098cc BMC 1100 version. Some running gear was common to other models, such as the MM rear axle from the MG TD.

## BEST BUY

Classic heaven. Lots of Morris Minors are in circulation, with oceans of parts, many specialists and no trouble for your local garage. The early MMs are the rarest, making these and the Series II the collector's choice, while the 1000 and 1.1 litre cars are a joy to own and use daily. Many saloons turned into convertibles, so make sure you know what you are actually buying. Front wings rust frequently, but more importantly, check under floors and the suspension hanger areas – rotten undersides can be expensive.

*The first Morris Minor 'traveller's car' was completed at Cowley in spring 1951. The Traveller was identical to the other Series II Minors, except for the Austin A-type rear axle.*

*The overseas market was resistant to composite bodywork, preferring steel, which influenced the Light Commercial Vehicle range of May 1953. The LCVs have a true chassis to compensate for lack of rigidity in comparison with saloons, with extended box sections either side of the engine.*

the **MORRIS MINOR** *1000*

Now better than ever

IMPROVED PERFORMANCE · INCREASED SAFETY

Publication No. H & E 58—34

*Fact and fiction: the author's old Traveller being craned aboard a Scottish ferry (above), while BMC sales literature suggests a more elegant departure. The 1000 certainly was 'better than ever', with the overbored A-series engine, a new gearbox and less significant, but still pleasing, updates: thinner windscreen side pillars for example and larger back screen, for better visibility. A word of warning from restoration expert Jim Tyler: an awful lot of Minors have been badly bodged, so dig around.*

**MANUFACTURER**
# FORD

Here's our Popular!

Ford **POPULAR**

| Cost | £2,260 |
|---|---|
| % swing | 19 |

| | |
|---|---|
| Spares | ★★★ |
| V.F.M. | ★★★ |
| S.R. | ★★★ |

A significant part of the classic car culture is the way period styling and mechanics instantly conjure up former eras – be it in your memory or just imagination. Extended fins or aerodynamic wedges, razor-edged panels or flowing curves, these are as essential as the performance. One of the true classic automotive shapes, the Sit Up and Beg Utility Ford, is captured in the 103E Prefect. Those who remember them will fondly recall that this Ford provided much needed transport – freedom rather than excitement. The factory policy was to continue employing what was, in effect, the 1930's Model Y body style, and to re-use common running gear so they could afford to promote claims to the world's lowest priced car. In 1954 the 103E was being advertised at just £275 less tax.

The Popular was the last incarnation of this traditional upright styling, married to the larger 1172cc sidevalve engine previously employed in the export Anglia and Prefect cars. With 36mpg and 60mph top speed, it was essentially a pre-war engine packaged together with the most deliberately basic trim levels. Painted bumpers and hub caps, reduced headlights, only the passenger seat tipped forward, one wiper, plastic finished floor coverings. Struggling for trim selling points the sales brochure boasted 'Window and windscreen space is generous. Both driver and passengers are well catered for'. More telling were lines such as 'The man with a tired pre–war car and increased running costs now drives and saves in a Popular'. This was Ford's key to over 150,000 sales

during times of great austerity. Even publications get model variants confused. The 1948–53 1172cc Prefect was the E493A, while the 933cc Anglia was E494A; the 1953–59 Popular, the 103E, was 1172cc.

## RELATIONS

Its roots are in the pre-World War I Model T, its grandparent, and body style was influenced by the 1932 Model Y and 1949 Anglia, but without the trim, and with the addition of the 1172cc engine.

## BEST BUY

Purely utilitarian, reliable and economic, it suffered rust chiefly to the rear, while the back axle was prone to wear. Vague steering is quite normal and a starter handle is insurance against 6 volt electrics. Ageing engines can smoke, notably from the oil filter. Virtually unbreakable, and with great pre-war character, it's a case of finding the right car. Approach the Ford Side Valve Owners Club for help.

### SPECIFICATIONS

| | |
|---|---|
| **ENGINE:** 1172cc | **SUSPENSION:** Transverse leaf |
| **BHP:** 30 | springs |
| **FUEL:** 36 mpg | **SPEED:** 60mph |
| **GEARBOX:** 3 speed manual– | **BODIES:** 2 door saloon |
| no 1st synchromesh | **YEARS:** 1953–1959 |
| **BRAKES:** Drum | **PRODUCTION:** 155,350 |

# MANUFACTURER
# BMC

The last genuine Austin-bodied model range, the A40/50/55 Cambridge, was withdrawn in the mid-fifties and replaced with this Farina design. It was launched in January 1959 as the A55, a four-door saloon using a 1489cc version of the B series engine. They kept the reliable elements of the retired model, while cleverly offering a touch of Italian flair with the Farina bodywork. The Austin and Morris versions were launched with the most pronounced tail fins of the range, along with individually adjustable bench seating, optional Borg Warner automatic gears, and a choice of floor or column gear change. The De Luxe version also boasted sun visors, a heater, screen washer, a clock, leather trim and full carpets. There was liberal use of fashionable chrome on bumpers, headlight surrounds, etc. and a bold, square meshed, full-width grille boasting the Austin badge. The dashboard was pretty basic, however, with two principal dials set into the painted facia with black vinyl on the top, a glove locker and a parcel shelf. The Countryman Estate version was launched the following spring, and in 1961 the A60 appeared. The 1961 revamp included handling modifications such as 1.5 extra inches on the wheelbase and wider tracking, while the engine was enlarged to 1622cc. The dashboard gained a simulated wood finish, the rear fins were reduced in scale, the front grille was widened to virtually full width, and the bumpers were also altered.

## RELATIONS

The body style was from Pininfarina, although BMC personalised the cars for each marque. The BMC B series engine and basic running gear, including the suspension, came from the 1954 A50 Cambridge.

## BEST BUY

They were well built cars, with trustworthy engines and rusting tends to be in obvious places. The earlier A55s are more economical, but improved performance makes the later A60s the better buys.

## SPECIFICATIONS

**ENGINE:** 1489cc; 1622cc
**BHP:** 52; 61
**FUEL:** 28–26mpg
**GEARBOX:** 4 speed,
  3 syncromeshed
**BRAKES:** Drum
**SPEED:** 78–81mph

**SUSPENSION:** Ind coil & wishbone / half-elliptic
**BODIES:** 4 door saloon, 5 door estates
**YEARS:** 1959–69
**PRODUCTION:** 900,000 – all Farina family

| | |
|---|---|
| Cost | £2,900 |
| % swing | 64 |
| Spares | ★★★ |
| V.F.M. | ★★★★★ |
| S.R. | ★★ |

## FORD EXECUTIVE
### THE VERY LAST ALL-BRITISH FORD

MANUFACTURER
# FORD

| Cost | £2,300 |
|------|--------|
| % swing | 3 |
| | |
| Spares | ★★★ |
| V.F.M. | ★★★ |
| S.R. | ★★★ |

A great many of these cars have either been left to rust – which they do well – or been worked to destruction. This is a pity, for these largely unloved Fords have a certain merit.

Following Ford's classic Mk II models, the same designer was invited to create a new, more upmarket range, but Ford then turned to the Italian designers, Frua, before eventually adopting their own in-house shape for the Mk IIIs. The simple, bold, styling brought little charm but at least gained some notoriety from use in the British television series *Z Cars*. Ford's insecurity showed, however, for although these Mk IIIs were launched in 1962, Ford had already started looking for a replacement a year before the Mk III launch. Codenamed the Panda, the Mk IV was the embodiment of the new UK Engineering Director's search for larger American-style saloons using V4 and V6 power plants. The 1966 launch of the Zephyr 4 and Zodiac 6 revealed a long, searching bonnet, a well-proportioned cabin and a neat curved rear. The huge boot was virtually concealed and the extended engine bay was partly filled by the spare wheel. Inside, the Zephyrs featured bench seating and column gear change as standard, (individual recliners and floor change were an option) while the Zodiac specifications were quite simply the alternative. In the Mk III's final year Ford introduced a fully loaded Executive version of the then Zodiac, but one year later it was axed by the Mk IV range. Just six months later at the London Motor Show Ford launched their new flagship – the top of the range version of the Mk IV Zodiac – the Executive.

This model enjoyed the best of everything Ford had to offer, including power steering, C4 automatic gearbox, quad headlights, auxiliary lamps, thick carpets, plush upholstery, a sunshine roof, disc braking and full independent suspension. There was also a distinctive single star in the middle of the grille identifying its status. Initially well received, the big Mk IVs rapidly dated and the fashion for huge slabs of bodywork and 1970s trim detail has yet to revive their fortunes. Despite the transatlantic flavouring, these Mark IVs were in fact the very last all-British Ford motor cars.

## RELATIONS

Most Fords are a development of the previous model, but the Mk IV range was an exception. It was really a new design manufactured under the guidance of Ford's Harley Copp.

## BEST BUY

Thirty-five years on, there are still quite a few around and you get a lot of car for your money. Body rust appears in all the usual places, and they are such unfashionable cars that new panels are not always easy to find. The V6 engine is stronger than the V4, and later Granada parts are useful replacements. They always wallowed on corners, but the later Executives had even softer suspension.

### SPECIFICATIONS

**ENGINE:** 2993cc; V6
**BHP:** 136bhp
**FUEL:** 21mpg
**GEARBOX:** 3 speed automatic: 4 speed manual
**BRAKES:** Disc
**SPEED:** 103mph

**SUSPENSION:** Ind MacPherson strut & coil/semi-trailing wishbone
**BODIES:** 4 door
**YEARS:** 1966–1971
**PRODUCTION:** 42,000
*(incl Zodiac)*

## MANUFACTURER

# VW

# GOLF GTI

### A SECOND BULLSEYE

Replacing a true classic is fraught with danger. VW, trying to fill the shoes of the world famous Beetle, faced a tough challenge, but fortunately Rudolf Leidling championed two Italian designs by Giugiaro which would eventually materialize as the Golf and the Scirocco models.

With the same wheelbase as the Beetle, the Golf united new hatchback styling with the existing 1,471cc Audi 80 engine mounted transversely. For the second time Volkswagen were right on the money. The standard car was launched in the spring of 1974 offering surprising amounts of room and just under 100mph performance. Its handling promised greater things, and 5,000 Sport Golfs were released in Germany in 1975 to qualify the car for Group 1 saloon competition. The 1975 Frankfurt Motor Show saw the prototype GTi, followed in June 1976 by the GTi itself using a four-speed gearbox. It represented a unique combination of fun, speed and practicality which was irresistible – providing you could get the insurance cover.

Left-hand drive versions reached the UK in 1977, and finally, right-hand drive cars were released in 1979, by which point over 100,000 had already been sold in Germany. Adding the Bosch K-jetronic fuel injection system to the Audi engine gave it 0-60 in just under nine seconds, and in 1981 a five speed gearbox added to the attractions. In the spring of 1982 the engine was enlarged to 1,800cc, marginally improving the figures and setting the basic specifications for the 1984 Mk II version. Smart, fast and understated the GTi perfectly suited the aspirational

1980s. By chance or design, Volkswagen had captured the public's mood and created a classic.

## RELATIONS

A brand new Giugiaro-designed prototype developed into the Audi 80-powered 1.5 Mk I Golf. Using the 110bhp Audi 80GTE power plant, it became the limited production German Golf Sporting to qualify for racing – the GTi rapidly followed.

## BEST BUY

They are well built cars, with few serious rust problems, although checking for engine or body damage is important. Because of its performance charms, the front suspension and drive shafts can take quite a pounding and the petrol filler neck is weak. The Campaign model is desirable, while later five-speed gearboxes are better than the early four-speed – though enthusiasm for the early cars makes virtually any good example collectable.

---

### SPECIFICATIONS

**ENGINE:** 1,588cc; 1,781cc
**BHP:** 110–112bhp
**FUEL:** 28mpg
**GEARBOX:** 4 & 5 speed
**SPEED:** 112–116mph
**BRAKES:** Disc/drum; Disc/disc

**SUSPENSION:** MacPherson strut, coil/trailing arm, torsion beam, coils
**BODIES:** 3 & 5 door hatchback
**YEARS:** 1976–1983
**PRODUCTION:** 600,000 (Mk I & Mk II)

---

| | |
|---|---|
| Spares | ★★★★ |
| V.F.M. | ★ |
| S.R. | ★★★★ |

### MANUFACTURER
# RENAULT

5,000,000 Minis breed a sense of invincibility and there is no doubting the car's unique values. Yet across the Channel the Renault 5 has achieved the same figure, despite being launched 13 years after the ubiquitous Mini. This does nothing to distract from the originality of Issigonis's ideas, but does serve to remind us that while we exalt the Mini, there are clearly merits within the Renault. Rust, poor quality, and abused examples are equally common to the Mini and the Renault 5. Yet the Mini Cooper and the Renault R5 Gordini perhaps provide a more interesting parallel. England's 'Swinging Sixties' and a successful BMC Competition Department naturally reinforced Britain's allegiance to the Mini Cooper, leaving the interesting Gordini in the dark. They are now being valued at less than half the figure of a standard Mini Cooper, yet the Gordini offers 93bhp against the Cooper's 55bhp or indeed 76bhp from the mighty 1275 S. Having owned two 1275s I later bought a bright blue Gordini which offered many of the same driving pleasures with the welcome additions of passenger refinements.

Around the rest of the world this sporting 5 is known as the Renault Alpine, but as Chrysler owns that name in the UK, it became the R5 Gordini. The engine is a bored out version of the Renault TS, with alloy cross flow head, a sports camshaft and a twin choked Weber carburettor. With the optimum power band around 4000 revs, a five speed gearbox used in the larger 16TX and 17TS was installed. The resultant 93bhp gets to the road through 5¼-inch lightweight wheels which are almost impossible to keep clean. A good sized tailgate and folding rear seats are infinitely more practical that the old Cooper S, while the high backed, side hugging front seats are really well upholstered competition seats. However, to anyone committed to the sporting front wheel drive principle, the real joy is in travelling fast through the gears…and the corners. It's a grown-up's Cooper S and a bargain at current prices.

## RELATIONS

Clearly Renault 5-based, with elements drawn from the larger Renault models such as the 16 and 17.

## BEST BUY

The main danger is the car's ability to be driven hard – which inevitably means examples may be abused. Luckily with the Gordini Turbo and the fire-eating rear-engined Turbo T2 offering raw excitement, it leaves this rapid and civilized French car for those seeking fun.

| Cost | £2,000 |
|------|--------|
| % swing | -27 |
| Spares | ★★★★ |
| V.F.M. | ★ |
| S.R. | ★★★ |

### SPECIFICATIONS

**ENGINE:** 1397cc
**BHP:** 93
**FUEL:** 30mpg
**GEARBOX:** 5 speed
**BRAKES:** Disc/drum
**SUSPENSION:** Double wishbone – Torsion bar and trailing arm

**SPEED:** 107mph
**BODIES:** 3 door 4 seater hatchback
**YEARS:** 1976 – 81
**PRODUCTION:** (5,471,709) Gordini 63,814

# MANUFACTURER
# FIAT

The early 1960s gave Fiat over 2,000,000 sales of their 850 range, and its last incarnation, the pretty Bertone-designed Spider, sold most of its 140,000 examples to the USA. Naturally, both Bertone and Fiat looked for another project and the design work culminated at the 1969 Turin Motor Show where they showed their 'Runabout'. Close to the eventual X1/9, this was a design exercise based upon the Autobianchi A112 chassis. It was the same year Bertone's breathtaking Lamborghini Miura was released, and the central principle of that Supercar was compressed into the diminutive Fiat X1/9 – the transverse mounted mid engine. The final car was unveiled after the 1972 Turin Motor Show and was based upon Fiat 128 Coupé components including the 1290cc engine. This fresh new sporting car offered a good deal including quite excellent handling thanks to the central engine position, a detachable Targa roof, all round disc brakes and independent suspension, plus two different luggage areas. Its problem was Fiat itself, who had reputedly been less convinced about its potential – they even deferred its announcement until after that Motor Show. They concentrated on reviving the American market and thus ignored Britain – despite the MG/Sprite/Spitfire boom. For the first five years UK models were imported and converted by Rathbourne, the Fiat and Abarth specialists.

From 1977, official RHD models began to filter in, and a year later Fiat announced the 1500 using the more powerful 85bhp Strada 85 unit. Along with the extra horsepower came a new five speed gearbox and overdrive. From the spring of 1982 Bertone took over the building and the 1983 VS1500 model boasted both electric windows and leather upholstery. Quick, nimble and highly individual, these cars suffered from lacklustre Fiat marketing and so still offer excellent value for money as a classic.

## RELATIONS

The Fiat X1/9 has original Italian design house styling based upon the Fiat 128 Coupé engine, gearbox and general specifications. The later 1500 model utilised the Strada 85 power train.

## BEST BUY

Opinions are divided between the two models. The interiors of all except the final version are very basic, while the 1500 suffered the US-imposed impact bumpers. Rust and Fiat were synonymous, so check carefully as panels are expensive. However, if you find a sound example and enjoy DIY, try boring out to 1650cc and adding twin Weber 40 DCNIF carbs.

### SPECIFICATIONS

| | |
|---|---|
| **ENGINE:** 1290; 1498cc | **SUSPENSION:** All Ind |
| **BHP:** 75 – 85 | Macpherson strut |
| **FUEL:** 30 – 37mpg | **BODIES:** 2 door sports Targa |
| **GEARBOX:** 4 & 5 speed | **YEARS:** 1972–89 |
| **BRAKES:** Disc | **PRODUCTION:** 180,000 |
| **SPEED:** 106mph | |

| | |
|---|---|
| Cost | £2,800 |
| % swing | -7 |
| Spares | ★★★★ |
| V.F.M. | ★★ |
| S.R. | ★★★ |

# SUNBEAM RAPIER IIIA

## ECONOMICAL AND SPACIOUS SPORTING BARGAIN

**MANUFACTURER**

# ROOTES

*The IIIA will actually cost considerably more than the average for the whole range quoted below – particularly the convertible.*

| Cost (I–V) | £2,750 |
|---|---|
| % swing | 30 |
| Spares | ★★ |
| V.F.M. | ★★★★ |
| S.R. | ★★★★ |

Pure Sunbeams were pre-1935 motors cars which were turned into disguised Hillmans and Hunters by the new owners, Rootes, who salvaged Sunbeam from the chaos of STD (Sunbeam, Talbot, Darracq) in that year. Under corporate ownership there was little respect for individual badges or traditions, and marque personalities were systematically eroded. The initial 1955 Sunbeam Rapier was very similar to a two door Hillman Minx even down to its radiator grille – which was all the more confusing as it pre-empted the actual Minx launch by seven months. The initial car used an up-rated 1390cc Hillman Minx engine, a four speed gearbox with standard overdrive, and conventional, but effective suspension and handling. This natural performer managed to finish fifth overall in the Monte Carlo Rally, and immediately afterwards Rootes launched the Series II. It had a new, more powerful, overhead valve 1494cc engine, the overdrive was reduced to an option, and the car had a grille design of its own as well as distinctive rear fins. Both this and the Series III were also offered in convertible form. The next stage in its development mirrored the newly launched Alpine. Thus, the Series III Rapier enjoyed the Alpine's close ratio gearbox, new aluminium cylinder head and front disc braking. The II and III sold well, but it was the Series IIIA which ultimately was the bestseller, despite the appearance of a Series IV with general improvements borrowed from the new Humber Sceptre, and even a Series V, which added a five bearing 1725cc unit. The IV actually had slightly more power, a new gearbox and different road wheels, but it was the Series IIIA which offered performance while retaining the classic hood-

ed headlights, the higher bonnet line and the option of a full convertible – although the saloon's pillarless side windows were also a nice touch.

## RELATIONS

In essence the Rapier was a Hillman Minx – including the drive train. Later models borrowed the engines and developments of the new Sunbeam Alpine and the Humber Sceptre. Many panels and parts were common to the Minxs and Gazelles.

## BEST BUY

They were built with generously thick metal so the inevitable rust ought not be terminal, though check particularly around the screen base and suspension mounts. Poor servicing may lead to worn steering and suspension if greasing has not been maintained. The overdrive is a real asset, though watch for oil leakage around the gearbox. Broken dash instruments can be costly to replace. Good convertible IIIAs are like hens' teeth now, and the saloon is also becoming a desirable classic.

### SPECIFICATIONS

**ENGINE:** 1592cc
**BHP:** 75
**FUEL:** 24mpg
**GEARBOX:** 4 speed
**BRAKES:** Disc/ drum
**SUSPENSION:** Ind Coil/wishbone – semi-elliptic

**SPEED:** 90mph
**BODIES:** 2 door saloon, convertible.
**YEARS:** 1961–63
**PRODUCTION:** 17,354 (total Rapier 65,050)

**MANUFACTURER**
# ROOTES

Humber was one of the original pioneering manufactures and were the subject of a takeover by the Rootes brothers in the late 1920s. Eventually in 1976 the company was bought by the Chrysler Corporation and it was then that both Humber and Sunbeam ceased to exist. Having created such distinguished transport it's sad that the final car to carry its proud badge was a re–badged and trimmed Hillman Minx – the Humber Sceptre. The penultimate Humbers, the Super Snipes, were a far more fitting tribute to decades of elegant transport.

Launched in 1958 the Super Snipe Mk I revealed a modern, slightly Americanised, monocoque constructed body using a new 2.6 litre engine supplied by Armstrong Siddeley. This engine was similar to the Sapphire 346's unit and its supply was part of commercial arrangements whereby Armstrong also worked on the Rootes Sunbeam Alpines. A three speed automatic gearbox, extensive interior fitments, plus both limousine and vast estate car variants, completed the initial two years' thrust until 1960, when the Series II gained a bored-out 3.0-litre engine and front disc braking.

A year later the Series III got the four headlight treatment, and this was followed by the Series IV, again upgrading both trim and performance. The final incarnation was the 1965–67 Series V, which involved much crisper roof line styling, dropping the wraparound rear window and further enhancing details. This was joined by the ultimate Humber Imperial version with all the traditional de luxe features undertaken by Thrupp & Maberly. The new American owners gave brief hope of a further V8

upgrade but instead the marque was laid to rest. They are discreet motor cars – a cocktail of elegant veneer, leather and picnic tables with just a twist of Americana in the chrome and body styling. Driving one is like drinking a good claret – something to savour rather than rush.

## RELATIONS

The engine was from the Armstrong Siddeley Sapphire 246, while the bodyshell was shared with its four cylinder twin, the Humber Hawk – all made on the old Sunbeam-Talbot production line at British Light Steel Pressings.

## BEST BUY

Spares for the initial 2.6 litre engine are getting scarce, though the larger engine/gearbox is little trouble. Rust is likely around wheel arches and sills. A poor body means some searching for panels. Buy the best you can afford – a IV or V offers greater performance, although there's a rewarding restoration project with any of them.

### SPECIFICATIONS

**ENGINE:** 2651cc; 2965cc
**BHP:** 105;121;124;128.5
**FUEL:** 20 –18mpg
**GEARBOX:** 3 speed; Auto on Imperial
**BRAKES:** Drum/ Disc; Drum Series II onward
**SUSPENSION:** Ind Coil/wishbone – semi-elliptic
**SPEED:** 92 –100mph
**BODIES:** 4 door saloon, estate, limousine.
**YEARS:** 1958–67
**Production:** 30,013

| | |
|---|---|
| Cost (II-III) | £2,700 |
| % swing | 6 |
| Spares | ★★ |
| V.F.M. | ★★★ |
| S.R. | ★★★ |

## FORD CAPRI

Pocket GT ... Thanks to Diana & a committee

### MANUFACTURER
# FORD

The Capri was a Detroit concept which evolved from a Ford think tank called the Fairlane Committee, so-called because it met at the Fairlane Hotel! Aimed at swelling the numbers of car-buying European 'baby boomers', it deliberately set out to create multi-package options with a long bonnet and short tail styling in the footsteps of the legendary Ford Mustang. Germany and the UK entered production in 1968 and the resulting car was an immediate success. The Mark I proved to be the lighter car with sculpted side panels and even dummy air vents in front of the rear wheel arches. Essentially, there were 1300cc and 1600cc + GT versions, as well as a V4 2000GT and a V6 3000GTS, plus a de luxe V6 called the 3000E. In addition, there was a German bored-out 150bhp racer, the RS2600, and briefly a UK homologation qualifying Cosworth version – the RS 3100.

The Mk II development programme was called Project Diana (after an inspiring Ford secretary) and the 1974 model changes included dropping the V4 in favour of the 2.0 litre Pinto unit, with four headlights, upgraded trim and a hatchback option – all designed to capture the young family market. There were S versions, Ghias, even one painted to match a leading package of cigarettes – every conceivable choice. The bodywork was slightly longer, higher, wider, and the trim was simplified. The 1977 Mark III took matters further with a changed grille and an altered bonnet line over the four headlights. Again, with this last incarnation there was a veritable roll call of options such as Capri Calypso, Cameo, Cabaret, Laser, Brooklands, even a Tickford.

Mid-way through the Mark III's lifespan, the interesting and very desirable high performance 2.8i was developed by Ford UK's Special Vehicle Engineering.

With sales approaching 2,000,000, Ford's concept was proved absolutely right. The Capri is still such a common sight on our roads it is hard to perceive its classic status. However, it is a pretty design, it is reliable and will increasingly evoke past times: All sure signs and even now, they are beginning to win concours show awards.

## RELATIONS

The Capri was an American design based upon the Mustang. The multiplicity of engines, gearboxes, etc. were drawn from US and European Ford factories.

## BEST BUY

The 'wide boy' image is already fading and their classic potential is still unrealised. Ford reliability and spares are good, while rust, lack of servicing and general abuse need considering. Choose the original sporting mid-Atlantic Mk I, the more domesticated Mk II or any of the refined Mk IIIs. If you like the original design, and a big engine then the underrated 3000E makes an interesting prospect.

| Cost (3000E) | £2,750 |
| --- | --- |
| % swing | -28 |
| Spares | ★★★★★ |
| V.F.M. | ★ |
| S.R. | ★★★ |

### SPECIFICATIONS

| | |
| --- | --- |
| **Engine:** 1297; 1593; 1996; 2994; 3091cc | **Brakes:** Disc/ drum |
| | **Speed:** 86 - 140 mph |
| **BHP:** 72 - 148 | **Bodies:** 2 door 2 + 2 coupe; hatchback coupé |
| **Fuel:** 20 – 30mpg | |
| **Gearbox:** 4 speed | **Years:** 1969–86 |
| **Suspension:** MacPherson strut– semi-elliptcal | **Production:** 1,886,647 |

MANUFACTURER

# STANDARD TRIUMPH

This is not a simple 1950s runabout just attaining classic eligibility, but the real thing, an example of new post-war styling and all the more interesting for it. The Standard Vanguard was the first genuine new post-war British car and was the result of impressive forward thinking. Money and resources were in very short supply, and so it was decided to create a single world car and push exports to draw in valuable foreign exchange. Two years in planning, the Phase I Vanguard closely resembled American styling, with items such as column gear changes increasing US sales. The immensely strong chassis, and even the generous ground clearance, were deliberate decisions to favour countries with poor road conditions. Because of export successes, it was not until 1950 that production capacity allowed British sales in any number. Effectively a six seater with a good boot, it proved successful in all walks of life. Estate versions were both cavernous and sturdy, giving them a long working life. The likes of HRH the Duke of Gloucester, Lord Mountbatten and Lord Brabazon all favoured the Vanguard. A competition team even entered the Monte Carlo Rally. The very first cars used only 1849cc, but all of these are thought to have been exported. The replacement 2088cc engine had wet cylinder liners and was actually common to the successful Ferguson tractor which Standard also manufactured. The basic model offered vinyl trimmings, while a fully-fledged example had leather, a heater, a radio and overdrive. In 1951 a change of bumpers, grille design, enlarged rear window, rear wheel spats and revised bonnet – termed the Phase 1A – helped keep customers interested until its final replacement in 1953 by the more conventional Phase II.

Somehow the car manages to address the period American bias while retaining a very British, stately, presence. When you climb into one you know you are in a real car. A fascinating classic to own or restore with few problems – providing you don't expect 1990s responses from it.

## RELATIONS

Standard visited the American Embassy to sketch current US car styles before creating the Phase I although the body is a Standard design. The 2088cc engine was also used in the Renown and would find its way into the TR2. With less stylised bodywork the Vanguard would continue in various guises through the 1950s.

## BEST BUY

A wonderfully strong chassis and body. Check for rust around the lower edges of the bodywork and in particular the rear – behind the wheels there is no chassis support. The post-1951 Phase 1A encapsulates all the model's best features. Reasonable spares and a good UK club are in support.

### SPECIFICATIONS

| | |
|---|---|
| **ENGINE:** 2088cc | **BRAKES:** Drum |
| **BHP:** 68 | **SPEED:** 80mph |
| **FUEL:** 25mpg | **BODIES:** 4 door saloon, estate, |
| **GEARBOX:** 3 speed | van, pick–up |
| **SUSPENSION:** Ind coil – semi- | **YEARS:** 1947 – 53 |
| elliptic | **PRODUCTION:** 184,799 |

| | |
|---|---|
| Cost | £3,200 |
| % swing | 8 |
| Spares | ★★★ |
| V.F.M. | ★★★ |
| S.R. | ★★ |

# RENAULT 4CV

GREAT EXCUSE TO VISIT FRANCE AND BUY

**MANUFACTURER**

# RENAULT

Louis Renault had witnessed the launch of the VW Beetle at the 1938 Berlin Motor Show and spent the years of the Nazi occupation planning his own super-economical model. Work started discreetly in 1940 and rear wheel drive was one logical decision for the secret prototypes. The little 4CV was unveiled at the 1946 Paris Motor Show. The engine was 760cc, water-cooled and married to a three speed gearbox, but such raw statistics have little to do with the car's central appeal. In a deeply depressed France the sight of an affordable four-door, four-seater car, must have been very seductive. It was frugal to run and positively glowed with Gallic charm. Within a year a Luxe version had been announced and the car's roof line rounded; a now rare convertible model was introduced in 1949 along with slight engine increases. As 14 years of production rolled by, numerous changes took place, including renaming the Luxe the Affaires, a Grand Luxe becoming the Sport; and in 1952 a Service model was launched. This was an absolutely basic version with no interior trim, hammock seating and just a dark grey paint option. At the other end of the scale, racing activity – including two Le Mans class wins - led to a competition model. Just 80 were made of this 1063cc, 32bhp car with specially constructed engines and four or five speed boxes, while the road-going Sports 4CV offered speeds into the 80s. The 4CV was a huge success, becoming the first Renault to sell a million examples and reaching over

500 produced in a single day. A Japanese production line made over 50,000 examples and another in London produced the model named the Renault 760 and 750. The slight cc change was to put the car into a 750cc category.

## RELATIONS

An original Renault concept which gave birth to many coach-built models including drophead, coupés, two door pillarless cars, and even a Gullwing coupé. The 1956 Dauphine also used the 4CV engine, gearbox and suspension.

## BEST BUY

Naturally with such a basic car many have rusted away; particularly watch floors, engine and suspension mountings. Body panels are difficult to find, but engines were made into the 1980s.

| Cost | £3,000 |
|------|--------|
| % swing | -8 |
| Spares | ★★ |
| V.F.M. | ★★ |
| S.R. | ★★★★★ |

## SPECIFICATIONS

| | |
|---|---|
| **ENGINE:** 747cc; 760cc | **SPEED:** 60mph |
| **BHP:** 17–21 | **BODIES:** 4 door saloon; convertible |
| **FUEL:** 50mpg | |
| **GEARBOX:** 3 speed | **YEARS:** 1947–61 |
| **BRAKES:** Drum | **PRODUCTION:** 1,105,547 |
| **SUSPENSION:** Ind wishbone/ coil – swing axle/coil | |

# MANUFACTURER
# SAAB

As an aviation company, Saab needed to diversify after 1945. Their 1947 prototype 18hp 764cc two stroke car could reach 70mph simply by using aviation knowledge and a body design so efficient that the drag factor was 0.30. Fifty years later, the new computer-designed Porsche Boxster boasted 'The best drag coefficient of all cars in its class – 0.31'. That's how far ahead Saab was in the 1940s. The first actual production Saab in 1949 was forced to remove its aerodynamic wheel spats because of snow accumulation, but still offered 0.32 and a power increase to 25hp to compensate. Monocoque construction, front wheel drive, hydraulic braking and full independent suspension were all utilized. Designed to feed the domestic economy market, its principles were decades ahead of other manufacturers, and international interest grew. The early 92/3 models evolved into the Saab 95 Estate (in UK 1960) and 96 Saloon (UK 1960/61), which were powered by an 841cc, three-cylinder, two-stroke offering 38bhp through front wheel drive. Early examples had three speed boxes with four speed as optional until 1965 – all via a column change. They were strong, they handled well, and in triple carb Monte Carlo or Sports versions they also included rev counter and disc brakes (standard on Saab from August 1966). Naturally, they made brilliant rally cars and victory after victory built up a lasting respect amongst enthusiasts. Despite competition successes, a public reticence towards two-stroke engines led in October 1966 to the Ford Taunus 1498cc V4 unit being fitted and two years later the two-stroke ceased production. The V4 Saab continued until late 1976.

## SPECIFICATIONS

**ENGINE:** 841cc (3 cyl); 1498cc (V4)
**BHP:** 38–55bhp
**FUEL:** 41–28mpg
**GEARBOX:** 3 speed + free-wheel: 4 speed
**BRAKES:** Drum: disc/drum
**SUSPENSION:** Ind wishbone, coil/dead axle, coils
**SPEED:** 74–95mph
**BODIES:** 2 door saloon: estate.
**YEARS:** 1959–1979
**PRODUCTION:** 730,607

## RELATIONS

The original prototype engine was inspired by the pre-war DKW. The 95/96 models took their cues from the previous 92/3 models, but as you might expect of such an advanced engineering company, though the 96 always looked much the same only basics like doors, boot lid, rear braking and some suspension elements remained unchanged. A highly original motor car.

## BEST BUY

The two strokes are collectors' favourites and are comparatively fast in multi-carb forms, but spares for these early 'Bullnose' cars are extremely scarce. The V4s have a more even power distribution making for an easier drive and spares are generally more widely available. The 95 Estate offered a third, rear-facing, row of seats; Erik Carlsson took this car on the 1961 Monte Carlo rally. A late V4 enjoys the fruits of all Saab's years of development.

| | |
|---|---|
| Cost | £3,300 |
| % swing | -20 |
| Spares | ★★ |
| V.F.M. | ★ |
| S.R. | ★★★★★ |

# MINI MOKE
## FIND A CREDIBLE EXCUSE

### MANUFACTURER
# BMC

Back in the mid-sixties BMC saw an opportunity to use the all-conquering Mini as the basis for a miniature Land Rover which would serve farmers, utility services and especially the military. Unfortunately it was rejected because of its impractical ground clearance and mere two-wheel drive. They experimented with independent engines for front and rear, but eventually admitted defeat and looked around for another market.

With no real purpose in life, small, fun and with occupants on display, it naturally became the plaything of the Swinging Sixties set. The conservative might of BMC had been trying to access this youth market for some time – indeed they actually ran a pair of fabric-covered Paisley Minis in order to look trendy. Known to embrace both the music and motoring worlds I was invited to run a Mini Moke in return for publishing accounts of its life in London's showbusiness world.

Production was unsustainable, however, and from 1966 it moved to Australia where it was instantly adopted as a genuinely useful vehicle. They soon increased the ground clearance with 13-inch wheels, and enlarged the engine to 1098cc with options of the 1275cc unit. 26,142 sales later, production moved again, this time to Portugal where another 9,277 were manufactured, this time with more refinements and the 998cc A Plus engine.

Like some orphan, it moved around the globe appealing to limited numbers over a total production run of 30 years. There are now rumours it might again be made – this time in Italy. Based on a simple light-

weight platform, it actually made for very nimble transport with all the Mini attributes, but with no serious weather or wind protection (the hood is virtually a tent). Thousands of owners had found justifiable excuses to own one, but almost without exception Mokes were really just great fun. They still are.

## RELATIONS

It's pure Mini, except for the platform chassis. Many of the Australian examples used a still larger power plant which was a derivative of the Cooper S unit.

## BEST BUY

The initial, more spartan, UK models are considered the best investment. The Portuguese cars are more refined, with roll-over bars assisting an improved soft top, high-backed seating and a compromise height with 12-inch wheels. Mechanically they are very simple and although rust is inevitable, virtually everything is a simple flat panel – so repairs are easy.

### SPECIFICATIONS

| | |
|---|---|
| **ENGINE:** 848cc; 998cc; 1098cc; 1275cc | **SUSPENSION:** Ind cone, wishbone, coil/cone, trailing arm |
| **BHP:** 34-65bhp | **YEARS:** UK: 1964-68 |
| **FUEL:** 40mpg | Australia: 1966-81 |
| **GEARBOX:** 4 speed | Portugal: 1980-94 |
| **BRAKES:** Drum | **PRODUCTION:** 14,518/26,142 |
| **SPEED:** 84mph | /9277 = Total 49,937 |
| **BODIES:** 4 seater utility | |

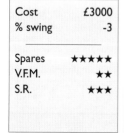

| | |
|---|---|
| Cost | £3000 |
| % swing | -3 |
| Spares | ★★★★★ |
| V.F.M. | ★★ |
| S.R. | ★★★ |

# MANUFACTURER
# VOLVO

'We design and we improve – but we do not invent', a philosophy declared by Gustaf Larson, one of the founding fathers of the Swedish Volvo organisation. True to his words, Volvo's history charts progressive improvement through just a handful of models. In the last 25 years they have relentlessly perfected transport for labradors and their owners – and it has worked. Now they are heavily investing in correcting that image through racing and advertising the 850. It has impressed new fans while the better informed just smile in the knowledge that Volvo's real sporting heritage pre dates the current macho chest beatings.

The distinctive PV544 has its roots in the Second World War. Sweden was neutral and allowed factories to continue manufacturing, so in 1944 Volvo unveiled their PV444 – named after the year of its launch. The car incorporated a 1414cc four-cylinder engine, independent front suspension, plentiful space for passengers and luggage (the seats even converted into beds), and an American-influenced body styling. Shadowing the Amazon specifications, the PV444 was then upgraded as a Sports version to an 85hp, 1.6 unit which went on to achieve class wins in race meetings across the USA. In 1958 this car became the impressive PV544, initially with the same 1593cc engine. and then from 1962 using a larger 1780cc powerplant. The sales pitch emphasised 'The car renowned for its repeated racing successes', stating that the PV544 was designed 'specially for passenger comfort and safety', and even listed rear seat belt attachments – perhaps current Volvo marketing isn't quite so innovative after all.

A great rally car in its day, strong, responsive and predictable, it makes an indestructible day-to-day classic which still enjoys a little competition. Sadly, import taxes made it too expensive to justify any right hand drive versions.

## RELATIONS

Volvo designer Erik Jern had previously concentrated on streamlined cars which, coupled with Volvo factory fascination with the USA, naturally led to the distinctive 'Hunchback' style, as it was nicknamed. The engine was rationalised with Amazon parts.

## BEST BUY

PV544s love to be driven, and mileage should not be a concern – the engine is so willing you can actually start in third! There was a factory option of three or four speed boxes. Bodywork was sturdy heavy gauge metal, the interior has uncomplicated trim. The Sports version is a lighter car.

## SPECIFICATIONS

**ENGINE:** 1414; 1598; 1778cc
**BHP:** 40 – 90
**FUEL:** 33 – 28 mpg
**GEARBOX:** 3 or 4 speed
**BRAKES:** Drum
**SUSPENSION:** Ind coil/wishbone – coil/rigid axle

**SPEED:** 59 – 98mph
**BODIES:** LHD 2 door saloon, estate & van
**YEARS:** 1944–58; 1958–65
**PRODUCTION:** 440,000

(Various basic & sports versions of each engine necessitate compression of figures)

| | |
|---|---|
| Cost (PV544) | £4,500 |
| % swing | 3 |
| Spares | ★★ |
| V.F.M. | ★★★ |
| S.R. | ★★★ |

# MATRA RANCHO
## A GENUINE UTILITY VEHICLE

### MANUFACTURER
# SIMCA

One of the major trends in the late 1970s and on through the 1980s was the strong preoccupation with appearances over and above utility. The Golf GTi and the spoiler-laden Porsche 911 were examples of cars deemed sufficiently expressive, yet rarely used to their full potential by their style conscious owners. The ubiquitous Range Rover too fell into this genre, though curiously it was initially launched in 1970 with distinctly unfashionably basic trim. The crop of rival vehicles which followed relentlessly offered four-wheel drive so as long as prosperity continued.

The French, with their spectacular sense of independence and love of simple logic, presented the motoring world in 1977 with their Matra Rancho. Like Citroën's indispensable 2CV, the Rancho perfectly fulfilled the role of a genuine utility vehicle. It was wisely based on the platform and running gear of Simca's hugely successful 1100 Alpine range, providing practical economies and splendid spares support. Intriguingly, its late 1970s part fibreglass body strongly echoed the current mass selling Discovery 4 x 4. It offered 90mph from its 80bhp

engine, and considerable interior space accessed from three doors. The two-tier roof added additional rear head room, and the second row of seating could be folded away providing quality storage. It offered a simple no-nonsense interior that every harassed parent, muddy child or wet dog could appreciate – all the basic utility functions without the cost, noise or price loading of four wheel drive.

## RELATIONS

The vehicle was actually based upon the transverse mounted front-wheel drive Simca 1100 pickup cab and chassis, with engine and transmission from the Chrysler Alpine S. Braking and suspension came from the Horizon and Alpine of the time. Essentially, this original design was the direct precursor of the French Espace.

## BEST BUY

Naturally, rust needs to be carefully checked, though fibreglass body sections reduce many of the problems – check sills and floors in particular. Ironically, these vehicles were so practical they were used hard so many are now looking pretty tired, even though they have only just become eligible as Classics. There were five subtle progressions in the model's life, as well as limited editions. Still very much in mid-life crisis, they have lost approximately a fifth of their value in recent years. However, properly restored a Rancho will prove thoroughly useful.

| Cost | £3,200 |
|------|--------|
| % swing | -22 |
| Spares | ★★ |
| V.F.M. | ★★ |
| S.R. | ★★★ |

### SPECIFICATIONS

**ENGINE:** 1442cc
**BHP:** 80bhp
**FUEL:** 25mpg
**GEARBOX:** 4 speed
**SPEED:** 90mph
**BRAKES:** Disc/drum
**SUSPENSION:** Ind wishbone, torsion bar/trailing arm, transverse torsion bar
**BODIES:** 3 door utility
**YEARS:** 1977-1984
**PRODUCTION:** 56,457

# MANUFACTURER
# VOLVO

This was the model which launched the Swedish company around the world. It was strong, it was safe, it was even considered beautiful – not a word readily associated with the previous PV 444. It also wasn't planned. The designer, 23-year-old Jan Wilsgaard, was asked to create a new model to precise management specifications. However, he also worked up his own ideas and presented them to Volvo alongside the required project. His boss pushed for the official car, but the remaining directors supported Jan's ideas and so the 120 Amazon was born. Far less simple was the factory attitude towards defining the models. In essence the P120 cars were four-door saloons, the 130s were the two-door versions, and the 220 were the estates. However, the 121s were single carburettors and 122s were the twins, irrespective of whether the car concerned had two doors, four doors, or was an estate vehicle!

The first UK cars in 1961 were four-door saloons and the 121 estates in 1962, both using the 1778cc engine and four-speed gearbox. 1964 saw 122 twin carb models with front disc brakes and the launch of the two-door 131; the 132 with twin carbs and two-door arrived the following spring. 1967 brought the 222 twin carb estates and the desirable 123GT with improved lighting, handling and power. As the model range matured, Volvo increased their safety features, introducing stronger door locks, padded dashboards, collapsible steering column and locks, and twin circuit braking. They were the first to provide seat belts as standard (including provisions for rear ones). As a practical classic that's different, easy to tinker with and costs little to run, a late disc-braked Amazon with twin carburettors will be hard to beat.

## RELATIONS

An all-original car, though the body styling began with Willys in the USA just before they were involved with Kaiser-Frazer. Legally, the name Amazon was not to be used outside Sweden because of ownership by the German motorcycle organisation Kreidler. Although thoroughly Swedish, many components were actually from the UK.

## BEST BUY

Virtually indestructible engines and build qualities suggest they will outlive all comparable vehicles. Naturally some rust will appear, but the worst problems might be finding replacements for the interior trim. The 123GT is the most sought-after, followed by the saloons and estates with the B20 power plant. Best of all are the extremely rare Rudd Speeds.

## SPECIFICATIONS

**ENGINE:** 1583cc, 1778cc, 1986cc
**BHP:** 85-118bhp
**FUEL:** 22-29mpg
**GEARBOX:** 4 speed: automatic
**BRAKES:** Drum; disc/drum
**SUSPENSION:** Ind coil, wishbone/live axle, Panhard rods, radius arms
**SPEED:** 88-107mph
**BODIES:** 2 & 4 door saloon: estate
**YEARS:** 1957-1970

| Cost | £3,800 |
| --- | --- |
| % swing | |
| Spares | ★★ |
| V.F.M. | ★★ |
| S.R. | ★★★★ |

# LAND ROVER SERIES I
## A MOTORING MASTERPIECE

### MANUFACTURER
# ROVER

Rover had been producing cars since 1904, but following the Second World War they, like other British manufacturers, were faced with massive shortages. Steel was at a premium and the government rationed materials, favouring work which generated vital export revenue. Rover design chief Maurice Wilks farmed in Anglesey where he had been using an American Willys Jeep. He became convinced Rover could manufacturer something better as a stopgap

LAND·ROVER IN ACTION

LAND-ROVER

*The 86-in Series One soft top (above) has the semaphore trafficators listed as an option in the early 1950s. This example belongs to enthusiast Nigel Weller. On the very earliest Series Ones, even the doors were an extra-cost option!*

| | |
|---|---|
| Cost | £4000 |
| % swing | 83 |
| Spares | ★★★★ |
| V.F.M. | ★★★★★ |
| S.R. | ★★★★ |

## SPECIFICATIONS

| | |
|---|---|
| **ENGINE:** 1595cc; 1997cc | **SUSPENSION:** Semi-elliptic |
| **BHP:** 50-52bhp | springs, beam axles |
| **FUEL:** 15-25mpg | **SPEED:** 65mph |
| **GEARBOX:** 4 Speed + | **BODIES:** Utility |
| transfer box | **YEARS:** 1948-1958 |
| **BRAKES:** Drum | **PRODUCTION:** 218,327 |

until proper car production resumed. Two Willys Jeeps were evaluated, and in 1947 a Land Rover prototype was created using a Rover 10 engine, slab sides of easier to source aluminium, and a central driving position to evade costly left- and right-hand drive versions. Innovative chassis design, permanent four-wheel drive, and the selection of the new 1596cc Rover P3 engine were all features of the vehicle unveiled at the 1948 Amsterdam Motor Show – though the central driver position was dropped. Public reaction was good, and within months the first of many options appeared: the seven-seater station wagon. The Ministry of Defence carried out trials which would lead to decades of Land Rover orders. The hard top followed in 1950. A year later, the 1997cc high torque engine arrived, and then in 1954, by public demand the 86-inch model was joined by a longer 107-inch wheelbase example. Two years later the 86 became 88 inches and the 107 became 109 inches providing additional engine bay space to accommodate the 2.0 diesel engine which appeared in 1957. Fifty years on and still in production, its simplicity of purpose and design singles it out as one of

*The Series One LWB Station Wagon was introduced in 1956; four doors, ten seats, 107-inch wheelbase.*

## BEST BUY

So many years have passed and with roughly 80% of Land Rovers going overseas, good Series Is are getting quite scarce. Body condition is easy to judge but check the more vulnerable chassis – any visible rust means more concealed. Really early fixed four-wheel drive cars have constant velocity joints which are rare, and early diesel spares getting tricky. Few short station wagons exist, but standard 80s are easier to find than the long versions. Particularly rare are the very early wooden-framed coachbuilt station wagons. Later Series are still excellent workers, but these first models are becoming venerated – they have risen very significantly in value during the last three years.

*An interesting example of of top-class restoration. This 80-inch Series One was discovered in a barn in the late 1980s. One part of the motivation for the painstaking renovation was that this particular vehicle had been used in the Great Train robbery of 1963!*

Britain's motoring masterpieces. Ignored by some motoring gurus, it is indeed a true classic by period, trustworthiness and through its originality. Overall production soars into seven figures but these early Series I are becoming rare and are small and slim in comparison to the current macho incarnations.

## RELATIONS

The basic idea was inspired by the American Willys Jeep, engines were from the P3 Rover, and body design/construction was born out of Rover initiatives with available post-war materials.

## MANUFACTURER
# VAUXHALL

VAUXHALL
VELOX/CRESTA PA
1950s STYLING MASTERPIECE

Car manufacturing history is packed with indifferent models pretending to be grand sports cars, badge-engineered to suggest that they go faster. Many tried to bait the US and home markets simultaneously; the Cresta PA had an up-front American style that caught the social mood to perfection, and brought transatlantic street culture to Britain. The Crestas were striking cars with long, low bodies, generous wrap-around windows, excesses of chrome, fins, and rear lamp clusters to match anything on American highways. The initial 2262cc in line six was replaced in 1960 with a larger 2651cc version, increasing power by 25 per cent. Both these units were tilted slightly downward at the rear to help provide identical headroom to the older and larger F series. — despite being 4.5 inches lower overall. These were fast cars for their day and comfortably accommodated six. A Velox version provided basic transport, while the Cresta with its heater/demister, washers, leather trim, carpets and underlays and a varieties of secondary lighting, was Vauxhall's rightful flagship. Distinguishing features included name-badging in gold, bonnet motifs, white wall tyres, stainless steel window trimming and gloriously flamboyant choices of duo-toned paintwork. Other markers were the 1959 changes from three to one piece rear window and replacing the initially straight grille with a larger curved version. From March 1958 there was also a Friary-bodied estate offering volumes of space.

## RELATIONS

The body style is original; the engine until 1960 was the same powerplant as in the old E series, but with automatic choke carburation. The Velox and Cresta were basically identical. Prefixes for the PAs pre-1960 are Velox – PAS and Cresta – PAD, while after 1960 they were PADY and PADX respectively.

## BEST BUY

The early smaller engined cars had unique elements such as the triple rear window, while the later ones were more powerful and actually boasted larger grilles and fins. Good examples are now rare and body panels are scarce.

| Cost | £3,950 |
|------|--------|
| % swing | 11 |
| Spares | ★★★ |
| V.F.M. | ★★★ |
| S.R. | ★★★ |

### SPECIFICATIONS

| | |
|---|---|
| **ENGINE:** 2262cc, 2651cc | **SUSPENSION:** Ind Coil - semi--elliptic |
| **BHP:** 83 – 113 | |
| **FUEL:** 21–25mpg | **SPEED** 90–95mph |
| **GEARBOX:** 3 speed or 2 automatic | **BODIES:** 4 door saloon; estate |
| | **YEARS:** 1957–62 |
| **BRAKES:** Disc /drum | **PRODUCTION:** 81,841 |

# MANUFACTURER
# TRIUMPH

**TRIUMPH GT6**

FLAWED BUT WORTHWHILE 1960s COUPÉ

The idea of combining the essence of the Spitfire, the Triumph 2000 engine and a diminutive E Type-styled coupé body was excellent. It was a 'Parts Bin' dream – which nearly turned into a nightmare simply because Triumph refuse to react to criticism.

In 1966, the year of the Mk I launch, there was a flood of orders but soon afterwards all the old Herald handling complaints magnified around the GT6. Despite knowing the limitations of the rear suspension in a modest family saloon, they pressed ahead selling the same specification in a 100mph+ sports car. To compound matters, the Spitfire front suspension had been softened on the GT6 to appease the American market – further aggravating the unpredictable handling. A leading British magazine reported that one US reaction was to ask if it was ' George III's revenge?'

Triumph capitulated, and the 1968 Mk II was a different story, with the rear suspension a Rotoflex double wishbone and a different suspension set up. It was expensive remedial action, but meant the Mk II suddenly brought the pretty coupé into bloom. Providing 30mpg, and over 100mph top speed, it had a sweet four-speed gearbox often with the overdrive option on 3rd and 4th – effectively giving it six gears. The cockpit was quite confined, but the rear storage was always useful.

In October 1970 the Mk III was born out of a Spitfire facelift. The body work was de–seamed, a larger windscreen added, and the rear chopped short which actually rather suited the coupé body. However in February 1973, with falling US sales, the factory reverted to a modified variant of the cheaper original rear suspension. The Rotoflex versions completed a very attractive coupé with excellent cruising manners and quite safe progressive handling. It also costs a fraction of its inspiration – the Jaguar E Type.

## RELATIONS

It had a Herald chassis, the Vanguard Six/Triumph 2000 engine, and Mk II engine improvements from parallel work on TR5. The Rotoflex double wishbone was inspired by the Cooper F1, while the GT6 gearbox was used in the Spitfire and Dolomite.

## BEST BUY

Unless it's an ambition, leave the Mk I alone. The Mk II and Rotoflex suspended Mk IIIs are definitely the best cars. Late Mk IIIs had marginally inferior handling, but improved trimmings. Lots of rust, but with a full-opening front end you can easily see many of the trouble areas. Mk I dash boards and seats are tricky to find, and many examples have acquired fibre glass bonnets. Engine/gearbox generally reliable.

### SPECIFICATIONS

**ENGINE:** 1998cc
**BHP:** 95;104
**FUEL:** 24; 30mpg
**GEARBOX:** 4 speed, optional o'drive
**BRAKES:** Disc/drum
**SPEED:** 106; 112mph

**SUSPENSION:** Ind coil/ wishbone – MkI swing axle MkII/early III Rotoflex: Later MkIII swing–spring axle
**BODIES:** 3 door coupé
**YEARS:** 1966–73
**PRODUCTION:** 40,926

| | |
|---|---|
| Cost (MkIII) | £4,800 |
| % swing | -2 |
| Spares | ★★★★★ |
| V.F.M. | ★★ |
| S.R. | ★★★ |

# TRIUMPH HERALD VITESSE

## TOWN MANNERS – OPEN ROAD ENJOYMENT

**MANUFACTURER**

# STANDARD-TRIUMPH

Standard-Triumph's enforced decision to bolt on (Michelotti-designed) Herald body panels to a separate chassis proved useful. It did mean occasional rattles and leaks, but at least panels were easily replaced. To the factory, convertibles, estates, and sporting versions were thus primarily a matter of bolting on differing non-stressed body parts. Perhaps the most successful of these variants was the Vitesse range which first appeared in May 1962. Superficially, it took just a side flash of paint and replacement front panels to provide four headlights and a fresh grille. It cost little and looked good, but the real bonus was that instead of just upgrading the Herald engine they installed a reduced bore 1596cc in–line six from the Standard Vanguard 6 model. Coupled to a pair of Solex carburettors, improved gearing, 9 inch front discs (and enlarged rear drums), this offered 90mph performance on a stiffened chassis – even though it was a full 1cwt heavier than the Herald. It was, indeed, sports car performance from an economical saloon platform. With the Vitesse, Triumph were revisiting their 1930s role as manufacturers of small sixes for the discerning. After carburettor changes, in 1966 came the 2 litre engine from the Triumph 2000 saloon, with 95bhp performance married at last to a new full syncromeshed gearbox and generally improved trim. This improved performance, however, accentuated the unpredictable behaviour of the rear swing axle and the factory were finally forced to remedy matters. The Mk II was announced in October 1968 with some trim changes, improved engine performance and the lower wishbone system

from the GT6 sports car. The Vitesse had reached its final form with 100mph+ performance, four seats, good storage and in–town manners. Through a fusion of models and ideas Standard-Triumph had moulded a thoroughly enjoyable, practical motor car.

## RELATIONS

Its roots are in the basic Herald. The Vitesse 6 engine came from the Standard Vanguard 6, while the later 2 litre models used the Triumph 2000 powerplant. The final Mk II versions employed improved suspensions from the Triumph GT6.

## BEST BUY

Bolt-on bodywork means easy DIY and some poor restorations. A good chassis is essential, next are sound mountings and front bonnet. Gearboxes do wear and body panels rattle. The Vitesse 6 is the poor relation, the 2 litre Mk II definitely the best, a Mk II convertible something to savour.

---

| Cost | £4,750 |
|---|---|
| (MkII Convertible) | |
| % swing | 8 |

| | |
|---|---|
| Spares | ★★★★★ |
| V.F.M. | ★★ |
| S.R. | ★★★★ |

---

### SPECIFICATIONS

**ENGINE:** 1596cc; 1998cc
**BHP:** 70; 104
**FUEL:** 30 – 24mpg
**GEARBOX:** 4 speed (early no syncro on 1st)
**BRAKES:** Disc/Drum
**SPEED:** 91; 101mph

**SUSPENSION:** Ind with transverse leaf/swing axle (post-1968 change to wishbone system)
**BODIES:** 2 door saloon; 2 door convertible,
**YEARS:** 1962–71
**PRODUCTION:** 51,212 disputed

## MANUFACTURER
# BMW

A classic 1950s BMW you can store at the end of your garage, that won't break the bank, that you dare to practise DIY on, you can remove an entire engine from in half an hour, tax for around £50, and cruise at 50+mph. The Isetta may have been a 'Bubble' car but the post-war recovery of BMW depended heavily upon this little Italian machine, and now their scarcity value, nostalgia for the 1950s and the enormous fun they offer make them a very serious classic choice for some. These micro saloons blossomed from a combination of limited manufacturing materials, a financial crisis, and the extreme petrol shortages following the Suez Crisis in 1956. A two seater with luggage storage, reduced road tax, 60 mpg and small enough to park at right angles to the curb is an attractive prospect, especially in our crowded 1990s cities. The Isetta originated from Iso in Milan and was launched in 1953 using a 236cc, 9.5hp two stroke engine with the paired rear wheels 26 inches closer together than the front ones. Its ingenious jointed steering column allowed the entire front of the car to hinge away as a wide single door. A year later BMW undertook German production using their 247cc four stroke yielding 12hp and as Milan production fell away the BMW model catered for exports. By 1957 BMW had opened a UK production line in Brighton's old railway buildings where employees negotiated a hundred steps to work and materials could only arrive by rail. In 1959 they switched to a three-wheeled configuration exploiting UK tax laws which considered any three wheeler under 8cwt a motorcycle, which paid less road taxation. Right-hand drive followed and then a two-door, four-seater model. Isetta means 'Little Iso' reflecting its originators, and it remained the quintessential mini car until in 1959 the Mini rewrote the rules.

## RELATIONS

Designed by the Italian motorcycle and scooter company Iso, the Isetta was licensed to bike producers BMW who installed their own engines. The 700 followed the 600, another rear engine in 1960. Soon after, the BMW 1500/1800 saw the Bavarian company enter their contemporary realm.

## BEST BUY

The Brighton factory produced around 30,000 using suppliers such as Lucas and Girling. The British Isettas had sliding side windows and swivelling quarter lights and used BMW 250 and 300 engines, which are strong; DIY should not be threatening, though rust can attack floors and lower bodywork.

### SPECIFICATIONS

**ENGINE:** 247cc; 298cc
**BHP:** 12; 13
**FUEL:** 65mpg
**GEARBOX:** 4 speed
**BRAKES:** Drum
**SUSPENSION:** Dubonnet Ind coils – Quarter elliptics/dampers

**Speed:** 52–58mph
**BODIES:** 2 seater saloon; roll top cabriolet
**YEARS:** 1955–62
**PRODUCTION:** 161,728 (UK 30,000)

| | |
|---|---|
| Cost | £4,600 |
| % swing | -14 |
| Spares | ★★ |
| V.F.M. | ★★ |
| S.R. | ★★★★★ |

## MANUFACTURER
# BMC

# MGB GT

PERFECT AFFORDABLE BRITISH SPORTS CAR

*The front end (above) is of course non-standard, but not that unattractive – certainly not as unsatisfactory as US regulations made the factory issue in 1974.*

BMC had struggled to find a suitable replacement for the MGA which utilised the existing 1622cc unit. Fighting off competition from cars like the Triumph TR3, young designer Don Hayter's simple 1958 design disposed of the restrictive MGA chassis, and within 10 weeks a full scale mock-up revealed the excellent lines of the MGB. At the next drawing table Dennis Williams battled deadlines to design the MG Midget, and ironically, a smaller MGB rear appeared on the Midget before the Roadster B itself was launched in 1962.

The MGB GT was unveiled in 1965 by which time the new BMC 1800 five bearing crankshaft was added to the MGB. So good was the B's design that no significant mechanical changes occurred until the late experiments with big engines. Excellent rack-and-pinion steering, the sturdy Series B engine, and the car's sheer versatility made it an instant favourite. Many consider the GT has the more graceful lines, yet on the classic market they are usually around 25 per cent cheaper than the roadsters.

In October 1969 there was a cosmetic update with Rostyle wheels, reclining seats, interior trimming and a revised chrome and matt black grille. 1967 had seen the start of a two year experiment marrying a strengthened MG to a 145bhp six-cylinder engine.

The MGC was to be twinned with an Austin-Healey 3000 replacement but Donald Healey would not co-operate. The resultant MG was not well balanced and certainly the Abingdon press car of the time (below right) gave me an eventful week. The regular B GT's popularity rolled on until threatened American legislation prompted the 1974 change to the large energy absorption black bumpers and raised suspension. Both these changes spoilt the car, reflected in much lower classic car prices. From 1973 to 1976 there was also an MGB GT V8 version using the 3.5 Rover engine which had more potential than the ill fated C but within a year it too was saddled with the damaging American modifications and lacked the visual excitement of the works racing Sebring bodywork.

## RELATIONS

With a modified MGA engine, gearbox and front suspension, the MGB GT used an updated version from the BMC 1800 from 1964; a new BMC Series C

| Cost | £5,000 |
|---|---|
| (GT 65-74 average) | |
| % swing | -17 |
| Spares | ★★★★★ |
| V.F.M. | ★ |
| S.R. | ★★★ |

### SPECIFICATIONS

**ENGINE:** 1798cc, 2912cc; 3528cc V8
**BHP:** 95 bhp; 145bhp; 137bhp
**FUEL:** 22 mpg; 18mpg; 25mpg
**GEARBOX:** 4 speed
**BRAKES:** Disc/Drum
**BODIES:** 3 door coupé
**SUSPENSION:** Ind coil/wishbone – semi elliptic
**SPEED:** 103 mph; 120mph; 125mph (B, C, V8)
**YEARS:** 1965 – 1980; 1967–69; 1973–76
**PRODUCTION:** 125,597; 4,449; 2,600

Roadster or GT? The market says the GT is inferior, worth considerably less, but this is no reflection on the lines of the GT. You pays your money – and 460,000 did just that …

engine for the MGC, and a Rover 3.5 for the MG GT V8. The Austin 3 litre gearbox was introduced from autumn 1967. The body styling was original.

## BEST BUY

The only drama is rust within the central body construction, so inspect prospective purchases carefully.

Repair can be extremely costly, but in dire situations new bodyshells are now available. Otherwise they are a joy to own. They are eminently practical, spares abound and the car lives up to John Thornley's dream (formerly of MG) of creating a 'poor man's Aston Martin'. Nearly forty years on, these cars are guaranteed to turn heads and are among the most popular classic cars around.

… plus another 9000 who opted for the MGC in the same bodyshell (half GT), with the 6 cylinder ex-Austin-Healey 3000 engines, from late '67 to late '69. Top speed was impressive at 120mph, but the low-speed torque was found wanting by the motoring press at the time. Autocar considered that 'somewhere in the large BMC complex it has lost the "Abingdon touch".' Prophetic words.

# TOYOTA MR2 MK I

*Forgotten Charms*

### MANUFACTURER
# TOYOTA

The SV-3 had been under development for almost a decade before it was finally launched in the June of 1984 as the Toyota MR-2 (Midship – Runabout – 2 seater). This was Japan's very first mid-engined sports car, and was firmly aimed at the market which had

| Spares | ★★★★ |
| V.F.M. | ★★★ |
| S.R. | ★★★★★ |

belonged almost exclusively to the mid-engined Fiat X 1/9. Although the MR-2 had a number of distinguishing features, it was the responsive twin cam engine which was at the heart of its success. Actually, Toyota had amazingly managed to use the same basic power plant in their front-wheel drive Corolla GT Coupé and the rear-wheel drive Corolla Hatchback, as well as this mid-engined car. For the MR-2 it was in twin overhead cam form, delivering 6,600 revs and

lots of attractive low- and mid-range punch, while remaining extremely tractable: it was still able to operate in fifth gear at just 16mph. The mid-engined position provided an ideal 55% rear/42% front weight distribution, even with the fuel tank ideally slotted amidships between driver and passenger. As a result, this was a sweet handling sports car, though as it dated from the early days of Japanese sports cars, we tend not to remember the MR-2. Though it certainly made a tremendous impact at the time, hailed by some as the model which marked Japan's coming-of-age in the car world.

In fact, they were fitted out virtually to saloon car specifications, with features such as electrically adjustable mirrors, heated rear screens, electric windows, audio systems, highly efficient heating systems, sensible wide doors and even eyeball vents.

From late 1986, Toyota added the T-Bar model, with two small stowable roof panels; it was effectively a Targa model. You could sit with the eager twin cam unit just behind you offering 0–60 in 7.7 seconds, great handling (at least in the dry!) and good fuel economy.

When it comes to the second generation, (picture opposite, below) the style is still there in spades, with the turbo offering a whole 65 hp more than the normally aspirated engine, but the latter actually has more torque at lower speeds. Elegant undoubtedly, and the cheapest mid-engine sports coupé around, but there are question marks regarding the handling which may preclude it from classic status in years to come. It's the usual story; some kind of ineluctable

Why does this car deserve a double page splash? Well maybe it doesn't, but as always, people can get really passionate about their cars. The car (opposite top) was owned by Osprey's Design Manager, as is the Mk II below. So we had no choice! The Mk I was bought more or less on its looks in 1991 for £10,000, sold after two years of trouble-free motoring for £9,000 …

… Which happy experience leads to the purchase of the revamped second generation, despite a long hard look at the Lotus Elan and the more expensive (new) MGF.

## SPECIFICATIONS

| | |
|---|---|
| **ENGINE:** 1587cc | **SUSPENSION:** MacPherson struts, coils |
| **BHP:** 122bhp | |
| **FUEL:** 29mpg | **BODIES:** 2 door sports |
| **GEARBOX:** 5 speed | **YEARS:** 1984-1989 |
| **BRAKES:** Disc | **PRODUCTION:** 166,104 |
| **SPEED:** 120mph | |

law states that a car which was designed to be an agile, highly manoeuvrable and affordable machine must in its second incarnation become bigger, more powerful and more expensive. Though *What Car?* magazine voted it the Sports Car of the Year in 1995.

But the MR-2 Mk 1's distinctive shape, superior build quality and abundant sporty charms all point to a successful future as a classic.

## RELATIONS

With its mechanical roots shared with the Corolla GT Coupé and the Corolla Hatchback, the car is very much a Toyota. Design cues such as the detachable roof reflect Porsche Targa tricks from the previous decade. The Fiat X 1/9 from 1972 a clear influence.

## BEST BUY

The initial fixed head coupés were actually sold from April 1985 and at that year's motor show they gained spoilers and colour coded skirts. A year later came the T-Bar, and a leather seating option, and

both models also enjoyed marginal improvement of specifications. In the United States and Japan a super-charged version also went on offer. In October 1988 the T Bar benefited from standard leather interiors, and in April 1990 the Mk I was replaced by a sub-stantially different vehicle. Mechanically quite sound, many MR-2s suffer from rust, most likely around door pillars. The electrics can also be problematic.

Electric window motors are weak and can be expensive to replace. A late T Bar gives you all the driving pleasure you can reasonably expect, while any good MR-2 Mk I should make an eventual classic.

# MG MIDGET
## EXTENDING SPORTS CAR OWNERSHIP

**MANUFACTURER**

# BMC

In creating the Frogeye Sprite, Donald Healey captured the small sports car market which had been the domain of MG Cars pre-war. Inevitably, when the Frogeye was due to be replaced an MG version was planned. The basic body/chassis continued, but Healey designed a more conventional front end treatment, while Abingdon was responsible for the new tail section. In fact, Dennis Williams' rear design was actually scaled down and borrowed for the MGB before being unveiled on the Midget. The Mk II Sprite was launched in June 1961 a month ahead of the Mk I MG Midget version, but both were powered by the same 948cc twin carb series A engines and equipped with just drum brakes. Conventional headlamps and an opening boot were radical departures from the more eccentric Frog. A year later, but still the Mk I Midget, the engine was upgraded to 1098cc, it gained front disc braking, an improved gearbox and some trim changes. The official step up to Mk II came in 1964 when the car gained another 3 bhp, semi-elliptic rear suspension and a more civilized interior including wind-up windows. Later in the same year, the famous 1275cc power plant was installed, boosting power to 65bhp and this model continued to attract new fans until matt black grilles, Rostyle wheels and fussy trimmings were introduced in 1970. This final Mk IV version was devised to appease the critical US market which was becoming obsessed with safety regulations. Big black rubber bumpers, higher road clearance and extra weight pushed the company into fitting the larger Triumph Spitfire 1500cc engine until the end in 1979. Like a corpse, the model had long separated from its spirit: an Austin Healey Sprite with MG badges and a Triumph Herald engine was hardly a purist's dream,

| SPECIFICATIONS | |
|---|---|
| **ENGINE:** 948cc; 1098cc; 1275cc; 1493cc | bone/quarter-elliptic leaf*, radius arms |
| **BHP:** 47–65bhp | **SPEED:** 85–101mph |
| **FUEL:** 28–45mpg | **BODIES:** 2 door sports |
| **GEARBOX:** 4 speed | **YEARS:** 1961–1974 |
| **BRAKES:** Drum: disc/drum | **PRODUCTION:** 135,903 |
| **SUSPENSION:** Ind coil, wish- | *Became half elliptic with Mk III from 1964. |

but at least it continued the MG tradition of extending economical sports car ownership.

## RELATIONS

Essentially a continuation of the popular Frogeye Sprite, with the BMC Series A engine which powered the Minor, Mini, etc. Suspension parts came from the A35/A40 and in the Mk IV form the 1500cc engine was from the Triumph Spitfire and 1500 coupled up to a Morris Marina-type gearbox.

## BEST BUY

Rust is the conventional enemy and strikes freely on these cars, though replacement parts – even bodies – are available. Front suspension is vulnerable, so check wishbones and king pins. Purists may hunt out the more primitive early examples, but it is the late Mk IIs and the 1275cc Mk IIIs which provide the best blend of performance and comfort – relatively speaking! The Mk IV has always been decried – and certainly its handling is less predictable, but a large number were sold and its depressed status provides bargain opportunities.

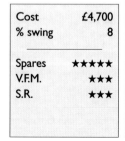

| Cost | £4,700 |
|---|---|
| % swing | 8 |
| | |
| Spares | ★★★★★ |
| V.F.M. | ★★★ |
| S.R. | ★★★ |

# MANUFACTURER
# JENSEN

Relatively unloved, this is the child of a marriage of convenience. Jensen built Healey bodies from the early 1950s until new US safety rules prompted the death of the Healey 3000 in 1967. The same laws axed the Sunbeam Tiger, Jensen's other contract, leaving them with troubled finances. Meanwhile, Donald Healey, less than impressed with Leyland's attempts to fill the big Healey void with their suspect MGC, had been developing a replacement model using the Vauxhall Victor 2.3, but tightening emission laws ruled it out. However, an American millionaire who had sold Healey 3000s approached Donald Healey as a backer for a replacement and eventually the wealthy Kjell Qvale bought 80% of Jensen, appointed Healey as Chairman and in just two-and-a-half years the Jensen-Healey was a reality. The Victor engine was unsuitable, BMW couldn't meet the projected production numbers, the German Ford V6 was too tall, and both Mazda and Volvo were considered before the new 1973cc Lotus was chosen. Dangerously, this had yet to appear in any car, but it fitted and would give 120mph. Jensen's skills provided a good monocoque body/chassis, and most other parts were derived from existing Rootes and Chrysler models. There was disappointment at the bland styling, but *Autocar* thought 'It is everything a Healey and a British sports car should be, simple in concept, basic in construction, sporting in performance and nimble through the curves'. It proclaimed it as a future classic, and certainly, a good one acquits itself well on the road.

Unfortunately, the under-developed Lotus engine proved seriously unreliable, and the car gained a poor reputation. Minor restyling in 1973 provided some fashionable matt black paint and wood graining,

## SPECIFICATIONS

| | |
|---|---|
| **ENGINE:** 1973cc | **SPEED:** 120mph |
| **BHP:** 144bhp | **SUSPENSION:** Ind wishbone, |
| **FUEL:** 23mpg | coil / live axle, coil |
| **GEARBOX:** 4 & 5 speed | **BODIES:** 2 door sports |
| **BRAKES** Disc/drum | **YEARS:** 1972–1976 |
| | **PRODUCTION:** 10,921 |

while 1974 saw the Mk II with a 5 speed gearbox and those huge American safety bumpers. It never recovered from its poor start and production ended in 1976 with most exported. A last-ditch effort with a Reliant GTE type Jensen GT sold just 473, but Mr Healey had removed his name.

## RELATIONS

The engine was the Lotus LV220 for the new Elite, the subframe, steering and brakes were standard Vauxhall, the suspension from the Firenza. The four-speed box came out of the Sunbeam Rapier H120 and the five-speed Getrag was used in BMWs.

## BEST BUY

Difficult to define. Rust problems exist in most 1970s cars and it's all down to restoration costs and your love for the model. The initial mechanical troubles are hardly a problem now – if it's still running it has done better than most. One has to balance inexpensive and distinctive classic motoring with major rebuild costs. Spares are not quite the problem you might expect, and the Martin Robey Group are even rumoured to be building new bodyshells.

| Cost | £5,200 |
|---|---|
| % swing | 5 |
| Spares | ★★ |
| V.F.M. | ★★★ |
| S.R. | ★★ |

# ROVER P5
### SOLID CREATURE COMFORTS

## MANUFACTURER
# ROVER

As the Rover 75 to 110 era – the P4 range – was nearing its end, the replacement plan was for a light, mass appeal model. Concepts included a V6 engine, front-wheel drive, rear-wheel drive, four-wheel drive, rear-engined – even a plan to place the gearbox under the seating. As time passed, and Rover failed to gain planning permission to expand production buildings, it was decided the P5 should be a quality car generating limited demand and thus less factory pressures. The V6 engine was dropped and the initial Rover 3.0 saloons were launched in 1958 using a revised 2995cc P4 unit. The strong design appealed to the more conservative customers and indeed prime ministers and royalty all favoured these charismatic cars. It employed unitary construction with a rubber isolated front sub-frame for the engine, gearbox and front suspension. This feature, and the exceptional

levels of interior comfort, made it supremely comfortable transport. The interior boasted three-way front seat adjustments, hide upholstery, mahogany veneers, a pull-out tool tray under the dash – it was simply the most luxurious car Rover had made– and immensely British. In 1962 the Mk II was given another 12bhp by a Weslake head, the suspension was lowered and a shorter gear lever fitted. Although identical to the saloon, the Coupé was also launched boasting a 2½inch lower roof line. To survive, however, they needed a more powerful engine and by

*The 1949 P4 had been known as 'Auntie Rover' – the kind of car your maiden aunt drove – upgrade to three litres, then V8, on the P5 helped to lose the tag.*

| Cost | £4,800 |
|------|--------|
| % swing | 26 |
| Spares | ★★★ |
| V.F.M. | ★★★ |
| S.R. | ★★★ |

### SPECIFICATIONS

**ENGINE:** 2995cc, 3528cc
**BHP:** 105, 160
**FUEL:** 20mpg – 18mpg
**GEARBOX:** 4 speed; automatic; overdrive option
**BRAKES:** Drum;Disc/drum (after 1959)
**SUSPENSION:** Ind wishbone & live axle semi-elliptic
**SPEED:** 96mph; 110mph
**BODIES:** 4 door saloon & coupé
**YEARS:** 1958 – 73
**PRODUCTION:** 48,241

*That doughty Buick 3.5-litre V8 engine would prove to be significant for Rover, not just in the P5 and P6; it powered the 1970 Range Rover and was an option in the Land Rover from 1979.*

chance an unloved aluminum V8 was spotted during a visit to Mercury Marine in Wisconsin and the engine design was licensed to Rover by Buick. In the interim, Mk II models provided even more creature comforts including individually sculpted front and rear seating with separate rear heating controls. The P5 was phased out in 1967 and the P5B (B for Buick) arrived bringing a massive 46bhp power increase, turning these cars into very desirable executive expresses. No existing gearbox could sustain the levels of torque, so only automatic was offered.

## RELATIONS

Designed by Rover, the car's initial engine was from the out-going P4 range, while the V8 came from Buick. MGB GT V8s, Morgan +8s, Range Rovers, TR8s, and the Rover SD1 all used this engine.

## BEST BUY

The serious danger is rust, particularly in bulkheads, wings, and sills – the usual concealed areas. The drive trains of both versions ought to be good for around 200,000 miles. Though these cars are excellent value, the quality of construction means that any major works can get expensive – buy the best you can and don't be seduced by the delightful American V8 power without considering that miles of hard driving gives an expensive 17 miles per gallon. A post-1965 3.0 litre is still good for around 100mph and in the same comfort.

# RELIANT GTE
## HONEST AND INTERESTING STYLESETTER

**MANUFACTURER**
# RELIANT

**Model families:**
SE5 – 1968-71
SE5a – 1971-75
SE6 – 1975-76
SE6B – 1979-86
SE8b (GTC) – 1980-86
Middlebridge – 1988-90.

| Cost | £5,250 |
|---|---|
| (Scimitar GTE SE6) | |
| % swing | -6 |

| Spares | ★★★★ |
|---|---|
| V.F.M. | ★★ |
| S.R. | ★★★ |

The innovative GTE attacks both head and heart. With all the basic bugs ironed out in the Ogle designed Reliant SE Coupé this subsequent sporting estate was very appealing. Fast, sturdy and exceptionally roomy it led others such as Volvo with its P1800 and Lancia Beta's HPE to copy the concept of practical, high speed transport. The strong fibreglass bodywork couldn't rust, the chassis was strong, the running gear all proven Ford. It appeared to have everything, yet never fully captured public imagination. In the '90s the heart recognises a highly individual sporting car, with good spares, plenty of room and best of all – extremely good value for money.

However, the head dispassionately records warnings of mixed build qualities and missing glamour. The attributes of reliability, together with the fold down rear seating meant many worked hard and so look tired. They also remain a bargain and so the costs of major restoration may well not sit easily with overall values. It would be wrong to assign the GTE's to serious DIY owners only, but tired cars could damage bank accounts.

The initial SE5 model ran until 1971 and featured the UK Ford V6 which was uprated from 128bhp to 138bhp in 1971–75 SE5a form. This minor revamp covered the dashboard, new tail lighting and a grille but left the four 5¾-in headlights – a hallmark of the first body styling. SE6 and SE6b ran 1975–76 and 1976–79 respectively, using a 4 inch stretched body style, larger outer headlights, black grille and eventually an improved braking set–up. A 1980 convertible – the SE8b, used Ford of Germany's 2.8 V6 which

kept interest alive until 1986. The cars undulating commercial fortunes saw two years in abeyance and then another company try one last incarnation – the Middlebridge, using the 2.9 Ford engine, 1988–90.

## RELATIONS

Body work an original Ogle design. The engines and some gearboxes were Ford, front suspension from the Triumph TR4/5/6, with Vitesse steering rack.

## BEST BUY

A realist's classic car usable day-to-day. Rustless bodywork doesn't mean the vital chassis and metal supports aren't vulnerable. Fibre glass patching, rippling, and cracks need watching – a good repaint is four figures. Interior trimming was never that durable and a major retrim too will be costly. If you are not too concerned about the thickness of burred walnut furniture but want honest, economical and practical classic transport then the GTE is just right. The early style body looks prettiest and feels more agile.

### SPECIFICATIONS

| | |
|---|---|
| **ENGINE:** 2994cc – 2792cc | **SUSPENSION:** Ind Coil – |
| **BHP:** 128 – 150 | live axle/coil |
| **FUEL:** 22–28mpg | **SPEED:** 116 – 123mph |
| **GEARBOX:** 4 speed, overdrive | **BODIES:** 3 door sports estate |
| standard post 4/74 | **YEARS:** 1968–86 / 1988–1990 |
| **BRAKES:** Disc/Drum | **PRODUCTION:** 9,705 |

**MANUFACTURER**

# BMC

After the war Austin's new managing director Leonard Lord was anxious to meet the inevitable demand for new cars. While many – including Austin – carried forward old designs, he also pushed development of new a brand new Austin A40 Devon saloon, launched in 1947. A strong chassis cradled a brand new 1200cc overhead valve engine and an equally new independent front suspension set up under a very modern 4 door body shell. The car and its derivatives sold roughly 450,000 in its five years.

Meanwhile the Jensen Brothers were evolving the luxury PW with the Austin Sheerline 4 litre unit. It was not ideal and Jensen returned to Austin with drawings for another sporting car based upon Austin's A70 chassis. There was an interesting solution: Jensen's 1950 4 litre Interceptor shared a body design with the 1950 Austin A40 Sports – which Jensen constructed. It was more an open tourer than a sports car with wind up windows and rear seating for children. Naturally it was based upon the A40 Devon rolling chassis with a modified 1200cc unit and twin SU carburettors for an additional 10mph. The initial cars were constructed with floor placed gear change but with the Devon's switch to column change in August 1951, so too did the A40 Sports. Indeed the entire interior was virtually the Devon and this same basic equipment would in time also appear in the A40 Somerset. During 1952 Leonard Lord also

encouraged Donald Healey to create an outright sports car based upon the Austin A90 Atlantic engine and that year's motor show saw a prototype Healey 100: the little A40 sports was dead in the water. Jensen's production line went on to build the Austin Healey 100. Subsequent years proved open touring cars were just as appealing as sports cars – the A40 Sports was the right idea at the wrong moment.

## RELATIONS

An Austin A40 Devon through and through with bodywork shared with Jensen's 1950 Interceptor.

## BEST BUY

Rare, simple, with common Devon mechanics for spares. So worth work. Engines good for 75,000 miles before anything serious; gearboxes sometimes tricky.

### SPECIFICATIONS

| | |
|---|---|
| **ENGINE:** 1200cc | **BRAKES:** Drum |
| **BHP:** 50 bhp | **SPEED:** 78mph |
| **FUEL:** 29mpg | **BODIES:** 2 door convertible. |
| **GEARBOX:** 4 speed | **YEARS:** 1950–53 |
| **SUSPENSION:** Ind Coil/wishbone – semi-elliptic | **PRODUCTION:** 4,011 |

| | |
|---|---|
| Cost | £5,000 |
| % swing | 2 |
| Spares | ★★ |
| V.F.M. | ★★★ |
| S.R. | ★★★★ |

# FORD ESCORT MK I

## MIXED BLESSINGS – ENDLESS CHOICE

**MANUFACTURER**

# FORD

Once upon a time our roads were littered with Mark I Escorts, but nowadays it's something of a shock to stop and consider when last you saw one. They have become a relatively rare sight and this has stimulated a collectable classic status for a range of cars that really needs more debate than this section allows.

The model was launched in January 1968 as a two-door replacement for the popular Ford Anglia 105E, with a 1098cc version of the Kent engine. For the first time Ford incorporated rack-and-pinion steering, a new German four-speed gearbox, and the basic model was joined by a De Luxe, with an Escort Super version boasting either the 1100cc or the Mk II Cortina's 1298cc power plant. Next up the scale, using the Super's engine, was the 1300GT with front discs, wider wheels and the stronger export bodyshell. The real performer was the Twin Cam, with the Lotus-Cortina unit squeezed into the Escort by Ford's Competition Department. In 1968 the lower range gained a De Luxe Estate with 1100 or 1300 units, and an automatic option.

A Super Estate appeared in 1969 and in the same year, a four-door saloon. In 1970 the De Luxe and Super were replaced by a base model, the Escort L, (1100 or 1300) plus a fully-loaded Super 1300XL. The Mark I ceased in 1974.

The Twin Cam cars, and indeed the GTs, were trimmed to the Super standards, although TCs were always two-door white cars with black interiors. After just 12 months the strong export body shell was replaced by the domestic version on the GTs and it was phased out during 1973. The 1600cc, 16 valve

Cosworth RS1600 was unveiled in 1970 pointing the way for future development. The AVO facility released a conventionally-tuned 1600 pushrod engined version of the RS1600 to commemorate the Escort's victory in the London–Mexico rally, which was joined a year later by a black 2 door 1300 facsimile of the Mexico which would eventually replace the GT Escort. As the GT ceased, a luxury Escort joined the range using Ford's E suffix. The RS2000 also appeared in 1973, using the Ford Pinto engine. Ford excelled at drawing the best from a model range without undue badge engineering but the legacy is a complex web of cars.

## RELATIONS

Although everything possible was adapted from the Cortina and Lotus-Cortina, the Escort was classed as an all-new car.

## BEST BUY

The GT Sports and 1300E are much the same car barring trim, the RS2000 and Mexico provide strong, simple engines, while the Twin Cams and RS1600s are more complex, as well as being the fastest. Straightforward and often long-lasting components make these Fords a prudent buy providing you find a decent bodyshell. They make excellent historic rally cars, although watch out for poorly disguised ex-rally cars when buying. The best balance of assets is probably an RS 2000.

| Cost | £6,500 |
|------|--------|
| (That frightened you - Twin Cam) | |
| % swing | 33 |
| | |
| Spares | ★★★★ |
| V.F.M. | ★★★★ |
| S.R. | ★★★★ |

# MANUFACTURER
# LOTUS

**LOTUS EUROPA**
A FINE IDEA FROM MANY SOURCES

Colin Chapman had the idea for a race-proven mid-engined format, a cheap sports car to compete with rivals such as the Midget – a kind of MGF of the late 1960s. Primarily designed as a replacement for the Lotus 7, the Europa construction was supposed to allow cheaper production. The reality was somewhat different, and between 1964 and 1966 the design grew, becoming 12 inches longer than the Elan, and 8.5 inches wider: Chapman had evolved a new model which competed with his own Elans. So it became the Europa and was intended for export, with Renault engines and the transmission fitted in France to save import duties. A steel backbone chassis with the new Renault 16 drive-train mounted behind the seating appeared to be a good package, but the S1 had seat cushions simply mounted on the floorpan, fixed windows, (so nothing opened) desperate rear vision, poor engine torque and barely room for the occupants. Approximately 300 were made before the Series II cars appeared. They used the proven 1558cc twin cam engine out of a Lotus-Cortina. The interior was altered to provide extra space, proper ventilation and improved gear changes, while the rear suspension was adjusted to compensate for the hard race configuration jarring the car – unfortunately using rubber cushioning which itself added to the handling cocktail. From 1972-75 there was a Europa Special with an enlarged twin cam engine offering 126bhp via a five-speed gearbox. As with much of Lotus' history it was a fine idea brought together with what was available and dragged into the public view through the company's separate competition activities.

## SPECIFICATIONS

**ENGINE:** 1470cc; 1558cc
**BHP:** 78-126bhp
**FUEL:** 25-33mpg
**GEARBOX:** 4 speed; 5 speed optional post-1972
**BRAKES:** Disc/drum
**SPEED:** 115–123mph

**SUSPENSION:** Ind wishbone, coil/radius arms, links, coils
**BODIES:** 2 door Coupé
**YEARS:** 1969-1975
**PRODUCTION** 9230

## RELATIONS

As expected, Lotus used what they could source. Body design was worked around available Ford Anglia bumpers, suspension was Elan-based, it used Triumph Herald steering and uprights, the chassis was a variant upon the Elan, while power trains were from the Renault 16 and the Ford Lotus-Cortina.

## BEST BUY

A very dangerous area. It is possible to create a fine classic from a Europa, but use the Lotus Owners' Club for guidance. For the first series they not only restricted breathing to save money, they also bonded the fibreglass body to the chassis – but this was not the case with later examples. Sold as kit cars in the UK, many examples will be subject to poor construction, and Lotus build quality itself was always variable. However, if you know what you are doing, a full restoration could be rewarding. Interestingly, the earlier cars are appreciating faster.

| | |
|---|---|
| Cost | £6,500 |
| % swing | 41 |
| Spares | ★★★ |
| V.F.M. | ★★★★ |
| S.R. | ★★★ |

## MANUFACTURER
# BMC

The union of Donald Healey's ideas and Austin production facilities reaped rich rewards with the Austin-Healey 100, so naturally there was enthusiasm for another joint project to capture the budget sports car market. Healey's team designed an affordable open seater utilizing the Morris Minor and Austin A35 parts bins, and powered by the BMC A Series engine. The result was a model of such simplicity, and such character, that it gave birth to a line of small BMC sports cars that would run for 30 years. Here we have the first truly mass produced small sports car.

Pop-up lights were too expensive, so lamp pods were used. There were no exterior door locks or handles, not even a boot lid, as stowage space was behind the seating. A brilliantly simple and responsive monocoque body/chassis – the first British mass mono-production – allowed the tried and tested A35 and Minor 1000 mechanical parts to shine. It was never a fast car, but it was affordable, open, and handled extremely well.

The entire front section hinged away, offering unrivalled access to the engine, and a long list of factory extras encouraged customization. Uprated carburettors, clutch, cams, valves, differential options, close ratio gears, firmer suspension and wire wheels were available, along with superchargers. It became a successful international competition car, while on Britain's roads thousands of proud owners drove with big smiles on their faces. In its brief production life virtually nothing was altered, making all the more dramatic the 1961 body change into a clone of the more conventional MG Midget.

### SPECIFICATIONS

| | |
|---|---|
| **ENGINE:** 948cc | **SUSPENSION:** Ind coil, wishbone/quarter-elliptic leaf, radius arms |
| **BHP:** 43bhp | |
| **FUEL:** 34mpg | |
| **GEARBOX:** 4 speed | **BODIES:** 2 door sports |
| **BRAKES:** Drum | **YEARS:** 1958-1961 |
| **SPEED:** 86mph | **PRODUCTION:** 48,999 |

Some cars receive rose-tinted write-ups by people who have forgotten the real-life nightmares of ownership. I owned a blue 'Frogeye' and it gave nothing but pleasure. This little car ranks among the most practical and genuine classics in the whole book.

## RELATIONS

The same inspirational parents as the Austin-Healey 100. The basic engine, gearbox, front suspension and axle were from the Austin A35, while the braking was from the Morris Minor, as was the steering. The rear suspension copied Jaguar thinking.

## BEST BUY

Americans and Japanese have bought up many of the best, but plenty are still around. Mechanical parts are rarely a drama, though gearboxes can be vulnerable. Rust is serious if in the rear bulkhead. A good bonnet is an asset as many have been replaced by fibreglass. Upgrade to 1275cc and conversions to disc brakes are common and not detrimental to values.

| | |
|---|---|
| Cost | £7,100 |
| % swing | 19 |
| Spares | ★★★★★ |
| V.F.M. | ★★★ |
| S.R. | ★★★★★ |

# MANUFACTURER
# BMW

It was BMW's development of their 1960s coupés which formed the foundations of their 1980s status. Fine engineering and a huge investment in competition ought to have been their magnetism but in the 1980s 'me' decade the password was style. It was the functional elegance of BMW coupés which was to cast its glow across even the most uninspiring 1980s BMW saloons. The pedigree began with the 1966 2000CS Coupé styled within BMW by Wilheilm Hofmeister. The car was based upon the standard 2000 saloon but these Karmann-built coupés were actually heavier than the saloon with consequently rather more style than performance. However the next generation of saloons presented two brilliant new 2,494cc and 2,788cc engines; and in September 1968 the first six-cylinder coupé appeared. They selected the 2788cc engine and front suspension from the big saloon and utilized the basic 2000 Coupé body but with a more aggressive front end treatment. This was the 2800CS which unlike the 2000CS both looked great and touched nearly 130mph. The quality interior with its panoramic visibility and elegant pillarless side windows simply added to the allure of what was really only an interim model: in 1971, BMW announced the larger 3.0 Coupé. The concept of rapid, refined, transport was now synonymous with BMW and the new 3.0 Coupé was able to offer over 130mph top speed while returning an average consumption of around 20mpg. Not content, later that year they added fuel injection creating a 200bhp, 140mph Executive Express. A complex game of option shuffling provided extra customer choice.

Pursuing further competition success they created a homologation model to qualify their race cars. These 1000 lightweights, (CSL) used perspex and aluminium along with highly tuned engines. The few that were imported to the UK were reportedly refitted with some luxuries making rapid and strange hybrids..

## RELATIONS

The 2000CS was based on 1960s four-cylinder saloons while the coupés from the 280 onward used the later saloon mechanics and powerplants. The factory designed 2000CL body extended through whole range with frontal amendments.

## BEST BUY

Despite all the build quality rhetoric these BMWs are prone to rust. Karmann failed to fully protect the body shells and concealed mud traps didn't help. Check sills carefully, the upper mountings of front suspension and test bulkhead through glove locker. 2.8 CS/3.0CS look alike, but old suspension inferior.

*The 3.0CSL (for lightweight) was a particularly fine example of the breed, but will cost you considerably more than the CS.*

## SPECIFICATIONS

**ENGINE:** 2788cc – 2985cc – 3003cc – 3153cc
**BHP:** 170; 200; 206
**FUEL:** 16 – 20mpg
**GEARBOX:** 4; 3 speed auto
**BRAKES:** Disc/drum – All disc

**SUSPENSION:** Ind Macpherson strut/coil – semi trailing/coil
**SPEED:** 128mph – 139mph
**BODIES:** 2 door 4 seat coupé
**YEARS:** 1966 – 75
**PRODUCTION:** 39,427

| Cost (3.0CS/CSi) | £6,500 |
| --- | --- |
| % swing | -11 |
| Spares | ★★★★ |
| V.F.M. | ★★ |
| S.R. | ★★★★ |

# LANCIA FULVIA COUPE

*DISCREET SPORTING PLEASURES*

## MANUFACTURER
# LANCIA

Lancia entered the 1960s as one of the Italian aristocrats. Unlike most companies they designed their Flavia range in–house complete with authentic boxer engine – Italy's first front wheel drive production car. Their next target was a replacement for their ageing Aprilia to be based around a new V4 power unit. This was the Fulvia and would become the last real company triumph before it was sold to the giant Fiat. The FWD Fulvia family stemmed from the 1963 Berlina saloon with its 1097cc version of the V4 and rather square body styling. Six years later, the second series saloon enjoyed engine development and some refinements but the gem was the coupé derivative unveiled in 1965 and which would become Lancia's flagship competition car. The coupé was based on a shorter wheelbase than the saloon, used a great many of the new Flavia parts and, much to the enthusiast's delight, that brand new Lancia V4 engine. Alongside the standard 80bhp model there was a tuned 1.2HF (High Fidelity) version sporting a matt black bonnet and no bumpers. In 1966 a similar pairing had the 1.3S Coupé at 1298cc with 93bhp while the faster 1.3 HF Rallye version pushed both bhp and top speed over the 100 mark. Considered by many to be the most desirable was the bored out 1969 1.6HFS which in rare instances were sold with a 132bhp output. It was in this year that Fiat took over and a Series Two

was developed for 1971. Detail refinements included raised outer headlights and kinder suspension. A UK de luxe trimmed model known as the 1600HF Lusso. A 1300 shell with 1600cc engine – the Fulvia Sports, also appeared in 1971 and became the fastest non-competition version. A final 1974-76 Series 3 model offered only minor alterations. Free revving, agile with excellent gearbox and handling plus good accommodation – almost a Cooper S in Italian garb.

## RELATIONS

Lancia's own body with transmission, steering, suspension and brakes from Flavia; V4 engine was brand new. The last true Lancia made. 2,600 special Zagato Sports version were also made between 1970–72.

## BEST BUY

Beautifully engineered cars and so most have been loved. Buy through Owners Club sources, to avoid rust – particularly costly around subframes. Many examples will have lightweight body panels which are prone to denting. Hand brakes a traditional grief.

*A very different front end treatment for the Zagato Sports special.*

| Cost (HF SII) | £11,250 |
|---|---|
| % swing | 38 |
| Spares | ★★ |
| V.F.M. | ★★★★ |
| S.R. | ★★★★ |

### SPECIFICATIONS

| | |
|---|---|
| **ENGINE:** 1216cc; 1231cc; 1584cc; 1298cc | **SUSPENSION:** Wishbone/ transverse leaf spring & dead axle/half elliptic |
| **BHP:** 80p – 115 | |
| **FUEL:** 34mpg – 22mpg | **BODIES:** 2 door, 4 seat coupé |
| **GEARBOX:** 4 & 5 speed | **YEARS:** 1965 – 76 |
| **BRAKES:** Disc | **PRODUCTION:** 140,205 |
| **SPEED:** 90 – 119mph | |

## MANUFACTURER
# FORD

Promoted as 'The Three Graces', wisely, Ford's MkIIs were a direct development from the successful Mk I. The monocoque bodies were 3" wider, 6.5" longer, although the central passenger section remained identical to the Mk I. Exterior trim helped differentiation, from the humble Consul to gold-plated trim on the Zodiac. The traditional bench seating fore and aft permitted six occupants, there was a column gear change and the engines were enhanced. An optional overdrive was available and carefully selected higher final drives helped fuel economy – ultimate cruising status came with any one of the three convertibles. The luxury Zodiac version was released some months later than the Consul and Zephyr soft tops, offering a number of extra fittings and the prestige of a power-operated roof. Naturally, there were continual detail changes over the years including a 1957 de luxe Consul with duotone paintwork and many dashboard refinements.

One really conspicuous alteration was the 1959 change to the car's profile, reducing the slightly bulbous roof pressing by 1.5". A disc brake option had become so popular it became a standard fitting from May 1961. Somehow those bench seats and the column change *inter alia*, chimed with the huge transatlantic invasion of UK culture. During May 1961 the Consul became officially known as a Consul Classic 315 which was part of plans to use the name Consul as a prefix to Ford family cars – The Ford Consul Classic and Capri is as far as it went.

## RELATIONS

Mk I! Improved engine, 'box, suspension, steering.

## BEST BUY

All three were strong working cars and the less stressed 6-cylinder versions in particular are solid.

*Rust inevitably is a problem, particularly around the floor, sills and front suspension mounts, and trim is becoming harder to replace.*

### SPECIFICATIONS

**ENGINE:** 1703cc; 2553cc
**BHP:** 59; 85
**FUEL:** 25mpg; 22mpg
**GEARBOX:** 3 & 4 speed
**BRAKES:** Drum (front discs post 61)
**SUSPENSION:** Ind Macpherson strut –
semi-elliptic
**SPEED:** 80mph; 90mph
**BODIES:** 2 door, 4 door saloon, convertible, estate
**YEARS:** 1956–62
**PRODUCTION:** 682,400

(1st figures – 4 cylinder Consul & 2nd – 6 cylinder Zephyr/Zodiac)

| Cost | £7,500 |
|---|---|
| (Consul MkII Conv.) | |
| % swing | 10 |
| | |
| Spares | ★★★ |
| V.F.M. | ★★★ |
| S.R. | ★★★ |

# MINI COOPER S
## TURNS DRIVERS INTO ENTHUSIASTS

## MANUFACTURER
# BMC

From its spectacular entrance in 1959 the Mini's place in motoring history was secure, and subsequent major competition triumphs defined the mythology; but its obsessive hold over enthusiasts appears illogical, given that almost every modern hatchback can comfortably outperform the very best. Certainly, the Mini represented optimum fun for an entire generation's youth and nostalgia is the wild card with any classic. However, there were genuinely special qualities about the sporting Minis which stood them apart. Grand Prix's wizard John Cooper identified the potential when loaned a pre-production Mini to attend the Italian GP. Race driver Roy Salvadori in that early Mini beat team manager Reg Parnell in his Aston Martin DB4GT down to Italy: and even at the circuit, the former chief Ferrari engineer disappeared in it for a run. The result was the 1961 997cc Mini Cooper and its 1964–69 998cc replacement, utilizing the ex-Riley and Wolseley Mini unit.

The real power and glory was within the confusing world of the Mini Cooper S range. I've been lucky enough to own two glorious examples and drive almost all the possible variants – indeed at one time

had the Rauno Aaltonen/Henry Liddon Works car, my all black 60s show stopper, and a custom-built Wood & Pickett de luxe version. The major difference between the fun Coopers and the more serious Cooper S's was the engine. All John Cooper's success with both Grand Prix racing (double World Championships) and his inspired work on the same BMC A engine in Formula Junior meant that the Cooper S engine was specifically created to perform. Everything was stronger, disc brakes bigger, wheels wider on the differing S models. The initial 1963 1071cc S was deliberately aimed at motor sport and offered a 70bhp high revving engine with bags of torque in the upper ranges. Just 4,017 were produced in its 13 month production life. However, in 1964 two new S's were launched. The 970 S was a

*The Cooper Car Company earned a small royalty on every car bearing their name; in 1971, when the original 'consultancy agreement' lapsed, about £2.*

| | |
|---|---|
| Cost (1275 S) | £7,500 |
| % swing | 10 |

| | |
|---|---|
| Spares | ★★★★★ |
| V.F.M. | ★★★ |
| S.R. | ★★★★★ |

## RELATIONS

Mini 1959 onward
Mini Cooper 1961–64 : 997cc
Mini Cooper 1964–69 : 998cc
Mini Cooper S 1963–64 : 1071cc
Mini Cooper S 1964–65 : 970cc
Mini Cooper S 1964–71 : 1275cc

## BEST BUY

It's a Mini so check rust in front and rear subframe mounting points, footwells, sills and around A posts. The enormous torque was always destroying the engine's top steady bar and thus damaging exhausts. Drive couplings too worked very hard: but the main issue is confirming exactly what you are buying: many Mini Coopers have been `upgraded' and there are few visual clues. The 1964 Hydrolastic suspension upset some of the older enthusiasts. The 1968 Mk II range brought the larger disc braking and a valuable all-synchromesh gearbox, which points to a post '68 1275cc S as the best option, but beware — if you buy an S, your driving outlook will never be the same again.

homologation exercise producing a mere 967 over just 10 months in order to claim a production class for 1 litre competition, with a screaming 6,500 rev range and an appetite for sprints and hill climbs. The other new S was the famed 1275cc version which remained in production until June 1971 – the last few were unbadged as British Leyland boss Donald Stokes thought that John Cooper's name was putting customers off! Very minor visual changes took place through the years other than the cosmetic 1967 Mini range upgrade to Mk II; but in late 1964, there was the controversial addition to all Minis of Hydrolastic suspension which altered ride characteristics.

Basic interiors, super discretion (virtually identical to the standard Mini) and sporting action within a runabout shell were the S characteristics but its divine status stemmed from the handling and through-the–gears performance. It was so responsive, so forgiving, it allowed us all to develop our own driving skills in a way no other affordable car could.

### SPECIFICATIONS

**ENGINE:** 970cc; 1071cc; 1275cc
**BHP:** 65; 70; 76
**FUEL:** N/A; 27mpg; 30mpg
**GEARBOX:** 4 speed – all syncromesh post 1968
**BRAKES:** Disc – Drum
**SPEED:** 92mph; 95mph; 97mph
**SUSPENSION:** Ind cones/wishbone & Ind trailing arm/cone Hydrolastic inter-connection after 1964
**BODIES:** 2 door saloon
**YEARS:** 1963 – 71
**PRODUCTION:** 45,442

## CITROEN DS
### GAMBLING ON HIGH STYLE

### MANUFACTURER
# CITROEN

This car has glamour and danger in equal measures. A jet black fully restored DS23 Pallas Décapotable (Drophead) is probably the most chic eligible classic car in the world – a triumph aesthetically and technically. Unfortunately, major repairs or restoration could cost you the price of another classic car. Inevitably, rusting combined with awesome levels of technical innovation, mean you need to buy with great care and guidance in order to enjoy the civilised pleasures of DS ownership. I've run three including a DS23 Pallas and the car's ride and comfort surpassed even that of the modern Bentley. However

unconventional, Citroëns – like equivalent humans – require an open mind and drivers quickly become enthusiastic or completely disenchanted.

The origins of this advanced car go back to André Citroën himself who lost money – and control of his beloved company – in the 1930s while struggling to develop and launch the Traction Avant with its revolutionary front wheel drive. After decades of the TA, the Bertone-designed D was presented to a stunned world at the 1955 Paris Motor Show. It was aerodynamically inspired, had an unstressed body of steel, fibreglass and aluminium, with disc braking and

*The top-of-the-range DS19 Pallas arrived in 1964, four years after the first production convertible. The subsequent DS23 Pallas was even more luxurious.*

| Cost | £7,750 |
|------|--------|
| (20/21/23 Pallas) | |
| % swing | 18 |
| Spares | ★★ |
| V.F.M. | ★★★ |
| S.R. | ★★★★★ |

*Autosport's review of the 1955 Paris Salon provides some indication of the impact Flaminio Bertoni's and André Lefebvre's design made, together with the technical brilliance the car evinced. 'The Paris Salon is the most important motor show in the world … Even more brilliant than usual, the tone of this year's show is set by the incredible new Citroën DS19. Futuristic but entirely functional, this startling machine at once renders half the cars of the world out of date.'*

an engine evolved from the TA. A one-spoke steering column, eye-level rear indicators, safety placement of the petrol tank and a super sensitive valve-controlled break button instead of a pedal, all contributed to its technical edge. Its famous hydropneumatic suspension ironed out every bump by combining pressurized gas and liquid while, as a by–product, creating variable ride height. The DS19 was joined by a basic ID19 in 1957 and then ID/DS minor developments took place until finally reaching the DS-only 23 model with 2347cc fuel injection. As you would expect from a French de luxe version, the Pallas offered great comfort, with limousine derivatives transporting successive French presidents during the 1960s.

## RELATIONS

Italian body design with Traction Avant-inspired engine and hydropneumatic suspension principles. Many D ideas appeared within subsequent Citroën based models such as the Citroën/Maserati SM, the Citroën CX and the GS.

## BEST BUY

Despite alloy, fibreglass and bolt–on body panels, rust is still an enemy, with the platform chassis particularly vulnerable at the rear and around sills. Engines last a long time and the suspension system is either fine or dreadful. The modest IDs are basic, but have less to go wrong. The self-levelling suspension is useful on the rare Safari estate car, while the dropheads are gold dust. Many good Ds were made at Citroën's Slough factory. The main body change was encasing the headlights from 1967 and incorporating swivel spotlights linked to the steering.

### SPECIFICATIONS

**ENGINE:** 1911cc; 1985cc; 2175cc; 2.347cc
**BHP:** 75 – 141
**FUEL:** 34 –18mpg
**GEARBOX:** 4 & 5 speed; semi automatic
**BRAKES:** Disc/drum

**SUSPENSION:** All ind Hydropneumatic springs
**SPEED:** 92mph – 120mph
**BODIES:** 4 door saloon; 2 door Cabriolet; 8 seater estate
**YEARS:** 1956 – 75
**PRODUCTION:** 1,456,115 (disp)

### A CHRONOLOGY

**1955** The Goddess is born: replete with constant height hydropneumatic independent suspension, variable ground clearance and removable panels on integrated bodywork. Length 4.81m. Weight 1215kg.

**1956** Paris Motor Show. ID19 on sale from May 1957.

**1958** DS Prestige and ID19 Estate.

**1959** Monte Carlo Rally. Victory for Coltelloni-Alexandre-Desrosiers team. New front wing ventilation grilles.

**1960** DS convertible.

**1961** 83bhp SAE engine.

**1964** DS19 Pallas.

**1965** SD19A and DS21. New radiator.

**1966** Pauli Toivonen victory at Monte Carlo.

**1968** DS20, ID20.

**1969** Fuel injection for DS21, D Super and D Special. Robert Neyret victory in Morocco Rally.

**1970** 5 speeds for DS21. Citroën-Maserati SM 2 + 2 sports saloon launched at Geneva, using Deesse technology and experience.

**1975** The last DS in the spring, the Maserati link broken in the autumn, and the SM abandoned as well.

# LEA FRANCIS LYNX

## It Died of Shame

## MANUFACTURER
# LEA FRANCIS

Originally a Coventry-based cycle company, Lea Francis produced their first motor car in 1903 and following the First World War became renowned for both racing and road cars of quality. They stopped production in 1935 and resumed in 1937 with the totally new 12 and 14 models. After the Second World War both motor cars developed into sporting models and the 18 was added to the range until the new double purchase tax forced them to cease production in 1954. In March 1960 the company was reactivated under the new chairman Kenneth Benfield to provide cars for connoisseurs. Within months a tubular chassis was created by the former Jaguar designer Jack Gannon, while Bristol Designs developed the bodywork, and Abbey Panels pieced it all together. It employed independent front suspension, along with a Ford Zephyr engine married to the Triumph TR3 gearbox, and it was equipped with overdrive, fresh air heating, screen washers and the promise of a full Perspex hard top. Incredibly, the car was designed and constructed from scratch in time for that year's motor show. It offered 2 + 2 seating with a tidy fold-away hood and degrees of interior refinement, as well as the promise of 80mph cruising and a 100mph top speed from the 2.5 litre, triple SU-fed Ford engine.

The problem with this reasonably equipped car from one of the industry's most respected pioneers was that it looked terrible. It's not just that it didn't appeal to me – and I actually saw it on the stand – nobody else liked it either. Nobody ordered one. It was a complete disaster.

## SPECIFICATIONS

**ENGINE:** 2553cc
**BHP:** 107bhp
**FUEL:** 21mpg
**GEARBOX:** 4 speed
**BRAKES:** Disc
**SPEED:** 100mph

**SUSPENSION:** Ind double wishbone, torsion bar / live axle, semi-elliptic
**BODIES:** 2 door roadsters
**YEARS:** 1980
**PRODUCTION:** 3

The frontal area was bleak and gutless centred around a circular air intake, while the tail fins looked as ill fitting as one of those old cornflake box cut-out models. Even the side profile, perhaps its best aspect, was dominated by bulbous side panels resembling pontoons. Conceived by the new chairman, who was apparently fond of Italian Ghia ideas, it not only lacked any styling grace it was, believe it or not, presented in mauve with all the chrome parts finished in gold plating. Plans for a four-door version were terminated – and so in time was the company.

## RELATIONS

Original body and chassis, with 2.5 Ford Mk II Zephyr engine married to a TR3 transmission.

## BEST BUY

The Lynx has a certain rarity value, as only three were ever produced! There was also some experimentation with a four-door V8 Tourer which would have been called the Francesa, had the company survived.

# MANUFACTURER
# JAGUAR

One Christmas day during this car's production life it snowed and I had to make an early morning drive to family in Oxford. Snowy landscapes, empty roads and the factory test Daimler V8 made that journey one of the more memorable ones in my life. Naturally it wasn't a classic then – just the first Daimler following Jaguar's takeover. Traditionalists discarded it as being just a Jaguar-bodied Daimler, oblivious of the fact that prior to the takeover a struggling Daimler had been seriously experimenting with this engine in a Vauxhall Cresta PA – now that really might have upset them. The Edward Turner-designed V8 was the key to everything. It had attracted fans in the flamboyant SP250 sports car, but both Daimler and Jaguar knew its value, and once the takeover was complete its installation in the current Jaguar sporting saloon was an obvious move. Fortuitously, this marriage created one of the most perfectly balanced cars, uniting glorious V8 power, a good Borg-Warner automatic gearbox, the classic Jaguar Mk II body and excellent levels of interior luxury.

Although outwardly only the traditional fluted grille distinguished the two models, the V8 provided an entirely different feel to the car. Everything from the racing Mk II Jaguars to Inspector Morse have conspired to keep this excellent Daimler something of a secret in the shadows of the Mk II – thus making good ones really excellent value.

There were changes to the automatic gearbox and axle ratios in the spring of 1964, and three years later the Jaguar manual box and overdrive became options. The only visible changes came in 1967 when it was re-named the V8-250, bumpers were slimmed down and interior trim slightly altered. By this point Jaguar had become part of British Motor Holdings and in July 1969, production ceased.

## RELATIONS

Glorious engine from the 1959 Daimler SP250 sports car, everything else from the famed Jaguar Mk II except the Daimler grille and badge work.

## BEST BUY

Buy a good one and you'll never want to sell it again, but take care in choosing – a mistake could make for costly restoration. The engine and gearbox are traditionally pretty trouble-free although corroded heads can give grief. The body naturally suffers from all the rust areas customary on the Jaguar cars. Check wings, sills, boot lid, the floor and the bottom of doors where drain holes can become blocked. The automatic suits the car and the post-1964 box had the extra D2 option, restricting it to 2nd and 3rd.

## SPECIFICATIONS

**ENGINE:** 2548cc
**BHP:** 140
**FUEL:** 20mpg
**GEARBOX:** 3 speed automatic; rare 4 speed manuals
**BRAKES:** Disc

**SUSPENSION:** Ind Coil/wishbone – semi-elliptic
**SPEED:** 110mph
**BODIES:** 4 door saloon
**YEARS:** 1963–69
**PRODUCTION:** 17,620

| | |
|---|---|
| Cost | £11,300 |
| (V8 Saloon) | |
| % swing | 30 |
| Spares | ★★★ |
| V.F.M. | ★★★★ |
| S.R. | ★★★ |

# VW BEETLE
## THE STREET CHAMPION

## MANUFACTURER
# VW

This, the world's bestselling car, emerged out of two still-born projects from Ferdinand Porsche's design company. These ideas eventually found an outlet within pre-war Germany for a state-funded 'People's Car'. After hostilities ended in 1945, the factory – within British-occupied territory – was encouraged back into production, and the first export model appeared in 1949 complete with 25bhp 1131cc air- cooled flat four engines. Mounted in the tail along with the gearbox, it used swing axles and torsion bar suspension all round. The original intentions were for the car to transport two adults and three children at up to 100kph (62mph) consuming not more than 33 mpg and priced at no more than RM 1000 (around £90). During the decades of production the car's appearance has changed very little, but around 78,000 individual changes have actually been made. Some, such as the larger rear window in 1957, were obvious, while four years later (less visibly) the engine was improved to 34bhp, lifting the top speed to around 70mph. In 1965 the De Luxe 1300 appeared with 1285cc, moving the bhp up to 40bhp; steering joints were also improved. By 1966 it had a 1493cc engine, taking the car to 80mph+ with improved suspension, disc brakes and a wider track; a year later a new 1200cc Basic was created without all the trimmings, but with improved suspension. The early 1970s witnessed a flood of changes with the arrival of the 1600cc 1302s and 1303s with disc brakes, and a move to Macpherson strut suspension. on the S. Although German production ceased in 1978 , it continued in Mexico, reopened in Brazil and in America a lookalike is rumoured for 1998 production. It's an extraordinary story of a car full of idiosyncrasies and flaws, yet essentially providing reliable transport – a true classic.

## RELATIONS

The Beetle is one of a kind, owing little if anything to anyone outside the Porsche studio's initial inspirations, although you can see a hint of the Beetle in the curvy silhouette of VW's later Karmann Ghia Ironically, those first still-born concepts involved motor cycle companies searching for new markets in the pre-war depression – hence the air-cooled engines.

*It is interesting to note that the cabriolet 1300s have actually fallen in value (below). The less fashionable older 1100s, in contrast, have shot up by 34% over the same four-year period.*

| Cost | £8,250 |
|---|---|
| (Cabrio 1301/2 L/S) | |
| % swing | -26 |
| Spares | ★★★★★ |
| V.F.M. | ★ |
| S.R. | ★★★★★ |

You can still buy a new Cabriolet today – the Bieber Cabriolet – providing an open four seater at a far lower price than, say, the Golf convertible, with a whole lot more character and none of the drawbacks of classic car ownership.

Why the less than professional snap shot below? Unashamed editorial corruption. This 1972 Beetle belonged to the editor's brother, and its imminent starring role here maybe helped the sale! More relevantly, one option for UK buyers is to import rust-free Beetles from California like this one. £4,000 to the door, a pricey respray, five year's trouble-free motoring, a tearful farewell for £3,800, private sale.

## BEST BUY

The Beetle has a sub-culture all of its own. Overall, the mechanics are generally safe, though check the crank case pulley to judge engine wear. Rust gets into the floor areas, sills and wings particularly on the desirable Cabriolets. Buying a Beetle is a great adventure, but first try one as the driving position is an acquired taste and performance limited.

### SPECIFICATIONS

**ENGINE:** 1131/1192/1285/ 1493/1584cc (post 1970 Macpherson strut/semi trailing)

**BHP:** 36 – 50

**BODIES:** 2 door, 4 door saloon

**FUEL:** 25mpg; 22mpg

**YEARS:** 1949–78 (1st export model to end of German prod line)

**GEARBOX:** 4 speed

**BRAKES:** Drum (front discs Post `70 )

**PRODUCTION:** 21,000,000+

**SPEED:** 65 – 80mph

**SUSPENSION:** All Ind torsion

# ALFA DUETTO SPIDER

*BEWARE OF LOVE AT FIRST SIGHT*

## MANUFACTURER
# ALFA ROMEO

*The unofficial name of the Duetto was 'Osso di Seppia' – cuttlefish bone – a nickname that stuck, at least in those lucky countries where a cuttlefish bone, and its shape, meant something.*

| Cost | £10,750 |
|------|---------|
| (1750 Spider Veloce) | |
| % swing | 36 |

| | |
|------|------|
| Spares | ★★★★ |
| V.F.M. | ★★★★ |
| S.R. | ★★★★★ |

This is an extraordinary car. Like the Mini and Beetle its long production run (27 years), has automatically earned it a powerful classic status. It was never the fastest car around and many critics were unkind about even its appearance and yet it captures the hearts of enthusiasts and romantics in equal parts.

Based upon the Giulia Sprint GT platform, this Italian two seater was launched at the 1966 Geneva Motor Show under the name Duetto – the result of a 140,501-entry competition to name the new Alfa. The body styling was the last complete design project undertaken by Battista Pininfarina and had roots in both the early fifties sports racing Alfa, the 6C 3000M, and the 1962 Giulette-based Super Flow 1 concept car. The heart of the Duetto was Alfa's all alloy 1570cc twin cam engine offering 109bhp and a memorable exhaust note. This, coupled with all round disc brakes and a beautiful five speed gearbox, made it an advanced model. While the Healey 3000 was revelling in its reputation as a wild sports car, the Duetto was creating a new sophistication with light gear change and steering, a relatively comfortable ride and a particularly successful folding soft top. In 1968 the Duetto name was dropped, and the engine slightly bored out to create the 1750 Spider – actually enlarged to 1779cc and adding another 9bhp. A number of additional changes were made to the suspension, electrics and braking, but nothing conspicuous occurred to the Pininfarina bodywork until the radical face lift in 1970 when the charismatic long tail was simply chopped off and replaced by an abrupt vertical rear reducing the boot by a full six inches.

The interior too was updated and the general tone of the car was more luxurious. The same year saw the launch of a 1300cc Spider Junior, with a more economical version of the same body, though only a few came to Britain. A year later the 2000 Spider was launched, taking the trusted engine to 1962cc. General refinements continued until it finally ceased production in 1993.

## RELATIONS

An original Pininfarina body style. The mechanics belong to the Giulia family of Alfas – the engine taken from the Sprint GT model.

## BEST BUY

The drive train is excellent, but rust eats into the complex body structure making it a dangerous car to buy in a hurry. The 1600s are the hard-core fan's choice, late models give more comforts. The initial 1750 Spider combined the most responsive engine with the last of those long boat–tails.

### SPECIFICATIONS

| | |
|------|------|
| **ENGINE:** 1290cc, 1570cc 1779cc 1962cc | **SUSPENSION:** Ind coil/wishbone & coil live axle |
| **BHP:** 89 – 132 | **SPEED:** 106mph –118mph |
| **FUEL:** 24mpg | **BODIES:** 2 door sports |
| **GEARBOX:** 5 speed | **YEARS:** 1966 – 93 |
| **BRAKES:** Disc | **PRODUCTION:** 82,500 |

# MANUFACTURER
# STANDARD

Triumph T.R.3 Sports

Standard-Triumph attempted to buy the Morgan Car Company in the early 1950s and having failed, rushed to assemble a competitive model. A pre-war Flying Nine chassis, Triumph Mayflower suspension, axle and steering, together with the Standard Vanguard 2 litre engine and gearbox, were all modified and squeezed into a new body for the 1952 Motor Show. The same show premiered the new Healey 100; a redesigned TR2 was finally unveiled at the 1953 Geneva Show. Reactions were good but work continued. The 1955 launch of the TR3 was really the model's coming of age. It gained a wider egg box styled grille, sliding side screens, a useful triple overdrive option and token extra interior space along with larger carburation and a step up in bhp. Within months there was also improvement to the back axle and front disc brakes added. Critical exports built up and the TR3 achieved virtually twice the TR2 sales in roughly the same life span. In 1958 further changes

unofficially created a TR3A – though it was not the factory term. These included a full width grille integrating the side lights, recessed headlights, lockable door handles and new seating. They also began to offer the enlarged 2138cc engine used in the successful works competition cars. In 1959 they re-tooled but waning US interest was pushing the company towards certain disaster – until Leyland bought in 1961. A brief US- only TR3B was released.

## RELATIONS

A cocktail of Flying Nine, Mayflower and Vanguard models and initial TRI prototype and TR2. Body style ends with TR3A but mechanics extend to TR4.

## BEST BUY

Pre 1956 Mayflower back axles can be troublesome as can the early front drum brakes and many will have been changed to match Triumph's upgrades. Best choice would be a 1958–61 TR3A enjoying 100bhp, disc brakes and those low cut door panels.

*During the industry rush to create affordable sports cars in the early 1950s, TR3 built much of its solid reputation through competition success. A staggering 90% of sales were exports. The engine and particularly the gearbox of most examples should be bomb proof, but beware poorly serviced front suspension.*

### SPECIFICATIONS

**ENGINE:** 1991cc
**BHP:** 95, 100
**FUEL:** 30mpg
**GEARBOX:** 4 speed
**BRAKES:** Drum; Disc/drum (after 1956)
**SUSPENSION:** Ind wishbone/ coil & live axle semi-elliptic
**SPEED:** 103mph
**BODIES:** 2 door sports
**YEARS:** 1955 – 61
**PRODUCTION:** 71,613

| Cost | £11,300 |
|------|---------|
| % swing | -6 |
| Spares | ★★★★ |
| V.F.M. | ★★ |
| S.R. | ★★★ |

# TRIUMPH TR5 PI

*IMPERFECT STAR*

## MANUFACTURER
# BRITISH LEYLAND

The methodical improvement of the TR range proved commercially rewarding, despite more exotic competition from cars such as the Austin-Healey 100. The simple, solid engineering of the early TRs, and the reliability of such well tested parts generated many fans, but by the 1960s the body styling was losing appeal. September 1961 saw the unveiling of the TR4 which disappointed some by continuing most of the old engineering, but did present a startling new Italian body from Michelotti. It may have used the trusted Vanguard engine, but it also boasted innovative features such as dashboard air flow ventilation years ahead of Ford, and a two part Targa hard top, preempting Porsche by some years. The body itself was much wider and created an improved boot area. Winding windows, adjustable steering column and in 1965, independent rear suspension, all gradually turned the TR into a comfortable touring car. Clearly next, the ageing Vanguard engine had to be replaced, particularly with strong new competition from cars such as the MGB. This pushed Triumph towards the next incarnation – the TR5.

At the heart of this model change was the six cylinder powerplant from the Triumph saloon which was shoe horned into virtually the same body as the TR4. What distinguished this installation was the first use of fuel injection in a British mass production car. It provided Triumph with excellent press reviews and the enthusiast with a smooth and powerful car capable of over 125mph. Coupled with the extra wide and spacious cockpit, those winding windows and the Targa roof options, this was a package which pushed

Triumph ahead of their rivals. Sadly, the Lucas fuel injection proved troublesome, and nervous garages did little to calm the mood of unease. The TR5 was the nearest Triumph got to an outright winner; production lastied just one year, so the car remains rare.

## RELATIONS

Italian Michelotti body styling, with most of the model carried forward from previous TRs. The engine came from the Triumph 2000 saloon range.

## BEST BUY

It's the rarest and the fastest TR, yet buy with some care. The separate chassis does multiply rust dangers and a careful inspection will save you many later shocks. The engine is not as robust as the old Vanguard unit and that fuel injection seriously bruised the car's reputation. Specialist TR firms have finally ironed out the problems which means you can now probably get more carefree enjoyment out of this very British sports car than the original owners.

| Cost | £11,750 |
|------|---------|
| % swing | 3 |
| Spares | ★★★★ |
| V.F.M. | ★★★ |
| S.R. | ★★★ |

### SPECIFICATIONS

| | |
|---|---|
| **ENGINE:** 2498cc | **SUSPENSION:** Ind |
| **BHP:** 150 | wishbone/coil & Ind semi |
| **FUEL:** 22mpg | trailing arm |
| **GEARBOX:** 4 speed | **BODIES:** 2 door sports |
| **BRAKES:** Disc/drum | **YEARS:** 1967–68 |
| **SPEED:** 125mph | **PRODUCTION:** 2947 |

## MANUFACTURER
# BMC

Stuck with the dated pre–war T series design and with BMC bosses giving priority to the new Donald Healey deal, MG were rapidly losing ground to their competitors. With racing privateer George Phillips, they explored a streamlined racing-bodied TD at Le Mans in 1951, and spurred on, quietly constructed further prototypes. BMC were concentrating on the Healey 100, and refused to consider developing the new car until 1954. To underline the car's racing roots, the launch was June 1955, and coincided with a Le Mans team of three MGAs. The fatalities that year, tragically, undermined further publicity, but the launch was, nevertheless, a huge success.

With solid chassis, steel bodies with aluminium bonnet, boot and doors, this MG was powered by a 68bhp, 1489cc Series B engine with sensitive rack and pinion steering and good drum brakes. Initially launched as a roadster with detachable hard top, Fixed Head Coupé versions followed in 1956. A powerful 108bhp Twin Cam version appeared in 1958 with disc brakes, bored out to 1588cc, but it proved unreliable and was dropped after just 2111 cars had been manufactured, and only 360 were sold in the UK. The following May, a pushrod version of the ill-fated Twin Cam became the hugely successful MGA 1600 MkI; the final incarnation was the 1961–62 1622cc Mk II version. A true MG, born out of sporting traditions, and reflecting the 1950s pre-occupation with streamlining, it has become a true classic. 101,081 MGAs were made – more than any other previous MG – and 80 per cent of them were sold in the USA!

## RELATIONS

Completely unlike any previous MG, body styling came from George Phillips' TD Special and the subsequent MG prototypes. The chassis was initially from the T series, and then evolved through racing experience. Competition successes with the MG Magnette ZA prompted the use of its engine, gearbox, back axle, and brakes. Steering and suspension was from the TF.

## BEST BUY

These cars are so good, that virtually any sound example will be a delight to own and drive. Unless you are mechanically experienced, steer clear of the Twin Cam versions. Inevitably, later cars had improved performance, but the body styling remained intact, apart from the recessed grille of the Mk IIs. A factory surplus of dropped Twin Cams produced a rare and very desirable de luxe version (1960–62) which was effectively a TC without the troubled powerplant: Only 395 were made.

*In comparison with the lack of movement of the 1958-60 fixed head coupé Roadster price as indicated below, the price for an early 1500 Roadster has increased by about 25% over the last four years, which takes it into the four-star value-for-money category.*

### SPECIFICATIONS

| | |
|---|---|
| **ENGINE** 1489cc; 1588cc; 1622cc; (TC 1588cc ohc) | **SUSPENSION** Ind–leaf sprung |
| **BHP** 68; 80; 93; (TC 108) | **SPEED** 95–113mph |
| **Fuel** 25–30mph (TC 22mph) | **GEARBOX** 4 speed manual |
| **BRAKES** Disc–drum; TC & De Luxe disc–disc | **BODIES** Open & coupé |
| | **YEARS** 1955–62 |
| | **PRODUCTION** 101,081 |

| | |
|---|---|
| Cost (fhc TC) | £13,200 |
| % swing | -10 |
| Spares | ★★★★★ |
| V.F.M. | ★★ |
| S.R. | ★★★ |

# LOTUS CORTINA MK I

BEWARE OF THE RACE PASSPORTS

## MANUFACTURER
# FORD

This car basks in former glories such as the 1964 British Saloon Car Championship, and with around a million roadgoing Mark I Cortina owners longing to emulate drivers like Jim Clark, Jack Sears, and Sir John Whitmore, its desirability was assured. The sporting Cortina GT was a workhorse offering disc brakes and Webers alongside four door practicality and even an automatic. The Lotus Cortina was a more precious item.

Ford wanted motor sport association and Colin Chapman needed a new engine for his forthcoming Elan. Using the basic Ford 1500 Kent engine, adding a twin cam cylinder head and uniting it with a close ratio gearbox created the 105bhp drive train that would grace both the Lotus Cortina and the Lotus Elan. Ford's interest in the Group 2 racing category meant quite a lot of race customization but homologation required 1000 models to be produced. So the initial Lotus Cortina bodies were transported to the Lotus factory for conversion. Aluminium housing for the diff, parts of the gearbox and clutch also saved valuable weight. The suspension was lowered, the steering ratio adjusted and a complete rebuild of the rear suspension replaced the leaf springs with coil and dampers, trailing arms and an A bracket. Externally, the classic white and green striped livery, the wider wheels, quarter bumpers and Lotus badging remained the same until production gave way to the Mk II in 1967. However, this was not the case under that bodywork. The 1000 qualifying cars were semi-racing examples, providing a track passport for the real racing Lotus Cortinas. Inevitably, many of these 1000

cars succumbed to weakness. The lightweight panels would crease if touched, and the rear suspension was fraught with troubles and wrecked differentials. Suspension reverted to leaf springing in 1964-5, panels were strengthened and a Ford gearbox replaced the tricky close ratio version. Thus, this hugely practical Cortina trailing competition glories made an interesting, if fickle classic.

## RELATIONS

Essentially a Ford Cortina with a Lotus Elan engine and gearbox.

## BEST BUY

Most value is placed on the early Lotus-built homologation cars, but these are potentially more troubled. The later cars are cheaper, still exciting and far more practical. Inevitably cars will have been driven hard and engine builds can be expensive. Rust attacks floors, sill, the engine area and suspension mounts, but fortunately the car is easy to work on.

| Cost | £12,400 |
|---|---|
| % swing | 20 |
| Spares | ★★★★ |
| V.F.M. | ★★★ |
| S.R. | ★★ |

### SPECIFICATIONS

| | |
|---|---|
| **ENGINE:** 1558cc | **SUSPENSION:** Coil/MacPherson |
| **BHP:** 105 | strut & semi-elliptic (see |
| **FUEL:** 21mpg | above) |
| **GEARBOX:** 4 speed | **BODIES:** 2 door saloon |
| **BRAKES:** Disc/drum | **YEARS:** 1963–66 |
| **SPEED:** 106mph | **PRODUCTION:** 4012 |

**MANUFACTURER**
# LOTUS

Colin Chapman was one of the country's most enterprising designers whose endless visions often ran ahead of business support. Outside the Lotus competition success, his dream was to create a sports car with wide appeal. His initial Lotus Elite was very desirable, but too expensive to produce. In 1958 he gained US orders for 1000 cars, but his body suppliers were contracted to supply just 250 per year and were already falling behind that quota. He adjusted to a far simpler concept, nearer to that of the Lotus 7, using a monocoque fibreglass body and the newly developed Lotus Ford twin cam engine. The Elan, launched at the 1962 Motor Show, had a simple backbone chassis, fully independent suspension, rack and pinion steering, disc brakes all round – everything beneath a beautifully simple open two seater body. It was replaced two years later by the Series II, which incorporated a number of customer-requested changes. In 1965 the first Fixed Head Coupé emerged as a Series III, complete with electric windows, while the Series II Sports continued, gaining a a Special Edition luxury option from January 1966. This SE package involved servo brakes, a close ratio gearbox and uplift to 115bhp. The inevitable open Series III arrived in June 1966, and both the Coupé and Sports synchronised again as Series IV in March 1968. Changes this time involved squared-off wheel arches, low profile tyres, a bonnet bulge to accommodate the Stromberg carburation, facia and rear light alterations. Some later examples reverted to Webers, and from January 1971 the final Elan – the Sprint – used Webers along with a big valve 126bhp

engine until a last change to Dellorto carbs: Sprints were duo-toned. These cars were perfectly balanced, lightweight sports cars, with great agility and a knack of making good drivers feel like great ones.

## RELATIONS

A Ford Cortina-based engine, original Lotus chassis and body, and with components from various sources such as the Triumph GT6, and suspension parts from the Ford Cortina.

## BEST BUY

It has a terrible reputation for fragility, but the body should be reasonable. Check the chassis for rust, particularly around the front suspension. Trim was always poor. Patchy engine reputation was never reflected when new, but is underlined by clumsy rebuilds or tuning. Set up properly, it is a sweet car, appreciated by, and ideally suited for the mechanically minded. The pretty fixed heads are cheaper and a good Series IV is a great classic.

### SPECIFICATIONS

| | |
|---|---|
| **ENGINE:** 1498cc; 1158cc | **SUSPENSION:** Ind wishbone/ coil –Wishbone/coil |
| **BHP:** 105 – 126 | |
| **FUEL:** 20mpg – 30mpg | **BODIES:** 2 door sports; fixed head coupé |
| **GEARBOX:** 4 speed | |
| **BRAKES:** Disc | **YEARS:** 1962 – 1973 |
| **SPEED:** 115mph – 120mph | **PRODUCTION:** 12,224 |

| | |
|---|---|
| Cost (SIV fhc) | £11,500 |
| % swing | 3 |
| Spares | ★★★★ |
| V.F.M. | ★★★ |
| S.R. | ★★★★ |

## MANUFACTURER
# ARMSTRONG-SIDDELEY

ARMSTRONG-SIDDELEY STAR SAPPHIRE · A DYING BREED

Cost £12,000
% swing 57

Spares ★★
V.F.M. ★★★★★
S.R. ★★★

A union of Armstrong-Whitworth and Siddeley Deasy, the very first Armstrong-Siddeley was the 1919 30 HP model. Ironically, it was their very last model which perhaps best encapsulated their aims. The Armstrong-Siddeley Star Sapphire was launched in 1968 with a price tag of £2,498 and impressive specifications all under an elegant and discreet body. They really were the final vestige of a very British way of automotive life. Built to the same standards as their aircraft work, the cars were trimmed in fine leathers and veneers, and were designed to appeal to the discreetly wealthy. This was a deliberate move to cater to those who would not wish to tout their wealth with vulgar new cars such as Jaguars, or overstate their position by driving a Rolls. Such customers certainly existed, and the Star Sapphire perfectly met their particular needs. However, they were a dying breed, and in June 1960 Bristol-Siddeley Engines Ltd announced it was not practical to continue, and production ceased just one month later, though spares continued to be produced for a further ten years.

Although the Star was heavy at 35.5cwt, the 4.0 litre Bristol engine developed a decent 165bhp and using twin Zenith carburettors it would happily cruise at 80mph with an absolute top speed of slightly over 100mph. Power steering, automatic gearbox, the 11.8 inch front discs and 12 inch rear drums were servo-assisted and enormous trouble was taken to sound proof the interior. It would accommodate up to six in considerable luxury, include separate heating arrangements for the front and rear of the car. For the last year there was also a seven-seater limousine version,

### SPECIFICATIONS

**ENGINE:** 3990cc
**BHP:** 165bhp
**FUEL:** 17mpg
**GEARBOX:** 3 speed automatic
**SUSPENSION:** Ind twin wishbone/semi-elliptic
**BRAKES:** Disc/drum
**SPEED:** 105mph
**BODIES:** 4 door saloon
**YEARS:** 1958-1960
**PRODUCTION** 980

though the factory's sense of decorum resulted in a less powerful engine than the saloon – 90mph was deemed 'quite sufficient' for such a sedate carriage of quality. If a finely constructed piece of bygone British motoring history appeals, then a Star Sapphire holds considerable charm.

## RELATIONS

These really were home-grown products, and Armstrong-Siddeley constantly pressed on with developments which were handed down through the range. They produced the first all-new post-war car in the UK (the Hurricane) and their 1956 Sapphires were the first British cars with power steering

## BEST BUY

The saloon only sold for the two years and so choice is all about condition. The car was beautifully over-engineered and the engine should last years. Sills can rust, but these are obvious and curable. Replacing poor interiors of such quality would be expensive.

## MANUFACTURER
# DOWNTON

**DOWNTON CLUBSPORT**

IT SHAMES PAST MACHINES

Performance Minis have always been the backbone to entry level motor sports. The Mini Coopers provided an off the shelf model and the fabled S versions went on to conquer the world. These factory pre–packed versions aside, an entire industry grew to provide conversions and DIY performance items. Probably the most respected example was Downton Engineering run by Daniel Richmond who even supplied the great BMC Competition Department. The global success of the Works Minis and countless privateers gave Downton an incredible reputation. Eventually the company faded and in 1993 Norfolk brothers Stuart and Paul Mickleburgh acquired the rights to the name and revived the same tradition of high standards with the BMC A engines. They even involved one of the original Downton Engineering talents Brian Slark and have now built up a range of fine Mini tuning and retro models. 1997 was the 50th year of the Downton trading name and they have combined the best of their Retro Mini work with modern performance tunning to create a Downton Anniversary model called the ClubSport. It may essentially be a retro styled 90s 1.3i with low key Downton green livery but driven in anger it shames past machines – even 1275 S's. A late 60s showroom model would offer around 75bhp whilst the Downton car is delivering 92bhp. The original was a joy to corner but this car is a pure delight. Balancing 12 inch wheels, ride height and a much lightened body takes high skill levels and even between my two test drives Downton had gone further, installing a 1.5 inch rear anti roll bar. It doesn't shake your teeth out yet the set-up allows a satisfying level of point and squirt into corners. There are chic

### SPECIFICATIONS

| | |
|---|---|
| **ENGINE:** 1310cc | **BRAKES:** Disc / Drum |
| **BHP:** 92bhp | **SPEED:** 110mph |
| **FUEL:** 33mpg | **BODIES:** 2 door saloon |
| **GEARBOX:** 4 speed | **YEARS:** Current |
| **SUSPENSION:** Rubber cone, Konis & anti roll | **PRODUCTION** N/A |

trim levels if you choose but it's as a 'drive to the event' club competition car that it's most seductive. The test car required just a couple of hundred pounds of changes to become a brilliant, competitive, and fully eligible amateur competition car.

## RELATIONS

The car is a direct descendant of the famed 1960s 1275cc Mini Cooper S but using the 90s 1.3i Mini as the central platform. Many components are Downton supplied accessories which follow closely the original BMC Special Tuning Dept range.

## BEST BUY

As these cars are generally built to order, prospects for second hand choice are bad. However Downton offer various levels of equipment depending on your plans – competition or road transport. Various trim and performance options are available and their Mk I Austin or Morris look front grilles adds an extra helping of nostalgia. Being Downton 50 Year anniversary models these cars are likely to remain desirable.

| | |
|---|---|
| Spares | ★★★★★ |
| V.F.M. | ★★★★ |
| S.R. | ★★★★ |

# SAAB 900 TURBO

### BRILLIANT – I JUST WISH IT HAD BEEN FOR SALE

## MANUFACTURER
# SAAB

Decades of enjoying press cars spoils you. It also destroys many day dreams as almost inevitably, fancied cars proved to have annoying traits, or didn't suit day-to-day life – something car buyers find out the hard way. It was an extraordinary shock when I found a SAAB fulfilling virtually all criteria for a perfect road car. The model concerned was one of the very last SAAB 900 Turbos before the current Vauxhall Cavalier cloned version. Called the Ruby, just 200 of these cars were imported as a final celebration of the 900's impressive 15 years in production. The range evolved out of the 99 through increased wheelbase and redesigned front end and has been offered in two, three, four and five door versions plus a convertible – all constantly improved in terms of safety and with regard to the environment: they were the first with asbestos free brakes pads. The 99 was the first mass production turbo. The engine remained the two litre but their policy of development took the power output from 100bhp up to the Ruby's 185bhp. The 900 had 16 valves from October 1984 and water-cooled turbos arrived in 1987 along with ABS; while in 1991 they introduced a 145bhp light turbocharged S engine option. Often as a car reaches old age the manufacturers add nothing but weight and badges, but with SAAB's constant evolution of a single range the final Ruby was a triumph. It came with their most powerful 1985cc full turbo engine, three door body, aero wheels, air conditioning and leather heated seats. With the turbo lag problems ironed out there was an endless stream of power; with near perfect steering (weighted 60% over

the front axle) excellent brakes and firm suspension it drove like a fine sports car while offering saloon comfort, space and traditional Swedish build quality. It's a great road car and its qualities combined with long life expectancy ensure eventual classic status. A stunning combination – I wish it had been for sale.

## RELATIONS

A naturally evolved model. First SAAB Turbo was the January 1978 99 model and the first 900 Turbo came in March 1979. The present day 900 is the GM based range introduced in 1993.

## BEST BUY

If you can find a Ruby, all finished in dark red mica–metallic paint, it's a gem, but any post-1988 water cooled turbo is interesting, though the 1989 go faster Carlsson version lacks class. Excellent build limits body troubles. Mechanical aspects are chiefly limited to clutch wear: see if it judders. Worn high mileage turbos expensive. Seek a good service record.

| Spares | ★★★★ |
| --- | --- |
| V.F.M. | ★★★★ |
| S.R. | ★★★ |

## SPECIFICATIONS

| | |
| --- | --- |
| **ENGINE:** 1985cc | **SUSPENSION:** Ind coil/wishbone – coil/trailing arms |
| **BHP:** 185 | |
| **FUEL:** 27mpg | **BODIES:** 3 door Saloon |
| **GEARBOX:** 5 speed | **YEARS:** 1978 – 1993 |
| **BRAKES:** Disc | **PRODUCTION:** 26,346 |
| **SPEED:** 130mph | |

# MANUFACTURER
# JOWETT

Jowett started production in 1906, and for decades made safe and reliable small cars and vans powered by twin cylinder engines. Based in Bradford (hence their Bradford vans), they emerged from the Second World War in need of a more contemporary image.

The 1946 prototype and 1947 production Javelin revealed highly advanced thinking for a company considered so conservative. The Javelin was an 80mph six-seater powered by a horizontally-opposed flat-four cylinder which, combined with front and rear torsion bar suspension, gave it notable handling and economy. This car was an important advance and, buoyed up by their progress, Jowett pressed ahead seeking further glory, and much-needed export income, from a new sports car.

The result was the Jowett Jupiter which was launched in 1950 with a special tubular chassis designed by Von Eberhorst – the man behind both Auto-Union and ERA success. An extra 10hp was added to the Javelin engine and this was installed ahead of the front wheels with the radiator behind. A four-speed gearbox and a modified version of the saloon's impressive suspension all provided a sports car well ahead of its time. The styling, however, appeared to be looking, Janus-like, pre- and post-war. The interior offered a bench seat, wood fittings and wind-up windows. Towards the end of 1952 a Series III engine assisted reliability, while that October the Mk IA Convertible was launched, with an improved interior, chassis configuration and even an external boot lid. It was too little, too late for a startlingly well-conceived car. It was too expensive and could

## SPECIFICATIONS

ENGINE: 1486cc
BHP: 60.5bhp
FUEL: 21.8–25mpg
GEARBOX: 4 speed
BRAKES: Drum
SUSPENSION: Ind wishbone, torsion bar/live axle, trail-
ing arm, torsion bar, Panhard rod
SPEED: 84 – 86mph
BODIES: 2 door, 3 seat sports
YEARS: 1950–1954
PRODUCTION: 899

not match Jaguar. It died away in 1953, although in their short life, the Jupiters achieved class wins and a second in the Monte Carlo Rally 1950-51.

## RELATIONS

Essentially the Jupiter is derived from the previous Javelin saloon with the addition of a racing-inspired tubular chassis. Their preoccupation with flat twin engines extended from 1906 to 1936 when the flat four arrived. A final effort to fend off disaster with a fibreglass Ferrari look-alike body – the Jupiter R4 – failed in the last year.

## BEST BUY

These cars are high on character and individuality, but need care given their age. Rust often appears in the rear as well as in the conventional places. Front suspension requires regular lubrication and some parts are difficult to find. The owners' club is invaluable. Late engines are a safer bet.

| Cost | £14,300 |
|---|---|
| % swing | 20 |
| | |
| Spares | ★ |
| V.F.M. | ★★★ |
| S.R. | ★★★★ |

## MANUFACTURER
# RENAULT

The term "real sports car" is often used by owners of overweight sporting legends massaging ageing egos. Just a precious few cars – like race horses – are genuine thoroughbreds requiring skilful mastering. One such car is the Alpine-Renault A110. It was rooted in competition and throughout its lifespan searched for the perfect engines for each task.

Jean Redélé, the son of a Dieppe Renault agent began competing in a Renault 4CV, particularly the sporting Type 1063 version. In his search for victory he discarded the heavy body and replaced it with a fibreglass shell. A Michelotti design pre–production model followed and a finished commercial version was unveiled at the 1955 Paris Motor Show. After some initial cars Redélé's vision finally crystallized in 1963. The A110 formula for success was a central backbone chassis, proven Renault components and literally a one-piece, lightweight fibreglass body. The engine was slung low behind the axle but cambered wheels, race-proven suspension and an incredibly light body conspired to create a true winner – competition versions were virtually transparent. It won races and rallies – even achieving a spectacular one, two, three victory in the 1971 Monte Carlo Rally. All independent suspension, 4- or 5-speed gearboxes, all-round disc brakes and a

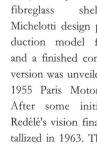

truly bewildering selection of engines were employed. As with the Donald Healey/BMC union, so Renault increasingly supported Alpine, turning them into the national sports car – even competing in the French colours. Naturally, Renault's involvement led to the subsequent cars, the GTA Turbo, the A310 and the final A610 becoming heavier and more comfortable; which leaves the lithe, undeniably beautiful yet fast A110 as the true classic masterpiece. If you are looking for something different, a connoisseur's classic and have the driver skills to get the best from its power and sensitivities, then the Alpine could well become your passion.

## RELATIONS

Italian Michelotti-inspired design with approximately 750 Renault components in every car, including a variety of their engines (see separate box above right). Francophiles might spot those Citroën Dyane front indicators! The history of Alpine Renault includes the engineering groundwork for the success of Williams Renault in Formula One today.

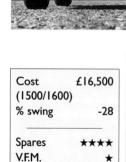

| Cost | £16,500 |
|------|---------|
| (1500/1600) | |
| % swing | -28 |
| | |
| Spares | ★★★★ |
| V.F.M. | ★ |
| S.R. | ★★ |

### SPECIFICATIONS

| | |
|---|---|
| **ENGINE:** 1300cc – 1600cc (competition variations) | **SPEED:** 110mph–130mph (competitions higher) |
| **BHP:** 58 – 170 | **SUSPENSION:** Ind wishbone/ |
| **FUEL:** 24mpg (competitions lower) | coil – Swing axle/coil |
| **GEARBOX:** 4 & 5 speed | **BODIES:** 2 door coupé |
| **BRAKES:** Disc | **YEARS:** 1963-77 |
| | **PRODUCTION:** 7,914 |

## DIEPPE FACTORY BUILT ALPINE–RENAULT A110 BERLINETTES

(LIMITED PRODUCTION ALSO TOOK PLACE IN BRAZIL, BULGARIA, MEXICO & SPAIN)

**1963–65** "1000" A110–950 (i) 956cc (55hp), 106mph, (Renault8/Floride S)

**1963–65** "1000" A110–950 Mignotet (i) 956cc (70hp), mph n/a, (R8/Floride S)

**1963–65** "1100" 80" (ii) 1108cc (55hp), 106mph, (Caravelle&R8)

**1964–65** "1100" (ii)1108cc (66hp), 109mph, (R8) – later called "Standard"

**1965–66** "85" (ii) 1108cc (85hp), 112mph, (Caravelle/R8)

**1965–na** "1100 Competition" (ii) 1108cc (90hp), 122mph, (R8Gordini)

**1965–76** "100" (ii)–1108cc (95hp), 121mph, (R8Gordini)

**1966–67** "Standard" (ii) 1108cc (66hp), 109mph, (R8)– was 1964/5 "1100"

**1966–na** "Standard Hautes Performance" (ii)1108cc (na), 116mph, (R8Gordini)

**1966–71** "1300" (iii) 1296cc (115hp), 134mph, (R8) called Super after 1967

**1967–69** "70" (ii) 1108cc (66hp), 109mph, (R8) – formally the "Standard"

**1967–71** "1300 S" (iii) 1296cc (120hp), 138mph, (R8) called Super after 1967

**1967–71** "1300 S Usine" (iii) 1296cc(na), 148mph, (R8) called Super after 1967

**1967–na** "1100GTH" (ii) 1147cc (110hp), mph n/a, (R8Gordini)

**1967–70** "1300" (iii) 1255cc, (105hp), 134mph, (R8Gordini)

**1970–71** "1300G" (iii) 1255cc (103hp), 134mph, (R8Gordini)

**1970–74** "85" (iii) 1289cc (81hp), 113mph, (Renault 12TS)– became "1300" until 1976

**1975–76** "1300" (iii) 1289cc, (81hp), 113mph, (Renault12TS) formally the "85"

**1967–68** "1500" (iv) 1470cc (82hp), 116mph, (Renault16)

**1969–70** "1600" (v) 1565cc (92hp), 122mph, (Renault16TS)

**1970–70** "1600" (v) 1565cc (102hp), 122mph, (Renault16TS)

**1970–73** "1600 S" (v) 1565cc, (138hp), 134mph, (Renault16TS)

**1970–73** "1600 S" (v) Group IV, 1596cc (172hp), 141mph, (Renault16TS)

**1973–74** "1600 S" (v) 1605cc, (140hp), 131mph, (Renault17TS)

**1973–74** "1800 S Group IV Usine" (v) 1798cc, (185hp), 158mph, (Renault17TS)

**1974–75** "1600 SC" – 1600Si (v) 1605cc, (140/145hp), 131mph, (Renault17TS)

**1976–77** "1600 SX" (v) 1647cc (109hp), 122mph, (Renault16TX)

### ALPINE–RENAULT GENERAL CLASSIFICATIONS

**(i)** A110 "1000"
**(ii)** A110 "Berlinette 1100"
**(iii)** A110 "Berlinette 1300" VA–VB–VC
**(iv)** A110 "Berlinette 1500"
**(v)** A110 "Berlinette 1600" VA–VB–VC–VD–VH

N.B. All Power ratings are in S.A.E. HP

Prepared with the assistance of Club Alpine–Renault

## BEST BUY

Engines sizes systematically grew from 956 to 1951 though the essential production models were around the 1300 & 1600 mark. Exclude the early 4-speed gearbox and be aware there were also Spanish-built examples. Almost inevitably, any A110 will have been driven hard, quite possibly in competition, and with most cars customized you should contact the Owners Club to help find one of these prized machines.

# PORSCHE 911
WE'VE SAID NICE ...

## MANUFACTURER
# PORSCHE

*Which 911 is pictured above? Does it really matter? Well, of course it does. Turbo convertible, 1985-89 with the paintwork provided at source (originally offered as decoration on the 935). 300 bhp for the eighties winners. Whatever the author's misgivings, there must be a few nineties winners out there who are stiill enamoured: there is a seven-month waiting list for the latest £64,000 911 Targa.*

I happily acknowledge the 911 as a very fine looking car and that, after the millions of Deutchmarks and hours of skilled German application, the machine is most beautifully engineered. However, we were saying that over 30 years ago, congratulating the company for effectively re-creating the same central design problem which existed on its predecessor. Hanging the engine at the very back and then adding more and more power over the years to compensate seems rather naïve. Yes, we should applaud their huge expenditure which off-set such flaws, but more thought at the time might have left funds for genuinely new models. Porsche staggered and fell trying to make a 'People's Porsche' with the 914/16. They virtually apologised for the 924 and have never convinced anyone about the 928. Only the upgrade of the 924 to the 944 stands the test of time, and even that was left with borrowed bodywork. Design teams with such appalling track records wouldn't survive anywhere else. However, it does seem that the latest incarnation 1997 Carrera is about as far as you can go in revamping an old design without abandoning it altogether. Every panel is different, it's a little bigger – 18.5cm longer, 3cm wider – though impressively 50kg lighter. The radical change is to water cooling for the flat six, which has had a civilising effect on the noise levels which some might regret. The problem of all that weight at the back is still there though.

The cars that came before this latest 175-mph slingshot are truly exciting to drive, and generate lots of the correct noises from both the engine compartment and bystanders, but they are expensive for something that is centrally flawed in its handling, with spartan basics for an interior, notchy, unattractive gear changes, excessive spares costs, poor ventilation and group 20 insurance. In the same time frame Jaguar created the Mk II, the E-Type, the Mk X, the 240/340/420 range, the XJ6, the XJS, the 220 and the new XK8. Even under-funded design teams like Lotus created the Lotus 7, the sports racers, the Formula Juniors, the FI cars, the Elite, the five Elans, the +2s, the Europa, the Elite SI, the Esprit range and the new Elise. The 911 has become like an obsessive body-builder pumping ever more irons and steroids to ensure continuing admiration – we've said nice. There must be employees in the Porsche design department with years of service, the Boxster notwithstanding, who have never ever been involved in a genuinely new car launch.

The 911 itself was launched to an appreciate public in 1963 (as the 901) and has journeyed through endless incarnations, systematically improving until its fashion status became the core sales impetus. It is indeed a very exciting and exacting driver's car but 35 years on there are now a range of temptations for the

| Cost | £17,000 |
|------|---------|
| (Carrera '73) | |
| % swing | 3 |
| | |
| Spares | ★★ |
| V.F.M. | ★★ |
| S.R. | ★★ |

## SPECIFICATIONS

| | |
|---|---|
| **ENGINE:** 1582cc: 1971cc | **SUSPENSION:** MacPherson |
| **BHP:** 90 – 80 | Strut/Torsion bar & Semi |
| **FUEL:** 28mpg | trailing/Torsion bar |
| **GEARBOX:** 4 & 5 speed | **BODIES:** 2 door Coupé: Targa |
| **BRAKES:** Disc | **YEARS:** 1965 – 69: 1975 – 76 |
| **SPEED:** 110mph | **PRODUCTION:** 32,399 |

# A CHRONOLOGY

**1963** Launch at Frankfurt Motor Show – as the 901
**1964** Initial production cars renamed 911 following Peugeot objections
**1965** 1991cc model with 130bhp,130mph and Solex carbs
First right hand drives reach Britain
912 launch with 1,582cc, 90bhp and 122mph
**1966** S version and Targa with 160bhp ventilated disc brakes and Webers
**1967** 911L launch with 110bhp, Sportomatic gearbox
911T launch with 1991cc, 110bhp and 125mph
**1968** 911S receives fuel injection and 170bhp
911T rises to 140bhp
911E with 140bhp replaces 911L
Targa gets fixed glass window
912 ends production
**1969** 911S to 2195cc, fuel injection 170bhp and 136mph )
911E to 2195cc, fuel injection 155bhp and 137mph
911T to 2195cc, Zenith carbs 125bhp and 128mph )
911L to 1991, 130bhp – last year
911 wheelbase stretched to 2268mm
Enlarged 5.5 inch wheel rims
**1970** New front air dam, galvanising undersides
**1971** 911S to 2341cc, 190bhp and 144mph
911T to 2341cc, 130bhp,and 129mph
911E to 2341cc, 165bhp and 140mph
New 915 gearbox
**1972** 911RS 2.7 Carrera launch with 2687cc
210bhp and 149mph
Enlarged rear wings and wheels for Carrera

**1973** 911T gets Bosch Kjetronic fuel injection
All models to 2687cc
911 replaces T and has 150bhp
911S replaces E and has 175bhp
**1974** 911 3.0 Carrera RSR Turbo launch at Paris Show with 260bhp and 153mph
**1975** 912E reintroduction with 1971cc, 80bhp and 110mph
**1976** Bodies now zinc coated
**1977** 911 3.3 Turbo, 3299cc, 300bhp and 160mph
**1980** 911SC 3.0 with 204bhp
**1982** Cabriolet body launched
**1983** 911 3.2 Carrera launched with 3164cc, 231bhp and 152mph
**1984** 3164 installed in non Turbo models with 231bhp
**1987** 959 launch with 2848cc, twin turbos, 4WD, 450bhp and 196mph
**1988** 911 3.6 Carrera 4 with 3600cc, 4wd, 250bhp and 155mph
Speedster begins short production run
**1989** 911 3.6 Carrera 2 with tiptronic gearbox and 159mph
**1990** 911 3.3 Turbo to 320bhp and 171mph
**1991** 911 3.6 Carrrera RS with 260bhp and 161 mph
911 Turbo servo steering and ABS introduced plus ABS
**1992** 911 3.3 Turbo S special with 355bhp
911 Carrera RS, essentially the Carrrera 2 with 260bhp
**1993** 911 3.6 Turbo with 360bhp and 175mph
911 Speedster limited edition version of Carrera 2
**1997** 911 3387cc Carrera, watercooled, 300bhp @ 6800rpm, 175mph

knowledgable enthusiast: the Honda NSX, for example, a better sports car with the wrong badge. The 911 doesn't invite DIY restorations, costs large sums to have rebuilt and requires all your attention, all the time, when driving. Magazines sell extra copies flaunting state-of-the-art Porsche features but virtually none remember the 912, which is identical to its contemporary 911 sister but used the 4-cylinder engine from the final trusted 356C model. The 912 will still get you to 110mph, give brilliant fuel consumption and with the lighter engine over the tail, not behave as badly. So the interior trim is basic – so it is for virtually all the 911s. It does, however, enjoy the early and pure body styling, its own cachet; and remember you could buy a good looking example for the cost of a hard top for the present 911 Cabriolet.

## RELATIONS

Designed by Dr Porsche's son Ferdinand it echoed most of the preceding 356C model and has been developed in-house over the decades. Other economy minded 911s include the 911T and 911S.

## BEST BUY

The 912 was launched in 1965 when the 356C was dropped. 1967 saw a Targa roof option and dual circuit braking, with longer wheelbase and five speeds following. It reappeared as the 912E (not the 911E) just for 1975 as an export using the larger fuel injected engine from the discontinued 914 model. If you get serious, check any Porsche obsessively for rust.

Take a deep breath and consider the following from the renowned journalist and author L.J.K. Setright:
'It is simply not possible to combine stablity in yaw and pitch, reliable braking on slippery surfaces, freedom from perturbation in cross-winds, high speeds, strong acceleration, agile handling and ease of control, all in a car of short wheelbase with rear-wheel drive, with the the major masses concentrated between and behind the axes of the rear wheels, with bodywork so shaped that the aerodynamic centre of pressure is well forward and shifts even further forwards as speed rises, and with suspension geometries that cause flexure of the springs to be accompanied by significant migrations of the instantaneous roll centres at front and rear.' *(Courtesy* Classic Cars, *September 1996.)* Presumably, behind that Winnebago of a sentence lie years of growing unease – and an intimidated sub editor … For decades, Porsche have added and subtracted 911 body parts to create new versions, just like so many toy models.

# DAIMLER SP250

*MORE DESIRABLE NOW THAN WHEN NEW*

### MANUFACTURER
# DAIMLER

This is a car that deserves careful attention. Daimler's unexpected excursion into the 1960s sports car market, with unconventional body styling, had little chance of survival particularly as Jaguar took over the company and within two years were to unveil their world beating E-Type. However the low production figures, its glorious V8 engine and a strong fibreglass body have combined to give the Daimler a very collectable status. Informed observers feel that approximately two-thirds of the total production are still in existence – and that's Rolls-Royce survivability. The powerful and lightweight Edward Turner-designed V8 was the envy of the industry and many cynics wrote referring to a fine engine test rather than a road test – thus utterly dismissing the unconventional styling or the natural Daimler concerns for passenger comfort. The car wasn't trying to be an Austin-Healey or a TR – it was a Daimler boasting leather trim, adjustable bucket seating, wind up windows, detachable hard top, standard disc braking, an automatic option. Daimler's independence disappeared within a year of the SP250's 1959 New York launch and despite good orders and reviews, the new Jaguar masters hardly wanted in-house competition for their imminent E-Type.

Briefly named the Daimler Dart, the initial A specifications offered full 120mph performance but the chassis proved to flex under stress and shortly after Jaguar's takeover the 1961 B version added extra

chassis and body strength, a full-width front bumper and detail refinements. Towards the end of its short life there was also a C spec, fitting as standard previous options such as a heater and even a cigar lighter. This unique car offers rapid and elegant touring with suspension and handling to suit: inevitably compromising finesse if driven in anger. Rare, comfortable, with wonderful engine and head turning retro style, it's more desirable now than when new.

## RELATIONS

Daimler body concept and new V8 engine; Jaguar controlled after 1960. Daimler had also owned Hooper who coachbuilt a prototype SP250 Coupé for the 1959 Earls Court show. Aimed at the US market, it preempted much of the MGB GT concept but was still born…Jaguar's fixed head E-Type was coming.

## BEST BUY

Sought after so choice is limited. Tap into the owners club network and try to find B or C versions. The engine wears well and the largely trouble-free fibreglass body is strong. Check rear sections of the chassis, around the steering box and front suspension.

| Cost | £14,300 |
| --- | --- |
| % swing | -8 |
| Spares | ★★★ |
| V.F.M. | ★★ |
| S.R. | ★★★★ |

### SPECIFICATIONS

| | |
| --- | --- |
| **ENGINE:** 2548cc | **SUSPENSION:** Ind |
| **BHP:** 140 | wishbone/coil& live axle |
| **FUEL:** 27mpg | semi-elliptic |
| **GEARBOX:** 4 speed; 3 speed | **BODIES:** 2 door sports |
| automatic | **YEARS:** 1959 – 64 |
| **BRAKES:** Disc | **PRODUCTION:** 2,645 |
| **SPEED:** 122mph | |

## MANUFACTURER
# GENERAL MOTORS

The 40 years of the Corvette is a story of competition – not motor sport, but pure commerce. Its catalyst was GM design chief and enthusiast Harley Earl's growing frustration at the European influx of sports cars such as the XK 120 and the Austin-Healey 100. Now, such is the UK/European love affair with '50s Americana that the era's body styling appears particularly attractive, but ironically the initial Corvette was a terrible compromise and only survived thanks to corporate pride in the face of Ford's new Thunderbird. It is the 1956–62 period that best represents the early cars. The Corvette first appeared as the 1953 Motorama show car. Fibreglass was used for development economy while the chassis and engine were ageing saloon items. A pre–war in–line 6 engine, negligible brakes and a two-speed automatic gearbox hardly amounted to a sports car. *Road and Track*, viewing it as a woman's car, drove the point home by suggesting a three-tone paint scheme and frilly curtains. Production staggered onward but unsold stock and mounting criticisms heralded a swift end: until Ford launched that Thunderbird, goading GM into competition. In 1955 the new V8 265 cubic inch saloon Chevrolet engine was squeezed into the Corvette adding 45bhp – and a 3-speed manual gearbox. Harley Earl and team then set about re–styling and in 1956 the car came of age. Deep elliptical grooves down the body sides appeared, a more aggressive front treatment with protruding headlights, a hardtop, winding or electric windows, upgraded tuning options and in best form a 120mph+ top speed. Each year it gained extra performance and the

styling actually became more Rock 'n' Roll – until the 1963 Sting Ray took over.

## RELATIONS

General Motors body styling with the rest a GM parts bin extravaganza. Initial in-line 6 dated back to the Depression; subsequent V8s from saloon range.

## BEST BUY

The 1953–55 car (see above) is interesting and collectable as a boulevard cruiser. The 1956–62 era is progressively more sporting until the Sting Ray. 4-speed manual from 1957 and from '58 quad headlights and a truly amazing cockpit worthy of any sports car. Basically trouble-free, but watch for accident damage beneath the (easily repairable) bodywork. With retrimming expensive and spares tricky, prioritise interior condition when choosing and join the club to tap into members' cars for sale.

*The interior is as important as the running gear and bodywork when buying, maybe more so.*

### SPECIFICATIONS

**ENGINE:** 3861cc; 4344cc; 4639cc; 5359cc
**BHP:** 150 –250 (360 bhp tuned)
**FUEL:** 13 – 25mpg
**GEARBOX:** 2 speed auto; 3 & 4 Manual
**BRAKES:** Drum
**SUSPENSION:** Unequal A

arms/coil – Live axle/semi-elliptic
**SPEED:** 106 – 120mph (135mph tuned)
**BODIES:** 2 door Sport; Hard Top
**YEARS:** 1953 – 1962
**PRODUCTION:** 69,475

| Cost | £19,000 |
|---|---|
| (Sting Ray '63-67) | |
| % swing | 8 |
| | |
| Spares | ★★★ |
| V.F.M. | ★★★ |
| S.R. | ★★★★ |

# MERCEDES 230–250–280 SL

HARD TO FAULT MIDDLE GROUND CLASSIC

### MANUFACTURER
# MERCEDES-BENZ

Mercedes–Benz entered the 1960s with some trepidation: while their once revered 300SL was dating fast, and the 190SL languished in the Gullwing's shadow, the competition was forging ahead, offering that all-important impressive top speed – once the Gullwing's domain – plus greatly improved creature comforts. In March 1963 they unveiled their answer, the 230SL. Inevitably there were mixed reactions and to many the title sports car was inappropriate. However as road testers and the public got behind the wheel, attitudes changed, for much of Mercedes' effort had gone into handling – never the Gullwing's strong suit. So much care in fact, that they even instigated the design of brand new tyres. The car was based on the floorpan, engine and equipment from the 220SE which some pointed to as an endorsement of the non sports car argument: forgetting a Works 220SE team came first, second and third in the 1960 Monte Carlo Rally. The engine was slightly bored out, with new camshaft, improved compression and fitted with fuel injection for 170bhp. Transmission was four speed with awkward gear ratios or the generally specified four speed automatic. Power steering was available, front disc brakes standard. Soft top was an option; or a solid five point fixing hardtop with extra tall door windows, which forced the hardtop roof sides to tilt upward – hence the famous Pagoda nickname. These finely built cars began to create a very wide customer base. In 1967 they answered lack of power criticism by putting their fuel-injected 2.5 into what was then called the 250SL. This also offered a choice of final drives, four and five speed boxes as

well as auto and disc brakes all round. Despite traditionally long runs, Mercedes took less than a year before eclipsing the 250SL with the 280SL. This was the last of the 6-cylinder SLs and the most popular, enjoying a power hike to 2778cc courtesy of the 280/300SE range. The 6-cylinder SLs make beautiful touring cars and basically safe investments.

## RELATIONS

Substantially based on the 220SE saloons with subsequent versions taking engines from the 250SE and finally the 280/300SE. Bodystyling is original.

## BEST BUY

The 230SL underpowered but actually more agile than the bigger engined cars which became increasingly heavy – and comfortable. Buy through recognised sources and with service history: mistakes are expensive. Rust limited to wings, sills, rear floor area.

| Cost | £19,300 |
|------|---------|
| (280SL) | |
| % swing | –1 |
| Spares | ★★★ |
| V.F.M. | ★★ |
| S.R. | ★★★ |

### SPECIFICATIONS

**ENGINE:** 2306cc; 2496cc; 2778cc
**BHP:** 150 – 170
**FUEL:** 17 – 25mpg
**SPEED:** 115 – 121mph
**GEARBOX:** 4 speed; Automatic; 5 speed 280SL
**BRAKES:** Disc/drum – Disc/disc after '67
**SUSPENSION:** Ind wishbone/coil – swing axle/coil
**BODIES:** 2 door roadster soft/hard tops
**YEARS:** 1963–67; 1966–68; 1967–71
**PRODUCTION:** 19,831; 5,196; 23,885

## MANUFACTURER
# FIAT

**FIAT ABARTH 850 TC**

AN INDIVIDUALIST'S CLUB CAR

Whether it was a Ford Galaxy battling the Mk II racing Jaguars, three wheeling Lotus Cortinas, John Rhodes burning Cooper S tyres or the latest Mercedes/Alfa tussle in the DTM, racing production cars have always held real fascination. Just to see familiar models tuned to perfection and thrashed to within inches of destruction brings out the gladiatorial instincts. Naturally this type of classic competition appeals to amateurs and leads to the quest for something different, something affordable to run. John Cooper's magic transformed the humble Mini into a world beating competition car while in Italy a man specialising in exhaust pipes achieved the same with even more modest machinery – the tiny 500 and 600 Fiat saloons. Carlo Abarth's Fiat-tuning gifts are truly legendary. The basic 600 saloon developed just 28bhp yet such was his skills that in its extreme TCR state it yielded 130bhp. There were over 7,000 class wins! The tiny saloons were reliable, fun and millions were sold creating a good supply of both cars and parts. The actual Works cars were the pinnacle of development and frequently changed livery from season to season which, combined with so many Abarth conversion kits, makes establishing a genuine Works car extremely tricky. I tried out just such a rarity, the 1966 Works 850 TC Corsa – the TC is Turismo Competizione. Having driven BMC Works Cooper S's I approached the drive with more amusement than excitement but within minutes the acceleration, the glorious noise, the rock steady suspension and disc braking in each corner of the tiny thing commanded great respect. They really are the giant killers

you read about and exceptional fun – though reverse in the initial gear position and actual first where second should be does keep you concentrating. The historic machine pictured is prepared and raced by Tony Castle-Miller at Middle Barton Garage who is the UK's Abarth specialist and can restore or build you any grade of Fiat Abarth. These cars win events, need little space, create large crowds and make you smile a good deal – an ideal clubman's classic.

## RELATIONS

The Fiat 500 and 600 were the replacements for the tiny Tipolino while Abarth's ideas blossomed under his own badge and as the tuning element for a wide range of manufacturers including Lancia and Ferrari.

## BEST BUY

If your quest is just for a hot road car then all the usual warnings about that virile Italian rust applies. If however you are tempted to prepare a modest but competitive race or hill climb car, talk to Barton.

### SPECIFICATIONS

**ENGINE:** 982cc
**BHP:** 93
**FUEL:** 4 gallon racing tank
**GEARBOX:** 5 speed
**BRAKES:** Disc
**SPEED:** 122mph
**SUSPENSION:** Wishbone/transverse leaf – Semi trailing/coil
**BODIES:** 2 door 4 seat saloon
**YEARS:** 1968
**PRODUCTION:** NA

| | |
|---|---|
| Spares | ★★★★ |
| V.F.M. | ★★★ |
| S.R. | ★★★★★ |

# FIAT COUPE 20V TURBO

FERRARI SPEED – PUNTO BOOT SIZE

## MANUFACTURER
# FIAT

| Spares | ★★★★★ |
| V.F.M. | ★★★★★ |
| S.R. | ★★★★★ |

Apart from the universally loved baby Fiat 500 and 600, Fiat motor cars are not often obvious classics. Many were just utility vehicles, and most attracted rust as if it were a design feature. So it is all the more rewarding to cite this stunning new Fiat Coupé as a future classic.

The history of the motor industry is chequered with breathtaking cars that failed to live up to their looks, and others which were mechanically excellent, but let down by poor styling. With this new coupé, Fiat have managed to bring the best of both worlds together in the one model. You may love or hate its distinctive appearance, but you won't forget it. In 20 years time this model will still stand out from the crowd of eligible classic cars.

To grow to true classic status, the chosen model must be useful, and become a much-loved friend. Astonishingly, this Fiat is really quite practical transport. It won't object to traffic congestion, doesn't consume unreasonable amounts of fuel and provides exceptional on-board space for its class. The boot has a greater capacity than that of the best-selling Punto, and the two occasional seats are a realistic proposition. Add to this growing list of advantages a 0-60 figure of just 6.0 seconds and a blistering top speed of 155mph, and classic status becomes compelling. The turbo comes in very early, providing exceptional performance low down where it's most useful on public roads, and the Brembo disc brakes are so powerful they are a talking point. Among motoring journalists, there is considerable respect for Fiat's success in rejoining the serious coupé market after so

## SPECIFICATIONS

| | |
| --- | --- |
| **ENGINE:** 1998cc | **SUSPENSION:** MacPherson |
| **BHP:** 220bhp | strut, crossbeam & trail- |
| **FUEL:** 28mpg | ing arms & coils |
| **GEARBOX:** 5 speed | **BODIES:** 2 door coupe |
| **BRAKES:** Disc | **YEARS:** 1996–current |
| **SPEED:** 155mph | **PRODUCTION:** N/A |

many years. The 1960s Fiat Dinos were their last performance cars, and before that the rare 1950s 8V models. Not only are they back, but they have succeeded in a bold and exciting manner.

## RELATIONS

Something refreshingly new from Fiat, with very few borrowed style features. The vibrant body colour dashboard follows in the traditions of MGA and earlier Alfa sports cars, while the non-turbo version of the 2.0 litre engine is also used within the top of the range Bravo/Brava/Marea

## BEST BUY

The standard version shares all the faster car's high styling, but the exceptional performance of the 20v Turbo model makes it the only choice – providing you don't mind paying the extra. However, the seduction of Ferrari performance may in time mean these examples get worked very hard. Also, the rear lamp clusters have the potential to trap water.

## MANUFACTURER
# FORD

**FORD PROBE**
A CONFUSED DOG

Just how could one of the giants of motor manufacturing so completely miss the spirit of a sporting car? Just imagine what a company like TVR would have created given Ford's resources. After the success of the Capri it was reasonable to expect something exciting, but the Probe failed, and prospective buyers voted with their (closed) cheque books.

With the Japanese taking great bites out of the domestic US market, the troubled motor colossi elected to try balancing their books with export priorities on cars such as the Viper and the Jeep. So the Probe was Ford of America's attempt to replicate a classic European sporting coupé. With Mazda as a partner they had a head start with the availability of the well established Mazda MX-6 floor pan and running gear as a basis. To this they added either the equally well developed V6 24 valve 2.5 Mazda engine, or their own Ford Mondeo 16 valve 2 litre unit. So far, it sounded a good bet, but from then on it all started to go horribly wrong.

Coupés are all about excitement wrapped in style and comfort – they should make strong statements. Not this one, however. The Probe is huge without offering any critical space: it is only 30 mm short of the Galaxy and that's an MPV. Engines are stifled by gearing that belongs in a Mondeo, and above all, the body style would not have got past the expresso boy in an Italian design house.

They utterly and completely missed the essence of a performance car. Yes, it's got the slender raked nose of a computer-generated approach to animation, but nowhere does it present a sense of latent power,

### SPECIFICATIONS

**ENGINE:** 1991cc; 2497 V6
**BHP:** 115-165bhp
**FUEL:** 37-29mpg
**GEARBOX:** 5 speed
**BRAKES:** Disc
**SPEED:** 127-136mph
**SUSPENSION:** MacPherson strut, coils/multi link strut, trailing arms
**BODIES:** 2 door coupé
**YEARS:** 1984-current
**PRODUCTION** N/A

of any restlessness, an eagerness to stretch out on the open road or cling to the curves of fast bends. There isn't even a single line or curve accentuating the coiled power around the rear wheels.

Who knows how many powerful computers and individuals contributed to the Probe? The prospects should have been brilliant. Ford could have adopted an adventurous new automotive style – but not this time. I hope that such a famous manufacturer will never again display such insensitivity to all of the sporting style cues.

## RELATIONS

Under the skin, much is actually a Mazda MX-6 – including the 24-valve engine option; the 2 litre is from the Mondeo. Built near Michigan in a joint venture with Mazda, it ought to have been a classic Ford but seriously failed.

## BEST BUY

The Mazda MX-6 and save the embarrassments.

# BENTLEY MK VI
## GREAT PERIOD COMFORT – AT A RISK

## MANUFACTURER
# ROLLS-ROYCE

Bentley Mk VI (above) with standard steel body. The four-door saloon was the first example of a Rolls-Royce 'factory' body; built by Pressed Steel and finished at Crewe.

| Cost | £17,000 |
|---|---|
| (Standard steel) | |
| % swing | 3 |
| | |
| Spares | ★★★ |
| V.F.M. | ★★★ |
| S.R. | ★★ |

Immediately pre-war, Rolls-Royce was developing a 4257cc prototype called the Corniche but hostilities stopped work. However, they used the war years to appraise ideas by loaning the prototypes to leading military and political figures. The resulting 1946 launch of the Mark VI was something of a revolution for this famous manufacturer. Driven by the conviction that traditional bespoke construction had to be replaced by production line methods, they appointed Pressed Steel at Cowley to construct this new four-door saloon with its strong channel section chassis, independent front suspension and a reworked version of the pre–war B60, 6 cylinder, 4257cc engine fitted with twin SU carburation. An initial novelty which they later discontinued was to chrome plate the bores to reduce wear. During 1951 there was an increase in the engine capacity to 4556cc, and the original by–pass oil filter system was replaced by a more conventional full flow arrangement. Rolls-Royce themselves used the Mk VI platform to continue the tradition of coachbuilding all the Silver Wraith bodies – although, by 1949, the logic of a more accessible prestige car led them to use the Bentley VI in R Type form as the basis for their Silver Dawn model. Undoubtedly the Mk VI offers excellent entry level Bentley enjoyment, but is it practical? In the 1960s Maurice Wiggin of *The Sunday Times* evaluated running costs of a then new 1963 Mini and a 1951 Bentley Mk VI – both then costing around £500. There was just an old half penny per mile difference, (see box) yet they were a world apart in quality and safety. 18 coats of paint, acres of veneer and leather, tables, a drawer full of tools, a remote operated rear window blind, even slightly raised rear seating. Decades on it is telling that both cars are true classics yet the Bentley is now worth 30 times its 1960s value, while the Mk I Mini has risen just six-fold – neither figure takes currency or inflation factors into account.

## RELATIONS

In-house body design with enhanced pre-war B60 engine. It gave birth to many coach-built examples, including desirable dropheads and to the later R Type, the famous Continental R (or more properly, the R-Type Continental, as 'Continental R' is the name given to the 1991 niche model) and the Rolls-Royce variants. The four-door saloon from Pressed Steel and finished at Crewe was later offered with a Rolls-Royce radiator as the Silver Dawn.

## BEST BUY

Buy the best you can afford, for it will be much cheaper than hunting out a bargain and meeting

### SPECIFICATIONS

| | |
|---|---|
| **ENGINE:** 4257cc – 4556cc | **BRAKES:** Drum |
| **BHP:** Never released | **SPEED:** 95mph |
| **FUEL:** 16 – 18mpg | **BODIES:** 4 door saloon; |
| **GEARBOX:** 4 speed | Coachbuilt versions |
| **SUSPENSION:** Ind coil/wish- | **YEARS:** 1946–52 |
| bone – live axle/half elliptic | **PRODUCTION:** 4964 |

## 1960s ANALYSIS OF COMPARATIVE RUNNING COSTS

|  | BENTLEY MK VI | MK I MINI |
|---|---|---|
| Depreciation: | £50.00 | £100.00 |
| Servicing: | £10.00 | £ 10.00 |
| Petrol: | £80.00 | £ 40.00 |
| Tyres: | £30.00 | £ 20.00 |
| Insurance: | £30.00 | £ 15.00 |
|  | £200.00 | £185.00 |
| Cost per mile (Based upon 6,000 miles) | 8d | 7½d |

Pounds, shillings and pence currency

painful restoration bills. A well maintained example will give enormous pride and pleasure to its owner. Mechanically there are no real problems though the post-1951 enlarged engine and changed oil flow is preferable. The enemy is rust and you need to check all the body mountings, the sills, the boot area, door bottoms and the wings. Ironically, the chassis generally escapes major troubles. The drophead coupé will cost you at least double the standard body version – multiply by five if you set your heart on an R-Type Continental with body from H.J.Mulliner (see pages 176-77). With the exception of the T-series saloons of the mid-1960s, the post-war Pressed Steel Mk VI is entry level for a classic flying wing. In 1930, Bentley had published a 'Resumé of Policy' as part of the celebration of victory at Le Mans: 'Participation in races [stamps] the Bentley … as a racing car. Nothing could be further from the truth. On the conrrary, as our racing successes have increased our cars have become more silent, more docile, more refined.' The Mk VI is faithful to that promise.

# ASTON MARTIN DBS

MORE MISPLACED CLASS PREOCCUPATION THAN ANY OTHER MARQUE

### MANUFACTURER
# ASTON MARTIN

Until the mid-eighties it was quite possible to buy a reasonable Aston Martin for a few thousand pounds but then the madness of the boom years saw their prices in particular soar through the roof. These are rare cars and so naturally valuable, but the unprecedented price rise told most about the owners. The world of Aston is probably riddled with more misplaced class preoccupations than other classic marque, though ultimately we all benefit when enthusiasts invest in restoring examples of our motoring heritage. Unfortunately, Astons enjoy the same cachet as a good country address, making them the ultimate accoutrement for successful types – who in turn attempt to cast an exclusion zone around the marque. This isolationism no longer applies to other prestige marques, but ageing executives and showbusiness types have used cheque books to try colonising

Aston Martin. The two models which missed their gaze were the DB2/4 which 'wasn't a DB4 darling', and the DBS which 'wasn't a V8'. The DB2/4 has now entered the investment stakes, but so far, the DBS remains just about affordable. A young Aston seat designer, William Towns, watched sports cars lose credibility as 2+2 versions got gradually longer. He sketched ideas for an initial 2+2 length car with an optional shortened sports version. His rare and

ultra long Lagonda proved the starting point, with the DBS the derivative. With the DB4/5/6 range rapidly dating, Aston used the Towns DBS design to give birth to the whole new family of V8s. However, that engine would take two years more to refine and so the 1967 DBS launch revealed the powerful Towns body styling, and used the excellent Talek Marek six-cylinder engine within an adapted DB6 chassis. The emphasis was on fast touring, and it offered four seats, practical luggage space and considerable comfort, aided by advanced de Dion rear suspension and an adjustable ride control. Although the heavy chassis and comfortable trimmings turned it into a heavy car, the steering was a delight, while speeds of 140mph was attainable. It's a wide, luxurious car, with timeless body styling – and that endlessly evocative Aston badge.

## RELATIONS

Towns designed the DBS and the 1970s Lagonda. The chassis, engine and other elements were taken

| Cost | £27,300 |
|---|---|
| % swing | 73 |
| Spares | ★★★★ |
| V.F.M. | ★★★★★ |
| S.R. | ★★ |

### SPECIFICATIONS

**ENGINE:** 3995cc
**BHP:** 282; 325 (Vantage version)
**FUEL:** 12mpg
**GEARBOX:** 5 speed: automatic
**BRAKES:** Disc
**SPEED:** 140mph: 150mph (Vantage version)

**SUSPENSION:** Ind wishbone/coil – de Dion axle & coil
**BODIES:** 2 door, 4 seater Coupé.
**YEARS:** 1967– 72
**PRODUCTION:** 899

from the DB6, while the famous V8 range followed afterwards, in September 1969. All those distinctively Aston coupés and convertibles are effectively related, from the DB4 which grew into the 4-litre DB5, DB6 and DBS.

## BEST BUY

These are only an economic buy if you don't have to face very expensive restoration. The six-cylinder cars enjoyed a good reputation, but rust crept into all the lower sections. However, spares are excellent and good specialist firms are helpful. The last batch of cars reverted to single rather than quad headlights, a DB3S grille and were called AM Vantage – in preparation for the arrival of the V8. Remember that the whole point about this model is that it *isn't* a V8, which keeps prices down. (It isn't as if the company was profiteering at the time – Sir David Brown was forced to sell out in the DBS's last year.)

*It's a DBS body (opposite, inset) but from 1978 and therefore has the V8. From 1969 to 1972 the DBS body with V8 engine was called the DBS V8, thereafter simply the V8, and had single headlights. The Aston two-door fastback coupé/convertible look had begun with the 3.7-litre DB4, which was launched in October 1958.*

MORGAN PLUS 8

TURNS LACK OF DEVELOPMENT INTO HIGH NOSTALGIA

## MANUFACTURER
# MORGAN

As a classic for restoration it's not hugely attractive; as a brand new car only the Rover engine is truly worthwhile – if you remove its style and romance, that is. It would be unforgiveable not to include a Morgan in a list of classic cars, and dishonest not to warn of endless troubles. The two truly impressive elements are a beautiful, timeless body coupled with the sense of history which the marketing prowess of the Morgan family has fostered. With precious few changes to the car, and meagre resources, they have outshone even Porsche in maintaining perpetual motion for a single design. After all, the Porsche 911 has been endlessly regurgitated to hold enthusiasts' attention, while the very absence of change in Morgan design is what maintains the company's quite astonishingly long waiting lists.

Concepts of a V8 Morgan actually go back to the 1930s, when H.F.S. Morgan ran an experimental 4/4 car with a flat head 22hp V8, but it was not until the 1960s when supplies of the TR engine were diminishing that the search for new powerplants led Morgan to the Cortina GT engine for the 4/4, and produced the Plus 8 in 1968, which used the lightweight 161bhp Rover P6B 3500 engine. Until 1972 a quite demanding Moss gearbox was used, before the five-speed Rover unit was installed. Three years later an alu-

minium lightweight Sports option appeared; 1976 changes including an overdrive to help fuel economy. The radiator was enlarged in 1979, a high lift cam was added in 1982. Constant small improvements continued with rack and pinion steering in 1983, and a fuel injection option adding extra power from 1984. Straight line performance takes your breath away – as does the desperate suspension. Why such sales figures for a car that combines 1930s (sliding pillar) front suspension and a present day alloy V8 engine – configurations which were never intended to work together?

A trip around the craftsman-filled Morgan factory helps to illuminate what is going on: it's like a living motor museum – timeless traditions are used to create masterpieces apparently ill-equipped for our motoring world. Ash frames left to season for at least a year in the factory wood shed, power tools rarely used, snips, shears and mallets to the fore; Morgans have been built at the same Malvern Link site since 1923. Just as Paul Simon borrows ethnic roots to sell his contemporary records, so Morgan turn their lack of development since the 1930s into high nostalgia.

| Cost | £18,500 |
|---|---|
| (Plus 8 1976) | |
| % swing | 13 |
| Spares | ★★★★ |
| V.F.M. | ★★★ |
| S.R. | ★★★ |

## SPECIFICATIONS

| | |
|---|---|
| **ENGINE:** 3528cc | **SUSPENSION:** Ind coil – |
| **BHP:** 157; 190 | live axle leaf |
| **FUEL:** 20mpg | **BODIES:** 2 door Sports |
| **GEARBOX:** 4 & 5 speed | **YEARS:** 1968 – to date |
| **BRAKES:** Disc/drum | **PRODUCTION:** 4000+ |
| **SPEED:** 124mph – 126mph | |

They really are hand-built with an extraordinary selection of tools to create delicious curves in wood and metal. The whole factory feels like some painstakingly productive time warp.

## RELATIONS

Born of the Morgan 4/4 which was first produced in the mid-1930s but powerered by Rover engines. The steering was modified with joints to clear the wider cylinder block. Dimensions slightly larger than the Plus 4, one inch wider and three inches longer.

## BEST BUY

Brand new. The earlier the car the more likely structural grief. Rust is a problem for body and chassis, the aluminium alternative is vulnerable to knocks. More significant is the virtually invisible wooden framework which rots and can only be replaced by stripping down the car and through the work of skilled craftsman – even Morgan concede bodies need attention every five years. The archaic sliding pillar front suspension, like the passengers, wear out quickly but the engines are generally trouble-free. The Rover V8 3528cc engine was employed 1968-76, followed by the SDI to 1987; the SDI Vitesse was used from 1983-1990 – then came the big change, to the Range Rover 3946cc V8.

Men with enough time; the detailed final checks of every car add to the traditional wait for delivery of a new Morgan.

## PORSCHE 356
### THE EPITOME OF FINE DESIGN

### MANUFACTURER
# PORSCHE

Some of the world's acknowledged masterpieces depict humble subjects such as bowls of fruit or views from the window – the artistry is in translating such simplicity through personal vision. Dr Ferdinand Porsche and his son Ferry achieved that transformation when they took the essence of the VW Beetle – another brainchild of Herr Doktor, and created the Porsche 356. The very first prototype used a space frame chassis, three abreast seating, and a mid engine. However, when production began in 1949 they used the VW floorpan and chassis, its suspension, gearbox and a modified version of the 1131cc flat-four engine – under a breathtaking aerodynamic coupé body. Over the following 18 years, it matured from a humble 40hp to the latest 2.0 litre Carrera offering 130hp, and more class, in the author's opinon, than a garage of 911s. Various changes occurred, including the 1954 launch of the stripped-down Speedster, before the next key upgrade to the 1955 356A. These retained the initial jelly mould body style, but were mainly 1600s powered by the 60bhp or 75bhp engines, while the first Carrera appeared offering 125mph from a 1498cc twin cam engine. The A was replaced by the 356B model in 1960 with higher bumpers, changed headlights, improved rear seating, larger brakes and rear window, but the same engine options until the Super 90 version which boasted 115mph. The Carrera 2 followed in 1962 boasting disc braking and a 130bhp powerplant. Two years later, the final incarnation was the 356C using the 1582cc engine, except for the 356SC which raised the output to 95bhp – the fastest standard 354. The last Carrera, the 2000GS, was by then yielding an impressive 130bhp. Maturing the modest VW concept to a high performance sports car took great technical skill given the engine's position. It took a lack of foresight to then nurture the same problems with the 911. The 356 dash layout is supremely functional, even pure, while the gear lever movement is a precision tool compared to the heavy and notchy 911s. Porsche lived just long enough to see what a true masterpiece he had created.

| Cost (356C) | £18,500 |
|---|---|
| % swing | 31 |
| Spares | ★★★★ |
| V.F.M. | ★★★★ |
| S.R. | ★★★★★ |

### SPECIFICATIONS

**ENGINE:** 1100cc – 1300cc – 1500cc – 1600cc – 2000cc
**BHP:** 40 – 130
**FUEL:** 35mpg
**GEARBOX:** 4 speed
**SPEED:** 84 – 125mph
**BRAKES:** Drum; Discs on C range cars & Carrera
**SUSPENSION:** Ind transverse torsion bars, swing axle
**BODIES:** 2 seater coupé, roadster, speedster, hard top
**YEARS:** 1949 – 65
**PRODUCTION:** 76,303 (all types)

## MODEL GUIDE

**PORSCHE 356** 1949–55
*Three engines sizes, split screen, original body style.*

| | |
|---|---|
| 1100 | 1086cc |
| 1300 | 1286cc |
| 1300 Super | 1290cc |
| 1300A | 1290cc |
| 1500 | 1488cc – Rise to 55/60bhp |
| 1500S | 1488cc – Rise to 70bhp |

**PORSCHE 356A** 1955–59
*Smaller engines now overhead valves – while Carrera is double overhead*

| | |
|---|---|
| 1300 | 1290cc |
| 1300 Super | 1290cc – Rise to 60bhp |
| 1600 | 1582cc |
| 1600 Super | 1582cc – Rise to 75bhp |
| Carrera | 1498cc |
| Carrera GT | 1498cc – Rise to 110bhp |
| Carrera 1600 | 1588cc |
| Carrera 1600GS | 1588cc – Rise to 115bhp |

**PORSCHE 356B** 1959–63
*Larger rear window, raised headlights, bumpers*

| | |
|---|---|
| 1600 | 1585cc – 60bhp |
| 1600 Super 75 | 1585cc – Rise to 75bhp |
| 1600 Super 90 | 1582cc |
| Carrera 1600GT | 1588cc |
| Carrera 2 2000 GS | 1966cc |

**PORSCHE 356C** 1963–65
*Fastest standard 356 plus all round disc brakes*

| | |
|---|---|
| 1600 | 1582cc |
| 1600SC | 1582cc – Rise to 95bhp |
| Carrera II 2000 GS | 1966cc – Rise to 130bhp |

## RELATIONS

Apart from the original body styling, all the basic ingredients stemmed from the VW Beetle. It bred over 20 body variants and was followed by the conveyor belt of 911s.

## BEST BUY

The car's addictive but be respectful of its handling. Excluding followers of the more specialist Carrera, Speedsters and the rare early 356s, there are three groups of enthusiasts: purists revere As, lovers of early style but more power like the Bs, while the refined C is the best all-rounder. (The subtle changes through the years make for great obsessional dating: the rear licence plate light went <u>underneath</u> in mid 1957!) Suspension and steering wear need watching, although the engine is long lasting. Rust is the traditional enemy, as are badly repaired cars. Buy from specialists or better still through the club and benefit from their knowledge of this great car.

*The 'Continental' script was added to some coupés and cabriolets in 1955.*

**COMPETITION CLASSIC**

## CATERHAM 7
### THE PERFECT START

MANUFACTURER
# CATERHAM CARS

The central flaw to competing for enjoyment, is that it means risking a cherished classic you've just spent years and too much money restoring. The alternative is to be rather more committed and invest in an outright competition machine. Colin Chapman's basic 1953 Mark 6 was a development of his early rough and ready trials models and provided a unique solution to the problem. With tax concessions favouring kit cars, he launched his street version – the famed Lotus Seven – with the Ford 100E engine in a lightweight tubular steel framed two seater. Using various engines it flew, and was loved on and off the race track, but full-blooded competition cars, and his desire for sports car recognition, reduced Lotus' commitment to virtually nil. Their London sales agent Graham Nearn thought differently, however, and bought the manufacturing rights in order to expand the interest. Caterham Cars have shone in the task, continually refining and improving the cars mechanically without spoiling the traditional appearance. Lotus Sevens officially ran from 1957 to 1973, with Caterham then progressively improving models, introducing engines such as the JPE, which achieved a world record for production cars with 0–60 in 3.44 seconds. One mark race series were introduced and complete packages of car kit for road or track, includ-

ing race harness, fire equipment, everything. You are 70 hours' construction work from pure adrenaline. They're low, and fast, with pin-point precision handling and offer that overwhelming confidence of new machinery. A very rare instant of a true classic – with full pedigree, unspoilt lines and modern equipment.

## RELATIONS

Pure breeding line back to that 1953 Lotus 6 with long list of engine suppliers.

## BEST BUY

A period Lotus VI or Seven will have been kit-built and well used, so only buy if you can service and restore. Caterham continued the Lotus S4 briefly until reviving the previous classic – the S3 – which remains their production model. Unless you want a workshop exercise, simply buy new with all Mr Nearn's brilliant aids such as finance link-ups, and race starter packs, even Rent-a-Seven with refund if you go on to buy. Go.on, 2-litre 7HPC, 130mph …

| | |
|---|---|
| Spares | ★★★★ |
| V.F.M. | ★★ |
| S.R. | ★★★ |

## SPECIFICATIONS

| | |
|---|---|
| **ENGINE:** 1397cc | **SPEED:** 112mph |
| **BHP:** 103 | **BRAKES:** Disc |
| **FUEL:** 40mpg | **BODIES:** Two seater sports |
| **GEARBOX:** 5 speed | **YEARS:** 1973 – to date |
| **SUSPENSION:** Ind coil/wishbone – coil/radius arms | **PRODUCTION:** Current |

## MANUFACTURER
# JOHN COOPER

**COOPER 500**

THE ORIGINAL BEGINNER'S FORMULA

During the Second World War there was much talk about creating a new street level of competition and this bred many informal events. A group of West Country enthusiasts pressed on further and presented a set of rules for an official formula – Formula 500. These allowed up to 500cc, one gallon of fuel, four wheel braking, a handbrake and optional bodywork. Initial examples were powered by JAP and Vincent engines, and among the first enthusiasts was John Cooper, whose car took just five weeks to build. Gradually the 500 Club grew, with Cooper's machines gaining dominance. The 1948 British Grand Prix incorporated a 500 support race with 26 entrants. Europe followed, and such growth required sanctioning by the governing bodies, new rules and the status of F3. A motor racing version of go-karts the open cockpits and lightweight bodies (min. 500lbs) made their epic duels very appealing to watch and the cars very tempting to own. Many great drivers ventured up through this formula, and even the godfather of present-day Grand Prixs, Bernie Ecclestone, became an owner. Cooper's dominance continued, but always there was the search to improve, with engineer Francis Beart creating his own version of the 1953 Cooper VIII with differing handling and body profile. Racing grew in cost and status over the remainder of that decade before being squeezed out by the birth of Formula Junior. With the overall growth in historic racing there is renewed interest in any single seater, and while the numbers of cars are now reduced, prices are still held down until race classifications provide a competitive class

structure. I was invited to Goodwood to enjoy rare time with the newly restored and unique Beart VIIA special (above) recently bought by a knowledgable Peter Altenbach whose next task is to replace the current JAP engine with an original Norton. It's extraordinarily small and fragile looking, but actually beautifully light and responsive with braking to tempt you ever deeper into corners. Stirling Moss remembers his eight Beart car wins in 1954 and anyone who has ever watched 500s racing knows just how much excitement they generate.

## RELATIONS

The formula's essence was anything goes, though inevitably they used motorcycle engines.

## BEST BUY

Brilliant progression from motor bikes or small DIY restoration. Present absence of competitive race class helps prices and less threatening hill climbs always available as economical christening – exactly where the formula came in.

### SPECIFICATIONS

| | |
|---|---|
| **ENGINE:** 498cc | **SUSPENSION:** Transverse leaf |
| **BHP:** 75 | **SPEED:** 95mph |
| **FUEL:** 15mpg (Methanol) | **BODIES:** Single seater |
| **GEARBOX:** 4 speed | **YEARS:** 1953 |
| **BRAKES:** Drum | **PRODUCTION:** NA |

| | |
|---|---|
| Spares | ★★★ |
| V.F.M. | ★★★★ |
| S.R. | ★★★ |

## MANUFACTURER
# LAMBORGHINI

The 1960s fashion for 2+2 seating caused manufacturers many headaches trying to adapt existing two seat sports cars to fit the famous pair of legless midgets. The rather sad sight of misshaped cars such as the E Type Jaguar 2 + 2 struggling to maintain original 2 seater imagery, has helped to cast a shadow over the concept. Lamborghini, however, managed to achieve a stunning 2 + 2 model. Indeed the Espada eventually turned into the second best selling Lamborghini of all time – behind the famed Countach. The original plan was to base the car upon the spectacular transverse-engined Miura and a Bertone prototype, called the Marzel, was displayed at the 1967 Geneva Motor Show. Space was created by halving the Miura's V12 and using large gullwinged doors. The car proved too heavy and too slow, and a semi monocoque design was used instead. Most of the mechanical parts came from the Lamborghini Islero, itself a development of the 400GT. This included their glorious V12 which must be one of the motoring world's finest engines.

Many of the prototype Marzel ideas were incorporated in the stunning 1968 Espada which turned heads around the world. I still remember my first sight of one, particularly from that overhead view. It looked long but was actually just four inches longer than other Lamborghinis and virtually the same as the present Honda Accord. It was wide, however, at just over 6 ft and extremely low, all exaggerating the feeling of interior space. Four leather bucket seats, extraordinary visibility, and good luggage space were complemented by a long list of items such as power

steering, optional automatic, air conditioning. The engine revs into the gods, creating sounds from an enthusiast's dreams and is silky smooth – all the way beyond 150mph. It underlined just how clumsy others were at approaching that 2 + 2 market.

## RELATIONS

Earlier front-engined Lamborghini V12 engines and mechanics married to the development of Bertone's Marzel prototype.

## BEST BUY

Well treated engines and gearboxes last well and all too common oil leaks actually preserve the chassis. Traditional Italian rust is a big worry so take an expert with you and steer clear of troublesome automatics. Good brightwork is valuable. Series I – III saw improving interior and power. Few true supercars will ever combine practical space, powerful, forgiving engines and awesome good looks as successfully as the Espada.

| Cost | £20,500 |
|------|---------|
| % swing | -6 |
| Spares | ★★ |
| V.F.M. | ★★ |
| S.R. | ★★★ |

### SPECIFICATIONS

| | |
|---|---|
| **ENGINE:** 3929cc | **BRAKES:** Disc |
| **BHP:** 325 – 350 | **SPEED:** 155–160mph |
| **FUEL:** 14–16mpg | **BODIES:** 2 door, 4 seater coupé. |
| **GEARBOX:** 5 speed | |
| **SUSPENSION:** Ind wishbone & coil all round | **YEARS:** 1968– 78 |
| | **PRODUCTION:** 1217 |

# MANUFACTURER
# FERRARI

Enter the world of fantasy, the mythological state of Ferrari ownership, if not the possession of the 308 specifically. Period Italian cars rust furiously, quality varies widely, spares are expensive, and the existence of a great competition past is no guarantee of anything except status. Did the MG's sporting heritage bias your MG 1100 purchase, the troublesome Alfetta appear wise because of their legendary GP cars? If you are investing good money try balancing logic with your heartbeat. Ironically, the 308GT4 is interesting because its 1973 body styling followed fashion not tradition. The net result is the least-loved production Ferrari and consequently one of the very best for value. There is no doubt this solitary Bertone/Ferrari adventure lacked the visual grace and romance of Pininfarina cars, but the decision ought to be seen in context. The wedge form and slabbed panels were forward-thinking then – think of the fashionable Fiat X1/9 ('72), or Lotus Esprit ('76); with a brand new V8 engine Ferrari were looking to the future. The car itself followed in the shadow of the Dino 246 which was losing ground to the new US emission laws, but used its multi–tubed chassis, transverse mounted mid-ships engine position, and similar all independent suspension. The 308GT4 was badged as a Dino, although its 155mph performance truthfully lifted it above second division Ferrari status. Poor American reaction to the car led to Ferrari badges being added and by 1978 these were factory-fitted on all cars. The important change was the new all aluminium 255bhp, 3 litre, quad cam engine, actually a descendant of the 1964 Grand Prix Ferrari 158

which gave John Surtees the World Championship. Brilliantly flexible, this gem of an engine can pull in 5th from 25mph yet take 6.9 seconds to propel you from 0–60 in anger. It also used toothed cam belts rather than traditional chains, thereby reducing engine noise. It has a functional period dashboard, but the plus two seating has the standard limitations of the genre, and some customers had the area carpeted for additional storage.

## RELATIONS

Ex-F1 engine, original Bertone bodywork, many other elements from the Dino 246.

## BEST BUY

Always remember it's just a 1970s Italian car with huge rust potential, poor wiring and perhaps an abused engine. The difference isn't the badge – it's the restoration bills. If you find a decent one, then it's undoubtedly the perfect first Ferrari, excellent value and virtually a supercar mechanical package.

### SPECIFICATIONS

| | |
|---|---|
| **ENGINE:** 2926cc | **SUSPENSION:** Ind wishbone/ |
| **BHP:** 255 | coil – all round |
| **FUEL:** 19mpg | **BODIES:** 2 door coupé |
| **GEARBOX:** 5 speed | **YEARS:** 1973 – 80 |
| **BRAKES:** Disc | **PRODUCTION:** 2,826 |
| **SPEED:** 154mph | |

| Cost | £20,000 |
|---|---|
| % swing | 20 |
| Spares | ★ |
| V.F.M. | ★★★ |
| S.R. | ★★ |

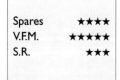

## CELICA GT
### WELL-HEELED GOOD LOOKS

### MANUFACTURER
# TOYOTA

As rivals jostle for position in the newly revitalized sporting market, Toyota have quietly built up a coupé tradition with the Celica. While other cars, such as Honda's CRX and Prelude, started out looking great and were re-designed into pale shadows of their former selves, Toyota have gone from strength to strength. The essence is a straightforward 2+2 configuration with a front wheel drive 2.0 litre engine. It seems unexceptional until you start to appreciate that it feels comfortable, safe, has a good boot, impressive storage with the back seats down, offers over 30mpg, a 60,000 mile warranty, and even child-proof locks. Much the same as your car? Well, the Celica also won the World Rally Championship twice, took victory in the 1996 RAC Rally, (one of 83 wins in 1996 alone) was '*What Car* Sports Coupé of the Year' twice and has been offered with 1.8, 2.0, 2.0 Turbo engines in coupé, convertible and four-wheel drive forms.

Toyota's reliability is enviable, and it's hard not to like a car that can take you to 137mph in relative haste, absorb so much luggage and still look so good. It's not until you actually hand wash one that you fully appreciate how virtually every inch of this pretty bodywork slopes and curves. It looks more expensive and more exotic than it is, which, combined with practical values, turns it into a favourite. (Though the GT-Four, 239bhp@6000rpm and 152mph is pretty exotic; while still providing 37.7 mpg at 56mph.) More than 25 years of development have created a car of rare versatility.

The 2.0 GT does not have the initial sparking acceleration of the 4WD and Turbo, but 0-60 is achieved in a useful 7.9 seconds, and its cruising performance is both comfortable and quick. Finely built, well respected in sport and on the road, the current Celica is proof that international manufacturers can still deliver an affordable car to be proud of.

## RELATIONS

The car developed through six generations with initial 1970 versions sharing much with the Carina under a new notchback body. The 1985 edition introduced the 16 valve twin cam engine, increasing performance and handling. In 1988 the then 140mph GT–Four paved the way for the competition cars.

## BEST BUY

Apparently more Celicas have been made than Ford Escorts, so the choice is enormous. Practical, hard wearing interiors and good body build ensure longevity, though the smaller 1800cc engines may have worked hard. A 2.0 GT with a service record is a dependable choice.

### SPECIFICATIONS

| | |
|---|---|
| **ENGINE:** 1998cc | **SUSPENSION:** MacPherson strut and coils |
| **BHP:** 168bhp | |
| **FUEL:** 31mpg | **BODIES:** 2 door 2+2 coupé; convertible |
| **GEARBOX:** 5 speed | |
| **BRAKES:** Disc | **YEARS:** 1993–current |
| **SPEED:** 134–137mph | **PRODUCTION:** N/A |

| | |
|---|---|
| Spares | ★★★★ |
| V.F.M. | ★★★★★ |
| S.R. | ★★★ |

# MANUFACTURER
# FERRARI

We tend to think that the great marques, like movie stars, are immune from everyday commercial pressures, but this is not so. Rivals such as Aston Martin and Lamborghini secured good market shares of the 1960s GT trade, and Ferrari needed a seductive 2 + 2 to regain lost ground. In 1967 their 365GT 2 + 2 was launched at the Paris Motor Show and boasted fully independent suspension and considerable attention to interior silence and comfort. Sales were encouraging, although few reached the USA, and in 1972 it was followed by the four cam 356GT4 2 + 2 which was longer, wider and luxuriously appointed. By now Fiat had invested in Ferrari, easing design and production finances, but rival +2 cars such as the Espada and Maserati's Indy had joined the battle. Ferrari retaliated in 1976 by launching a further improved version of the 356GT4 called the 400GT with striking new bodystyling by Pininfarina successfully slimming a necessarily large Ferrari. Among the more controversial features was the American Cadillac automatic gearbox – an unthinkable addition in the minds of many purists. The fact four seat executive expresses were ideal candidates for such equipment and the fact that both Rolls Royce and Jaguar were using the box all missed the traditionalists. However, it sold surprisingly well, and in 1979 it became the 400i with the inclusion of Bosch fuel injection Revisions in 1982 improved the interior, power, self levelling rear suspension and even provided dual air conditioning – all added attractions to this 150mph dream. Finally, in 1985 it went to 4943cc, received another interior refit and a greater

luggage area as the 412. Although purists consider it unloved, the +2 range was actually the longest Ferrari production run, ending in 1989.

## RELATIONS

It started with the 1964 500 Superfast, through the 365GT 2 + 2, the 365GTC/4 and the 365GT4 2 + 2 – the actual 400 range, like all the others, was Pininfarina-designed. The engine was the classic 60 degree V12 which powered all their masterpieces and optional automatic was from the Cadillac.

## BEST BUY

Most examples have either found appreciative homes or are unloved, bargain Ferraris on some non-specialist forecourt. Don't even think about them, as restoration is painfully expensive. Contact a recognised Ferrari dealer or the excellent owners club and take your time. While some Ferraris belong on posters this is really usable – though its one disgrace is fuel consumption of around 10mpg.

---

### SPECIFICATIONS

| | |
|---|---|
| **ENGINE:** 4,23cc; 4943cc | **SUSPENSION:** Ind A arm/coil all round |
| **BHP:** 315 – 340 | **SPEED:** 150mph |
| **FUEL:** 9 – 12mpg | **BODIES:** 2 door, 4 seat coupé |
| **GEARBOX:** 5 speed manual & 3 speed automatic | **YEARS:** 1976 – 89 |
| **BRAKES:** Discs | **PRODUCTION:** 2,386 |

| | |
|---|---|
| Cost | £19,500 |
| % swing | -11 |
| Spares | ★★ |
| V.F.M. | ★★ |
| S.R. | ★★ |

## AUSTIN HEALEY 3000
### MOST PEOPLE'S DREAM

MkI BN7 59-61 2,825

MkI BT7 59-61 10,825

MkII BN7 61-62 355

MkII BT7 61-62 5,095

MkIIA BT7 ,

(conv) 62-63 6,113

MkIII BJ8 63-64 1,390

MkIII BJ8 64-67 6,322

BN7 = 2 seater, BT8 = 2+2

Total production: 42,925

| Cost | £21,000 |
| --- | --- |
| (Mk III) | |
| % swing | 18 |
| Spares | ★★ |
| V.F.M. | ★★★ |
| S.R. | ★★★★ |

### MANUFACTURER
# BMC

There is a mythological status surrounding this car and it is hard to rationalise. It's just 7bhp more powerful than the 100/6, and uses the very same body. Yet there's no denying that owning a 100/6 would be good, but owning a Healey 3000 is most people's dream. Perhaps the car's popularity is the perfect example of an endorsement of a manufacturer's investment in motor sport. It should also be said that as the model increased in power and sophistication, so it also fell more and more out of step with modern designs such as the E-Type or TR4. It became the last of the powerful cars requiring mastery.

The 1952 London Motor Show launch of the 100/4, and the commercial union between its creator Donald Healey and Austin, led to enormous success – the 100/4 is itself a brilliant classic. In 1956 the Healey 100/6 used the 6-cylinder BMC C engine, leading in March 1959 to the enlarged 2912cc 3000 model which boasted front discs, a fresh badge and a lift of just 3mph. April 1961 saw a brief Mk II moving to 132bhp with triple SU carbs behind a revised grille, followed in February 1962 by a Mk IIA returning to less temperamental twin carburation. This was the new 'convertible' model with a fold-away soft top, curved screen, quarter lights and wind-up windows; with this car the 2+2 configuration became the only model available. The final Mk III arrived in November 1963 with a fresh full width wooden dash and a further lift to 148bhp. The last Phase II version from May 1964 until production ended in 1968, had a re-designed rear suspension. The development may be prosaic, but a good 3000

### SPECIFICATIONS

**ENGINE:** 2912cc
**BHP:** 124–148bhp
**FUEL:** 20mpg
**GEARBOX:** 4 speed
**BRAKES:** Disc/drum
**SPEED:** 112–121mph
**SUSPENSION:** Ind coil, wishbone / live axle, half-elliptic leaf, Panhard rod
**BODIES:** 2 door sports, 2+2 sports
**YEARS:** 1959–1968
**PRODUCTION:** 42,925

really is something to treasure. More than that, it really is as good to drive as in your dreams.

## RELATIONS

The engine has its roots in the ill-fated 1949 Austin Atlantic, while the design and bodywork is actually the same as the previous Healey 100s. Successes in motor sport bred suitable improvements, and items such as disc brakes were needed to compete with opposition from the likes of the TRs.

## BEST BUY

These cars may be high on your wish list, but mid-value ones with concealed rust mean a re-build not just repair – this can be very costly. The Mk II (BN7/BT7) triple SUs offered urgency and continual tuning attention, while the late Mk IIIs (BJ8 – Phase II) provided maximum power and GT amenities. The market prices show these last Healeys posting the best gains over the last three years.

# MANUFACTURER
# VOLVO

**SOMETHING SPECIAL**

# VOLVO T5 ESTATE

It is a mistake to assume that only the bright and shiny sports models become loved. Three of the leading post-war classics are the MGB, the ubiquitous Mini and the Morris Minor, none of which were actually head-turners. The Minor estate served families loyally, and the modern-day Volvo estate is very much its contemporary equivalent. It has an unrivalled reputation for reliability and safety, and though it is not glamorous, nor was the Minor Traveller.

Earlier Volvos estates generated little excitement, and the latest V versions are beginning to slip away from the classic signature bodyshape. However, the 850 T5 perfectly mixes domestic values with impressive performance figures. It's not just 145mph speeds or the acreage of storage space, but hundreds of tiny details which have matured this car into something special. It's the little weather cover over the tailgate lock, the shaped carpet protector exactly where your right sole rubs the wheel arch, the warnings if the rear seat hasn't latched back fully. The ergonomics are brilliant, and even when new to the car all the controls fall to hand. Its rigidity and silence on the road masks the phenomenal cruising speeds, and the sophisticated Delta link rear suspension deals not only with enormous loads but smooths out the FWD characteristics.

It is a car of enormous versatility, and after a serious drive you realize it is tough to find an equal.

## RELATIONS

The continuous evolution of Volvo allows you to trace its lineage back more than 40 years to their first PV445 Duett which used a strong box frame and was even offered in a twin carburettor Sports version. 90,000 of those Duetts led to 73,000 Amazon estates, then to 270,000 145s and 959,151 245s before this impressive 850 was unveiled in 1991.

## BEST BUY

The first cars were GLTs, 20 valve five-cylinder models with a stiff chassis; the GLE was the slightly less sporting version with 10 valves and a gentler suspension set-up. By the end there were 2.0 10 valve, 2.5 10 valve, 2.5 20 valve, a Turbo Diesel, the T5, an 850AWD (all-wheel drive) and the seriously quick 850R – all engines transverse-mounted and FWD. The standard 850s hold values well, and the 2.5 10 valve offers the best torque and economy, though the T5 is highly desirable. They are heavy on tyres; and check suspension and gears if a towbar is or was fitted. The Estate outsells the saloon 2 to 1 – either are worth consideration.

## SPECIFICATIONS

| | |
|---|---|
| **ENGINE:** 2319cc Turbo | asymmetric shockers/Delta link, trailing arms |
| **BHP:** 225bhp | **SPEED:** 143–149mph |
| **FUEL:** 29.5mpg | **BODIES:** 4 door saloon: 5 door estate |
| **GEARBOX:** 5 speed: automatic | **YEARS:** 1992–1997 |
| **BRAKES:** Disc | **PRODUCTION:** 59,228 |
| **SUSPENSION:** Struts, | |

| | |
|---|---|
| Spares | ★★★★★ |
| V.F.M. | ★★★★ |
| S.R. | ★★★★ |

# AUSTIN-HEALEY 100/4
## A SLICE OF MOTORING HISTORY

**MANUFACTURER**
# AUSTIN-HEALEY

The Austin-Healey 100/4 is the epitome of a classic sports car, although its evolution owed much to chance. Donald Healey built sporting cars with Riley engines but knew they were due to be phased out. He also knew that there was a gap in the market, particularly the American market, with a niche between the Jaguar XK 120 and the MG waiting to be filled. Healey wanted to produce the first 100mph car that was affordable by the average motorist. His friend Leonard Lord, chairman of Austin, had produced a failure, the Austin Atlantic, and was left with an underused factory and components. That engine started life as a pre–war six cylinder range for light trucks, and re–appeared as a four cylinder for the Champ Jeep, before being enlarged for the abortive Atlantic. Donald Healey, his son Geoff and Barrie Bilbie worked secretly from home, combining new car ideas and the spare Austin engine. Healey insisted that the the frame had to be as rigid as possible, and the car had excellent roadholding for its time. The chief design problem was in building a car light enough to perform well, but strong enough to cope with the heavy mechanical components inherited from the Atlantic. Just two chassis and a single car

were in existence as the 1952 Earls Court International Motor Show approached, and the one car was so late being finished it missed the pre-publicity. However, it was an instant success. The New York Motor Show voted it Car of the Year, the Miami World's Fair gave it the Grand Premier Award, and over 3000 orders swamped their modest factory. An astute Leonard Lord stepped in and it became the Austin-Healey – the rest as they say is history. Lord's intervention instantly cut the car's price by £50 as a consequence of mass-production. In 1954 Healey developed 50 lightweight competition versions called the 100S (Sebring), and within a month the first examples scored a 1–2–3 in a Sebring Series littered with D Type Jaguars and Ferraris. The 100M (Le Mans) followed, with a modified engine, suspension and a louvred bonnet which maintained the sporting imagination until the BMC Competition department grasped the Healey 3000. The initial 100/4 examples were designated BN1, switching to BN2 in 1955 with the change to a four speed A90 Westminster box. In 1956 the six cylinder Westminster engine replacement became the BN4.

| Cost | £20,000 |
| --- | --- |
| % swing | 12 |
| Spares | ★★★★ |
| V.F.M. | ★★ |
| S.R. | ★★★ |

## SPECIFICATIONS

| | |
| --- | --- |
| **ENGINE:** 2660cc | **SUSPENSION:** Ind wishbone/ |
| **BHP:** 90 | coil – Live axle/half elliptic |
| **FUEL:** 25mpg | **SPEED:** 102mph |
| **GEARBOX:** 3 speed + O/D | **BODIES:** 2 door sports |
| on 2nd/3rd: 4 Speed | **YEARS:** 1952 – 1956 |
| **BRAKES:** Drum | **PRODUCTION:** 14,012 |

This car was slower, heavier, a 2 + 2 and not popular – so BMC reverted to two seats, a power increase
and BN6 status.

The car I tried was Peter Banham's beautifully prepared Historic Rally 100/4 with S specifications, (this
page and below left) although a partially opened bonnet dispersed the engine's incredible heat rather than
the S's louvres. Driving such a classic is the height of
motoring pleasure: the car drives beautifully and
looks terrific..The engine torque is so great that virtually everything can be achieved in top gear. Change
down, floor the throttle, and it stirs the latent beast
in both car and driver. Healey's initial aim was to
produce 'a very fast everyday car with genuine sporting characteristics, capable of 100mph, which would
also be exceptionally cheap and easy to maintain'; he
succeeded on every count.

## RELATIONS

Original Healey bodywork, Austin Atlantic engine
with the Westminster gearbox and the famed Healey
3000s to follow from 1959.

## BEST BUY

Solid and well built, with long lasting mechanical
parts, the main problem is rust generally around the
floors and chassis areas. Replacement panels are
tricky and any serious restoration work is likely to
requiring expert hands. However, good ones last and
last while giving enormous pleasure to driver and
admirers. Watch out for claims of S or M Types –
there are many conversions. The early BN1s are
excellent value.

# AC ACE

## THE PUREST OF SPORTS CARS

### MANUFACTURER
# AC CARS

*One of our panel of 'Car of the Year' judges, (above) Simon Taylor in his long-nosed Ace 2.6.*

'The Great British Sportscar' is a phrase grossly overused by all the leading magazines. We are, however, blessed with both our pre-and post-war sports car legacies – the Morgans, Healeys, the value-for-money Jaguars and yet, for me, the purest celebration of the British sports car is the 1950s AC Ace. It may have grown up into a rough and ready supercar thanks to Carol Shelby, but the initial Ace captured a sense of agility, with its long sloping bonnet and haunched rear quarters, all the classic signals of a true sports car within a body of supreme grace. With the lowered nose of the 1961 Ford-powered version, the Ace was truly beautiful. However, a new AC was needed as both AC's boss, William Hurlock and the Buckland Tourer were nearing retirement. Next door to the body shop, a young racing engineer, John Tojeiro, was preparing cars which were regular winners in British sports car racing. One customer had commis-

sioned a two seater body based upon the 1949 Ferrari 166 Barchetta, and he was persuaded to show this example to AC who fell in love, bought the car and the licence to manufacture. Tojeiro immediately built the first example for the 1953 London Motor Show – using the 40-year-old AC two-litre engine. Reactions were excellent – the rare all-independent suspension and fine handing were thanks to Tojeiro's competition experience, and a simple ladder-type chassis saved sufficient weight to allow a well trimmed interior. The production version appeared in mid-1954, with a subtly strengthened chassis and minor body modifications. With superb roadholding and handling, it set new standards at a time when no other British sports car had all-independent suspension. It weighed only 16.5 cwt and could easily top 100mph. Experts agreed that the car's compact yet powerful body looked even better than the Ferrari which had inspired it. As its status grew, it needed a new engine, and so AC began fitting the two-litre Bristol engine developed from the BMW 328. This eased racing developments and one race driver was

| Cost | £32300 |
|------|--------|
| % swing | -12 |
| Spares | ★★★ |
| V.F.M. | ★★ |
| S.R. | ★★★★ |

ACLAND & TABOR LTD.
WELWYN BY-PASS
HERTS.
Tel: WELWYN 481-2-3

**AC** BRISTOL

### A.C. "ACE BRISTOL" 2-Seater Sports

A.C. Cars Limited in co-operation with the Bristol Cars Limited offer the well-known 6-cylinder Bristol Engine, complete with Gearbox as an optional extra both in the Ace and Aceca Chassis.

A.C. CARS LTD                    SURREY
THAMES DITTON                    ENGLAND

## SPECIFICATIONS

(Ace engine : Bristol engine : Ford engine)

**ENGINE:** 1991cc – 1971cc – 2553cc
**BHP:** 75; 125; 170
**FUEL:** 21–25mpg
**GEARBOX:** 4 speed
**BRAKES:** Drum: Front disc after 1957

**SUSPENSION:** Ind Transverse leaf/wishbone
**SPEED:** 103mph/ 120/ 130mph
**BODIES:** 2 door sports; coupés
**YEARS:** 1953–63 : 1956–63 : 1961–63
**PRODUCTION:** 223 : 463 : 37

Ken Rudd who drew the best from the Bristol unit, and then inspired the factory to install his tuned Ford Zephyr engine. Bristol switched production to an American V8 powerplant and AC turned to Rudd's idea thus creating the 2.6 litre Ace. Its short stroke permitted the lowering of the bonnet to the classic position, but very few of these supreme versions were made before Shelby squeezed in a 4.2 V8 and caused such excitement AC had to drop all cars to meet the Cobra demand.

## RELATIONS

The body was Ferrari-inspired, and initially the 1919 AC-designed 2 litre engine was used. A BMW-influenced Bristol engine followed, ending up with the 2.5 Ford Zephyr unit, before the Ace gave birth to the powerful V8 Cobras.

## BEST BUY

Styling remained constant, front discs came after 1957, and the last cars had the lowered noses; but the real deciding factor is the engine. The AC unit is desirable, the Bristol eager to work hard, while the fastest, the Ford, naturally has spares more readily

available. Coupé bodies were called Aceca and if you're tempted, a quarter of the Aces produced were right hand drive. Despite the age of the cars, many have only passed through a few owners, production numbers were so low, and most are known – so use the club or specialists to check histories.

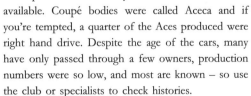

*The traditional single cam six (above) was fitted to 223 of the Aces. Tony Bancroft's car, (left) with 1950s competition modifications – short exhaust, bonnet air scoop and wing vents – has the Bristol engine.*

**MANUFACTURER**

# BRISTOL

*Pace* SAAB, aerospace engineering works to tolerances beyond any mass production car's dreams; but the Bristol has a genuine aerospace background. In 1945 the Bristol Aeroplane Co. tried to retain their workforce and use redundant hangar space by building cars. The 1947 Bristol 400 was based upon the pre–war BMW 328. An airfield for testing and a private wind tunnel aided development, and in 1949 the 401 appeared, mechanically the same, but with a new lightweight alloy streamlined body, tube framing and little superfluous trim. Beautifully built, the 402 convertible version appeared later in the same year, followed in 1953 by the 403 looking much the same, but with increased power, braking and a new gearbox. The series became heavier with the four-door 405 and again with the 406 which used additional bhp to maintain pride. After this the Bristol range moved to the big 250bhp Chrysler V8 and the custom-built tourer reputation was established. However, between 1953 and 1955, Bristol's spirit of adventure led them to cut the wheelbase from 9ft 6in to 8ft and build a beautiful aluminium two-door body over an ash frame, incor-

porating a one-piece bonnet and a nose deliberately inspired by the Brabazon aircraft. The 404 was introduced at the '53 London Motor Show. This was Bristol's answer to the DB4GT six years before Aston produced it. With two true seats, a sloping roofline, and tiny tail fins, it was capable of 110mph in considerable luxury. It was powered by their excellent two litre engine with triple carbs and a delightful gearbox, and every part was manufactured by Bristol. This is a connoisseur's classic, rare, and finely made.

## RELATIONS

The initial 400 was basically a rebodied 328 BMW, developing through to the 406 before turning to V8 Chrysler power from 407 to present day.

## BEST BUY

Body rust is not a huge problem, although the concealed ash frame members need checking for rot. The chassis is hardy, and most aspects are reliable. Bristol know about most cars, and are very approachable.

| Cost | £28,500 |
|------|---------|
| % swing | -6 |
| Spares | ★★★★ |
| V.F.M. | ★★ |
| S.R. | ★★★ |

### SPECIFICATIONS

| | |
|---|---|
| **ENGINE:** 1971cc | **SUSPENSION:** Ind Transerse |
| **BHP:** 105 – 125 | leaf – Torsion Bar/Live axlel |
| **FUEL:** 20 – 25mpg | **BODIES:** 2 seater coupé |
| **GEARBOX:** 4 speed | **YEARS:** 1953 – 55 |
| **BRAKES:** Drum | **PRODUCTION:** 52 (disputed) |
| **SPEED:** 105mph – 110mph | |

# MANUFACTURER
# FERRARI

It turns heads, quickens hearts, prompts dreams and desires just outside your reach – well maybe. You sit in traffic staring down the bonnet of your Merc diesel estate and flirt with a straight swap for one of these stunning scarlet machines. The 308 GTB was in some ways inferior to the technically similar 308GT4, but the seduction of the near perfect Pininfarina body fuses with Ferrari legend. A Porsche is sold to us through advertising and style makers – Ferrari really is different, for when did you last see them advertising in your colour supplement?. They've made their business competition and sporting cars and they simply rely upon you climbing into a Ferrari cockpit and absorbing the decades of experience. The 308 has impeccable handling, responsive controls without ever feeling flimsy. The four cam alloy engine doesn't howl like some, but you know it's working and when you floor the pedal and grab the gear lever and the car feels ready for anything. The car was launched in 1975 in the shadow of the poorly received Bertone-bodied GT4, but the new version was immediately praised for its stunning bodywork. So critical is the combination of implied power and grace that the same car's two bodies caused completely different reactions.. The 308 GTB was joined two years later by a Targa topped GTS primarily to please the appreciative American market. The four Weber carbs were replaced by Bosch fuel injection between 1980–82, losing performance but in 1982 a four valve per cylinder 308GTB Qv model restored reputations with its 240bhp. An upgraded GTB/GTS – the 328, appeared for four years before Ferrari

moved on. These are Ferraris to dream about; beaten up or unloved examples are affordable, but if you are ever going to give yourself that prancing horse key ring – this is the car.

## RELATIONS

Spiritual descendant of the loved 248 Dino, and actual development of the 1973 Bertoned bodied 2 + 2 308 GT4. Matured into the 328 and then the V8 was used in the extremely rare and exciting 288GTO

## BEST BUY

Fibreglass bodies were used in the first year – 150 for the UK. The 308 was in production for an entire decade, although there are only 2000 right hand drive cars. Avoid the fuel injection version and the Targa GTS are 20 per cent more expensive. Naturally there's rust and other important points, but really it's about budgets. Get experienced help and always, always remember the most important asset is a good service history.

## SPECIFICATIONS

**ENGINE:** 2926cc
**BHP:** 240 – 255
**FUEL:** 20mpg
**GEARBOX:** 5 speed
**BRAKES:** Disc
**SPEED:** 154mph

**SUSPENSION:** Ind double wishbone coil all round
**BODIES:** 2 door coupé; targa
**YEARS:** 1975 – 1985
**PRODUCTION:** 19,555

| Cost | £26,500 |
| --- | --- |
| % swing | -5 |
| Spares | ★★ |
| V.F.M. | ★★ |
| S.R. | ★★★★ |

# JAGUAR V12 E-TYPE
## COMFORT AND PEDIGREE

## MANUFACTURER
# JAGUAR

The impact of the 1961 E-Type at the Geneva Motor show is hard to over-estimate. I was at art school and we all sat around in the common room just staring at the magazine pictures – it was stunning and probably fired more dreams than any other post-war car. An impressive competition tradition with the C- and D-Types, and a near-exhausted era of XK sports cars inevitably set the stage for something new, but the brilliance of the concept leant heavily upon an aviation man, Malcolm Sayer, who was inclined to sketch design ideas onto anything – even the walls. The monocoque construction of the D-Type was a starting point, while the need for increased power was resolved by the inspired decision to use the excellent V12 engine from the still-born prototype competition XJ13. Sayer's aircraft background drove his interest in aerodynamics and he was even known to stop en route to the MIRA test track to buy sticky tape and balls of wool to study wind movement from a tandem car. Thus the sleek E-Type cut through the air – urged forward by the 272bhp V12 at speeds virtually twice most equivalently priced road cars. The initial 3.8 litre engine came from the XK150S with a

period Moss gearbox and narrow wheel tracks. It leaked, didn't stop, but was agile and sparse – it's the purist's dream machine. As the 4.2 Series II it became compromised and middle-aged as it tried to accommodate US regulations. A 9 inch extended wheelbase offered the 2 + 2 configuration. For some, the Series III V12 was the model's dotage, while for others it became the most desirable of them all. Everyone agreed that a serious hike in performance and prestige was needed and the V12 was shoehorned into the extended +2 wheelbase, along with wider wheels, flared wings, power steering, automatic option, and a visual meanness to match the 145mph performance. From the pure sports car Series I, it crawled through Series II to emerge as a stunning Grand Tourer. It broke a pre-war tradition by making an accredited 'real sports car' comfortable.

## RELATIONS

Spiritually born of the XK120, through C- and D-Types to the Series I E-Type, the V12 E-Type had a

### SPECIFICATIONS

| | |
|---|---|
| **ENGINE:** 5343cc | **SUSPENSION:** Ind wishbone/Torsion bar – Ind coil/wishbone |
| **BHP:** 272 | |
| **FUEL:** 16mpg | |
| **GEARBOX:** 4 speed | **BODIES:** 2 door 2 + 2 roadster: coupé |
| **BRAKES:** Disc | |
| **SPEED:** 146mph | **YEARS:** 1971 – 75 |
| | **PRODUCTION:** 15,290 |

| | |
|---|---|
| Cost | £38,500 |
| (V12 Roadster) | |
| % swing | 18 |
| | |
| Spares | ★★★★ |
| V.F.M. | ★★★ |
| S.R. | ★★★★★ |

The E-Type was introduced in March 1961, replacing the XK150 which had been in production since May 1957. It is easy to forget that both cars were similarly powered.

The V12 was a quantunm leap forward from the original 3.8 and 4.2. The four cam V12-engined racing XJ13 of 1966 was a technically advanced design scotched by BMC amalgamtion.; but it provided the 5.3-litre ohc power for the 1971 III Series E-Type (and the XJ12 saloon in the following year).

perfect pedigree, with body styling from the E2A prototype and a legacy for the XJ.

## BEST BUY

This is where the romance ends. Experts find diagnosing trouble within the complex body very hard, so don't even consider the solitary 'bargain' on a general dealer's forecourt. They probably look good, but opening the bonnet may reveal a can of mechanical worms. Use the strengths of the owners' club, or specialists such as XK Engineering who are ex–factory. Buy the best you can afford and remember coupés are cheaper than roadsters. All are expensive on fuel, parts and restoration, but owning a good one will make you feel pretty special.

# PORSCHE BOXSTER

THE MOST COMPLETE EXAMPLE OF A 90S SPORTS CAR

## MANUFACTURER

Porsche have been through some very strange times. Their engineering prowess has never been in doubt, nor their commitment to competition development, but for a very long time their instincts for marketing have failed them. It's true they sold motor cars, but they failed to deliver models to match the market-place. They just soldiered on with their ageing 911 – relentlessly adding bits to flatter the owners' pride. Launching a modest front-engined, water-cooled 924 was really the abduction of a planned Audi and pro-motional indecision left it floundering for a market position. The assault on the Supercar world with their 928 was the scheduled introduction of a replacement for the elderly 911, but its 'rapid armchair' image left it as a wannabee SL Mercedes. Only the front-engined 944 combined performance, great handling and some semblance of a fresh approach.

### SPECIFICATIONS

| | |
|---|---|
| **ENGINE:** 2480cc | **SUSPENSION:** MacPherson |
| **BHP:** 204bhp | strut, transverse arms |
| **FUEL:** 30mpg | and coils |
| **GEARBOX:** 5 speed | **BODIES:** 2 door sports: |
| automatic | hardtop |
| **BRAKES:** Disc | **YEARS:** 1996–current |
| **SPEED:** 149mph | **PRODUCTION:** N/A |

Unfortunately it suffered from the basic styling of the little ex-Audi models. So they plugged along for another decade or so with the ill-conceived, yet relentlessly improving, 911. The appearance of the Boxster concept at the 1993 Detroit Motor Show was therefore highly significant. However, three further years would then pass before the brand new Boxster was unveiled at the 1996 Paris Motor Show.

It may have been an extraordinarily long wait for something truly fresh from Stuttgart, but the Boxster was certainly worth it. Who knows if it's thanks to new teams or the release of old Porsche executives from their cobwebs, but this car brims with class and appeal. It does not have the extrovert body styling 911 fishtail fans would have hoped for, but something far more sophisticated. It's discreet, extremely aerodynamic and immensely practical. They have hung on to the con-cept of water cooling, but placed the brand-new flat six boxer engine amidships, allowing German engi-neering to perfect truly outstanding roadholding characteristics. The design is so effective, the hood stores directly over the engine with the resultant space

| | |
|---|---|
| Spares | ★★★★★ |
| V.F.M. | ★★★★★ |
| S.R. | ★★★★★ |

*It's a sports car, so the interior trim is black. Simple. Just another one of those laws. The rev counter, not speedo, dominates.*

generating astonishing luggage capacity both front and rear. There are more ostentatious modern sports cars, more expensive ones, even faster ones, but the Boxster currently represents the most complete example of a 90s sports car.

## RELATIONS

An entirely new Porsche, though the design ancestry includes the neglected late 1960s mid-engined 914/6, the early 1950s Spyder and the factory's first sports car designs for a mid-engined model – dated 1947.

## BEST BUY

At this point there is just one model, but Porsche's tradition of continuous development ensures many progressions from this Boxster which will, in time, make this first incarnation very valuable.

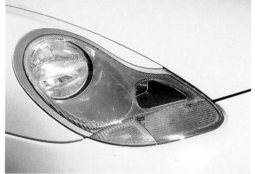

*Look back to, for example, the pretty RS60 of 1959 for a close genetic link with this front end. In 1986, there were exciting reports of a new Porsche mid-engined two seater sports car, codename 984, scheduled for sale in 1989 …*

# MANUFACTURER
# MASERATI

MASERATI BORA
*A FORGOTTEN VINTAGE*

During the 1960s, the fashion in fast cars became increasingly mid-engined. This presented difficult compromises for designers juggling lost luggage, seating and rear vision with desired high performance and handling. It also created some cars that looked seriously fast. The forgotten personification of this breed is the Maserati Bora. The company were main players in World Sports Car championships until withdrawing in 1957. Their Works car, the mighty V8 450S, was the spiritual ancestor of the Bora, although the intervening years saw action for the famous sports/racer the Birdcage Maserati and the F1 Cooper Maseratis. Citroën took control of Maserati in the mid-sixties, bringing fresh investment and requirements leading to the powerful and smooth V8 which was destined for the new mid-engined supercar. Giulio Alfier, who was involved with the classic F1 Maserati 250F, devised a complex monocoque two seater coupé with all the main elements mounted on an isolated frame. There was no pretence of 2 + 2 seating, but reasonable luggage storage up front, all independent suspension, disc braking and styling by Giugiaro who had created the classic front-engined Ghibli and the dramatic mid-engined De Tomaso Mangusta. The V8

engine had chain-driven twin cams per bank, alloy block, a bank of four carbs hurling 310bhp towards the tarmac via a five-speed gearbox. The advantage over rivals was the engine's forgiving nature, and thanks to impressive flexibility it can negotiate most conditions in a single intermediate gear. Understated, classy, but just waiting to fly, this 165mph supercar offers a great deal.

## RELATIONS

Body by Giugiaro at Ital Design, with V8 engine rooted in the racing 450S, and some components such as the pressured braking system from Citroën. The 1975 V6 Merak SS was a Bora derivative.

## BEST BUY

The car barely changed over its production life as the slight increase in engine capacity merely off set American emission control modifications. The chief enemy is rust, and apart from obvious body areas check suspension and engine mounts.

| Cost | £36,000 |
|------|---------|
| % swing | 65 |
| Spares | ★★ |
| V.F.M. | ★★★★★ |
| S.R. | ★★★ |

## SPECIFICATIONS

| | |
|---|---|
| **ENGINE:** 4719cc; 4930cc | **SUSPENSION:** Ind wishbone/coil all round |
| **BHP:** 310 – 320 | |
| **FUEL:** 14mpg | **BODIES:** 2 seater coupé |
| **GEARBOX:** 5 speed | **YEARS:** 1971 – 78 |
| **BRAKES:** Disc | **PRODUCTION:** 571 |
| **SPEED:** 160–165mph | |

# MANUFACTURER
# JAGUAR

During the post-war recovery period William Lyons needed a new engine to power a fresh range of family cars. Starting with XA, theory became trial engines by version XF, finally maturing into the XK design. The new cars would be the Mk IV through X, and the now revered Mk II saloons. As part of development 200 aluminum sports cars were built as test beds based upon a cut-down Mk V saloon chassis. Using the new 3447cc, 160bhp XK engine, a staggering 120mph was achieved, thus creating the XK 120's name. The impact of this car at the 1948 London Motor Show was colossal, and orders flooded in defying notions of only 200 cars. In 1950 a slightly altered steel production version emerged with further performance options for the Fixed Head, Drophead and Roadster bodywork. In 1953 the XK140 was unveiled with improved cabin space by moving the engine forward, rack and pinion steering, redesigned grille, an uprated engine and an automatic gearbox option. By 1957 the ultimate XK was ready. The 150 enjoyed sleek modern lines, a refined grille and light treatment, a single wraparound windscreen and, thanks to development in the competition C-Type, the XK150 became the first production car with disc brakes. Fixed and Dropheads initially matched the old 140 power, but in the second year came the Roadster and the S versions with new head, triple carbs, 250bhp and over 130mph which was approaching Ferrari performance for half the price. The final 1959 versions used a 3.8 engine developing 220bhp with 265bhp for the S option. It had wind-up windows, limited slip diff (S only) mohair hood

design and an air of high speed refinement which became the very hallmark of Jaguar's tradition. Driving a completely rebuilt 3.4 Drophead example was just wonderful. All the joys of that long bonnet, the period interior and yet virtually an E-Type performance was magical.

## RELATIONS

Original Jaguar body styling wedded to one of the most important post-war engines which powered numerous successful saloons, the XK sports range and the awesome Le Mans-winning C- and D-Types.

## BEST BUY

At this level it's largely about finances and aesthetics. The three body styles give choice, though the Fixed Head outsold the other two, and is half the Roadster's price. The S models provide the extra excitement but don't buy anything without guidance.

---

### SPECIFICATIONS

**ENGINE:** 3442: 3781cc
**BHP:** 190 – 265
**FUEL:** 18mpg
**GEARBOX:** 4 speed
**BRAKES:** Disc
**SPEED:** 124mph – 136mph

**SUSPENSION:** Ind wishbone/torsion bars – Live axle/semi-elliptic
**BODIES:** 2 door sports; fixed and drophead
**YEARS:** 1957 – 1960
**PRODUCTION:** 9,395

---

| | |
|---|---|
| Cost | £52,500 |
| (150S 3.8 Roadster) | |
| % swing | 3 |
| Spares | ★★★ |
| V.F.M. | ★★★ |
| S.R. | ★★★★ |

# ASTON MARTIN DB6
## IMPROVING ON BOND

### MANUFACTURER
# ASTON MARTIN

The legendary growth of the Aston Martin DB series to preternatural status tends to prevent us viewing the cars clearly. Aston Martin's formidable competition presence disguised a troubled company. Despite the marketing coup of the DB5 in a Bond movie, this car was presented as a touring model, but had only a tenuous claim to four-seater capacity. Sales figures for the DB5 were poor, and having committed the marque to a presence in the touring market, Aston Martin's solution was to adapt the car.

The 1965 DB6 was the result – in all but a few mechanical details still a DB5. Four inches were added to the wheelbase; there was a choice of automatic transmission at no extra cost, air conditioning, new dial-a-ride Selectaride shock absorbers, electric windows and new facia arrangements. The engine was bored out to 4.0 litres and the previously elite Vantage engine carburation was installed as standard. The DB6 became a fast car with a top speed to match the famed DB4GT, but development had shown high speeds were destabilizing the new model, so they redesigned the DB5's tail section to incorporate a raised tail as a spoiler – an idea drawn from the DP Project competition car. The Mark I achieved more sales in three years than the entire five years of standard DB4s.

There was a short period in July 1969 when a Mk II DB6 actually ran alongside the incoming DBS model. However, the DB6 ended in November 1970. The drophead version was called Volante, and until mid-1965/6 they were actually based upon the DB5 bodies. After that they were known as Volante Mk Is

with conversions on the proper DB6 bodyshell, while the Mk IIs had slightly shaped wheel arches to fit around the DBS wheels.

## RELATIONS

It is essentially a DB5 with slightly stretched bodywork and increased power output to compensate for extra luxury fittings. The last examples used many items from the subsequent DBS model.

## BEST BUY

The Mark Is have increased in value by a third over the last few years. A handful of coachbuilt estates still exist, and the triple Weber-equipped Vantage-engined models add status. With so many parts and tasks costing serious money, call the owners' club for advice before contemplating a purchase. The alloy engine can crack, so oil pressure is an important gauge. Chassis rust and even water build-up in the doors can be expensive.

### SPECIFICATIONS

| | |
|---|---|
| **ENGINE:** 3995cc | wishbone/live axles, coil |
| **BHP:** 282– 25bhp | **SPEED:** 148mph |
| **FUEL:** 13–15mpg | **BODIES:** 2 door coupé: |
| **GEARBOX:** 5 speed: | convertible: estate |
| automatic | **YEARS:** 1965 – 1970 |
| **BRAKES:** Disc | **PRODUCTION:** 1,755 |
| **SUSPENSION:** Ind coil, | |

| Cost | £35,800 |
|---|---|
| % swing | 48 |
| Spares | ★★ |
| V.F.M. | ★★★★ |
| S.R. | ★★★★★ |

**MANUFACTURER**

# ASTON MARTIN

**NMY 486**

Early in 1947 David Brown bought Aston Martin, and a few months later Lagonda Cars, and then set about building them up as *the* sporting and luxury British marques. The first post-war Motor Show in 1948 included Aston's DB1 – a tiny production of two-litre alloy-bodied Drophead Tourers, while Lagonda designer Frank Feeley was exploring shortened competition coupé versions. Using both the two-litre and the Bentley-designed Lagonda 6-cylinder engines, these cars carved a reputation on the international race circuits. Named the DB2 Mk I, the eventual production coupé was launched in the spring of 1950, rapidly followed by the faster Vantage version and the Drophead, creating capacity production for the factory. Occasional rear seating became the fashion and somehow Aston managed, within the same wheelbase, to deliver the 1955 DB 2/4 Mk II, (the 4 denotes seating) while establishing the often copied opening rear hatchback. During the early 1950s outright competition cars were the DB3s (never production road models) and much of that experience was poured into the final Aston Martin DB2 model – the DB Mk III launched at the Geneva Show. Produced between 1957–59 this model has, until more recent times, been largely overlooked – masked by the world-beating DB4 which followed. The Mk III had the final (and much revised) version of the Lagonda-based, originally W.O.Bentley-designed, engine, the DBA, which produced 162bhp; 180bhp versions were to be offered later. Frank Feeley re-styled the front of the car, using an enlarged version of his elegant DB3S grille and this shape was reprised in the dashboard layout. The DB2 two seater and the DB 2/4 Mk III represent pure classic Astons – before high fashion and show business coloured their personas.

## RELATIONS

Born of the DB2 road car, with Lagonda designer Frank Feeley's body styling, this car led directly to the famed DB4, 5 and 6.

## BEST BUY

Generally these are very sturdy cars. Rust does eat into traditional areas, while the suspensions needs expert checking. The spares position is excellent. It is important to check for horizontal cracks half way down the engine – particularly as the Mk III has its own unique block.

*The DB2 from the beginning of the decade used the Lagonda engine. Beautiful bodywork from ex-Lagonda stylist Frank Feeley.*

| SPECIFICATIONS | |
|---|---|
| **ENGINE:** 2922cc | **SUSPENSION:** Ind trailing |
| **BHP:** 162 | links/coil – Live axle/Panhard |
| **FUEL:** 18 – 21mpg | rod/coil |
| **GEARBOX:** 4 speed | **BODIES:** 2 door, 2 + 2 Drop- |
| **BRAKES:** Disc/Drum | head: coupé: hatchback |
| **SPEED:** 120mph | **YEARS:** 1957– 59 |
| | **PRODUCTION:** 551 |

| | |
|---|---|
| Cost | £39,000 |
| % swing | 26 |
| Spares | ★★★★★ |
| V.F.M. | ★★★ |
| S.R. | ★★★★ |

# RANGE ROVER

'INAPPROPRIATE' LUXURY STIGMA COULD RUN AGAINST IT.

### MANUFACTURER
# ROVER

When it was launched in 1960, the original Range Rover (now retrospectively called Classic) made a great impression. So much space, glass and power, along with country practicalities like rubber matting and easy-clean seating. Power steering was available from 1973, four doors an option after 1981, then automatic and five speed gearboxes. Bodywork was mainly aluminium, reducing rust, and the huge ground clearance both protected it and enabled efficient cross-country usage. Originally, there was to have been a four-cylinder and a V8 version, but the price differential was not wide enough, and so as the years passed, this vehicle, designed by Spen King and David Bache, moved progressively further up-market, until its rivals became the Mercedes, or the Lexus. It is a highly successful commodity, but sadly, perhaps inevitably, it has becomed estranged from its original concept. It is so comfortable that stepping out into the countryside itself could look like a mistake. From your high, air-conditioned, glass-tinted vantage point, the wilderness beyond the Home Counties can provide fine views. The present incarnation boasts a fresh ladder frame chassis, new suspension, revamped engines and body styling.

It would be churlish not to define such an original and successful motor car as a future classic, but deep down I have my doubts. The next 20 years could well see its excessive cabin area regarded as more of an ugly curiosity. The application of abundant luxury may even look out of place – as the huge Jensen Interceptor proved – and the associated social stigma could run against it as the years pass.

## SPECIFICATIONS

**ENGINE:** Classic: 3528cc V8
New: 2497cc; Diesel / 3950cc/4554cc V8
**BHP:** Classic:– 135bhp
New: 190bhp –225bhp
**FUEL:** Classic: 15mpg
New: 27mpg–17mpg
**GEARBOX:** Classic: 4 speed manual; 4WD
New: 5 speed manual / 4 speed auto; 4WD
**BRAKES:** Classic: Disc
New: Disc & ABS

**SUSPENSION:** Classic: Coils & beams
New: Electronic air suspension, beams
**SPEED:** Classic: 95mph
New: 105mph – 125mph
**BODIES:** 2 and 4 door utility hatchback
**YEARS:** Classic 1960 – 1995
New 1994 – current
**PRODUCTION:** Classic – 317,615
New – current

## RELATIONS

A logical (but more comfortable) extension of the famous Land Rover, it initially used the successful lightweight alloy ex-Buick V8 engine, which developed 144bhp, and now employs the powerful BMW-based 2.5 litre turbo diesel or Rover's 4.0 or 4.6 HSE V8s offering up to 225bhp.

## BEST BUY

Range Rovers are constantly in demand, although the very early vehicles are now showing their age badly. There were also many early gearbox problems. Of the more recent cars, the Turbo diesel makes most sense if you don't mind paying a £35,000 price tag for a vehicle without an automatic option, leather seating or air conditioning.

| Spares | ★★★★★ |
| V.F.M. | ★★★ |
| S.R. | ★★★ |

# MANUFACTURER
# JAGUAR

## JAGUAR XK8
### DOESN'T HAVE TO WAIT...

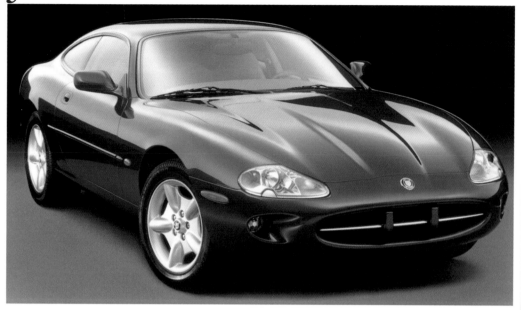

It's all like a good movie. Started by one man with loads of enthusiasm, Jaguar was built up by Sir William Lyons from motorcycle side-cars and rebodied Austin Sevens. First the slinky SS100 sports cars, then buying Daimler, Guy, Coventry-Climax and Meadows, before integrating with BMC. Then, as in any great story, followed the dark period – the British Leyland years. Morale, production quality and investment all plummeted. Miraculously, the company regained independence, sought public support through the stock market, and staggered on, only to be consumed by the dark shadows of a multinational – the Ford Motor Company. But wait … they didn't eat them up, but instead fed and nurtured the company back to its present rude health. Everyone likes happy endings, and none more than the enthusiasts now celebrating the birth of yet another classic Jaguar – the XK8.

Is it as good as those before? Does an automatic gearbox offend? It really doesn't matter because virtually every Jaguar is desirable. Their great tradition as rapid transport – for everyone from Le Mans racing drivers to Great Train Robbers – is only part of the story. Somehow, they have always managed to offer refined cars at a price to dismay the opposition. Whereas an Aston Martin or a Ferrari is a car to be ogled from afar, a Jaguar sports car has always been just about achievable.

The XK8 doesn't disappoint. It offers silky smooth V8 power, (the first in Jaguar's history) along with an impressive five-speed automatic gearbox, sophisticated suspension and a cockpit of considerable

### SPECIFICATIONS

**ENGINE:** 3,997cc
**BHP:** 290bhp
**FUEL:** 23.3mpg
**GEARBOX:** 5 Speed automatic
**BRAKES:** Disc
**SPEED:** 154mph
**SUSPENSION:** Wishbone and coils
**BODIES:** 2 door 2 + 2 Coupé; Convertible
**YEARS:** 1996–current
**PRODUCTION:** N/A

refinement. It feels fast, safe and powerful – all Jaguar trademarks. The electric roof on the convertible is so well insulated you actually forget it isn't metal. When new, E-Types were often considered 'too flash' but have now matured into admired thoroughbreds. An assured future classic, the XK8 won't have to wait for such recognition.

## RELATIONS

The very name reminds us of its ancestry, and design integrity has been maintained with the body styling. The engine is the first of a brand-new range, transmission is evolved from the ZF gearbox, but the XK8 also uses a much-modified XJS floorpan.

## BEST BUY

Deciding between coupé and convertible is a happy personal dilemma. Having driven both, the coupé has it for me both visually, and through offering a more spacious and useful cabin. It's also a little cheaper!

| | |
|---|---|
| Spares | ★★★★★ |
| V.F.M. | ★★★★★ |
| S.R. | ★★★★★ |

# LAMBORGHINI COUNTACH

THE WORLD'S MOST BEAUTIFUL MOTORING FOLLY

### MANUFACTURER
# LAMBORGHINI

In truth this is probably the most useless car in the book. It emulates competition machinery yet it's not a circuit machine, its excessive speed and fuel consumption have no place in our motoring world, and with neither wing mirrors, nor three-quarter vision negotiating public roads is a lottery – reversing simply unwise. Yet this car has become an icon among classic cars. It would be easy to leave it to the mercies of a *Top Gear* script were it not for the mechanical achievements beneath that 1mm thick aluminium bodywork. It was designed to follow in the footsteps of the celebrated, but imperfect transverse-engined Miura and the same basic team revealed their plan with the Countach prototype at the 1971 Geneva Motor Show. Its futuristic wedge shape and upwardly hinged doors caught everyone's attention, while the decision to place the V12 engine backwards, mounting the gearbox in the cockpit and devising an internal drive shaft through the sump to the final drive was an inspiration. This dismissed the need for long gear lever linkages, it brought all the weighted aspects of the car within the wheelbase, and greatly improved handling – a Miura failing. As significant as the prototype was the three year delay to production, during which every aspect was reviewed. Air intakes were installed over the rear haunches to increase cooling, and an enhanced Espada 4.0 litre was substituted for the unreliable 5.0 litre engine, marginally reducing top speed. Extraordinary discrepancies between manufacturer and different road testers' top speed figures abound in print, but all are agreed it was then the fastest road car. The Countach LP400 was unveiled early in 1974 and four years later the 400S saw improved tyres, enlarged wheel aches and nose spoiler, a tail mounted wing, and improvements to suspension. In 1981 the LP500S introduced the 5.0 litre engine (actually 4754cc) and dashboard changes, while the 1985 Quattrovalvole offset sapping US emission laws with the enlarged 5167cc, four-valve-per-cylinder 455bhp unit, hurtling the car into the 180mph zone. It is one of great motor cars to test drive or to admire – if not live with on today's roads.

## RELATIONS

The classic Miura/Espada V12 with unique space frame chassis and Bertone body.

## BEST BUY

Don't. Buy the model, the poster, or CD Rom ride, but leave this unique car to show business and museums. The cognoscenti consider the simpler 400 lines superior to later cluttered models.

| Cost | £56,250 |
|---|---|
| (LP400) | |
| % swing | 29 |
| Spares | ★★ |
| V.F.M. | ★★★ |
| S.R. | ★★★★ |

### SPECIFICATIONS

**ENGINE:** 3929cc: 4754cc: 5167cc
**BHP:** 375: 455
**FUEL:** 12mpg
**GEARBOX:** 5 speed
**BRAKES:** Disc
**SPEED:** 180 – 190mph
**SUSPENSION:** Ind wishbone & coil all round
**BODIES:** 2 door coupé.
**YEARS:** 1973–79: 1978–82 – 400 models 1982–85: 1985–89 – 500 models
**PRODUCTION:** 2199

# MANUFACTURER
# MERCEDES-BENZ

The 300SL Roadster isn't so much the sister car to the legendary Gullwing, as its progeny. The Roadster may not boast those top-hinged doors, it but did enjoy important improvements over the Gullwing. Just ten 300SLs started out as competition cars as Mercedes wanted to wave the sporting flag again, but with little development funding, they had to take the engine, gearbox, suspension etc,. from their then current saloon, the 300 Series. Naturally the engine was refined with a new dry sump, triple carburation, competition camshaft, new valves, and manifolds but its 160bhp+ wasn't enough alone. So they designed a complicated tubed space frame chassis, and tilted the engine through 45 degrees to reduce height. Keeping the car this low, however, meant extra strengthening along the chassis sides, creating huge door sills and not enough room above them for conventional doors – hence the half-height gullwings. The result of this body and chassis combined, along with the engine developments, gave Mercedes an instant competition winner. An enterprising American tried to order 1000 road versions, and this was enough to tempt the factory into production in 1954, with a largely steel bodied version which was successful, if hugely expensive. However, critics questioned the door design – escape in a road accident would be impossible, the windows did not open, and it was difficult getting in and out with any decorum. Gullwing production ended in 1957, and was replaced by the 300SL Roadster which looked identical, (roofline apart) but was substantially reworked. The space frame chassis was redesigned to permit conventional full height doors, fuel injec-

tion was added, there were important rear suspension improvements; a hard top and enhanced interior all contributed to an increasing GT role. Blisteringly fast in their day, it's their original design which promotes status, not their sophistication. Yes, it is one of the world's supercars, but it's a considerable sum of money to invest in a model with that much power and unstable handling. Attractive styling, flawed manners – buy a house instead.

## RELATIONS

New body styling over engine, gearboxes and other components from the 300 range.

## BEST BUY

If you are seriously considering this level of investment, first join the Owners' Club and draw on their knowledge and contacts. Repairs and restoration are very expensive. If you are not seduced by those Gullwings, then the later Roadster is technically improved and 20 per cent cheaper.

### SPECIFICATIONS

**ENGINE:** 2996cc
**BHP:** 250
**FUEL:** 16mpg
**GEARBOX:** 4 speed
**BRAKES:** Drum – Discs from 1961
**SPEED:** 155mph

**SUSPENSION:** Ind double wishbone/coil – high pivot swing axle (low pivot after 1961)
**BODIES:** 2 door sports: hardtop
**YEARS:** 1957– 63
**PRODUCTION:** 1858

| | |
|---|---|
| Cost (Roadster) | £109,000 |
| % swing | 29 |
| Spares | ★★★ |
| V.F.M. | ★★★ |
| S.R. | ★★★★ |

### MANUFACTURER
# ROLLS-ROYCE

The Bentley Mk VI was the first product of Rolls-Royce's post-war shift to building complete cars, and evolved between 1952 and 1955 with the more elegant R Type. This improved Mk VI featured an elongated rear section and boot, the bigger 4566cc engine, an optional automatic gearbox and some dashboard changes. Like its predecessor, it attracted a number of coachbuilt models – none more successful than the Mulliner Continental R. Numerous legends exist about its design inspiration, though fastback models were hardly new. Having bravely entered the world of 'production' cars, Rolls needed to impose superiority anew. The competition was blossoming, with the first Jaguar XK; the first of the Porsche 356s; the initial road-going Aston Martin DB2 with its tubular framework; the alloy-panelled, tube frame, and

*Of all the post-war Bentleys, surely the R-Type Continental is the one which would have received the nod of approval from W.O. Design work began in 1950 with the intention 'to exhibit those characterstics which appeal to the connoisseur of motoring.'*

| Cost | £88,500 |
|---|---|
| (H.J.Mulliner) | |
| % swing | 1 |
| Spares | ★★ |
| V.F.M. | ★★★ |
| S.R. | ★★★★ |

## SPECIFICATIONS

**ENGINE:** 4556cc; 4887cc
**BHP:** Never released
**FUEL:** 16 – 20mpg
**GEARBOX:** 4 speed manual & automatic
**BRAKES:** Drum
**SUSPENSION:** Ind coil/wishbone – live axle/half elliptic
**SPEED:** 120mph
**BODIES:** 2 door, 4 seat coupé; coachbuilt versions
**YEARS:** 1952–55 (a few later)
**PRODUCTION:** 208

Italian-designed Bristol 401. In this context, a streamlined, aluminium-bodied, R-Type, constructed around a tubular frame, was intelligent rather than inspired. It was the style and detail, however, which made this car stand apart from virtually all others in motoring history. They sent engineers to Italy to study coachbuilding practices and went to considerable lengths to create a truly aerodynamic shape while retaining the vital dignity of the marque. Less than two inches height reduction was permitted on the famed grille, and yet they managed to created a supremely quiet 120mph four seater, taking hills in top gear. All but a handful were the same Mulliner design, though Farina, Graber, Park Ward and Franay all built examples. The four years of production were discreetly divided into classifications but only a compression increase in 1953 and the move to the larger bore 4887cc engine in 1954 were significant. It's a hard task to explain exactly what justifies the car's status without experiencing the feel of the car from behind the wheel. What makes the difference between an off-the-peg suit and a tailor-made one? Subtle qualities, details, a feeling. Couple these with Bentley engineering, 20mpg and four hand-made leather armchairs, and the car was a rare motoring achievement: owners had to agree not to compete in them.

## RELATIONS

Essentially a 1952–55 R-Type Bentley and engine, the Continental had a lightweight framework and streamlined body from Mulliner and other coachbuilders. Of the 208 built, 193 had the Mulliner sports Saloon body. Farina's interpretation was perhaps one of the most successful of the other 15 with thick C-pillars and 'straighter' lines nose to tail.

## BEST BUY

With so few built and astonishing price tags, the condition of a Continental R is likely to be excellent. Pure driving bliss and rarity value will continue to keep them highly collectable. The donor car – the saloon R-Type, is a far more accessible classic, with a longer, more elegant rear section than the Mk VI, but there are the same concerns over rust. Later Continental S-Types are humble, rebodied saloons by comparison. As the years passed, the original intentions of producing a lightweight sporting saloon were traduced: customers demanded too many extras! Radios, automatic transmission, bigger seats …

LOTUS 21

ENTRY TO F1 – FOR THE PRICE OF A PORSCHE

## MANUFACTURER
# LOTUS

*The sreamlined shape first seen with the 1960 Lotus 20 was a winner, and continued to reappear almost unchanged in the 21 (F1), 22 (FJ), 24 and 25 (F1), 27 (FJ), 29 (Indy) and 33 (F1).*

| Spares | ★★ |
| V.F.M. | ★★★ |
| S.R. | ★★★ |

There is a very special place reserved for F1. The World Championship is a roller coaster of events creating mythological status for man and machine, with a TV audience recently quoted as 589,808,000. Depending on age, certain teams or drivers fire the imagination, while a string of superheroes transcend everything: Ascari, Fangio, Moss, Clark, Prost and Senna. Cars, too, attain the same status – the Mercedes W196, the Maserati 250 F, the shark-nosed Ferrari 156, the Lotus 25 and even the team managers such as Enzo Ferrari, Frank Williams, and Colin Chapman become household names. The unimaginable costs of building and racing a competitive Grand Prix team is outside our understanding, but relentless racecar development and changing rules actually produce a stream of retired cars. Now, with the huge growth in historic competition, grids of ex–F1 cars are filled with enthusiasts savouring the excitement at a fraction of the original cost. It's still not cheap, but for the cost of a Porsche Carrera you could own the genuine article and drive a motoring legend.

Each specific car represents a precise window of time for the marque. This beautiful Lotus 21, restored by Alan Baillie, is a fine example. The first F1 Lotus was the Coventry Climax 16 looking not unlike the old Vanwall and performing double duty for F1 and F2. The same dual Formula design operated for the Lotus 18 which was based on a space frame chassis with the 237bhp 2.5 F1 Coventry Climax engine set behind the driver. It appeared at the Brands Hatch Boxing Day meet just five weeks from the drawing board, and during 1959 Moss, Clark, Surtees and Ireland brought the car on – even delivering GP victories. At season's end rules changed, limiting engines to 1.5 litres, and while teams protested, Ferrari employed their Formula II V6 engine and developed the 129 degree V6 1.5. Lotus' new V8 was not yet ready and an interim car using Mk II version of the 4-cylinder FPF Climax engine was married to a new ZF gearbox. Though the FI Lotus 21 shared much with its Formula Junior

## SPECIFICATIONS

**ENGINE:** 1498cc
**BHP:** 151
**FUEL:** 5mpg (approx)
**GEARBOX:** 5 speed
**BRAKES:** Disc
**BODIES:** Single seater

**SUSPENSION:** Ind coil/wishbone – coil/radius arms
**SPEED:** 150mph (varied with gearing)
**YEARS:** 1961
**PRODUCTION:** 11

*The fuel tank was immense in relation to the rest of the 21, running along the left hand side and crossing under the seat. It was a nightmare to make leakproof, wrapping itself around each chassis tube. A secondary tank was squeezed in behind the right hand front wheel.*

sister, the 20, it was wider, with 30 gallon fuel storage including a third tank doubling as the driver's seat. The space frame was smaller gauge, oil pipes actually ran within each other, but terminated through separate outlets, oil and water cooling ran through the internal monocoque skin with supply pick-ups at each end. A car full of ideas which would later blossom into the mould-breaking full monocoque V8 Lotus 25. Early GPs saw misfortunes for Ireland and Clark, though Moss, still in the underpowered interim 18–21, won an impressive Monaco GP and again at a rainsoaked Nurburgring. The full Lotus 21 saw him at Monza along with five Ferraris sitting on the front three rows, but two laps in Von Trip's Ferrari and Clarke's Lotus touched, and Von Trip, along with 14 spectators, died in the ensuing accident. The season ended with the combined efforts of 18–21s and full 21s becoming runners up in the Constructors' Championship, with further successes in the winter's South African events before Lotus turned to what would be next season's V8 Lotus 24. Seven cars were built for the Works team plus just four others. One for Rob Walker/Stirling Moss, one for Jack Brabham and one for South African Syd van der Vyver which was written off and

eventually replaced in 1964 by the factory for privateer Aldo Scribante, which makes the car we feature a later chassis number than the 1963 Type 24s.

## RELATIONS

Lotus operated a constant development programme with this car directly descended from the Lotus 18 and bodywork shared with the Formula Junior 20.

## BEST BUY

Obviously with limited productions all F1 cars are highly collectable – particularly with good histories. Owning a Grand Prix car isn't difficult, – but you do need knowledgable mechanical help. However, for the price of a luxury road car you could buy a 4-cylinder example, join the world's most exclusive club – and enjoy the real excitement of historic competition.

*The 21 had the four cylinder Coventry Climax engine; the imminent V8 was not yet ready.*

# ASTON MARTIN DB7

## A BEAUTIFUL BALANCE OF NOSTALGIA AND TECHNOLOGY

### MANUFACTURER
# ASTON MARTIN

From a 1947 advert in *The Times,* David Brown bought a bomb-damaged factory and the Aston Martin name. He leant his initials to one of the most prized series of sporting cars ever produced, but in 1972 the DB prefix was replaced by the initially irksome V8 series and Brown sold up. A decade and a half of troubles and changing ownership led to Ford buying the company. With both Jaguar and Aston Martin owned by Ford, cynics saw a grim future. Under the new team, however, a series of inspired decisions were made to reposition the marque without loss of credibility. Ex-Ford designer Ian Callum crafted a stunning new coupé body, incorporating strong shadows of former DB4 glories, while ensuring four seats, a good boot and the powerful elegance synonymous with Aston Martins. TWR used the 3.2-litre straight 6, twin cam engine similar to the Jaguar XJR, but incorporating a unique 24 valve head, Zytec electronic management and an Eaton supercharger combining to produce 335bhp and 165mph. Sat upon the same sized chassis as the XJS, the finished car incorporated weight-saving panels where practical, and used the Rolls-Royce paint shop to complete the task. The quality of the interior, and the introduction for the first time of a veneered Aston dashboard,

combined to offer relative exclusivity for a fraction of a custom-built Aston's price. They also sought the blessing of David Brown himself, and then re-established the distinguished line with the DB7 name. The striking convertible Volante model followed and with record production under way, (the first DB7 to reach the vital US market is pictured left) the factory now talks confidently of further DBs, even racing versions. Ford have been shrewd, and there is little doubt that the DB7 has firmly re–established Aston Martin and created an instant classic model.

## RELATIONS

TWR Design styling, primarily Jaguar XJ parts, including basic chassis and engine.

## BEST BUY

It's too early to discuss second-hand models. Such is the delight at the DB7, a number of teething troubles have not been reported by the press – so perhaps the early models ought to be viewed with caution.

| | |
|---|---|
| Spares | ★★★★ |
| V.F.M. | ★★★★ |
| S.R. | ★★★★ |

### SPECIFICATIONS

| | |
|---|---|
| **ENGINE:** 3239cc | **SUSPENSION:** Ind wishbone |
| **BHP:** 335 | & coil all round |
| **FUEL:** 25mpg | **BODIES:** 2 door coupé: twin |
| **GEARBOX:** 5 speed | turbo coupé: convertible |
| **BRAKES:** Disc | **YEARS:** 1994 – to date |
| **SPEED:** 165mph | **PRODUCTION:** Current |

## MANUFACTURER
# FERRARI

There is something rather strange about love affairs with motor cars. We have here a £166,000 machine which can take you to the threshold of 200mph and yet leaves you discussing its beauty. Perhaps that is one of the things which stands Ferrari apart. The contrasts of such brutal road power and the sweeping grace of Pininfarina's styling are seriously seductive. The 456GT is considered by many commentators – including the author – to be one of the most stunning cars from Maranello for a very long time. It's simplicity conceals not only a wealth of glorious details but also two usable rear seats and a boot that will accept five suitcases – provided, naturally. With the return to a powerful front-engined Grand Tourer it's easy to proclaim it the 90s Daytona but the 456 has those extra seats and so its natural predecessor is the 1971-72 365GTC/4. That 2+2 used a 4,390cc V12 generating 320bhp. Just 500 were produced before it was replaced. The 456 boasts a new 65 degree lightweight V12 offering considerably greater power with 442bhp at 6,250rpm which is then married to a 6 speed gearbox rear mounted in order to help provide a near perfect weight distribution. The classic wishbone suspension has triple set–ups, electronically controlled, whilst the massive ventilated disc brakes owe their origins to the 512 TR.

It is simplicity itself to just reel off specifications to impress – but with Ferrari it's all genuinely rooted in their engines, not gimmickry. However, all the technical jargon is forgotten the moment you hear a 442bhp V12 Ferrari engine fire up – it gathers crowds like a circus parade. For the chosen few who

### SPECIFICATIONS

| | |
|---|---|
| **ENGINE:** 5,474cc V12 | **SUSPENSION:** Double wishbones, coils & dampers |
| **BHP:** 442bhp | |
| **FUEL:** 14mpg | **SPEED:** 193mph |
| **GEARBOX:** 6 speed manual: Automatic | **BODIES:** 2 door Coupé |
| | **YEARS:** 1993 – Current |
| **BRAKES:** Disc: ABS | **PRODUCTION:** N/A |

climb through those six gears there is a sound, an experience, of unparalleled excitement. 50mph in 1st, 75mph in 2nd through to 165mph in 5th – with another gear in hand. With four persons on board you will have to settle for 186mph but leave your friends at home and two of you can flee into the night at a claimed 193mph. Classic status was guaranteed the moment the 456 was unveiled.

## RELATIONS

Perfect pedigree – being a front engined V12 Ferrari designed by the incomparable Pininfarina studio. It borrows heavily on the famed Daytona but actual lineage is closer to 365GTC/4. The 456GT's massive V12 engine is now shared with Ferrari's 199mph flagship two seater – the 550 Maranello.

## BEST BUY

Obviously it's too young to make any worthwhile comment. The only real option is the later automatic version, if you find six gears too much hard work.

| Spares | Details, details |
|---|---|
| V.F.M. | ★★★★ |
| S.R. | ★★★★★ |

# SMALL WONDERS

## *Economy Scale*

As our roads become more and more congested with ever more anonymous cars the attraction of highly individual small models keeps growing. The Ford Ka, the Fiat Cinquecento, the Renault Scenic are now carrying the flags of economy and practicality formerly the domain of the little Fiat 500s, the Mini, the Citroëns, Renault, MG. Many of these cars still hold enormous attraction both for day-to-day use and as classic cars in their own right. Not surprisingly the model collectors market too reflects this love affair with these highly individual small cars and here are examples of some of the best models currently available in the model shops.

**ABOVE** Economy and Space – *These French cars provided extraordinary accommodation plus performance from tiny engines. On the left is a Vitesse Limited Edition model of the 1953-54 Citroen 2CV (Model No: L084A) with the early grille shape, no rear side windows and strange gearchanges. In the centre is a later 1966 2CV complete with fully retracted roof. This too is a Vitesse Limited edition (Model No: L108C) and shows the later grille, additional windows – the real life version also boasting a modest power increase and classic Citroën body roll. On the right is Renault's rival, the 4, which had front wheel drive, sealed cooling, the same push-pull gearchange and equally alarming suspension. Here is the 1961-62 Vitesse example (Model No: L105B) complete with twin sun roofs which each hinge towards the centre.*

**LEFT** Extended Family – *One of the cornerstones to classic small cars are the baby Fiats. Here on a hand painted cobbled street display from Heirloom Crafts is the tiny blue Fiat 500F from its launch year of 1965. The F enjoyed a small power increase along with doors which at long last hinged from the front. This model again is one of Vitesse' Limited Edition range (Model No: L094B). On the right is the fascinating Fiat 600 Multipla from 1956 which was based on the Fiat 600, used forward mounted controls and was a genuine minibus with seating for up to 6 and even taxi versions. This model is from the Italian company Brumm (Model No: R250).*

**TOP LEFT** Final Fling – *The Fiat 500 R was the last of the true baby Fiats and naturally boasted the most performance – 62mph with courage, using many items from the more modern 126. This beautifully detailed model is still in its Vitesse display case and features a retracted roof. (Model No: L130C).*

**BOTTOM LEFT** Bigger Babies – *Seen here on another of Heirloom's excellent detailed display settings are open and closed roof versions of the slightly bigger Fiat 600. Many perceive little difference between 500s and 600s but the cars are quite defined – not least because the 600 is a conventional water cooled engine as opposed to the tiny air cooled 500's. Both these models are from Detail Cars – a part of Corgi. (Blue/white closed car Model No: ART 315; the open topped 600 Model No: ART 313.)*

**TOP, CENTRE** Scarlet Idol – *The Mini was, still is, one of the most loved of the small cars and no example more glamorized the range than the famous Works Cooper S. Here is a stunning Vitesse example (Model No L067) of the 1968*

*Monte Carlo Rally car complete in its full works colours, rally plates, front and rear lighting, tiny BMC rosettes and even the Liddon/Aaltonen crew names legible on the wings.*

**TOP, RIGHT** Going Upmarket – *The Mini range was largely defined by engines and performance, but Wolseley and Riley versions enjoyed exclusive body changes. Here a Vitesse miniature of the 1966 Series III Riley Elf reveals the changed proportions with extended bonnet and boot, dedicated Riley front grille work and full width walnut dashboard – all faithfully shown in this tiny ⅟₄₃rd scale version (Model No: 055B).*

**BOTTOM, RIGHT** Confused but Pretty – *This delightful Details Cars model of an MG Midget is in fact an early prototype for their production model of a 1969 open left hand drive Mk IV (Model No: ART421). The interior work is good and even a luggage rack is mounted to the boot lid. The Detail Cars brochure, as did the real mark IV, show fully curved rear wheel arches. Watch out in the shops for the completed model to see if corrections were made!*

*Full details of these hand built displays from:*

**Ian H Thomson**
**Heirloom Crafts**
**Coalmoss Farm**
**Ythanbank**
**Ellon**
**Aberdeenshire**
**Scotland.**
**AB41 7TT**

# RAISING STANDARDS

## *"A dramatic achievement by designers and engineers" – reads the launch brochure ... The public didn't know the half!*

Reginald W. Maudslay, founder of the Standard Motor Company, thought big. The company's Articles of Association defined its future operations to include 'Locomotive engines, cycles, boats and engines of every description, whether worked by steam, gas, oil or electricity, or any other form of power or energy, and including aerial or aeronautical machines, builders and fitters of ships and other vessels.' However, he was also an extremely conservative man and favoured tried and tested approaches – indeed the company name was reputedly drawn from his pursuit of 'reliable standards'. Renowned for dependability, Standard even supplied parts to rivals such as Jaguar, Saab, Morgan and TVR. Among its acquisitions was the Triumph Motor Co. in 1944, and among important individual successes was the 1950s Standard 8.

Originally to have been called Beaver, the 803cc Standard 8 was launched in 1953 in such a basic form that it lacked a heater, second windscreen wiper or even an opening boot. The idea was to offer the hard-pressed post-war public an utterly reliable no frills means of transport. Both Volkswagen's Beetle and Citroen's 2CV triumphed with this approach, but even at £481 the British public weren't sold – that is until the De Luxe arrived in 1954. A 948cc version complete with winding windows also appeared which was called the 10 and for the rest of that decade a range of lightly trimmed 8 and 10s thrived. They achieved a victory in the 1955 RAC Rally with Jimmy Rae, numerous international class wins followed in the Tulip Rally, the Monte Carlo Rally and subsequent RACs. By 1957, Gold Star versions were including extra power and even an opening boot. The 10 was renamed the Pennant.

The 8 and 10 had been dating fast compared with the Austin A30, Ford Anglias and the Morris Minor and by 1957 Standard were ready to prepare a replacement – naturally embracing the modern cost-saving unit construction technique which the chassisless A30 enjoyed. A problem was immediately encountered, as the 8 and 10 bodies had been built by Fisher & Ludlow, which Leonard Lord had just acquired for his expanding BMC. Standard, who were not equipped for body building, would have to look elsewhere. The obvious alternative was Pressed Steel but their order books were full, and Standard's own Mulliners was unsuitable for such large scale production. A complete rethink was needed. Future design issues were also unresolved as the key stylist had stormed out of the company. The decision was made to revert to old technology and continue to use the separate chassis and 948cc Standard 10 engine as the basis for the new model. Then, it was hoped, fresh bodywork could be devised and built up around those proven parts. Call that a plan?

As fate would have it a certain Captain Flower visited the factory in 1957 seeking Standard engines

220

*The basic S model was a move in February 1961 to counter the British recession and naturally appealed as an ideal second car for use by the 60s ladies who lunched (frugally).*

## Luxury on a shoe-string

The Herald 'S' has a prestige value and a luxury out of all proportion to its modest cost. But you have to take this car out on the road to taste its comfort to the full. To find how delightfully easy it is to drive. How the all-round independent suspension smooths out the worst road and gives you the safest, surest cornering. How the 25-ft. turning circle solves most of your parking problems. How the 93% all-round visibility is the nearest thing to eyes in the back of your head. Refinements such as these lift the Herald 'S' right out of the economy class.

and chassis for his Meadows car project. Co-operation was conditional on seeing a real Meadows, so the Captain delivered working drawings and then a finished car. It transpired that the design work was from the Italian firm of Vignale, using Giovanni Michelotti ideas. Standard's in-house design efforts to replace the 8 and 10 were floundering, so their rejected ideas were presented to Michelotti for reworking. Critical time passed; eventually, Standard executive Harold Webster who was on his summer motoring holiday in Italy called on Michelotti in his studio, leaving the family in the car. It was a September afternoon in 1957. The Italian endorsed the rejection of Standard's designs and together the two men sat to consider fresh ideas. By midnight, the Triumph Herald Coupé was a recognisable drawing and Harold's forgotten family were asleep in the car. On his return from vacation he was carrying a set of drawings for the Herald saloon, coupé, estate and convertible. The board approved the concepts and by that Christmas a black/metallic silver Coupé prototype was concealed in the Standard factory.

The next stage was to resolve the construction nightmare. In the end the body was treated as separate sections which could be farmed out to different factories and then simply assembled like some giant Airfix kit in Standard's factory. Their own Mulliners took care of all it could, Pressed Steel, Fisher & Ludlow both contributed some panels, as did Liverpool's Hall Engineering and Chatwood Milner plus Birmingham's Forward Radiator Company. It was a clever solution with hidden future advantages, but inevitably resulted in many logistical hitches and frequent build quality problems.

Stuck with the old power plant and chassis Webster's team was anxious at least to embody some new specifications which led to an independent wishbone front suspension allowing a turning circle of just 25 feet, a valuable selling point. Independent rear suspension was achieved via a very basic swing axle employing a transverse leaf spring – a set-up which would be responsible for body roll problems and unnerving rear wheel tuck–in. However, given all the obstacles Standard were satisfied with their

The wonders of the new Herald 1200

## Big engine

1147 muscular cc's put 43 BHP (gross) under the bonnet of the new Herald 1200. This 21% increase in engine capacity gives you smoother driving in all traffic conditions. Less work on the gear stick, exceptional flexibility in top gear, with vivid acceleration throughout the range.

Yet the extra power brings negligible increase in petrol consumption; partly because the new Herald 1200 is only 28 lb. heavier than its predecessor.

More power to the Herald means longer engine life, and effortless *safer* driving, with a reserve of power in hand.

## Little maintenance

Petrol, oil, air and water are all the Herald asks for 3,000 miles of happy motoring. Brilliant design has reduced Herald servicing needs to a minimum. To the average owner this means a routine check only three or four times a year, and the low price maintenance voucher book,

which is good for 48,000 miles, enables this work to be carried out by any convenient Standard-Triumph Distributor or Dealer. No car needs less routine maintenance and for the do-it-yourself owner the Herald's unrivalled accessibility makes it all so easy.

*It really was a perfect car to promote, offering unheard of visibility, an extraordinary turning circle, modern body design and, thanks to those bolt-on panels, differing body styles could be achieved without excessive costs being passed on.*

efforts when they unveiled the Herald in April 1959. Ironically it wore a Triumph badge in order to take commercial advantage from the rising status of the TR sports cars. The press and public reaction was good and with its crisp styling and colours, its exceptional all-round 93% visibility and still rare all independent suspension, it presented an appealing package. Unfortunately, the early cars often suffered from poor panel fitting, creating water intrusion and rattles: even greater problems lay in wait. They bought both Fisher & Ludlow and Hall Engineering

– previously sub contractors building Herald body parts. Dedicated to the private car market, they extracted themselves from longstanding contracts to build Ferguson Tractors. Standard built a new assembly plant and were approaching self sufficiency when in 1960 the British economy took a steep dive, leaving Standard Triumph vulnerable.

Lord Stokes' acquisitive Leyland Motors were looking to expand and in 1961 they absorbed the company. "Although at the time" explained Stokes "we from Leyland were comparative innocents in the sophisticated world of the private motor car, the concept of the Herald appealed to our engineering thinking." They inherited the launch coupé and two door saloon as well as the 1959 twin carb version (effectively the coupé state of tune) plus the convertible, initially just for export. Under its powerful new owners the Herald range blossomed and before long the factories were struggling to keep up with demand. To defeat the recession a basic Herald S was introduced in February of 1961 and this model alone survived the 1961 switch to the larger 1147cc Herald 1200 and 12/50 models – offsetting the inevitable extra weight of a separate chassis. These models brought in excess of 300,000 more sales. The forced need to employ bolt-on body panels actually offered easy body style variations and by this point the range included 1200 saloon, coupé, convertible and estate.

*How different all those modern angles looked in comparison to the older, more homely curves of the Morris Minor. Triumph managed to turn every aspect into a selling tool including their enforced use of an old chassis. The one piece opening bonnet was particularly welcomed by the rising numbers of DIY car mechanics.*

## Triumph Herald Model 'S' all the details of the finest money's worth on four wheels

 Safety steering column

 93% all-round visibility

Real chassis

 13 cu. ft. Boot

72 seat positions

Service 3000 miles only

3000 miles

4 wheel independent suspension

25ft turning circle

STANDARD TRIUMPH
A Member of the Leyland Motors Group

**Body.** 2-door, 4-seat, 4-light saloon. Steel panelled specially treated to resist rust. Two winding windows and pivoting anti-draught ventilators.
P.V.C. leathercloth upholstery. Separate front seats, driving seat adjustable for height, rake and leg length — 72 positions.
Large, easily read instrument dial with speedometer, trip mileometer, fuel gauge, ignition, oil pressure and main beam warning lights. Interior light with courtesy switches to both doors. Direction indicator warning light in facia. Direction indicators (self-cancelling) and driving lamps operated by finger-tip switches on steering column.

**Dimensions**
| | | |
|---|---|---|
| Length | 12 ft. 9 in. | 3890 mm. |
| Width | 5 ft. 0 in. | 1525 mm. |
| Height | 4 ft. 4 in. | 1320 mm. |
| Wheelbase | 7 ft. 7¼ in. | 2320 mm. |
| Track | 4 ft. 0 in. | 1220 mm. |
| Ground clearance (static laden) | 6¾ in. | 170 mm. |
| Turning circle | 25 ft. 0 in. | 7·7 metres |
| Boot | 13 cu. ft. | 365 cu. m. |
| Fuel tank | 6¼ galls. | 29·58 litres |
| Cooling system | 8½ pints | 4·8 litres |
| Weight (dry) | 15 cwt. | 760 kg. |

**Engine**
4-cyl. O.H.V. Bore 63 mm., stroke 76 mm. Capacity 948 c.c. Compression ratio 8 : 1. Single downdraught carburettor. 4-speed gearbox, synchromesh on 2nd, 3rd and top. Gear ratios: top 4·875, 3rd 7·09, 2nd 11·99, 1st and reverse 20·82. Final drive 4·875.

**Performance**
NETT 34½ B.H.P. at 4,500 r.p.m. Torque 575 lb./in. at 2750 r.p.m. (Equivalent to 125 lb./sq. in. B.M.E.P.)
GROSS 38½ B.H.P. at 4,500 r.p.m. Torque 615 lb./in. at 2750 r.p.m. (Equivalent to 134 lb./sq. in. B.M.E.P.). Maximum speed 68-70 m.p.h. (110-112 k.p.h.). Piston speed at maximum road speed 2,580 ft./min. at 5,190 r.p.m.

**Suspension**
Independent front suspension, coil springs controlled by telescopic-type dampers. Swing-axle type independent rear suspension with transverse leaf spring.

**Chassis**
Double backbone steel-girder chassis. Steel disc wheels. 5·20" × 13" tubeless tyres. Girling hydraulic brakes.

**Optional Extras**
Leather seating. Twin carburettors. Heater. Screen washers.

Every precaution has been taken to ensure accuracy, but the Manufacturer accepts no liability for errors or omissions.

12 MONTH GUARANTEE. STANPART SERVICE ALL OVER THE WORLD

**Conditions of Sale**
The goods manufactured by Standard-Triumph Group are supplied with an express warranty which excludes all warranties, conditions and liabilities whatsoever implied by Common Law, Statute and otherwise. The Manufacturer reserves the right to vary the list prices at any time and all goods are invoiced at the prices current on day of delivery, ex-works. The Manufacturer reserves the right on the sale of any vehicle to make before delivery without notice any alterations to or departures from the specification, design or equipment detailed in its various publications.

Printed in England. 341/961/U.K. 50m.

## Are you in on the secret of the new Vitesse?

*(0-60 in 12.5 seconds)*

Outwardly the changes to the new Vitesse are slight, 3 little badges that sport the 2 litre sign. It has the same strong, lightweight body as its predecessor. But under the bonnet it is a very different story, with the new 2-Litre 95 BHP engine. This energy in a 18¼ cwt car gives new meaning to power-weight ratios. If cars could be judged on statistics alone, 20 — 40 in 7.7 seconds, 40 — 60 in 8 seconds would prove the case for the new 2-Litre Vitesse as the nimblest lightweight 4-seater saloon. But figures are only half the story. Have a test-drive, and discover that the pleasure of the new Vitesse cannot be measured with a stopwatch.

In the May of 1962 came the Vitesse with its underbored 6 cylinder 1596cc Standard Vanguard engine, standard front wheel disc brakes and the distinctive twin headlights set diagonally in the Herald bonnet. Next arrived the Herald 12/50 with a high compression head on the 1147cc engine, discs and additional luxury fittings including a sun roof. By 1964 the basic S was dropped and later the same year the pretty coupé also died. This sacrifice was made in the name of the company's two seater sports car based on the Herald – the Spitfire. Standard Triumph had actually developed the prototype but that project was abandoned through lack of funds until new BL blood spotted it under dust sheets and promptly funded its production. 1964 ended with BL replacing the Mk I Spitfire with the Mk II. In September 1965 the Vitesse was given the 1998cc Triumph 2000 engine, perhaps the most desirable Herald package. Having run coupé-styled Spitfires in races, they unveiled the good looking GT6 – a coupé version of the Spitfire which also utilized the mechanics of the powerful new 2.0 litre Vitesse and boasted classic bonnet bulge and 100+mph top speed. However the appealing GT6 had one serious problem – it also shared the Herald's vulnerable rear swing axle suspension and was universally criticised for its suspect handling. Meanwhile, the Spitfire gained further power and refinement in Mark III guise and August 1967 saw the 1200 convertible and 12/50 replaced by the 13/60 using the same 1296cc engine as fitted to the Mark III Spitfire. Such had been the outcry at the GT6 handling that in the autumn of 1968 the 104bhp Mark II version was announced. Its fresh suspension involved a new lower wishbone suspension set-up which was an expensive remedial investment for BL but significantly improved both the GT6 and the 2.0 litre Vitesse. Sadly as the GT6 sales eased off unforgivably BL moved onto a Mark III GT6, reverting to cheaper Spitfire type rear suspension before killing it off in 1973 – having sold 40,926. The Vitesse ceased in 1971 completing the Herald-bodied era with total platform sales of over 568,717. Such was the export appeal of the little Spitfire that it continued on until 1980 selling around 314,332. Triumph itself did not survive de-nationalization and slipped into the motoring history books in 1983, leaving the appealing Herald range, born of the humble Standard 8, as a lasting reminder of its ingenuity and determination.

*The more powerful Vitesse models were particularly desirable and enjoyed the distinction of those twin headlights. This promotion picture would have been risky using the first production cars, which suffered from poor panel fixture and readily took water on board.*

# CULTURALLY
*You don't even need a car to be part of it*

Rallying really requires a public warning sticker – for it's compulsive. Temptations exist with racing but that world is isolated and clear cut, dedicated machinery on dedicated circuits. Rallying feels much closer to real life, familiar road cars, country tracks, but with that smell of excitement. There are no more powerful motor sport images than peering over the crew's shoulders, wrestling with steering, loose intercom cables thrashing under the impact of heavy landings whilst forest tracks hurtle towards the screen.

The mystique was born in the 60s, a time when the might of BMC and Ford Competition Departments battled it out for supremacy on events such as the Alpine, Acropolis and the Monte Carlo. This was the world of scarlet and white Works Cooper Ss pushed to their limits by a succession of unpronounceable Scandinavian heroes earning more than Cabinet Ministers; of Works Cortinas backed by a 26-strong Ford

factory team offering everything – literally hundreds of spare tyres at the ready, each ice stud alone costing sixpence to install! There was great commercial prestige in such competition and the road cars actually benefitted from this savage testing. The road Cortina was said to have had 52 small body changes as a result of problems encountered at events. Each Works driver was required to fill out a 25 page debriefing questionnaire after every rally to pinpoint anything troublesome.

This spectacular sport is now followed by millions, yet the serious do-or-die stuff doesn't represent the majority of events. It's at club level that so much enjoyment is gained, whether it's leisurely treasure hunts or more competitive timed club rallies – all possible without destroying your road car. The opportunity to gently stretch both car and driving skills is genuinely tempting, particularly when shared with another enthusiast and with rival crews. This is where rally driving thrives.

Unfortunately, although getting involved is actually very simple, there are desperately few clues how to start. Basically the RAC MSA govern all motor sport and they perceive as 'Road Rallies' anything from treasure hunts to economy runs, essentially run on public roads, usually at night, working to a time schedule and with navigational challenges. You can use any standard car, the driver aged 17 or more with conventional licence whilst the navigator can be any age over 14. 'Special Stage Rallies are more serious and expensive with competitive high speed stages on private land with both car and crew needing to be correctly fitted out and with motor club membership and RAC credentials.

The same basic framework applies to Classic car events with Road Rally events ranging from the most modest to the giant RAC Norwich Union event. There are age of car criteria such as the loosely applied 20-year minimum for the Norwich Union, the Historic Special Stage categories which sub-divide each side of 1968, Post Historic, then full bore FIA international events splitting pre- and post-1972. It gets more complicated on occasion: would your car have been eligible for the '62 Monte Carlo Rally, for example? From the outset it all looks a nightmare, but in fact the cobweb of regulations actually creates an environment for enjoyment

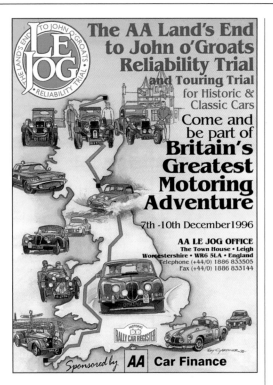

for everyone, from the dedicated rallyist through to novices – your car and experience automatically define your entry point.

However much you may feel you are the next Colin McCrae, once you enter the world of rallies, it is the camaraderie and not the competition itself that gets you. Put dozens of

*Certainly not a full blown Works Cooper S, but this modest 850 Austin Mini can still provide enormous pleasure in motor club events. So much of the enjoyment within the rally world is the shared experience, and the humblest of cars can be your entry ticket to that culture.*

maybe just help; marshalling is a brilliant way to get on the front line and watch all the tricks close-up. The RAC MSA publish a booklet listing every recognized club, and there is also the Historic Rally Car Register, a repository of enthusiasm. If you have any interest in classic cars and rallies, as driver, navigator or even marshal, £28 for HRCR membership opens the door to everything – including detailed advice.

For many years, acquiring competition driving skills was a self-schooling process, during which you progressively improved from club to national levels. The more you progressed, the more intense the competition and greater the risks, until you were either forced to stop or begin investing for real in a dedicated competition car. Over the years, this process has become ever more expensive as Works teams and sponsors fought with their cheque books for the ultimate prize of winning rallies. However, whilst commerce has turned mainstream rallies into a spectator sport, things are actually much better for classic cars, as there is now a boom in events and runs – plus the rather more elaborate rallies such as the London-Cairo-Cape Town, costing over £12,000 to compete, or the super tough 1,000 miles Corse Retro.

*Listening to World Champion Roger Clark provides a vivid insight into the complex mixture of skill, fun and fear which is the powerful rally cocktail ...*

enthusiasts and their cars together anywhere – even without a chance to compare driving skills – and a great time is guaranteed. Thus the actual key to involvement isn't heroic cockpit stuff, not even owning a car – it's being part of it. First step is to join a motor club and then

*... Once in the cockpit he runs through safety features before we set off on an initiation trip to remember, in the hands of this master craftsman ...*

The school car was a fully prepared Peugeot 306 Xsi which offered a reassuring mixture of strength and agility to any novice about to drive hard over rough ground. It is remarkable just how quickly you get over the violence and noise and begin to really concentrate on mastering the driving techniques.

These have revitalized the rallying world without the overpowering presence of Works teams and their sponsors. Even such a blue riband event as the Monte Carlo Challenge has seen a modest Standard just ten seconds from an outright win, and a three-man crew in an Austin A90 finishing in the top ten. This last year, over two-thirds of the entries were novices. The organisers even offered a training and familiarization weekend. The largest motor sport entry in the world is actually the RAC Norwich Union Classic Car Run.

All these opportunities prompt enthusiasts to look for basic rally handling training. Unfortunately, choosing an establishment is rather hit and miss. The motor sport governing body, the RAC MSA, feels unable to recommend specific schools, so they just list them all. There are two different stages at which you can benefit from such training. Firstly, as soon as you decide to enter even road events, take the opportunity to go somewhere safe – in someone else's car – and learn with an instructor exactly how to maintain control. Many younger drivers for instance may never have driven a car without ABS and yet any 'pressing-on' in a classic is going to actually require brake lock-up to set the car into corners.

The other effective time for tuition is after you have entered a few Special Stage events and you begin to realize that others are getting home quicker. Then a good school will help to sharpen your skills.

I decided to explore the Silverstone Driving Centre, where amongst its directors is the legendary rally World Champion Roger Clark, who for so many years dominated rallying as the Works Ford driver. Although not himself an instructor, I was to enjoy the rare privilege of sampling a school car and stages with the maestro. Despite breathtaking wins – 26 international, 23 nationals, four RAC Rally

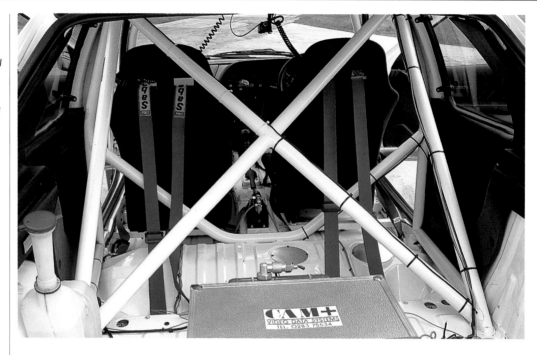

There are just so many levels of events open to the enthusiast, from modest afternoon runs to demanding reruns of famous international rallies. The Historic Rally Register is an ideal place to start asking the questions.

championships, his relaxed, easygoing manner gives you the feeling you're just off for a run in the country together. In fact you head to the far corner of the Silverstone estate where they have established a rally handling stage of rough tarmac laid out as a vague double figure eight. Alongside is a briefing room. Pupils of both sexes, ranging from young enthusiasts to those in their sixties, all start out with a briefing. They are given instruction in the value of using the

car's weight to full advantage, the causes and effects of over- and understeer and the infamous hand brake turn. Then for those on a half day course the handling area becomes their stage. Initially they are asked to drive it as though visiting a shopping centre – to familiarise with car and surfaces. Then each of the three pupils is required to put the foot down and explore the best lines and techniques. In the waits between turns there is time to consider where you're getting it wrong, watch other people's techniques and talk things through with a second instructor in the briefing room.

Clark and I strap ourselves into the new, stripped-out and fully protected Peugeot 306 XSi. On board video recording is available to study later and there is an intercom between the two helmets.

For this World Champion there is no initial pretend drive to the shops. He drops the clutch and the surprisingly lithe machine instantly screams to life. We zig zag around the corners and curves with apparently ever increasing abandon. On board the combined effect of noise and being thrown about is very dramatic and it is really quite shocking that the car remains so obedient.

As you begin to realize the world isn't ending, the cold logic of the briefing strikes home: using the ever shifting weight of the car to advantage, the value of the front end power forcing the rear to behave, the critical importance of braking and

Another charm of the sport has always been its appeal to a wide age range. These two pictures span decades of the author's life and yet the excitements remain just the same.

changing in a straight line and not whilst the geometry is upset within a corner. The experience is vivid and I realise the pupil waiting time between runs must be valuable for collecting thoughts. Roger Clark however has other ideas and we swap seats immediately. Strangely, the more power you apply the more secure it all feels, you still cannot believe it isn't going over but gradually you begin to build up an understanding of both your own skills and the character of the car. The master sits coolly beside me, still smiling and enjoying the sensations. He pushes me to wider approaches and even later turns into corners, catapulting us further across the exits with a slingshot effect. Techniques and personal skills are vividly focused upon for these intense and dramatic laps but when you finally stop the overall feeling is of absolute undiluted fun. Grown up fun, that makes you smile as you walk away several inches taller than on arrival.

In a school environment, nothing this dramatic would initially greet a novice, much more personal tuition would have taken place before the final practical. For those who undertake a full day's course, the afternoon session involves a detailed briefing followed by the advanced gravel special stage.

This is a 2-kilometre medium fast stage and embraces slippery surfaces, steep gradients, many turns including a great handbrake turn at the half-way point. For pupils there are indi-

vidual drives as well as an instructor-driven exhibition run. This is much more demanding and closer to what you see on the TV. Even if you never sit in a competition car again, this single drive is worth the investment and, if by chance it's to your liking, be warned that it becomes addictive.

Roger Clark approaches such special stages with a glint in his eye. Like a warrior finally spotting his prey he tightens his helmet and stares down the rough track. You cannot be prepared for the next few minutes. This is a World Rally Champion in his very own playground. The Peugeot takes off like a scalded animal. We plunge down into a dip, ground the car with teeth grinding impact and catapult up

**The Monte Carlo Challenge**

*How do I get an entry? What preparations do I need?*

Andrew Actman and Mick Briggs battle through blizzard in Sprite

Sir David Steel drove hard but broke Riley's diff

Left: Third files at hands of John Aan de Stegge. Above: oops – Betschart slips up in Healey 100

Above: chains essential for Ashleys to haul Delage up the snowy cols. Right: Abrams look saloon concours with authentic A90

**1997 8 1997 MONTE CARLO** Challenge

THE TOUGHEST WINTER CLASSIC CHALLENGE

**February 9-14**

Far left: Ewing and West battle with wayward Minx. Left: en route to record seventh Coupe des Alpes, Sandra Holt in ex-works MGA

Photos from Classic and Sportscar, April 1996.

Through coaching, and intense bouts of driving, you are by the end of a full day's training basically equipped to climb onto the first rungs of competition. A second advanced day's course is recommended about a month later; and perhaps most appealing of all is the one-to-one coaching available from two hours to an entire day. Under such conditions you could even bring your own, suitably prepared, classic car to the special stage where you can be shown techniques in the school car and then transfer to your own to apply them. Virtually all classic cars were rear wheel drive and such coaching in the different handling characteristics would have lasting value, both on public roads and in any classic club events you decide to enter.

Such adventure does sharpen the appetite and, if a spell as a rally marshal or club official won't do, then decisions have to be made. Do you want to be the driver or the navigator? Co-drivers also need training. Attending Don Barrow's Navigation School is a good way to start: though ultimately little will prepare you for map reading at 100mph over rough ground in the dead of night, except doing it.

The RAC, the school and your club can steer you through all the required documentation. You will need to buy personal items of kit such as helmet, flameproof suit, shoes etc, which are actually statutory requirements.

For these turn to one of the established suppliers such as Demon Tweeks who are now in

the other side, corners, markers, everything flashes by to a soundtrack of unforgettable violence. The handbrake turn point sees us plough back up the stage into a solid cloud of our own dust. According to the school a high proportion of the pupils receive the day as a birthday present: it's worth the wait. For a while we changed seats and I too enjoyed the adrenalin rush of pitting self and car against the terrain.

*This book's dedication refers to XUJ 564 having a hard time – so here's the proof!*

their 26th year of trading, which gives you peace of mind, and actually sponsor the HRCR Championship. They will sort you out correctly according to the standard requirements of your level of competition.

The remaining burning question is naturally the car, and here both cash and your level of competition experience become the salient factors. The highly enjoyable Classic runs and road events are all generally achievable in a well maintained standard classic car. Having chosen carefully, you will then have both a classic eventing vehicle and a practical second road car. My personal recommendation for such a double existence would be one of the later Mk II Farina Austin A40s, which are in effect a practical hatchback body over a Sprite.

If on the other hand you are serious enough to want to emulate the big boys and enter Historic Special Stage Rallies then you have to ask yourself some searching questions. In truly competitive form such cars are really best used only on rallies and the degree of tuning and alteration favours building one up from an unfinished restoration project. Alternatively, an equipped, ready-to-go car could be bought at the end of a season through magazines such as *Autosport, Motoring News* or *Classic Weekly*.

As a sport there is little to beat the sheer excitement and personal satisfaction of finishing, let alone winning an event. However, the

rally world brings a great deal more that just that to your life – an interest, a broad circle of friends with the same obsession and a strange sense of humour. What else could possibly lead peole to visit empty forests in the dead of night whilst rain, snow and winds numb the senses, to go nowhere fast!

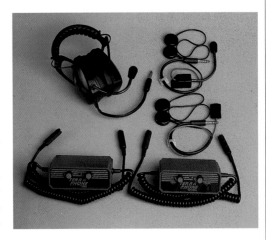

## BUDGET GUIDELINES

RAC Licences according to required grade
£10– £35 approx

| | |
|---|---|
| RAC Motor Sports Club Directory | £3.00 |
| RAC Starting Motor Sports Introduction | £3.00 |

**Typical Personal Rally Equipment from Demon Tweeks**

| | |
|---|---|
| Sparco Racing low cut suede shoes | £65.00 |
| Sparco Sprint 2 layer fireproof race suit | £195.00 |
| Sparco Budget suede gloves | £24.00 |
| Sparco Pro Jet open face helmet | £136.00 |
| Sparco Open face, double layer balaclava | £16.00 |
| Terraphone open face – open face intercom | £79.79 |
| Sparco fireproof socks and underwear | £72.00 |
| Sparco Chic kit bag | £26.00 |
| Sparco Co–driver bag | £32.00 |
| Sparco extreme rally jacket | £130.00 |
| | |
| Total Package costs | £775.79 |
| + VAT and Delivery | |

Demon Tweeks kindly offers readers a saving of £77.58 on this package, so the discounted total is £698.21 + VAT & Delivery

**Typical Silverstone Rally School Charges**

| | |
|---|---|
| Rally weekday course | £110.00 |
| Rally weekend day course | £115.50 |
| Rally Open Day | £121.00 |

Includes one to one tuition and practical.
All inclusive of indemnity

## CONTACTS

*The Rally Schools, Motor Clubs and competition licence details*

**RAC MSA**
Motor Sports House
Riverside Park
Colnbrook
Slough
SL3 0HG
Tel: 01753 681736

**BEST GENERAL CLASSIC CAR RALLY CLUB**

**Historic Rally Car Register**
Tibberton Court
Tibberton
Gloucester
GL19 3AF
Gen Secretary: Alison Woolley
Tel: 01452 790649

**RALLY SCHOOL TUITION**

**Silverstone Driving Centre**
Silverstone Circuit
Nr Towcester
Northants
NN12 8TN
Tel: 01327 857177

**INTERNATIONAL RALLY/RACE WEAR SUPPLIERS**

**Demon Tweeks**
75 Ash Road South
Wrexham Industrial Estate
Wrexham
Clwyd
LL13 9UG
Tel: 01978 664466

# LA DOLCE VITA

*A low mileage Ferrari for around £500 a month from a main dealership which isn't going to treat you like some lesser mortal … impossible? Not if you know who to ask for.*

The Ferrari phenomenon is unapproachable. Every marketing executive has stretched imaginations and budgets in the vain attempt to build up a similar status for their company. No one has come close. The car has a mythical status, a global ability to stir emotions and inspire dreams. Despite actually being a small organisation, the identity is so famous some experts claim it's the third most instantly recognised brand name in the world behind Coke and Rolex watches (though Harley-Davidson kick up quite a fuss about these beauty contests). Ferrari is only half the age of many car manufacturers, having started in 1940; it doesn't bother advertising and Enzo Ferrari introduced the first cars with very little interest in how they looked, only how they performed. The whole Ferrari ethos is the antithesis of most manufacturers, for it doesn't solicit custom: owners and admirers are drawn like moths to a candle. The driving force is competition which was the central passion in Enzo Ferrari's life, running the successful Alfa competition team before venturing out on his own.

Ferrari is the only company to have competed in every Grand Prix World Championship season since its inception in 1950. In 36 years they have gained over 100 victories, a record number of poll positions, nine Driver's World Champion titles, Manufacturers titles – they hold the Grand Prix world records for virtually every aspect of F1 racing and uniquely are the only team to build entire race cars themselves. The chassis is Ferrari, the suspension, the gearbox and that famous engine – all designed and constructed by their own team of craftsmen. Naturally this wins credibility, and every time one of their grand prix cars is victorious so interest rises in owning a roadgoing Ferrari.

Much of the public's obsession was prompted by the Sports and GT racing cars, because they bore a passing resemblance to road models. Sports Prototypes screaming past chequered flags a decade or so ago sowed the seeds of desire in a whole generation who now perhaps dream of a lottery win and a chance to own a similar low, scarlet machine. Even in Sports and GT racing the record was incredible, with nine Le Mans wins, eight Mille Miglia victories, seven Targa Florio – it's no wonder getting behind the wheel of a Ferrari remains the ultimate dream for the world's enthusiasts.

So has this mythical status got completely out of control? Have we all been mesmerized by track performance and the eulogies of privileged journalists into believing a Ferrari is unobtainable? Certainly the new road cars are rare and expensive whilst the occasional trade advertisement for a middle-aged example etches 'Expensive Maintenance' deeply in one's subconscious. Ferrari's single-minded pursuit of high performance and competition had somewhat isolated the handful of official sales outlets left to trade on their success. It bred a sales team sub-culture whose code was 'befriend the wealthy and maintain the

elitism', but this began to hurt even Ferrari. The air of superiority surrounding the Ferrari sales arms might once have been fitting, but in the 90s there are far too many attractive high performance rivals with marketing and sales armies soliciting new custom. Admiring Ferrari F1 victories from behind the barriers is natural, but almost consequently being made to feel like an intruder in a Ferrari salesroom is no longer acceptable.

Under the watchful eye of Graypaul owner Frank Sytner (ex BMW Touring Car maestro), there is one man who understands that the Ferrari affair does not only touch the super rich; a man who admits he cannot afford a Ferrari yet is so passionate about them it verges on reverence. Mario Vignali is from Naples but lives in Loughborough, England, where

*The classic Pininfarina styling provides great strength and purpose. Continuing respect for the conventions of Ferrari lines is easy to see – compare this 328 rear elevation with the picture of the brand new 355 on page 67.*

*Powerful detailing on the 328 includes this deep side intake which is shared with the 200mph twin turbo F40. Thanks to Pininfarina's influence most Ferrari bodies are evolutionary rather than revolutionary.*

*Mario Vignali – the successful face of Ferrari's more approachable customer policy. Working for Frank Synter, he has helped turn Graypaul into the number one UK used Ferrari dealership.*

*The engine housing skilfully fuses with sloping roof buttresses, air spoiler, and rear window. The success of such models depends on all the individual elements being brought together without causing distractions from the whole.*

his heartfelt convictions as Graypaul's Sales Manager influence all those around him. The company was founded in the 1960s as a small Ferrari restoration business, grew into a Service Agency in 1973 and was awarded the coveted status of full authorised dealership in 1983. Mario joined the company in 1995 and after six months he discovered it had ceased to be just a job and had become "a matter of love" – his words. He works in a modest office literally squeezed between the showroom and one of the largest Ferrari workshops in Europe. His passion for these cars is palpable: like Ferrari themselves, he

doesn't sell the product so much as the excitement they generate. He is quiet, courteous and mightily impressive, for Graypaul is now not just a major new car dealership but also the UK's Number I for used Ferrari: it has been for three years. They enjoy a staggering 80% repeat business with customers – an extraordinary nine out of ten clients trusting him so implicitly they buy sight unseen. Yet the same man has broken with tradition and opens the Ferrari showroom at weekends, inviting teenagers on tours of the premises. Unlike certain outlets he has turned Graypaul into a real home for enthusiasts, whatever their age or income. He mentions a lorry driver who had always dreamed of owning a Ferrari. With Mario's encouragement the man saved, really saved, towards a Dino 328. Eventually, the dream was realised, but there was not the money to insure it, so Graypaul used their £60,000 transporter to move the Dino free of charge to the man's home until it could be taxed and insured. Now he saves up and comes in to buy accessories.

This refutation of the old elitism is approved of by Ferrari's UK Managing Director Stuart Robinson. Equally passionate about these motor cars, Stuart has placed strong emphasis on changing dealership attitudes in the four years he has been the UK chief. According to him, 70% of success is the product and 30% the skilful dealerships. With just 3,500 Ferrari's built a year, dealer/customer relationships have to be excellent to prevent frustrations. "In the last two years" he points out "we have increased our first time ownership by a substantial 35%," so it's very important that waiting lists are honourably overseen, no matter how important any individual customer. Mario understands this – he's currently planning customized jigsaws of any future owner's Ferrari and intends sending them a piece at a time, so the jigsaw is completed upon the car's delivery!

I watch this man with a mission as he switches from his lorry driver story to organise a private jet day trip to the famed Maranello factory so that

*The 328's 3185cc Ferrari V8 engine which produces 270bhp and offers a top speed of around 150mph. It may not be the fire eating V12 so associated with Ferrari, but these smaller V8 cars are inevitably much lighter and as a result fast enough for most and extremely agile.*

another client can select paint colours. No one's background appears to influence him – only their love for his precious motor cars. Such is the confidence he has in the cars – and indeed his bosses have in him – that sales pressure doesn't exist. Two years to mature a sale is OK.

Such a unique opportunity to get honest answers isn't to be wasted. I ask what would be his model suggestion, following that lottery win?

On his pet subject the words flow freely and he begins to shatter some illusions. The best 'starter' Ferrari is either the 308 or 328, but not the troubled 308 GTSi of 1980-2 which used a fuel injection prone to dropping off tune. These, and the unpopular 308GT4, are often listed as the cheapest

Ferraris but might prove expensive to maintain. The 328 GTS (targa) and GTB from 1986 were excellent extensions of the range, the B with the stiffer bodyshell. Their popularity was so great that even after years of production the line finally ended with a two-year waiting list still existing. His highest recommendation is the 308QV, 1982-86 which offered more power, Daytona style seating, quad valves, along with the charm of being the last version to use the period chrome and toggle switch gear.

A salesman called Robin appears and I am escorted out to drive a scarlet 1989 328GTB with 10,000 miles on the clock. Naturally I've seen them before but when actually climbing into one you are struck with how slender, even delicate, they are close up – the

*Though the basic bodystyle has remained been retained through the 308 and 328 range, the 1982-86 version – the 308QV – employed quad cam technology and was the last 308 to use its lovely period chrome and toggle switch gear.*

*The grandest dream would involve this 512TR. Scarlet, 6ft 5 in wide, screaming to 175mph and, thanks to stable values, it can also be attained through financing by the not quite so super rich. There are a number of supercars around but very little can match the sophisticated blend of beauty and power that is a V12 Ferrari.*

*The TR stands for Testarossa of course, and the lineage is quite clear, though there have been some serious refinements to the engine: the 4.9-litre flat twelve provides 428bhp to the original redhead's 362.*

*The engine castings were strengthened to allow higher revs for longer periods, and the pistons and liners were changed to increase compression ratio from 9.3:1 to 10.1:1. With the use of aluminium alloy, the weight went down by 100 lbs. A new exhaust system and catalytic convertor has meant the the engine and gearbox could be lowered by an inch, which improved handling. Fuel economy also improved, by about 10%.*

classic Pininfarina styling is so famous the car almost feels familiar. Once inside the cockpit appears quite large and the driving position splendid, though offset pedals are disconcerting and the famous open-gated gearbox is a little threatening. However once out on the open road the whole experience rapidly becomes second nature. It's hard to know what driving a Ferrari is supposed to feel like – such is the hype that goes before it. It's actually quite quiet, even normal until you build up the confidence to press on. As the engine opens up, the wonderful sounds just behind your seat increase in volume. The roadholding becomes astonishing: It's like an exotic go–kart round corners and as the countryside moves by faster and faster you suddenly realise you are flicking through that gearbox as though it's been your transport for

years. These smaller engined V8 Ferrari develop 270bhp from their 3185cc units providing a top speed of 150mph and an agility the bigger Supercars cannot enjoy. From the outside it was a 44-inch high Italian thoroughbred slicing through the countryside; from the driver's seat it was pure magic.

Mario searches my face for reactions to his beloved machine. A car such as that late version 328 doesn't lose value and is therefore an ideal subject for finance packages. You may think a £50,000 Ferrari is unachievable; but an example of a Graypaul payment scheme shows that they could place this car in my hands – permanently – for between £500 and £600

a month over four years with a £10,000 deposit. Such generally available schemes involve a last 'balloon' payment of something like £27,000 for this example. Usually these schemes need careful consideration because of rapid depreciation, but in the present market such a Ferrari is not losing ground. So after four years of driving, say, 6,000 miles p.a., this 328 ought to sell for around £34,000 (assuming suitable condition). Thus £500 a month could place you in the most exclusive of motoring clubs for four glorious years with enough change at the end for another deposit.

According to Mario, all too often these cars are stored in garages, causing dried out gaskets and subsequent trouble. At least 6,000 miles a year is good

*If you go faster than a Testarossa, you better be able stop faster, or at least as well. The discs are bigger, drilled, and the air scoops and ducting are more effective. Bosch ABS is fitted, but if you want to feel what's happening more directly, switch it off.*

*The traditional open gate gear change is incredibly intimidating and for a while you find yourself taking your eyes off the road.*

No illusions. The cockpit of
a car this serious is not the
scene of excessive luxury.
There is air conditioning
and the windows are
electric, the steering is not.
No cupholders!

for them and, because so many owners have a number of cars, you ought to be able to pick up a good Ferrari with extremely low mileage. I press him on the frightening prospect of servicing and he quietly explains all his cars are sold with a series of Charter Points and undertakings about the car's condition. With disarming honesty he explains cam belts need replacing every three years, which costs £2,000. However on a 6,000 miles a year car the annual service bill would be around £500-£600 and viewed as a three-year outgoing – including cam belts, the yearly service cost is a highly creditable £1250 – a figure he suspected less than for his girlfriend's Ford.

So bought under the safety net of this main Ferrari dealership the eight-year-old Ferrari 328, with just 10,000 miles on the clock, could cost me £500 a month in repayments and £100 a month on basic service – with the reassurance it's likely to hold its value throughout my finance period. It's not hard to see why Mario and Graypaul have reached that number one dealership status.

He sits at his desk surrounded by photographs of glowing customers with their new Ferraris, tables laden with models and a prized, dedicated photograph from Michael Schumacher. "Listen, isn't this wonderful." From a concealed audio system he plays a CD of a V12 Ferrari being driven hard – his face relishing the aggressive sounds. "Sometimes I play this just to remind me, you always know that sound, Ferrari is different."

"I have something special for you," his face registering the anticipation. I turn and beyond the glass wall I set eyes on a scarlet 512TR – the 175mph, 6ft 5inch wide Supercar boasting 428bhp from their legendary V12 engine.

The next hour belongs is unforgettable. On the forecourt it has the such a commanding presence, the spectacular Pininfarina bodystyling with all the vents, fins and those massive rising wheel arches. The light reflecting across the complex body, the world famous prancing horse badges derived from a 1st World War fighter ace's mascot – these are all integral to the

However hard-nosed you
are, the sound and per-
formance of a Ferrari V12
will get to you. To have over
400bhp howling just behind
your head is perfection.
The scarlet rocker covers
are the traditional identifi-
cation of a Testarossa – a
Redhead.

Ferrari experience. No one has consistently created models of such stunning beauty, such coiled and powerful styling and then applied world-beating performance and handling.

The 512TR was the 1992-94 Supercar replacement for the 1980s Testarossa. Though similar, it was Ferrari's answer to the increasingly powerful Porsche 911 Turbo and the Lamborhhini Diablo. The example I was offered was one of the last, with just 5,000 miles on the clock, and looked virtually new. The interior is uncluttered but does boast electric windows, air conditioning and Connolly leather but not power steering. Visibility is unexpectedly good for the size of vehicle and after a few miles you really

*Not the light cluster of the top-of-the-range 512TR of course, but it has that that magic badge to set the pulse racing.*

forget the sheer scale of the car around you. The suspension provides huge amounts of grip but is still able to iron out the worst of the bumps. The brakes are drilled out and ventilated to keep them as cool as possible. Without being there it's hard to convey the extraordinary presence of the glorious V12 engine. Resting just behind you, it's like a living thing – it can calmly pull away in any gear from 10mph and yet press the accelerator and second gear will hurl you to 85mph, third to over 110mph and as the rev counter swings past 4,000 revs the mighty engine starts howling – a sound so powerful it will remain with you, haunt you. The impact of the experience is hard to convey and returning to the amiable Mario to be told it could be yours for the same price as a Mercedes SL or CL is momentarily compelling. The great V12 masterpiece may well be unsuitable for most drivers and their pockets, but the gentle passions of Graypaul opens up new opportunities to ask questions and genuinely explore the real possibilities of Ferrari ownership.

*Graypaul's workshops are about as close to Supercar heaven as you are going to get without a VIP pass to Ferrari inself. Even in the back yard (below) there are sophisticated £60,000 covered transporters to take care of your dream car – mine's the 512TR!*

# CENTRES OF POWER

## Jaguar's XK Masterpiece

Spending nights on a roof appears an unlikely setting to plan an engine so important it can justifiably be called a 'World Classic'. It's true a long drive, or walk, can sometimes provide a purple patch of inspiration but stationed on a war time factory roof all night fire–watching is something of an extreme. However Jaguar's William Lyons did just this – ensuring where possible his closest colleagues shared the same shift. The conundrum was that Jaguar were then using ageing Standard engines and after the hostilities they wanted their own modern power plant. Also to be taken into account, with fuel likely to remain in short supply, legislation might well favour those companies manufacturing smaller, more economical units.

A number of key issues had to be addressed:

1) Detailed studies had identified two core Jaguar market sectors requiring engines
2) The two engines needed common manufacturing parts/lines to be cost effective
3) Jaguar's actual performance levels had begun to lose their 1930s status.
4) The engine needed to look modern and powerful.

Understanding the market was obviously vital to survival with post war material shortages and uncertainty over public interest. Exports were clearly going to be critical and the daunting US market would require a large engine whilst other more depleted nations would favour less gas guzzling. Research proved both core strands of Jaguar loyalty were within the medium price group and so two power plants had to be created – without bankrupting the company. The solution was to find a pair of exciting new units with a large number of interchangeable parts and ideally capable of using shared production lines. It was narrowed to three options: (i) a 4 cylinder doubling to also make a V8 (ii) a 6 cylinder with a pair creating a V12 and (iii) a 4 cylinder plus a 6 cylinder version. In the end the last pair were chosen partly because it best matched the existing

The aluminium XK120 (opposite) as launched in October 1948. This is number nine off the Coventry production line.

Brothers under the skin (left). The mould breaking XK road cars covered themselves in glory, but the competition variation – the classic C-Type – attained pre-eminence immediately, winning Le Mans at its first attempt in 1950 and then taking 1st, 2nd & 4th two years later. This lightweight C was driven to that fourth place by Peter Whitehead and John Stewart.

core Jaguar market and crucially it represented the most economical cross-usage of components.

Having largely exhausted development of their current engines it was critical that these new power plants firmly reposition the company's cars at the forefront of performance and style. As a target a full sized saloon had to be capable of an honest 100mph without any extra tuning. This signalled considerably greater engine stress at the higher end and an arbitrary peak speed for the power curve was fixed at 5,000 revs. Later Jaguar were to successfully test a production unit by sustaining a fully loaded engine at 5,000 revs for 24 hours with regular 2-hourly 5 minute bursts at 5,250, 5,500 and 6,000 revs. The engine oil remained stable at 130°C. and the resultant engine strip-down revealed no ill effects.

Designing a totally new powerplant was a more common phenomenon in the United States than in Europe, but under Bill Heynes, Jaguar took the plunge. Each possible design was given an alphabetic code prefixed with an X for experimental. The XA to XE possibilities never got further than the draughtsman's board so XF was in fact the first constructed. This was a hugely important engine – even though it never went into production. It was a 4 cylinder unit of 1,360cc and was used successfully to test the head and valve gear. Perfectly matching Jaguar's vision of an ultra modern, high efficiency engine, it was a twin overhead cam unit – something up until that point very much the exclusive signature of supercars and competition machinery. This XF also boasted hemispherical combustion chambers

which was again a technical raid on the exotic parts bin and offered excellent valve throat flow, virtually cancelled flow turbulence and, being an entirely symmetrical shape, required just a single cutter to manufacture. Thus the XF engine was an excellent start, but did highlight weakness in the crankcase design at sustained high speeds.

The XG unit was based on the existing Standard engine then in use on their production cars. It was again a 4 cylinder engine of 1,776cc, this time push rod with head, valve gear and inlet ports based on the successful pre war competition proven BMW 328 cylinder head. However flow figures through the vertical ports were disappointing whilst the rods and rockers could not be silenced enough for use in a quality Jaguar saloon range. Back again to the

XK120 DHC (Drop Head Coupé) cockpit. As with the fixed head model, the dash was of walnut veneer and the handbrake was the racing 'fly-off' type. announced in March 1951, 1,765 Drop Heads were built to late 1954.

drawing board, more variations, until the significant XJ emerged. This was yet again a 4 cylinder unit this time of 1,996cc and proved to be the landmark prototype leading to the famed production engine. It returned to the twin overhead cam configuration and was the subject of a great deal of experimentation, particularly with valves and camshaft drives. The scent of success urged the team forward and it was

one of these experimental 'J' engines which was lent to Major Goldie Gardner to break the world 2 litre land speed record at Jabek. Apart from a raised compression ratio of 12 : 1 and modified pistons, this was a standard engine which reached 176 mph at a maximum of 6,000 revs from its 146bhp.

Having hit upon a successful formula a further XJ engine was built, this time with 6 cylinders and a capacity of 3,182cc. It was a pretty much an engineering triumph, but suffered from a troubling lack of torque at low speeds – something that would not suit the planned new Jaguar sporting saloons. The solution was to increase the stroke – raising the unit to 3,442cc and thus giving birth to the final incarnation, the classic XK engine.

The engine development resolved, Jaguar were faced with a timing problem. The existing models were overdue for retirement and the Mark V was only to serve as a filler before the planned 1951 launch of a truly new range for the XK engine. Shrewdly, it was realised the performance capabilities

of this still secret engine could catapult Jaguar into the limelight and so it was decided to reveal it without delay at the 1948 Motor Show – within a limited edition sports car. 200 were to be built in aluminium, around a shortened Mk V saloon chassis and fitted with the 4 cylinder engine – called the XK100. William Lyons rushed through a body design but only one example was actually fitted with the 4 cylinder unit, Jaguar eventually favouring the 120mph 6 cylinder version – hence the name change to Jaguar XK120.

The car was an immediate success and demand clearly outstripped the planned 200 run so the factory was tooled up for full production. Inevitably there was a delay meeting this demand and some critics began doubting the astonishing performance claims. So in the spring of 1949 a press trip was arranged to Belgium to witness a Works driver produce a top speed of 133mph with a virtually standard XK120 Super Sports – as it was termed. The driver underlined the engine characteristics which had been

striven for in development by returning from the speed run at 10mph in top gear. The sense of excitement generated by the new car fed on itself. Its first race at Silverstone was a 1-2 result and Lyons instigated a system providing Jaguar-prepared competition cars to successful privateers, who promptly scored victory after victory around the world to enhance the reputation of the marque.

The 1950 Le Mans, in particular, showed the XK potential, so for the following year Jaguar themselves entered the fray by creating the racing C-type. The road car was over-engineered for racing so a new, lighter space frame chassis was used under a wonderful body styled by Malcom Sayer. The front suspension was much the same though the rear was re-worked. Rack and pinion steering appeared, along wih 200bhp and a top speed of around 143mph. Three cars were prepared just in time for the 1951 race and though two fell by the way the third driven by Peter Walker/Peter Whitmore was the outright victor; whilst Stirling Moss repeatedly broke the lap record before retiring. So began Jaguar's fabulous post-war competition involvement with the XK engine. The next year was a failure, but in 1953 they took 1, 2 and 4 at Le Mans.

1951 had seen the first of the coupés (the XK120) which boasted many refinements normally associated with grander saloons whilst a year earlier the Mark VII saloon had also been launched using the same engine. As prescribed it boasted 100mph+ motoring with great comfort and proved a favourite with the vital US market. Again, the publicity garnered by its achievements both in international rallies and production car races was exploited to the full.

In 1953 a third XK120 body style was introduced, the Drop Head Coupé, which offered rather more upmarket open car motoring; though the model itself

*In 1956 Ron Flockhart and Ninian Sanderon brought Jaguar a 4th Le Mans victory with the Ecurie Ecosse D-type; in the same year, the factory were also victorious. That autumn Jaguar withdrew from international motor sport.*

ABOVE *The production of road going D-types didn't use up all the available body shells so the deluxe XKSS was designed to use them up. Just 16 were dispatched before a devastating factory fire destroyed the shells.*

*The XK road cars become more and more civilized, For the XK150s (above right) greater weight was offset by greater power.*

only ran for a single year before all three XK120 variations were dropped in favour of three new cars – the XK140s. These were ostensibly the same package with various small trim changes in response to criticisms and more usefully, the replacement of the old steering with rack and pinion. A shift in engine position helped revamp the interior space and offer token 2+2 seating. Meanwhile the priceless promotional value of competition glories had led the factory in 1953 to build a development of the C-type race car, which looked not unlike the eventual E-Type and was christened the C/D. In the following year the fabled D-type emerged, uniting the XK store of knowledge with structural wisdoms from the aircraft industry. The body construction was a revolution with a central stressed tub of riveted aluminium and the power plant/suspension mounted on a separate sub frame. Malcom Sayer designed the bodywork helped by the width reducing innovation of a dry sump. Disc brakes were also introduced and collapsible fuel tanks fitted. The XK engine was given greater power through use of larger inlet valves, reworked exhaust manifolds and a changed camshaft resulting in 250bhp. Their first Le Mans in 1954 was a disaster, with all three of the works cars apparently

suffering from sand in their fuel tanks, but for 1955 they further pushed the engines to 275bhp and extended the bonnet by 7.5 inches earning them the nickname the long nosed Ds. This was the year of the hellish accident costing 81 lives. It was yet another Jaguar victory, this time for Mike Hawthorn and Ivor Bueb. In October 1956 Jaguar announced withdrawal from competition, having proved their point to say the least, and created limited edition versions of their race cars: however, in 1957 privateers Ecurie Ecosse scored yet another Le Mans victory with their own D-type.

So, although their initial objective was to launch two generations of modern sporting saloons Jaguar had accidentally created a world-beating two seater sports car, two generations of Le Mans winning race cars and a single powerful sporting saloon, the Mark VII. The saloon was large and with great care could just about return 23mpg, making it of limited appeal in the still recovering European markets. Thus in 1955 Jaguar turned to the less important half of their plan – a more compact Jaguar saloon.

The Mark I, 2.4 saloon was naturally intended to have the new XK100 4 cylinder engine, but despite development work the smaller engine couldn't quite achieve the required noise levels or indeed balance, so it was decided to shorten the stroke of the proven 6 cylinder XK engine to create the 2,483cc version. It still developed 112bhp yeilding 0-60mph in 14 seconds and just qualified for that 100mph+ target with a top speed of 101.5mph. The body was totally new and – borrowing from competition experience – saved weight through a stressed unitary construction, whilst still ensuring Jaguar levels of comfort through the introduction of rubber buffering between the body and the separate sub frame. Approaching 20,000 would be sold of the 2.4; and more significantly, it had given birth to a family of small, agile luxury saloons that would eventually eclipse the bigger models. The following year, 1957, saw them upgrade the larger saloon into a Mark VIII with a B type head, twin exhausts and a power boost of 50bhp on the original 1954 Mark VII. There were chrome embellishments, a full width front screen, a switch to manual hold specific gears on the automatic box and, for those in the back, fold down picnic tables. This was a year of mixed fortunes at Jaguar, for February 12th witnessed the devastating fire which destroyed a quarter of the factory buildings and more than 270 cars – mainly Mk VIIIs and the latest version of the compact saloon – the Mark I, 3.4. This was the logical extension of the smaller 2.4, but it used the

successful standard XK 3.4 engine, twin SU HD6 carburettors and boasting 120mph luxury motoring. Yet again, the package also made a fine competition car with the factory encouraging privateers to spectacular victories. Independent race teams such as Lister also took a keen interest in the standard XK engine, successfully boring it out to 3.8 in order to get ahead. Incredibly, the factory had a hard time selling its limited edition racing D-types. By late 1956 they had devised a limited road going version of the D-type called the XKSS, to use up the engines and rolling chassis. The factory fire destroyed the donor cars, XKSSs and even the tooling, so the 18 which exist are much treasured.

1957 also saw the move from the XK140 to the new fixed and drophead coupé XK150. By now, the body styling was naturally beginning to date and the platform was losing ground to more modern opposition. However the incredible XK engine continued to deliver the goods. The XK150s – the roadster appeared the next year – were initially all equipped with the 3.4 unit followed in 1959 by larger 3.8 versions – all available with Weslake tuned high performance heads, with triple SU carbs and lightened flywheels under the banner of 'S' versions. In the optimum 3.8 S form this ten-year-old engine was offering 265bhp and speeds approaching 140mph. The cars had become rather Grand Tourers with plenty of discreet power and excellent four wheel disc braking. So whilst the factory released an even larger

See the New

JAGUAR 4·2 LITRE 'E' TYPE

*on Stand 116 Earls Court*

saloon, the Mark IX – powered by the newly enlarged 3.8 XK engine, minds were also firmly fixed on replacing the XK150.

The successful compact Jaguar blossomed into full maturity during 1960 with the release of the classic Mk II models – the 2.4, 3.4 and 3.8 versions. Talented reworking of the Mk I bodystyling created the stunning features of the Mk II with its slim

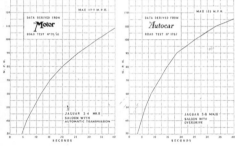

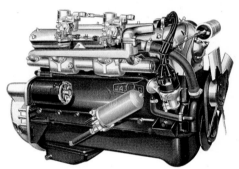

## THE WORLD FAMOUS XK ENGINE

Acknowledged throughout the world as a perfect expression of engineering efficiency, the Jaguar XK engine has carried works entered and privately owned and entered Jaguar cars to success after success on the racetracks of the world including no less than five record-breaking victories in the most gruelling race of all—the Le Mans 24-hours International Grand Prix d'Endurance.

In either 2.4 litre, 3.4 litre or 3.8 litre form, it incorporates every desirable feature available in the light of present day knowledge of automobile engine design. Twin overhead camshafts act directly upon valves set at 70° in hemispherical combustion chambers contained in a specially designed aluminium head incorporating Weslake patents. The finely balanced massive crankshaft is carried in seven exceptionally large bearings of 2⅜ ins. diameter thus ensuring complete absence of vibration or "whip". The most stringent inspection is applied throughout every stage of manufacture and assembly, and every engine is subjected to a 4-hours bench test followed by a road test check.

No engine in the world has earned a higher reputation for longevity and complete reliability under all conditions than the Jaguar XK.

This is the 3.4 litre twin overhead camshaft XK engine. With a capacity of 3,442 c.c. (210 cu. ins.) it develops 210 b.h.p. at 5,500 r.p.m. The 3.8 litre engine has 87 mm. bore × 106 mm. stroke with cubic capacity of 3,781 c.c. (230.6 cu. ins.) and develops 220 b.h.p. at 5,500 r.p.m. Both with compression ratio 8 to 1.

Acceleration and maximum speed figures from "Autocar" and "Motor" road tests. At the time of printing this catalogue, no road test figures for the 2.4 litre model from independent sources were available.

The 2.4 litre engine has the same bore dimension (83 mm.) as the 3.4 litre but has a shorter stroke (76.5 mm.). With a capacity of 2,483 c.c. it develops 120 b.h.p. at 5,750 r.p.m.

window pillars, enlarged glasswork and wider rear track. The interior enjoyed a new dashboard. Mechanically the 3.8 provided most excitement offering 0-60 in 8.5 seconds, a top speed of 125mph and even a limited diff. Inevitably this was a seductive race car with an impressive list of fans including Roy Salvadori, Stirling Moss, John Surtees, Bruce McLaren, Graham Hill and Jack Sears.

As if this one engine had not enjoyed a long enough working life, in 1961 it became very much a part of the next chapter in the Jaguar story. First it was used within the huge and oddly styled Mark X in the same level of tune as for the last S Type XK150 and then, in similar form, under the bonnet of the Malcolm Sayer-designed E-Type. Having originally chosen the engine development package of 4

cylinder/6 cylinder, the rapidly growing US enthusiasm for large V8 motor cars had been causing concern at Jaguar. They knew something very special was needed but it still had to use the existing engines. The E-Type was their answer, which was strongly related to the racing D-types. The body strengths and construction were similar, the still rare disc braking, the race proven engine, brought together with fresh elements such as independent rear suspension. In its earliest form it was a smaller car than we would recognise and used the 2.4cc engine but by the unveiling in 1961 it, like so many models before, was fitted with the 3.4 XK engine. Although the car appeared utterly new, the engine was effectively the 3.8S XK150. Thanks to the E's wind-cheating form, 150mph was now possible and a 0-60 time achievable in 6.9 seconds.

Equally predictable under its skin was the 1963 S Type saloon, which was essentially the 3.4 and 3.8 XK engine under revised Mk II bodywork involving changes to the nose, a lower overall profile and a semi Mark X rear section. Its one distinct advance over the Mk II was the inclusion of Jaguar's new independent rear suspension and, as a result, the ride was much improved.

The Mark X now required improvement and so too did the E-Type – leading Jaguar to turn once again to the trusty XK engine – this time reworking the block to provide an increase to 4.2 litres. Greater flexibility rather than further speed served the huge Mark X well, but the E-Type switch to this unit was viewed as no improvement. However, at the same time the 4.2 E-Type did gain a decent all synchromesh gearbox, slightly easier positioning for taller drivers and an improved interior. The tinkering with this beautiful car continued with the arrival of the extended 2 + 2, an attempt to embrace the family man and then spread across the model ranges. August 1966 saw the S-Type turn into the interim 420 saloon, incorporating further Mark X features and the 4.2 engine, which still managed to yield 115mph top speed. Shortly afterwards the 2.4 and 3.4 Mark IIs were updated to the 240 and 340 saloons but were actually downgraded in quality, whilst the Mark X turned into the 420G and Limousine.

Jaguar's winning ways were beginning to falter as the products aged. September 1968 was the starting point for their next model wave with the unveiling of their all new XJ6 saloon designed for the still secret V12 – this would also provide the last generation of E-Type. The car incorporated everything available. The E-Type/Mark X rear suspension, the rubber cushioning between sub frame and body, the stressed monocoque construction, the refined cockpit glazing of the Mk IIs and the all-round disc braking. The initial XK engines were the 4.2 and the virtually

square 2.8, yielding 180bhp whilst staying just under the European capacity limit which triggered surcharging. The Series II version from 1973 utilized the 4.2 engine which had enjoyed some changes. The head stud anchorage was improved to minimize gasket troubles, there were fresh transmission options and revised cooling. 1973 also saw the appearance of a two door XJ6 Coupé, again using the 4.2. Despite the obvious future success for the XJ saloon, and the V12 engine, the writing was on the wall for Jaguar. The stigma and discontent generated by the later years under Lord Stoke's BL regime led to key figures leaving. The government even stepped in during 1974 and commissioned the Ryder Report. The golden era was over and with it passed away the glorious XK engine, which had served the company for 38 years in a glittering array of their finest motor cars.

*The XK engine was so good it didn't need to be revamped out of all recognition even for the 'aircraft on four wheels', the D-type. Same capacity of 3442cc, identical block and cylinder head, triple Weber carbs boosting power to 250bhp @ 6000 rpm, additional oil pump and oil cooler. A large triple dry-plate clutch and crankshaft torsional vibration damper replaced the flywheel.*

## 132·6 M.P.H. ON PUMP PETROL · · ·

On May 30th, 1949, an entirely standard Jaguar 3½ litre XK 120 Sports Two-Seater, running on pump fuel, attained a speed of 132.6 m.p.h. over a flying mile on the Jabbeke-Aeltre Road in Belgium. This speed was officially timed by the Royal Automobile Club of Belgium and is the fastest ever recorded by a standard production unsupercharged car.

*Early displays to confound doubting critics over claimed performance figures included a 1949 press demonstration in Belgium to prove top speed. 'Soapy' Sutton, their test driver, was in fact to achieve a staggering 132.9mph.*

# PRICE GUIDE
## *1993–Present-day Fluctuations*

As 1997 Yearbook owners know, the following list of cars and prices is the result of a concerted effort to produce as stable and informative a listing as possible. Different price guides often feature identical cars showing 50% or 60% pricing discrepancies: despite faithfully reflecting their sources.

The fact is that a tired old money pit to one person is a highly desirable machine to another. All any price guide can therefore hope to achieve is a stable measure of current trends. We chose 1993 as our starting point to avoid the distortions of the speculators of the late 1980s and early 1990s. There is always of course, the dating minefield to contend with. Different publications, clubs, manufacturers, everyone clings to their own start or end date, be it the first overseas unveiling, the first announcement at home or the first sale. Do not be too disappointed with apparent anomalies in any database: as you learn more about your favourite cars, the model changes and upgrades will fix their history more precisely.

We sourced every available car price for 1993, then averaged out the safest figure, in consultation with the experts. We have repeated the exercise for 1998 and then applied the official Bank of England adjustment for the pound's value over the intervening years. These figures are therefore as accurate as we can make them, with the unique bonus of a valuation percentage swing, revealing just which models are gaining and which are losing ground in the market.

Last year there was a strong surge in the prices of the UK domestic 'shopping' models at the expense of the supercars. The same trend is in evidence this year, proving humble motor cars such as the Austin 1800/2200 (+66%) and its Morris equivalent (+117%) are worthwhile, affordable classics, if the word 'affordable' ever means anything in the classic car world. To underline the point, some BMC Farina saloons are posting 50% rises and slightly earlier domestic machinery such as the Morris Isis Estate rose by a huge 190%; even the little Ford Popular 100E increased in value by 83%.

More specifically, there are some fascinating signals. The booted Mini, in Wolseley Hornet form, has risen 22%, whilst the clearly less attractive Riley Elf version lost 19%, which begs the question about just which one of these virtually identical cars is the better oprion. Minis themselves are a mixed bag:-20% for the unloved 1275GT, +50% for the Mk II Minis. In general the larger saloons such as Mercedes and most Jaguars are losing ground, though the Daimler Sovereigns all showed +100% increases and the rarer BMWs performed very well indeed.

Reflecting the triumph of modern Alfa Romeos, many of their classic sporting saloon models are showing significant gains; rival Audi's GT Coupé dived 42 points. Aston Martins have also performed well, perhaps in the reflected glory of the DB7. The (more) affordable DBS moved ahead strongly and the Bond glamour of DB5 and DB6 continues to work its magic. The great Ferraris are still in the clouds.

As to bargains: two excellent sporting cars are dropping in value and thus look like atractive prospects. One is the evergreen MGB GT and the other the wholly underrated Porsche 944. Whether you are itching to look up your beloved marque or model, or simply intrigued by market trends, we hope that you find the following pages of interest.

| MANUFACTURER | ACTUAL CAR | YEAR FROM | YEAR TO | PRESENT VALUE | 1993 VALUE | VALUE SWING |
|---|---|---|---|---|---|---|
| A.C. | 2 LITRE DROPHEAD | 1949 | 1956 | 10000 | 8500 | 0.0787 |
| A.C. | 2 LITRE SALOON | 1947 | 1956 | 6000 | 5500 | 0.0003 |
| A.C. | 3000ME | 1979 | 1984 | 14333 | 15000 | −0.1238 |
| A.C. | 428V8 | 1965 | 1973 | 24833 | 23500 | −0.031 |
| A.C. | 428V8dhc | 1965 | 1973 | 31666 | 32500 | −0.1066 |
| A.C. | ACE AC | 1953 | 1963 | 32333 | 33750 | −0.1215 |
| A.C. | ACE BRISTOL | 1956 | 1963 | 41833 | 40250 | −0.047 |
| A.C. | ACE FORD RUDDSPEED | 1961 | 1963 | 42666 | 38750 | 0.0096 |
| A.C. | ACECA AC | 1955 | 1963 | 23333 | 18750 | 0.1411 |
| A.C. | ACECA BRISTOL | 1955 | 1963 | 28333 | 23750 | 0.0939 |
| A.C. | COBRA 289V8 | 1962 | 1968 | 94000 | 82500 | 0.0448 |
| A.C. | COBRA 427V8 | 1965 | 1968 | 128333 | 110000 | 0.0698 |
| A.C. | COBRA MkIV | 1981 | 1987 | 53000 | 40000 | 0.215 |
| A.C. | GREYHOUND | 1959 | 1963 | 16838 | 17000 | −0.0918 |
| ALFA ROMEO | 1300 GT JUNIOR fhc | 1966 | 1976 | 7916 | 5000 | 0.4517 |
| ALFA ROMEO | 1600 GT JUNIOR | 1974 | 1977 | 8000 | 5000 | 0.4671 |
| ALFA ROMEO | 1750 BERLINA SALOON | 1967 | 1972 | 5400 | 2500 | 0.9809 |
| ALFA ROMEO | 1750 GTV | 1967 | 1972 | 8900 | 6250 | 0.3058 |
| ALFA ROMEO | 1750 SPIDER VELOCE | 1967 | 1971 | 10750 | 7250 | 0.3596 |
| ALFA ROMEO | 2000 SPIDER | 1958 | 1961 | 11000 | 11000 | −0.083 |
| ALFA ROMEO | 2000 SPIDER VEL0CE dhc | 1971 | 1978 | 11500 | 7500 | 0.406 |
| ALFA ROMEO | 2000 SPRINT COUPE | 1960 | 1962 | 10166 | 6500 | 0.4341 |
| ALFA ROMEO | 2000GTV | 1970 | 1977 | 6500 | 6250 | −0.0464 |
| ALFA ROMEO | 2600 BERLINA SALOON | 1962 | 1968 | 7000 | 3500 | 0.8339 |
| ALFA ROMEO | 2600 SPIDER | 1962 | 1965 | 12250 | 10750 | 0.0449 |
| ALFA ROMEO | 2600 SPRINT COUPE | 1962 | 1966 | 8416 | 7000 | 0.1024 |
| ALFA ROMEO | 2600 SZ ZAGATO | 1965 | 1966 | 35000 | 25000 | 0.2837 |
| ALFA ROMEO | ALFASUD SPRINT | 1976 | 1983 | 3166 | 1500 | 0.9352 |
| ALFA ROMEO | ALFASUD Ti SALOON | 1974 | 1979 | 2833 | 1500 | 0.7317 |
| ALFA ROMEO | ALFETTA 1.6 GT | 1976 | 1979 | 2250 | 1500 | 0.3753 |
| ALFA ROMEO | ALFETTA GT/GTV/GTV6 | 1976 | 1987 | 3250 | 5500 | −0.4582 |
| ALFA ROMEO | GIULIA GTA | 1965 | 1969 | 30000 | 25000 | 0.1004 |
| ALFA ROMEO | GIULIA GTV | 1965 | 1968 | 9000 | 8500 | −0.0291 |
| ALFA ROMEO | GIULIA SS | 1963 | 1966 | 17500 | 25000 | −0.3581 |
| ALFA ROMEO | GIULIA TZ ZAGOTA | 1963 | 1967 | 850000 | 75000 | 9.3922 |
| ALFA ROMEO | GIULIA SPIDER | 1962 | 1965 | 11000 | 10000 | 0.0086 |
| ALFA ROMEO | GIULIA SPRINT/GT JUNIOR | 1962 | 1972 | 7958 | 5250 | 0.39 |
| ALFA ROMEO | GIULIA Ti/SUPER | 1962 | 1973 | 4833 | 3750 | 0.1817 |
| ALFA ROMEO | GIULIETTA BERLINA | 1955 | 1963 | 5666 | 4000 | 0.2989 |
| ALFA ROMEO | GIULIETTA SPIDER | 1955 | 1962 | 11668 | 10000 | 0.0699 |
| ALFA ROMEO | GIULIETTA SRINT COUPE | 1954 | 1965 | 10337 | 8000 | 0.1849 |
| ALFA ROMEO | GIULIETTA SS | 1957 | 1962 | 17500 | 22500 | −0.2868 |
| ALFA ROMEO | MONTREAL | 1971 | 1977 | 10500 | 15500 | −0.3788 |
| ALFA ROMEO | SPIDER DUETTO | 1966 | 1977 | 11333 | 7500 | 0.3856 |
| ALLARD | J2 | 1950 | 1952 | 52500 | 42500 | 0.1327 |
| ALLARD | J2X | 1951 | 1952 | 52500 | 85000 | −0.4336 |
| ALLARD | K1/K2/K3/ | 1946 | 1953 | 22000 | 16500 | 0.2226 |
| ALLARD | L/P | 1946 | 1953 | 21166 | 12500 | 0.5527 |
| ALLARD | M/M2X | 1947 | 1953 | 23338 | 17500 | 0.2228 |
| ALLARD | P1/P2 | 1949 | 1954 | 19000 | 10250 | 0.6998 |
| ALLARD | PALM BEACH 21c/21z | 1952 | 1956 | 20000 | 10000 | 0.8339 |
| ALLARD | PALM BEACH MK11 | 1956 | 1960 | 25000 | 18000 | 0.2736 |
| ALPINE–RENAULT | A108 BERLINA | 1961 | 1964 | 15000 | 17500 | −0.214 |
| ALPINE–RENAULT | A110 1,300 MODELS | 1966 | 1971 | 17336 | 15500 | 0.0256 |
| ALPINE–RENAULT | A110 1500/1600 MODELS | 1967 | 1977 | 16500 | 21000 | −0.2795 |
| ALPINE–RENAULT | A110 956 | 1959 | 1968 | 10000 | 8500 | 0.0787 |
| ALPINE–RENAULT | A110 BERLINA | 1964 | 1967 | 12000 | 12500 | −0.1197 |
| ALPINE–RENAULT | A110 GT4 1108 | 1963 | 1968 | 7000 | 7000 | −0.083 |
| ALPINE–RENAULT | A310 1600 | 1972 | 1976 | 7000 | 7000 | −0.083 |
| ALPINE–RENAULT | A310 V6 | 1976 | 1985 | 8750 | 11000 | −0.2706 |
| ALVIS | TA14 dhc | 1946 | 1950 | 14500 | 13500 | −0.0151 |
| ALVIS | TA14 SALOON | 1946 | 1950 | 10500 | 10000 | −0.0372 |
| ALVIS | TA21 dhc | 1950 | 1955 | 16000 | 15000 | −0.0219 |
| ALVIS | TA21 SALOON | 1951 | 1955 | 10500 | 8000 | 0.2036 |
| ALVIS | TC21/100 | 1950 | 1955 | 11500 | 15000 | −0.297 |
| ALVIS | TC21/100 dhc | 1950 | 1955 | 18500 | 17500 | −0.0307 |
| ALVIS | TD21 | 1956 | 1963 | 13166 | 14750 | −0.1815 |
| ALVIS | TD21 dhc | 1956 | 1963 | 23250 | 21500 | −0.0084 |
| ALVIS | TE/TF21 dhc | 1963 | 1967 | 28000 | 23750 | 0.081 |

| MANUFACTURER | ACTUAL CAR | YEAR FROM | YEAR TO | PRESENT VALUE | 1993 VALUE | VALUE SWING |
|---|---|---|---|---|---|---|
| ALVIS | TE/TF21 SALOON | 1963 | 1967 | 15083 | 13125 | 0.0537 |
| AMPHICAR | AMPHICAR | 1961 | 1967 | 7500 | 6000 | 0.1463 |
| ARMSTRONG SIDDELEY | HURRICANE | 1946 | 1953 | 11000 | 7500 | 0.3449 |
| ARMSTRONG SIDDELEY | LANCASTER | 1946 | 1952 | 8500 | 6000 | 0.2991 |
| ARMSTRONG SIDDELEY | SAPPHIRE 234/236 | 1956 | 1958 | 9500 | 4000 | 1.1779 |
| ARMSTRONG SIDDELEY | SAPPHIRE 346 | 1953 | 1959 | 11500 | 6000 | 0.7576 |
| ARMSTRONG SIDDELEY | STAR SAPPHIRE | 1959 | 1960 | 12000 | 7000 | 0.5719 |
| ARMSTRONG SIDDELEY | WHITLEY | 1950 | 1953 | 9000 | 4250 | 0.9417 |
| ASTON MARTIN | DB1 dhc | 1948 | 1950 | 50000 | 25000 | 0.8339 |
| ASTON MARTIN | DB2 | 1950 | 1953 | 32335 | 26250 | 0.1295 |
| ASTON MARTIN | DB2 dhc | 1951 | 1953 | 43334 | 35000 | 0.1353 |
| ASTON MARTIN | DB2/4 MK1 | 1953 | 1955 | 28339 | 22250 | 0.1679 |
| ASTON MARTIN | DB2/4 MK1 dhc | 1953 | 1955 | 40666 | 35000 | 0.0654 |
| ASTON MARTIN | DB2/4 MK11 | 1955 | 1957 | 28332 | 26250 | −0.0103 |
| ASTON MARTIN | DB2/4 MK11 dhc | 1955 | 1957 | 40666 | 35000 | 0.0654 |
| ASTON MARTIN | DB2/4 MK111 | 1957 | 1959 | 39000 | 28250 | 0.2659 |
| ASTON MARTIN | DB2/4 MK111 dhc | 1957 | 1959 | 51666 | 33750 | 0.4037 |
| ASTON MARTIN | DB4 | 1958 | 1963 | 41833 | 31250 | 0.2275 |
| ASTON MARTIN | DB4 dhc | 1961 | 1963 | 56500 | 42500 | 0.219 |
| ASTON MARTIN | DB4GT | 1959 | 1963 | 125000 | 95000 | 0.2065 |
| ASTON MARTIN | DB5 | 1963 | 1965 | 51500 | 27250 | 0.733 |
| ASTON MARTIN | DB5 dhc | 1963 | 1965 | 65500 | 38500 | 0.56 |
| ASTON MARTIN | DB6 MK1 | 1965 | 1969 | 35833 | 22250 | 0.4767 |
| ASTON MARTIN | DB6 MK11 | 1969 | 1970 | 36337 | 26250 | 0.2693 |
| ASTON MARTIN | DB6 Volante Convertible | 1966 | 1970 | 63333 | 51250 | 0.1332 |
| ASTON MARTIN | DBS | 1967 | 1972 | 27335 | 14500 | 0.7286 |
| ASTON MARTIN | DBS V8 | 1969 | 1972 | 28750 | 17750 | 0.4853 |
| ASTON MARTIN | DBS V8 SALOON | 1972 | 1991 | 26500 | 23250 | 0.0451 |
| ASTON MARTIN | V8 OSCAR INDIA | 1979 | 1985 | 33500 | 32500 | −0.0548 |
| ASTON MARTIN | V8 VANTAGE | 1978 | 1985 | 36500 | 37500 | −0.1075 |
| ASTON MARTIN | V8 VOLANTE | 1978 | 1985 | 49250 | 45000 | 0.0036 |
| AUDI | 60/70/80/90/100 | 1965 | 1976 | 1425 | 1475 | −0.1144 |
| AUDI | GT COUPE | 1981 | 1984 | 2200 | 3500 | −0.4236 |
| AUDI | QUATTRO TURBO | 1980 | 1989 | 6333 | 6750 | −0.1397 |
| AUSTIN | 1100 | 1963 | 1974 | 1375 | 925 | 0.3627 |
| AUSTIN | 1300 MK-111 | 1967 | 1974 | 1525 | 1075 | 0.3012 |
| AUSTIN | 1300GT | 1969 | 1974 | 2125 | 1225 | 0.5906 |
| AUSTIN | 1800/2200 | 1964 | 1975 | 1483 | 817 | 0.6644 |
| AUSTIN | 3 LITRE | 1967 | 1971 | 2233 | 1875 | 0.0919 |
| AUSTIN | A125 SHEERLINE | 1947 | 1954 | 7000 | 4250 | 0.5102 |
| AUSTIN | A135 PRINCESS | 1947 | 1958 | 7750 | 5250 | 0.3537 |
| AUSTIN | A30 | 1953 | 1956 | 2033 | 1425 | 0.3082 |
| AUSTIN | A30 COUNTRYMAN | 1956 | 1959 | 2350 | 1650 | 0.3063 |
| AUSTIN | A35 | 1956 | 1959 | 2266 | 1525 | 0.3626 |
| AUSTIN | A40 DEVON/DORSET | 1947 | 1952 | 2633 | 1650 | 0.4636 |
| AUSTIN | A40 FARINA MK1 | 1958 | 1967 | 1866 | 1625 | 0.053 |
| AUSTIN | A40 SOMERSET | 1952 | 1954 | 2600 | 1875 | 0.2714 |
| AUSTIN | A40 SOMERSET CONVERTIBLE | 1952 | 1954 | 5000 | 4000 | 0.1463 |
| AUSTIN | A40 SPORTS | 1950 | 1953 | 5000 | 4500 | 0.0187 |
| AUSTIN | A55/A60 CAMBRIDGE | 1959 | 1969 | 2929 | 1633 | 0.6446 |
| AUSTIN | A70 HAMPSHIRE | 1948 | 1950 | 3433 | 1925 | 0.6355 |
| AUSTIN | A70 HEREFORD | 1951 | 1954 | 3183 | 1925 | 0.5164 |
| AUSTIN | A90 ATLANTIC | 1947 | 1952 | 7833 | 5250 | 0.3682 |
| AUSTIN | A90 ATLANTIC dhc | 1949 | 1952 | 11338 | 7250 | 0.4339 |
| AUSTIN | A90/95/105 WESTMINSTER | 1954 | 1959 | 3116 | 1600 | 0.7857 |
| AUSTIN | A99/A110 WESTMINSTER | 1959 | 1968 | 3066 | 1725 | 0.63 |
| AUSTIN | GIPSY | 1958 | 1967 | 1750 | 1750 | −0.0828 |
| AUSTIN | MINI 1275GT | 1969 | 1980 | 1750 | 2000 | −0.1976 |
| AUSTIN | MINI COOPER | 1961 | 1964 | 4950 | 4500 | 0.0086 |
| AUSTIN | MINI COOPER 1071S | 1963 | 1964 | 6700 | 5750 | 0.0684 |
| AUSTIN | MINI COOPER 1275S | 1964 | 1971 | 7500 | 6250 | 0.1004 |
| AUSTIN | MINI COOPER 970S | 1964 | 1965 | 7283 | 5500 | 0.2142 |
| AUSTIN | MINI COOPER MK11 | 1964 | 1969 | 4383 | 3500 | 0.1483 |
| AUSTIN | MINI MK1 | 1962 | 1967 | 2650 | 2500 | −0.0279 |
| AUSTIN | MINI MK1 COUNTRYMAN | 1960 | 1967 | 2750 | 1800 | 0.4009 |
| AUSTIN | MINI MK11 | 1967 | 1969 | 1625 | 1000 | 0.4895 |
| AUSTIN | MINI MOKE | 1964 | 1981 | 3000 | 3000 | −0.0831 |
| AUSTIN | MINI SEVEN | 1959 | 1961 | 3016 | 2500 | 0.1064 |
| AUSTIN | NASH METROPOLITAN | 1954 | 1961 | 4500 | 4000 | 0.0316 |

| MANUFACTURER | ACTUAL CAR | YEAR FROM | YEAR TO | PRESENT VALUE | 1993 VALUE | VALUE SWING |
|---|---|---|---|---|---|---|
| AUSTIN | NASH METROPOLITAN dhc | 1954 | 1961 | 5833 | 4750 | 0.1261 |
| AUSTIN HEALEY | 100/4 BN1/BN2 | 1952 | 1956 | 20000 | 16250 | 0.1285 |
| AUSTIN HEALEY | 100/6 BN4/BN6 | 1956 | 1959 | 16666 | 12750 | 0.1986 |
| AUSTIN HEALEY | 100M | 1954 | 1956 | 21500 | 20250 | −0.0264 |
| AUSTIN HEALEY | 3000 MKI | 1959 | 1961 | 18750 | 15000 | 0.1462 |
| AUSTIN HEALEY | 3000 MKII | 1961 | 1963 | 21750 | 16750 | 0.1907 |
| AUSTIN HEALEY | 3000 MKIII | 1963 | 1968 | 25083 | 19500 | 0.1795 |
| AUSTIN HEALEY | 3000 MKIIA | 1962 | 1963 | 21000 | 17000 | 0.1327 |
| AUSTIN HEALEY | AUSTIN SPRITE | 1970 | 1971 | 4150 | 4500 | −0.1544 |
| AUSTIN HEALEY | SPRITE MKI FROGEYE | 1958 | 1961 | 7133 | 5500 | 0.1892 |
| AUSTIN HEALEY | SPRITE MKII | 1962 | 1964 | 4766 | 3850 | 0.135 |
| AUSTIN HEALEY | SPRITE MKIII | 1964 | 1966 | 4833 | 3750 | 0.1817 |
| AUSTIN HEALEY | SPRITE MKIV | 1966 | 1970 | 4166 | 3600 | 0.0611 |
| BENTLEY | CORNICHE dhc T2 | 1977 | 1984 | 40000 | 33750 | 0.0868 |
| BENTLEY | CORNICHE fhc T2 | 1977 | 1981 | 35000 | 28750 | 0.1163 |
| BENTLEY | MK6 dhc | 1951 | 1952 | 39000 | 35000 | 0.0217 |
| BENTLEY | MK6 STANDARD STEEL | 1946 | 1952 | 17000 | 15000 | 0.0392 |
| BENTLEY | PARK WARD dhc | 1959 | 1962 | 44000 | 40000 | 0.0087 |
| BENTLEY | R TYPE 4.5 LITRE dhc P/W | 1952 | 1955 | 39500 | 38500 | −0.0592 |
| BENTLEY | R TYPE 4.5 LITRE SALOON | 1952 | 1955 | 18500 | 12500 | 0.3571 |
| BENTLEY | R TYPE CONTINENTAL HJM | 1952 | 1955 | 88500 | 80000 | 0.0144 |
| BENTLEY | S SERIES SALOON | 1955 | 1959 | 21333 | 16000 | 0.2226 |
| BENTLEY | S1 CONTINENTAL MPW fhc | 1955 | 1959 | 68000 | 80000 | −0.2206 |
| BENTLEY | S1 CONTINENTAL PW dhc | 1955 | 1959 | 110000 | 80000 | 0.2608 |
| BENTLEY | S2 CONTINENTAL PW dhc | 1959 | 1962 | 44000 | 45000 | −0.1034 |
| BENTLEY | S2 FLYING SPUR HJM | 1959 | 1962 | 46500 | 40000 | 0.066 |
| BENTLEY | S2 STANDARD STEEL | 1959 | 1962 | 15500 | 15500 | −0.0831 |
| BENTLEY | S3 CONTINENTAL FLYING SPUR | 1962 | 1965 | 51500 | 47500 | −0.0058 |
| BENTLEY | S3 CONTINENTAL MPW | 1962 | 1965 | 40250 | 55000 | −0.329 |
| BENTLEY | S3 CONTINENTAL MPW dhc | 1962 | 1965 | 55500 | 55000 | −0.0747 |
| BENTLEY | S3 STANDARD STEEL | 1962 | 1965 | 21083 | 21500 | −0.1008 |
| BENTLEY | T SERIES CORNICHE MPW dhc | 1965 | 1977 | 30000 | 30000 | −0.083 |
| BENTLEY | T SERIES CORNICHE MPW fhc | 1965 | 1977 | 22500 | 19750 | 0.0446 |
| BENTLEY | T SERIES SALOON | 1965 | 1967 | 11500 | 10000 | 0.0545 |
| BENTLEY | T2 SERIES SALOON | 1977 | 1981 | 18333 | 15250 | 0.1023 |
| BERKELEY | B60 /B65 | 1956 | 1957 | 2650 | 2000 | 0.215 |
| BERKELEY | B90 | 1957 | 1959 | 2200 | 2375 | −0.1506 |
| BERKELEY | B90 dhc | 1957 | 1959 | 2500 | 2500 | −0.0829 |
| BERKELEY | B95/105 SPORTS | 1959 | 1961 | 3400 | 2500 | 0.2472 |
| BERKELEY | T60 | 1959 | 1961 | 2400 | 1500 | 0.467 |
| BMW | 1500/1800 | 1962 | 1972 | 2700 | 2500 | −0.0095 |
| BMW | 1502/1600–2/1602 | 1966 | 1977 | 3000 | 2600 | 0.0582 |
| BMW | 1502/1602 TOURING | 1966 | 1977 | 3000 | 2400 | 0.1464 |
| BMW | 2000 | 1966 | 1972 | 2830 | 2625 | −0.0115 |
| BMW | 2000CS | 1965 | 1969 | 4125 | 4500 | −0.1595 |
| BMW | 2002 CABRIO | 1971 | 1973 | 6625 | 6500 | −0.0655 |
| BMW | 2002 TURBO | 1973 | 1974 | 11500 | 11250 | −0.0627 |
| BMW | 2002/2002Ti | 1968 | 1975 | 4666 | 3563 | 0.2007 |
| BMW | 2500/2800 | 1969 | 1977 | 2750 | 2500 | 0.0088 |
| BMW | 2800CS | 1968 | 1971 | 4625 | 5750 | −0.2625 |
| BMW | 3.0CS/CSi | 1971 | 1975 | 6500 | 6750 | −0.117 |
| BMW | 3.0CSL | 1972 | 1975 | 10750 | 7100 | 0.3884 |
| BMW | 3.3L SALOON | 1971 | 1977 | 4200 | 3000 | 0.2836 |
| BMW | 501 | 1952 | 1956 | 13000 | 6500 | 0.8338 |
| BMW | 501 V8/502 | 1955 | 1963 | 16000 | 8000 | 0.834 |
| BMW | 503 COUPE | 1956 | 1959 | 32000 | 9250 | 2.1721 |
| BMW | 503 dhc | 1956 | 1959 | 40000 | 14250 | 1.574 |
| BMW | 507 | 1957 | 1959 | 72000 | 90000 | −0.2664 |
| BMW | 600 | 1958 | 1959 | 1000 | 1000 | −0.0834 |
| BMW | 628CSi | 1979 | 1990 | 3000 | 5000 | −0.4498 |
| BMW | 633CS | 1976 | 1990 | 3950 | 5000 | −0.2756 |
| BMW | 635CSi | 1976 | 1990 | 6250 | 5250 | 0.0917 |
| BMW | 700 | 1960 | 1965 | 1600 | 1625 | −0.0971 |
| BMW | ISETTA | 1955 | 1962 | 4666 | 5000 | −0.1443 |
| BMW | M1 | 1978 | 1981 | 65000 | 72500 | −0.1779 |
| BOND | 875 | 1966 | 1970 | 1450 | 1000 | 0.3291 |
| BOND | BUG | 1970 | 1974 | 1916 | 1500 | 0.1711 |
| BOND | EQUIPE 2 LITRE | 1967 | 1970 | 2933 | 2250 | 0.1952 |
| BOND | EQUIPE 2 LITRE dhc | 1967 | 1970 | 3700 | 3250 | 0.044 |

| MANUFACTURER | ACTUAL CAR | YEAR FROM | YEAR TO | PRESENT VALUE | 1993 VALUE | VALUE SWING |
|---|---|---|---|---|---|---|
| BOND | EQUIPE GT4/GT4S | 1963 | 1970 | 2233 | 1775 | 0.1534 |
| BORGWARD | BIG SIX | 1959 | 1961 | 8000 | 4500 | 0.63 |
| BORGWARD | ISABELLA COUPE | 1955 | 1961 | 8000 | 5000 | 0.4671 |
| BORGWARD | ISABELLA TS | 1954 | 1961 | 4000 | 4000 | −0.083 |
| BRISTOL | 400 | 1947 | 1950 | 22500 | 21250 | −0.0291 |
| BRISTOL | 401 | 1948 | 1953 | 20500 | 9500 | 0.9788 |
| BRISTOL | 403 | 1953 | 1955 | 20500 | 13750 | 0.3671 |
| BRISTOL | 404 | 1953 | 1955 | 29000 | 28500 | −0.067 |
| BRISTOL | 405 | 1954 | 1958 | 18750 | 13250 | 0.2976 |
| BRISTOL | 406 | 1958 | 1961 | 18750 | 12250 | 0.4035 |
| BRISTOL | 407 | 1962 | 1963 | 16550 | 15000 | 0.0117 |
| BRISTOL | 408 | 1964 | 1965 | 16550 | 15500 | −0.0209 |
| BRISTOL | 409 | 1966 | 1967 | 16550 | 16000 | −0.0515 |
| BRISTOL | 410 | 1968 | 1969 | 18000 | 16500 | 0.0003 |
| BRISTOL | 411 | 1969 | 1976 | 20500 | 14750 | 0.2744 |
| BRISTOL | 412 | 1975 | 1982 | 18750 | 13250 | 0.2976 |
| BRISTOL | 603 | 1976 | 1982 | 17500 | 20000 | −0.1977 |
| CATERHAM | SEVEN | 1974 | 1982 | 8875 | 10000 | −0.1862 |
| CHEVROLET | CORVETTE | 1953 | 1954 | 20000 | 23750 | −0.2278 |
| CHEVROLET | CORVETTE | 1955 | 1957 | 14000 | 15500 | −0.1718 |
| CHEVROLET | CORVETTE | 1958 | 1962 | 13000 | 13250 | −0.1003 |
| CHEVROLET | CORVETTE | 1963 | 1967 | 19000 | 16000 | 0.0889 |
| CHEVROLET | CORVETTE | 1968 | 1972 | 14250 | 13250 | −0.0138 |
| CHEVROLET | CORVETTE | 1973 | 1976 | 7250 | 8250 | −0.1942 |
| CHEVROLET | CORVETTE | 1976 | 1982 | 8100 | 9250 | −0.1971 |
| CITROEN | AMI 6 | 1961 | 1969 | 1900 | 1750 | −0.0042 |
| CITROEN | 2CV | 1948 | 1971 | 2250 | 2000 | 0.0316 |
| CITROEN | 2CV | 1971 | 1991 | 1416 | 1000 | 0.2979 |
| CITROEN | AMI 8 | 1969 | 1979 | 787 | 1125 | −0.3586 |
| CITROEN | AMI SUPER | 1973 | 1976 | 1200 | 1350 | −0.1848 |
| CITROEN | BIG 15/LIGHT 15 | 1935 | 1957 | 8916 | 7750 | 0.0549 |
| CITROEN | BIG 6 | 1939 | 1955 | 12250 | 8000 | 0.4042 |
| CITROEN | BIJOU | 1959 | 1964 | 2375 | 2125 | 0.025 |
| CITROEN | CX | 1974 | 1989 | 2500 | 2200 | 0.0421 |
| CITROEN | DS CONVERTIBLE | 1963 | 1971 | 17750 | 10000 | 0.6275 |
| CITROEN | DS19/ID19/DW19 | 1956 | 1965 | 6766 | 4438 | 0.3979 |
| CITROEN | DS20/21/23 PALLAS | 1966 | 1975 | 7750 | 6000 | 0.1845 |
| CITROEN | DYANE 4 | 1967 | 1974 | 800 | 900 | −0.1853 |
| CITROEN | DYANE 6 | 1968 | 1984 | 1050 | 1000 | −0.0376 |
| CITROEN | GS | 1970 | 1986 | 750 | 1000 | −0.3126 |
| CITROEN | SAFARI ESTATE | 1957 | 1975 | 6166 | 4000 | 0.4136 |
| CITROEN | SM lhd | 1970 | 1975 | 15000 | 11750 | 0.1706 |
| CLAN | CRUSADER | 1972 | 1974 | 2983 | 2500 | 0.0943 |
| DAF | 44 | 1966 | 1975 | 700 | 1200 | −0.4652 |
| DAF | 46 | 1974 | 1976 | 850 | 1000 | −0.2209 |
| DAF | 55 | 1968 | 1972 | 850 | 925 | −0.1576 |
| DAF | 55 COUPE | 1968 | 1972 | 1500 | 1800 | −0.2359 |
| DAF | 66 | 1972 | 1975 | 850 | 925 | −0.1576 |
| DAF | 750/33 | 1962 | 1975 | 750 | 1125 | −0.3888 |
| DAIMLER | 2.5 LITRE V8 SALOON | 1963 | 1968 | 11333 | 8000 | 0.2991 |
| DAIMLER | 250 V8 | 1959 | 1964 | 14333 | 13250 | −0.0810 |
| DAIMLER | CONQUEST CENTURY | 1954 | 1958 | 4166 | 4000 | −0.0449 |
| DAIMLER | CONQUEST ROADSTER | 1954 | 1956 | 10500 | 11250 | −0.1442 |
| DAIMLER | DB18 CONSORT | 1950 | 1953 | 5333 | 6000 | −0.1849 |
| DAIMLER | DB18 SPORTS | 1949 | 1953 | 11666 | 15250 | −0.2985 |
| DAIMLER | DOUBLE SIX | 1972 | 1973 | 5625 | 3375 | 0.5281 |
| DAIMLER | DOUBLE SIX 2 | 1973 | 1978 | 5400 | 3375 | 0.467 |
| DAIMLER | DOUBLE SIX COUPE | 1975 | 1977 | 9250 | 8833 | −0.0398 |
| DAIMLER | DOUBLE SIX VP | 1972 | 1973 | 7500 | 3500 | 0.9649 |
| DAIMLER | MAJESTIC 3.8 | 1958 | 1962 | 5083 | 4500 | 0.0357 |
| DAIMLER | MAGESTIC MAYOR DR450 LIMO 4.5 | 1959 | 1968 | 6583 | 5333 | 0.1319 |
| DAIMLER | REGENCY MK1 | 1951 | 1952 | 5700 | 3500 | 0.4933 |
| DAIMLER | REGENCY MK11/111 | 1954 | 1956 | 5500 | 4500 | 0.1206 |
| DAIMLER | SOVEREIGN 1 2.8 | 1969 | 1973 | 7750 | 2500 | 1.843 |
| DAIMLER | SOVEREIGN 1 4.2 | 1969 | 1973 | 5583 | 2500 | 1.0481 |
| DAIMLER | SOVEREIGN 2 3.4/4.2 | 1975 | 1978 | 6625 | 2500 | 1.4303 |
| DAIMLER | SOVEREIGN 2 4.2 COUPE | 1975 | 1977 | 8166 | 5000 | 0.4975 |
| DAIMLER | SOVEREIGN 420 | 1966 | 1970 | 8000 | 6000 | 0.2227 |
| DATSUN | 240Z | 1969 | 1971 | 7833 | 6000 | 0.1972 |

| MANUFACTURER | ACTUAL CAR | YEAR FROM | YEAR TO | PRESENT VALUE | 1993 VALUE | VALUE SWING |
|---|---|---|---|---|---|---|
| DATSUN | 240Z | 1971 | 1974 | 5666 | 4750 | 0.0938 |
| DATSUN | 260Z | 1973 | 1978 | 4000 | 3500 | 0.0479 |
| DATSUN | 260Z 2+2 | 1974 | 1979 | 3500 | 2250 | 0.4262 |
| DATSUN | 280ZX | 1978 | 1981 | 3250 | 3000 | −0.0067 |
| DATSUN | 280ZX 2+2 | 1978 | 1981 | 2583 | 2500 | −0.0525 |
| DE LOREAN | DE LOREAN | 1980 | 1981 | 14500 | 12500 | 0.0637 |
| DE TOMASO | DEAUVILLE | 1970 | 1988 | 11500 | 8000 | 0.3182 |
| DE TOMASO | LONGCHAMP | 1972 | 1990 | 11500 | 8000 | 0.3182 |
| DE TOMASO | MANGUSTA COUPE | 1967 | 1972 | 30125 | 27500 | 0.0045 |
| DE TOMASO | PANTERA COUPE | 1970 | 1989 | 27500 | 20000 | 0.2608 |
| DELLOW | MKI/II/III | 1949 | 1957 | 8000 | 7000 | 0.0479 |
| DKW | 1000S | 1958 | 1963 | 5000 | 1500 | 2.0562 |
| DKW | F102 | 1964 | 1966 | 1000 | 1500 | −0.3888 |
| DKW | JUNIOR | 1959 | 1965 | 1500 | 5000 | −0.7249 |
| DODGE | CHARGER 440 | 1967 | 1972 | 11000 | 11250 | −0.1034 |
| ELVA | COURIER | 1951 | 1961 | 6750 | 2000 | 2.0949 |
| ELVA | COURIER MKIII/MKIV | 1962 | 1969 | 7250 | 3500 | 0.8994 |
| FACEL VEGA | EXCELLENCE | 1958 | 1964 | 25000 | 18750 | 0.2226 |
| FACEL VEGA | FACEL 2 | 1962 | 1964 | 50000 | 28750 | 0.5947 |
| FACEL VEGA | FACEL 3 | 1963 | 1964 | 8000 | 10000 | −0.2665 |
| FACEL VEGA | FACEL 3 CONVERTIBLE | 1963 | 1964 | 12000 | 10000 | 0.1003 |
| FACEL VEGA | FACELLIA | 1961 | 1963 | 8875 | 8750 | −0.0699 |
| FACEL VEGA | FACELLIA dhc | 1960 | 1963 | 15000 | 13000 | 0.0581 |
| FACEL VEGA | FVS | 1954 | 1959 | 16500 | 17500 | −0.1354 |
| FACEL VEGA | HK500 | 1958 | 1961 | 23000 | 25000 | −0.1564 |
| FAIRTHORPE | ELECTRON MINOR | 1957 | 1973 | 3900 | 2750 | 0.3004 |
| FAIRTHORPE | TX GT/S/Ss | 1967 | 1973 | 4400 | 3500 | 0.1527 |
| FALCON | CARIBBEAN | 1957 | 1963 | 2000 | 2000 | −0.083 |
| FERRARI | 212 | 1951 | 1953 | 150000 | 110000 | 0.2504 |
| FERRARI | 250 CALIFORNIA SPIDER lhd 59 | 1959 | 1963 | 350000 | 200000 | 0.6047 |
| FERRARI | 250GT LUSSO | 1962 | 1964 | 105000 | 120000 | −0.1977 |
| FERRARI | 250GTE 2+2 | 1956 | 1964 | 40000 | 35000 | 0.0479 |
| FERRARI | 250SWB LIGHTWEIGHT | 1959 | 1963 | 600000 | 250000 | 1.2007 |
| FERRARI | 275 GTS SPIDER lhd | 1965 | 1966 | 120000 | 115000 | −0.0432 |
| FERRARI | 275GTB | 1965 | 1966 | 135000 | 112500 | 0.1004 |
| FERRARI | 275GTB/4 | 1966 | 1968 | 205000 | 187500 | 0.0025 |
| FERRARI | 275GTB/4 SPIDER lhd | 1966 | 1968 | 800000 | 400000 | 0.8339 |
| FERRARI | 308 GTB | 1975 | 1981 | 26500 | 25500 | −0.0471 |
| FERRARI | 308 GTB SC fibreglass | 1975 | 1977 | 30000 | 32500 | −0.1536 |
| FERRARI | 308 GTS qv SPIDER | 1983 | 1985 | 32000 | 32500 | −0.0971 |
| FERRARI | 308 GTS SPIDER | 1975 | 1981 | 27500 | 31000 | −0.1866 |
| FERRARI | 328GTB | 1981 | 1988 | 37250 | 37000 | −0.0769 |
| FERRARI | 330GT | 1964 | 1967 | 25000 | 29000 | −0.2095 |
| FERRARI | 330GTC | 1966 | 1968 | 45000 | 67500 | −0.3887 |
| FERRARI | 365 GT4 2+2 | 1972 | 1976 | 25500 | 25000 | −0.0647 |
| FERRARI | 365 GTC/4 | 1968 | 1974 | 52000 | 57500 | −0.1707 |
| FERRARI | 365GT 2+2 | 1967 | 1971 | 38000 | 30000 | 0.1615 |
| FERRARI | 365GTB/4 DAYTONA | 1968 | 1974 | 91000 | 85000 | −0.0183 |
| FERRARI | 365GTB/4 DAYTONA SPIDER | 1968 | 1974 | 250000 | 250000 | −0.083 |
| FERRARI | 365GTC | 1967 | 1970 | 60000 | 72500 | −0.2411 |
| FERRARI | 400GT | 1976 | 1985 | 19500 | 20000 | −0.106 |
| FERRARI | 410 SUPERAMERICA | 1955 | 1960 | 137500 | 120000 | 0.0507 |
| FERRARI | 500 SUPERFAST | 1964 | 1966 | 100000 | 100000 | −0.083 |
| FERRARI | 512 BB BOXER COUPE | 1973 | 1984 | 62000 | 77500 | −0.2664 |
| FERRARI | DINO 206GT | 1968 | 1969 | 53500 | 65000 | −0.2453 |
| FERRARI | DINO 246GT | 1969 | 1974 | 52500 | 35000 | 0.3754 |
| FERRARI | DINO 246GTS SPIDER | 1972 | 1974 | 51000 | 45000 | 0.0392 |
| FERRARI | DINO 308GT4 2+2 | 1973 | 1980 | 20000 | 15000 | 0.2226 |
| FERRARI | MONDIAL | 1981 | 1986 | 23000 | 22500 | −0.0627 |
| FERRARI | MONDIAL CABRIO | 1984 | 1986 | 30000 | 32500 | −0.1536 |
| FIAT | 124 COUPE | 1966 | 1972 | 3783 | 2750 | 0.2614 |
| FIAT | 124 SPIDER lhd | 1966 | 1982 | 6083 | 4600 | 0.2125 |
| FIAT | 128 3P | 1975 | 1978 | 2500 | 2875 | −0.2026 |
| FIAT | 130 | 1969 | 1976 | 2750 | 3000 | −0.1595 |
| FIAT | 130 COUPE | 1971 | 1970 | 4266 | 6500 | −0.3982 |
| FIAT | 131 MIRAFIORI | 1974 | 1984 | 1366 | 1000 | 0.2521 |
| FIAT | 1500 CABRIO | 1963 | 1967 | 7000 | 3500 | 0.8339 |
| FIAT | 1500S/1600S | 1959 | 1975 | 5375 | 4500 | 0.0952 |
| FIAT | 2300S | 1961 | 1968 | 5250 | 4000 | 0.2036 |

| MANUFACTURER | ACTUAL CAR | YEAR FROM | YEAR TO | PRESENT VALUE | 1993 VALUE | VALUE SWING |
|---|---|---|---|---|---|---|
| FIAT | 500 TOPOLINO | 1948 | 1955 | 5300 | 6000 | −0.19 |
| FIAT | 500/500D/500F | 1957 | 1975 | 2516 | 2500 | −0.077 |
| FIAT | 600/600D | 1955 | 1970 | 2533 | 2000 | 0.1614 |
| FIAT | 850 COUPE | 1965 | 1972 | 2150 | 1750 | 0.1268 |
| FIAT | 850 SPIDER | 1965 | 1973 | 3733 | 2850 | 0.2011 |
| FIAT | DINO 2000/2400 lhd | 1967 | 1973 | 7666 | 9000 | −0.219 |
| FIAT | DINO 2000/2400 SPIDER | 1967 | 1973 | 13500 | 14500 | −0.1463 |
| FIAT | MULTIPLA | 1955 | 1966 | 5000 | 2250 | 1.0375 |
| FIAT | X 1/9 | 1972 | 1989 | 2800 | 2750 | −0.0664 |
| FIAT | X 1/9 1500 | 1979 | 1985 | 3583 | 3500 | −0.0613 |
| FIAT ABARTH | 595 | 1963 | 1971 | 5000 | 1200 | 2.8197 |
| FIAT ABARTH | 595/695SS | 1963 | 1971 | 5200 | 1500 | 2.1785 |
| FORD | 500 SKYLINER | 1957 | 1958 | 13000 | 15000 | −0.2053 |
| FORD | ANGLIA 100E | 1953 | 1959 | 1600 | 1125 | 0.304 |
| FORD | ANGLIA 105E | 1959 | 1967 | 1783 | 1733 | −0.0566 |
| FORD | CAPRI 109E/116E | 1961 | 1963 | 4000 | 2625 | 0.3971 |
| FORD | CAPRI 1600/2000 | 1969 | 1974 | 1400 | 1000 | 0.2832 |
| FORD | CAPRI 2.8iV6 | 1981 | 1987 | 3500 | 4000 | −0.1976 |
| FORD | CAPRI 2000GT | 1969 | 1974 | 1650 | 1500 | 0.0086 |
| FORD | CAPRI 3000E | 1970 | 1974 | 2750 | 3500 | −0.2795 |
| FORD | CAPRI 3000GT | 1969 | 1974 | 2100 | 2500 | −0.2296 |
| FORD | CAPRI 3000V6 | 1969 | 1974 | 1500 | 1000 | 0.3749 |
| FORD | CAPRI GT | 1962 | 1964 | 4000 | 2750 | 0.3338 |
| FORD | CAPRI RS3100V6 | 1973 | 1974 | 5450 | 5000 | −0.0006 |
| FORD | CLASSIC 109E/116E | 1961 | 1962 | 2216 | 1575 | 0.2899 |
| FORD | CONSUL MKI | 1951 | 1956 | 2450 | 2125 | 0.0574 |
| FORD | CONSUL MKI CONVERTIBLE | 1952 | 1956 | 7000 | 5750 | 0.1162 |
| FORD | CONSUL MKII | 1956 | 1962 | 3100 | 2750 | 0.0337 |
| FORD | CONSUL MKII CONVERTIBLE | 1956 | 1962 | 7516 | 6250 | 0.1027 |
| FORD | CONSUL/GRANADA MKI | 1972 | 1977 | 1891 | 1350 | 0.2846 |
| FORD | CORSAIR | 1964 | 1965 | 2183 | 1450 | 0.3808 |
| FORD | CORSAIR 2000E | 1967 | 1970 | 1800 | 1375 | 0.2 |
| FORD | CORSAIR GT | 1964 | 1965 | 1833 | 1500 | 0.1204 |
| FORD | CORSAIR V4 GT | 1966 | 1967 | 1400 | 1400 | −0.0832 |
| FORD | CORTINA 1600E | 1968 | 1970 | 3700 | 2750 | 0.2337 |
| FORD | CORTINA GT MKI | 1963 | 1966 | 3083 | 5250 | −0.4615 |
| FORD | CORTINA GT MKII | 1966 | 1970 | 2016 | 1450 | 0.2751 |
| FORD | CORTINA MKI | 1962 | 1966 | 1450 | 1400 | −0.0504 |
| FORD | CORTINA MKII | 1966 | 1970 | 1175 | 1150 | −0.063 |
| FORD | CORTINA MKIII | 1970 | 1976 | 900 | 825 | 0 |
| FORD | CORTINA MKIV | 1976 | 1979 | 800 | 1000 | −0.2667 |
| FORD | CORTINA MKV | 1979 | 1982 | 800 | 1200 | −0.3888 |
| FORD | CORTINA SAVAGE | 1968 | 1970 | 9250 | 6750 | 0.2566 |
| FORD | ESCORT 1300E | 1973 | 1975 | 2100 | 2000 | −0.0371 |
| FORD | ESCORT GT | 1968 | 1973 | 2233 | 1700 | 0.2044 |
| FORD | ESCORT MEXICO | 1970 | 1974 | 4416 | 3000 | 0.3496 |
| FORD | ESCORT MKI | 1968 | 1975 | 1200 | 1200 | −0.0833 |
| FORD | ESCORT MKII GHIA | 1975 | 1980 | 1800 | 2100 | −0.214 |
| FORD | ESCORT RS1600 | 1970 | 1974 | 7750 | 4250 | 0.6721 |
| FORD | ESCORT RS1800 | 1975 | 1977 | 9625 | 8000 | 0.1033 |
| FORD | ESCORT RS2000 MKI | 1970 | 1974 | 4833 | 4500 | −0.0153 |
| FORD | ESCORT RS2000 MKII | 1976 | 1980 | 4333 | 5750 | −0.309 |
| FORD | ESCORT SPORT | 1971 | 1975 | 2500 | 2175 | 0.054 |
| FORD | ESCORT TWIN CAM | 1968 | 1971 | 6538 | 4500 | 0.3321 |
| FORD | ESCORT/ESQUIRE/100E ESTATE | 1956 | 1960 | 1933 | 1250 | 0.4182 |
| FORD | GRANADA COUPE | 1974 | 1977 | 2183 | 2000 | 0.0009 |
| FORD | GRANADA GHIA | 1972 | 1977 | 1966 | 1500 | 0.2017 |
| FORD | LOTUS CORTINA MKI | 1963 | 1966 | 12416 | 9500 | 0.1985 |
| FORD | LOTUS CORTINA MKII | 1967 | 1970 | 4933 | 4500 | 0.0051 |
| FORD | MUSTANG 289 | 1964 | 1966 | 6000 | 6000 | −0.083 |
| FORD | MUSTANG 289 CONVERTIBLE | 1964 | 1966 | 8000 | 8000 | −0.083 |
| FORD | MUSTANG 289 FASTBACK | 1964 | 1966 | 7000 | 7000 | −0.083 |
| FORD | PERFECT 107E | 1959 | 1961 | 1825 | 1250 | 0.339 |
| FORD | PERFECT/ANGLIA | 1940 | 1953 | 2250 | 2000 | 0.0316 |
| FORD | PILOT | 1947 | 1951 | 6166 | 6250 | −0.0954 |
| FORD | POPULAR 100E | 1960 | 1962 | 1600 | 800 | 0.8349 |
| FORD | POPULAR 103E | 1953 | 1959 | 2266 | 1750 | 0.1876 |
| FORD | SHELBY MUSTANG GT350 | 1966 | 1967 | 17000 | 20000 | −0.2206 |
| FORD | SHELBY MUSTANG GT500 | 1966 | 1967 | 24000 | 28500 | −0.2278 |

| MANUFACTURER | ACTUAL CAR | YEAR FROM | YEAR TO | PRESENT VALUE | 1993 VALUE | VALUE SWING |
|---|---|---|---|---|---|---|
| FORD | ZEPHYR 4 MKIII | 1962 | 1966 | 2333 | 2000 | 0.0697 |
| FORD | ZEPHYR 4 MKIV | 1966 | 1972 | 1616 | 1125 | 0.317 |
| FORD | ZEPHYR 6 MKIII | 1962 | 1966 | 2933 | 2500 | 0.0759 |
| FORD | ZEPHYR 6 MKIV | 1966 | 1972 | 1983 | 1675 | 0.0854 |
| FORD | ZEPHYR MKI | 1951 | 1956 | 34000 | 2625 | 10.8757 |
| FORD | ZEPHYR MKI CONVERTIBLE | 1952 | 1956 | 7766 | 7000 | 0.0173 |
| FORD | ZEPHYR MKII | 1956 | 1962 | 4100 | 3417 | 0.1004 |
| FORD | ZEPHYR MKII CONVERTIBLE | 1956 | 1962 | 7916 | 6667 | 0.0887 |
| FORD | ZODIAC EXECUTIVE | 1966 | 1972 | 2350 | 2100 | 0.0262 |
| FORD | ZODIAC MKII | 1956 | 1962 | 4333 | 3650 | 0.0884 |
| FORD | ZODIAC MKII CONVERTIBLE | 1956 | 1962 | 8250 | 6583 | 0.1492 |
| FORD | ZODIAC MKIII | 1962 | 1966 | 4066 | 2875 | 0.297 |
| FRAZER NASH | LE MANS REPLICA/REPLICA 2 | 1948 | 1953 | 102500 | 77500 | 0.2128 |
| GILBERN | GENIE | 1966 | 1970 | 4750 | 4500 | -0.0322 |
| GILBERN | GT COUPE/1800 | 1959 | 1967 | 3900 | 3125 | 0.1444 |
| GILBERN | INVADER | 1969 | 1974 | 5541 | 4750 | 0.0697 |
| GINETTA | G15 | 1968 | 1974 | 6416 | 4000 | 0.4709 |
| GINETTA | G21 1800/1800S | 1971 | 1978 | 6833 | 4500 | 0.3922 |
| GINETTA | G21 3LITRE | 1971 | 1975 | 6750 | 5250 | 0.179 |
| GINETTA | G4 1498 | 1967 | 1968 | 15500 | 7500 | 0.8951 |
| GINETTA | G4 997 | 1961 | 1968 | 15000 | 7750 | 0.7747 |
| GORDON KEEBLE | GKI/II | 1964 | 1967 | 21500 | 20000 | -0.0143 |
| HEALEY | ABBOTT dhc | 1950 | 1954 | 24000 | 13250 | 0.6609 |
| HEALEY | ELLIOTT | 1946 | 1950 | 14000 | 15000 | -0.1441 |
| HEALEY | NASH HEALEY | 1951 | 1954 | 21500 | 15000 | 0.3143 |
| HEALEY | SILVERSTONE | 1949 | 1950 | 32750 | 25000 | 0.2012 |
| HEALEY | TICKFORD | 1950 | 1954 | 14000 | 7250 | 0.7706 |
| HEINKEL | CRUISER TROJAN | 1956 | 1965 | 3600 | 4000 | -0.1747 |
| HILLMAN | AVENGER | 1970 | 1976 | 800 | 750 | -0.022 |
| HILLMAN | AVENGER TIGER | 1972 | 1973 | 2750 | 3000 | -0.1595 |
| HILLMAN | CALIFORNIAN | 1953 | 1956 | 2500 | 2000 | 0.1463 |
| HILLMAN | CALIFORNIAN dhc | 1953 | 1956 | 3700 | 5000 | -0.3215 |
| HILLMAN | HUNTER | 1966 | 1967 | 1000 | 1000 | -0.0834 |
| HILLMAN | HUNTER GLS | 1972 | 1976 | 1750 | 2000 | -0.1976 |
| HILLMAN | HUNTER GT | 1970 | 1973 | 1516 | 1500 | -0.0733 |
| HILLMAN | HUSKY MKI/2 ESTATE | 1954 | 1960 | 1325 | 1250 | -0.0279 |
| HILLMAN | IMP CALIFORNIAN | 1968 | 1970 | 1600 | 1150 | 0.2759 |
| HILLMAN | IMP/SUPER IMP | 1963 | 1976 | 1150 | 975 | 0.0818 |
| HILLMAN | MINX MKI–VIII | 1940 | 1956 | 1550 | 1500 | -0.0526 |
| HILLMAN | MINX SI–IIIC | 1954 | 1963 | 1583 | 1375 | 0.0553 |
| HILLMAN | MINX SI–IIIC CONVERTIBLE | 1954 | 1962 | 3566 | 4000 | -0.1825 |
| HILLMAN | MINX SV–VI | 1963 | 1967 | 1200 | 925 | 0.1893 |
| HILLMAN | NEW MINX | 1967 | 1977 | 900 | 850 | -0.0291 |
| HILLMAN | SUPER MINX SI–IV | 1962 | 1966 | 1200 | 875 | 0.2579 |
| HILLMAN | SUPER MINX SI–IV CONVERTIBLE | 1962 | 1964 | 3583 | 2750 | 0.1947 |
| HONDA | S600/S800 | 1966 | 1970 | 4133 | 2500 | 0.5161 |
| HONDA | S600/S800 CONVERTIBLE | 1967 | 1970 | 7333 | 4250 | 0.5821 |
| HONDA | Z COUPE | 1970 | 1975 | 3500 | 700 | 3.5872 |
| HRG | 1100/1500 | 1939 | 1955 | 20000 | 35000 | -0.476 |
| HUMBER | HAWK I–IV | 1957 | 1968 | 3433 | 3250 | -0.0313 |
| HUMBER | HAWK III–VI | 1947 | 1957 | 3625 | 3500 | -0.0503 |
| HUMBER | PULMAN LIMO | 1945 | 1953 | 6150 | 4000 | 0.4099 |
| HUMBER | PULMAN/IMPERIAL | 1953 | 1954 | 6600 | 5000 | 0.2103 |
| HUMBER | SCEPTRE I–II | 1963 | 1967 | 1866 | 1783 | -0.0401 |
| HUMBER | SCEPTRE III | 1968 | 1976 | 1550 | 1300 | 0.0931 |
| HUMBER | SNIPE | 1945 | 1946 | 3425 | 3600 | -0.1276 |
| HUMBER | SUPER SNIPE | 1947 | 1952 | 3425 | 4000 | -0.2148 |
| HUMBER | SUPER SNIPE I | 1958 | 1959 | 3875 | 4000 | -0.1116 |
| HUMBER | SUPER SNIPE II–III | 1960 | 1964 | 2733 | 2375 | 0.0552 |
| HUMBER | SUPER SNIPE IV | 1953 | 1956 | 4166 | 4000 | -0.0449 |
| HUMBER | SUPER SNIPE CONVERTIBLE | 1949 | 1952 | 11000 | 8500 | 0.1866 |
| HUMBER | SUPER SNIPE IMPERIAL | 1965 | 1967 | 3125 | 2125 | 0.3487 |
| ISO | FIDIA | 1967 | 1974 | 9000 | 12000 | -0.3123 |
| ISO | GRIFO | 1969 | 1974 | 3500 | 34000 | -0.9056 |
| ISO | LELE | 1969 | 1974 | 14000 | 14000 | -0.083 |
| ISO | RIVOLTA | 1962 | 1970 | 17000 | 15000 | 0.0392 |
| JAGUAR | 1.5 | 1945 | 1949 | 12250 | 12500 | -0.1014 |
| JAGUAR | 2.5 | 1946 | 1949 | 14500 | 15000 | -0.1136 |
| JAGUAR | 240 | 1968 | 1969 | 8500 | 6250 | 0.2471 |

| MANUFACTURER | ACTUAL CAR | YEAR FROM | YEAR TO | PRESENT VALUE | 1993 VALUE | VALUE SWING |
|---|---|---|---|---|---|---|
| JAGUAR | 3.5 | 1946 | 1949 | 19375 | 20000 | −0.1117 |
| JAGUAR | 340 | 1967 | 1968 | 12833 | 8000 | 0.471 |
| JAGUAR | 420 | 1966 | 1968 | 8083 | 5750 | 0.2889 |
| JAGUAR | E TYPE 3.8 ROADSTER | 1961 | 1964 | 34166 | 32500 | −0.036 |
| JAGUAR | E TYPE fhc 3.8 | 1961 | 1964 | 23333 | 21250 | 0.0069 |
| JAGUAR | E TYPE S1 4.2  2+2dhc | 1966 | 1968 | 16250 | 13000 | 0.1462 |
| JAGUAR | E TYPE S1 4.2 fhc | 1965 | 1968 | 21583 | 17500 | 0.1309 |
| JAGUAR | E TYPE S1 4.2 ROADSTER | 1965 | 1968 | 27666 | 24000 | 0.057 |
| JAGUAR | E TYPE S1/S11  2+2 | 1967 | 1968 | 16250 | 12500 | 0.192 |
| JAGUAR | E TYPE S1/S11 fhc | 1967 | 1968 | 22000 | 17500 | 0.1527 |
| JAGUAR | E TYPE S1/S11 ROADSTER | 1967 | 1968 | 31000 | 27500 | 0.0337 |
| JAGUAR | E TYPE S11 2+2 | 1968 | 1970 | 15416 | 11250 | 0.2565 |
| JAGUAR | E TYPE S11 fhc | 1968 | 1970 | 18833 | 12500 | 0.3815 |
| JAGUAR | E TYPE S11 ROADSTER | 1968 | 1970 | 26338 | 20000 | 0.2076 |
| JAGUAR | E TYPE V12 fhc | 1971 | 1975 | 18500 | 16500 | 0.0281 |
| JAGUAR | E TYPE V12 ROADSTER | 1971 | 1975 | 38500 | 30000 | 0.1768 |
| JAGUAR | MK V  3.5 CONVERTIBLE | 1949 | 1951 | 29166 | 24750 | 0.0806 |
| JAGUAR | MK V 2.5 | 1949 | 1951 | 16833 | 11500 | 0.3422 |
| JAGUAR | MK V 2.5 CONVERTIBLE | 1949 | 1951 | 24500 | 21250 | 0.0572 |
| JAGUAR | MK V 3.5 | 1949 | 1951 | 20083 | 16000 | 0.151 |
| JAGUAR | MK V11/V11M | 1951 | 1956 | 13250 | 11250 | 0.08 |
| JAGUAR | MK V111 | 1956 | 1959 | 14750 | 9000 | 0.5028 |
| JAGUAR | MK X 3.8 | 1961 | 1964 | 10333 | 5750 | 0.6477 |
| JAGUAR | MK X 4.2/420G | 1964 | 1970 | 7500 | 5750 | 0.196 |
| JAGUAR | MK1 2.4 | 1955 | 1959 | 9833 | 8000 | 0.1271 |
| JAGUAR | MK1 3.4 | 1957 | 1959 | 13666 | 9750 | 0.2852 |
| JAGUAR | MK11 2.4 | 1959 | 1967 | 12416 | 7750 | 0.469 |
| JAGUAR | MK11 3.4 | 1959 | 1967 | 17666 | 10250 | 0.5804 |
| JAGUAR | MK11 3.8 | 1959 | 1967 | 20500 | 15750 | 0.1935 |
| JAGUAR | MK1X | 1958 | 1961 | 14416 | 6250 | 1.115 |
| JAGUAR | S TYPE 3.4 | 1964 | 1968 | 10668 | 6250 | 0.5651 |
| JAGUAR | S TYPE 3.8 | 1964 | 1968 | 12000 | 7000 | 0.5719 |
| JAGUAR | XJ 12 COUPE 5.3 | 1975 | 1978 | 8916 | 8000 | 0.022 |
| JAGUAR | XJ12 S11 | 1973 | 1979 | 5266 | 3750 | 0.2875 |
| JAGUAR | XJ12 S111 | 1979 | 1986 | 5425 | 12500 | −0.602 |
| JAGUAR | XJ12 S1 5.3 | 1972 | 1973 | 5066 | 4000 | 0.1614 |
| JAGUAR | XJ6 4.2 S1 | 1968 | 1973 | 4833 | 2500 | 0.7729 |
| JAGUAR | XJ6 COUPE 4.2 | 1975 | 1978 | 7666 | 5750 | 0.2225 |
| JAGUAR | XJ6 S1 2.8 | 1968 | 1973 | 4066 | 2500 | 0.4916 |
| JAGUAR | XJ6 S11  3.4 | 1973 | 1979 | 4316 | 3250 | 0.2178 |
| JAGUAR | XJ6 S11  4.2 | 1973 | 1979 | 4516 | 3533 | 0.1721 |
| JAGUAR | XJ6 S111 3.4/4.2 | 1979 | 1986 | 3250 | 10000 | −0.702 |
| JAGUAR | XJS | 1975 | 1986 | 5041 | 7750 | −0.4036 |
| JAGUAR | XJS 3.6 CABRIO | 1984 | 1987 | 8000 | 10000 | −0.2665 |
| JAGUAR | XJS V12 | 1981 | 1987 | 5500 | 7500 | −0.3275 |
| JAGUAR | XJS V12 CABRIO | 1985 | 1986 | 10000 | 12500 | −0.2664 |
| JAGUAR | XK 120 dhc | 1953 | 1954 | 34666 | 25000 | 0.2715 |
| JAGUAR | XK 150 3.4 ROADSTER | 1958 | 1960 | 41500 | 35000 | 0.0872 |
| JAGUAR | XK 150 3.8 dhc | 1959 | 1960 | 48500 | 30000 | 0.4824 |
| JAGUAR | XK 150 3.8 fhc | 1959 | 1960 | 35000 | 19750 | 0.625 |
| JAGUAR | XK 150 3.8 ROADSTER | 1959 | 1960 | 52500 | 46500 | 0.0353 |
| JAGUAR | XK 150 dhc | 1957 | 1960 | 35338 | 21250 | 0.5249 |
| JAGUAR | XK 150S  3.4 ROADSTER | 1958 | 1960 | 46500 | 40000 | 0.066 |
| JAGUAR | XK 150S 3.4 dhc | 1959 | 1960 | 46250 | 36250 | 0.1699 |
| JAGUAR | XK 150S 3.4 fhc | 1959 | 1960 | 29000 | 23500 | 0.1316 |
| JAGUAR | XK120 ALLOY | 1949 | 1950 | 67500 | 50000 | 0.2379 |
| JAGUAR | XK120 fhc | 1951 | 1954 | 39335 | 20250 | 0.7812 |
| JAGUAR | XK120 ROADSTER | 1950 | 1954 | 40100 | 30000 | 0.2257 |
| JAGUAR | XK140 dhc | 1954 | 1957 | 32833 | 22250 | 0.3531 |
| JAGUAR | XK140 fhc | 1954 | 1957 | 24339 | 17250 | 0.2938 |
| JAGUAR | XK140 ROADSTER | 1954 | 1957 | 42500 | 31250 | 0.2471 |
| JAGUAR | XK150 3.4 fhc | 1957 | 1960 | 24500 | 16250 | 0.3825 |
| JAGUAR | XK150S 3.8 ROADSTER | 1959 | 1960 | 52500 | 46500 | 0.0353 |
| JAGUAR | XK150S 3.8 dhc | 1959 | 1960 | 48500 | 38500 | 0.1551 |
| JAGUAR | XK150S 3.8 fhc | 1959 | 1960 | 33000 | 26250 | 0.1528 |
| JENSEN | 541 | 1953 | 1959 | 14166 | 11250 | 0.1546 |
| JENSEN | 541R | 1957 | 1960 | 14833 | 9750 | 0.395 |
| JENSEN | 541S | 1961 | 1963 | 12500 | 11750 | −0.0245 |
| JENSEN | CV8 MK1/11/111 | 1962 | 1966 | 16000 | 14750 | −0.0053 |

| MANUFACTURER | ACTUAL CAR | YEAR FROM | YEAR TO | PRESENT VALUE | 1993 VALUE | VALUE SWING |
|---|---|---|---|---|---|---|
| JENSEN | FF MKI/II/III | 1967 | 1971 | 22666 | 16000 | 0.299 |
| JENSEN | INTERCEPTOR I | 1967 | 1969 | 13000 | 6000 | 0.9869 |
| JENSEN | INTERCEPTOR 2 | 1970 | 1972 | 12668 | 7000 | 0.6594 |
| JENSEN | INTERCEPTOR 3 | 1972 | 1976 | 13323 | 8000 | 0.5272 |
| JENSEN | INTERCEPTOR CONVERTIBLE | 1974 | 1976 | 29000 | 22500 | 0.1818 |
| JENSEN | INTERCEPTOR COUPE | 1975 | 1976 | 33000 | 12000 | 1.5216 |
| JENSEN | INTERCEPTOR SP | 1971 | 1976 | 19000 | 10000 | 0.7422 |
| JENSEN HEALEY | JENSON HEALEY CONVERTIBLE | 1972 | 1976 | 5166 | 4500 | 0.0526 |
| JENSEN HEALEY | JENSON HEALEY GT | 1975 | 1976 | 5916 | 5750 | -0.0566 |
| JOWETT | JAVELIN | 1947 | 1953 | 6500 | 6250 | -0.0464 |
| JOWETT | JUPITER dhc | 1950 | 1954 | 14345 | 11000 | 0.1958 |
| LAGONDA | 2.6/2.9 | 1947 | 1958 | 16000 | 10750 | 0.3647 |
| LAGONDA | 2.6/2.9 CONVERTIBLE | 1951 | 1956 | 21500 | 19000 | 0.0376 |
| LAGONDA | RAPIDE | 1961 | 1964 | 24750 | 23500 | -0.0343 |
| LAMBORGHINI | 350 GT | 1964 | 1966 | 65000 | 62500 | -0.0464 |
| LAMBORGHINI | 400 GT | 1966 | 1968 | 52500 | 45000 | 0.0698 |
| LAMBORGHINI | COUNTACH LP400 | 1973 | 1982 | 56250 | 40000 | 0.2895 |
| LAMBORGHINI | COUNTACH LP400S | 1974 | 1989 | 53500 | 45000 | 0.0902 |
| LAMBORGHINI | ESPADA I–II | 1968 | 1973 | 19500 | 15000 | 0.1921 |
| LAMBORGHINI | ESPADA III | 1973 | 1978 | 20500 | 20000 | -0.0601 |
| LAMBORGHINI | ISLERO | 1968 | 1969 | 32500 | 20000 | 0.4901 |
| LAMBORGHINI | JALPA | 1982 | 1986 | 24000 | 27500 | -0.1997 |
| LAMBORGHINI | JARAMA | 1970 | 1978 | 30000 | 12000 | 1.2924 |
| LAMBORGHINI | MIURA SV | 1971 | 1975 | 87500 | 125000 | -0.3581 |
| LAMBORGHINI | MIURA/MIURA S | 1966 | 1971 | 76500 | 75000 | -0.0647 |
| LAMBORGHINI | URRACO P250 COUPE | 1970 | 1979 | 15750 | 16000 | -0.0974 |
| LAMBORGHINI | URRACO P300 COUPE | 1970 | 1979 | 27500 | 27500 | -0.083 |
| LANCHESTER | 14 LEDA | 1951 | 1954 | 7500 | 3000 | 1.2922 |
| LANCHESTER | LD10 | 1946 | 1951 | 4000 | 2250 | 0.63 |
| LANCIA | APPIA | 1953 | 1963 | 5875 | 7000 | -0.2304 |
| LANCIA | APPIA ZAGOTA | 1957 | 1961 | 30000 | 27500 | 0.0003 |
| LANCIA | APRILIA | 1937 | 1949 | 14000 | 15000 | -0.1441 |
| LANCIA | AURELIA B10 | 1950 | 1951 | 9500 | 85000 | -0.8975 |
| LANCIA | AURELIA B12 | 1954 | 1955 | 15500 | 12500 | 0.137 |
| LANCIA | AURELIA B20 | 1951 | 1958 | 19166 | 17500 | 0.0042 |
| LANCIA | AURELIA B21/22 | 1951 | 1954 | 10000 | 10000 | -0.0831 |
| LANCIA | B24 CONVERTIBLE | 1955 | 1958 | 38000 | 30000 | 0.1615 |
| LANCIA | B24 SPIDER | 1955 | 1958 | 60000 | 45000 | 0.2226 |
| LANCIA | BETA COUPE | 1973 | 1984 | 1733 | 3000 | -0.4704 |
| LANCIA | BETA HPE | 1975 | 1984 | 2000 | 2500 | -0.2663 |
| LANCIA | BETA SPIDER | 1977 | 1982 | 3416 | 3750 | -0.1648 |
| LANCIA | FLAMINIA | 1957 | 1970 | 6000 | 8250 | -0.3331 |
| LANCIA | FLAMINIA CONVERTIBLE | 1959 | 1967 | 38000 | 12000 | 1.9036 |
| LANCIA | FLAMINIA COUPE | 1959 | 1967 | 12500 | 12500 | -0.083 |
| LANCIA | FLAMINIA GT | 1959 | 1967 | 21000 | 20000 | -0.0372 |
| LANCIA | FLAVIA | 1961 | 1966 | 2750 | 3167 | -0.2038 |
| LANCIA | FLAVIA 2000 | 1970 | 1974 | 3750 | 2750 | 0.2504 |
| LANCIA | FLAVIA 2000 COUPE | 1969 | 1975 | 5000 | 3500 | 0.3099 |
| LANCIA | FLAVIA COUPE | 1962 | 1968 | 4875 | 6000 | -0.2549 |
| LANCIA | FLAVIA ZAGOTA | 1963 | 1967 | 22500 | 25000 | -0.1747 |
| LANCIA | FULVIA COUPE S1/S11 | 1965 | 1976 | 9750 | 4083 | 1.1895 |
| LANCIA | FULVIA HF SI | 1968 | 1970 | 20000 | 20000 | -0.083 |
| LANCIA | FULVIA HF SII | 1971 | 1972 | 11250 | 7500 | 0.3755 |
| LANCIA | FULVIA ZAGOTA | 1968 | 1972 | 12937 | 10625 | 0.1165 |
| LANCIA | GAMMA | 1977 | 1984 | 1600 | 1500 | -0.022 |
| LANCIA | GAMMA COUPE | 1977 | 1984 | 3250 | 3250 | -0.083 |
| LANCIA | MONTE CARLO | 1975 | 1984 | 6583 | 4900 | 0.2318 |
| LANCIA | STRATOS | 1974 | 1975 | 63000 | 50000 | 0.1554 |
| LAND ROVER | SI | 1948 | 1958 | 4000 | 2000 | 0.834 |
| LAND ROVER | SII/11A | 1958 | 1971 | 3750 | 2500 | 0.3756 |
| LEA FRANCIS | 12/14 hp | 1946 | 1954 | 10000 | 6500 | 0.4106 |
| LEA FRANCIS | 12/14 hp COUPE | 1947 | 1948 | 12000 | 7500 | 0.4672 |
| LEA FRANCIS | 14 hp SPORTS | 1947 | 1949 | 16250 | 15000 | -0.0066 |
| LEA FRANCIS | 14/70 | 1949 | 1953 | 10916 | 10000 | 0.0009 |
| LEA FRANCIS | 2.5 dhc | 1950 | 1954 | 18500 | 14500 | 0.1699 |
| LOTUS | CORTINA LOTUS MKII | 1967 | 1870 | 4933 | 4500 | 0.0051 |
| LOTUS | ECLAT SI COUPE | 1975 | 1980 | 3833 | 4500 | -0.219 |
| LOTUS | ECLAT S2.2 | 1980 | 1982 | 4083 | 6000 | -0.376 |
| LOTUS | ECLAT SPRINT | 1975 | 1975 | 3916 | 5500 | -0.3471 |

| MANUFACTURER | ACTUAL CAR | YEAR FROM | YEAR TO | PRESENT VALUE | 1993 VALUE | VALUE SWING |
|---|---|---|---|---|---|---|
| LOTUS | ELAN PLUS 2 | 1967 | 1969 | 7083 | 6750 | −0.0378 |
| LOTUS | ELAN PLUS 2 | 1969 | 1971 | 7500 | 8500 | −0.1909 |
| LOTUS | ELAN PLUS 2S 130 | 1971 | 1974 | 8750 | 9000 | −0.1085 |
| LOTUS | ELAN SI dhc | 1962 | 1964 | 14166 | 14000 | −0.0722 |
| LOTUS | ELAN SII fhc | 1964 | 1966 | 12000 | 11500 | −0.0431 |
| LOTUS | ELAN SIII dhc | 1966 | 1969 | 13667 | 11750 | 0.0666 |
| LOTUS | ELAN SIII fhc | 1966 | 1969 | 12000 | 11750 | −0.0635 |
| LOTUS | ELAN SII dhc | 1964 | 1966 | 13668 | 11250 | 0.114 |
| LOTUS | ELAN SIV dhc | 1968 | 1971 | 13000 | 12750 | −0.0651 |
| LOTUS | ELAN SIV fhc | 1968 | 1971 | 11500 | 10250 | 0.0288 |
| LOTUS | ELAN SPRINT dhc | 1971 | 1973 | 14500 | 14000 | −0.0503 |
| LOTUS | ELAN SPRINT fhc | 1971 | 1973 | 13125 | 11750 | 0.0243 |
| LOTUS | ELITE | 1958 | 1963 | 25750 | 22500 | 0.0494 |
| LOTUS | ELITE SI | 1974 | 1980 | 3416 | 4000 | −0.2169 |
| LOTUS | ELITE S2.2 | 1980 | 1982 | 4250 | 5000 | −0.2206 |
| LOTUS | ESPRIT SI | 1976 | 1978 | 5333 | 6500 | −0.2477 |
| LOTUS | ESPRIT SII | 1978 | 1980 | 5750 | 7000 | −0.2468 |
| LOTUS | ESPRIT TURBO | 1980 | 1981 | 8500 | 9250 | −0.1574 |
| LOTUS | EUROPA SI/IA | 1966 | 1969 | 6334 | 4125 | 0.4079 |
| LOTUS | EUROPA SII | 1969 | 1971 | 6583 | 5250 | 0.1499 |
| LOTUS | EUROPA TWIN CAM/SPECIAL | 1971 | 1975 | 10250 | 10125 | −0.0717 |
| LOTUS | LOTUS CORTINA MKI | 1963 | 1966 | 12416 | 9500 | 0.1985 |
| LOTUS | SEVEN SI | 1957 | 1961 | 13500 | 16000 | −0.2263 |
| LOTUS | SEVEN SII/III | 1961 | 1969 | 12416 | 11750 | −0.0311 |
| LOTUS | SEVEN S4 SPORTS | 1969 | 1972 | 6833 | 5000 | 0.2531 |
| LOTUS | SIX | 1953 | 1956 | 15000 | 13750 | 0.0003 |
| MARCOS | 1500/1600/1800 GT | 1964 | 1968 | 8750 | 7000 | 0.1462 |
| MARCOS | 2 LITRE | 1969 | 1972 | 7000 | 5000 | 0.2837 |
| MARCOS | 3 litre | 1969 | 1972 | 9833 | 8250 | 0.0929 |
| MARCOS | MANTIS | 1970 | 1971 | 4750 | 5000 | −0.1289 |
| MARCOS | MINI MARCOS | 1965 | 1972 | 3266 | 2650 | 0.1301 |
| MASERATI | 3500 GT lhd | 1958 | 1964 | 30250 | 17500 | 0.585 |
| MASERATI | 3500 GT SPIDER | 1958 | 1964 | 42500 | 35000 | 0.1134 |
| MASERATI | BORA | 1971 | 1978 | 36000 | 20000 | 0.6505 |
| MASERATI | GHIBLI | 1967 | 1973 | 27500 | 30500 | −0.1732 |
| MASERATI | GHIBLI SPIDER dhc | 1967 | 1973 | 43250 | 50000 | −0.2068 |
| MASERATI | INDY | 1969 | 1974 | 23000 | 17500 | 0.2051 |
| MASERATI | KHAMSIN lhd | 1973 | 1982 | 26000 | 16750 | 0.4233 |
| MASERATI | KYALAMI lhd | 1976 | 1983 | 12500 | 10000 | 0.1462 |
| MASERATI | MEREK/MEREK SS | 1972 | 1983 | 19500 | 16500 | 0.0837 |
| MASERATI | MEXICO | 1967 | 1972 | 26500 | 18500 | 0.3135 |
| MASERATI | MISTRAL | 1964 | 1970 | 32500 | 30000 | −0.0066 |
| MASERATI | MISTRAL SPIDER lhd | 1964 | 1970 | 44000 | 37500 | 0.0759 |
| MASERATI | QUATTROPORTE | 1967 | 1971 | 10250 | 12250 | −0.2327 |
| MASERATI | QUATTROPORTE II | 1975 | 1977 | 13000 | 15000 | −0.2053 |
| MASERATI | SEBRING SERIES SI/II | 1962 | 1966 | 25000 | 15500 | 0.4789 |
| MATRA | BAGHEERA | 1973 | 1979 | 3625 | 3250 | 0.0229 |
| MATRA | MURENA/MURENA S | 1980 | 1984 | 6000 | 5250 | 0.048 |
| MATRA | RANCHO | 1977 | 1984 | 3200 | 3750 | −0.2176 |
| MAZDA | RX2 | 1970 | 1978 | 3000 | 2200 | 0.2505 |
| MAZDA | RX3 | 1971 | 1978 | 3000 | 2000 | 0.3755 |
| MAZDA | RX7 | 1978 | 1985 | 6500 | 4500 | 0.3244 |
| MERCEDES BENZ | 190/190D | 1961 | 1965 | 3866 | 3000 | 0.1815 |
| MERCEDES BENZ | 190/200 | 1956 | 1968 | 4000 | 3500 | 0.0479 |
| MERCEDES BENZ | 190SL | 1955 | 1963 | 22500 | 16250 | 0.2696 |
| MERCEDES BENZ | 200/200D | 1965 | 1968 | 4200 | 3000 | 0.2836 |
| MERCEDES BENZ | 220 | 1951 | 1954 | 10750 | 12000 | −0.1786 |
| MERCEDES BENZ | 220 | 1968 | 1976 | 4500 | 5000 | −0.1748 |
| MERCEDES BENZ | 220 CABRIO | 1951 | 1954 | 18500 | 20000 | −0.1518 |
| MERCEDES BENZ | 220A | 1956 | 1959 | 6750 | 7500 | −0.1747 |
| MERCEDES BENZ | 220A CABRIO | 1956 | 1959 | 10500 | 12500 | −0.2298 |
| MERCEDES BENZ | 220S | 1956 | 1959 | 8500 | 10000 | −0.2206 |
| MERCEDES BENZ | 220S CABRIO | 1956 | 1959 | 18000 | 17500 | −0.0569 |
| MERCEDES BENZ | 220S COUPE | 1956 | 1959 | 16000 | 11500 | 0.2758 |
| MERCEDES BENZ | 220S/SE | 1959 | 1965 | 9500 | 10000 | −0.1289 |
| MERCEDES BENZ | 220SE | 1958 | 1959 | 11000 | 11500 | −0.1229 |
| MERCEDES BENZ | 220SE CABRIO | 1958 | 1959 | 20500 | 20000 | −0.0601 |
| MERCEDES BENZ | 220SE COUPE | 1958 | 1959 | 17500 | 17500 | −0.083 |
| MERCEDES BENZ | 220SEb | 1960 | 1965 | 14250 | 12500 | 0.0453 |

| MANUFACTURER | ACTUAL CAR | YEAR FROM | YEAR TO | PRESENT VALUE | 1993 VALUE | VALUE SWING |
|---|---|---|---|---|---|---|
| MERCEDES BENZ | 220SEb CONVERTIBLE | 1960 | 1965 | 24000 | 19500 | 0.1286 |
| MERCEDES BENZ | 220SEC | 1959 | 1965 | 15500 | 15000 | −0.0525 |
| MERCEDES BENZ | 230/230S | 1965 | 1968 | 7500 | 10000 | −0.3123 |
| MERCEDES BENZ | 230SL/250SL | 1963 | 1967 | 16000 | 14500 | 0.0118 |
| MERCEDES BENZ | 250 | 1968 | 1972 | 4200 | 6500 | −0.4075 |
| MERCEDES BENZ | 250CE/280CE | 1968 | 1973 | 6750 | 5750 | 0.0764 |
| MERCEDES BENZ | 250S/250SE | 1965 | 1969 | 5933 | 10000 | −0.456 |
| MERCEDES BENZ | 250SE/280SE CABRIO | 1965 | 1971 | 19500 | 18625 | −0.04 |
| MERCEDES BENZ | 250SEC/280SEC | 1965 | 1971 | 13250 | 11500 | 0.0565 |
| MERCEDES BENZ | 280S/SE | 1968 | 1972 | 5533 | 4500 | 0.1273 |
| MERCEDES BENZ | 280SL | 1968 | 1971 | 19332 | 18000 | −0.0152 |
| MERCEDES BENZ | 300 CABRIO D | 1951 | 1957 | 32000 | 40000 | −0.2664 |
| MERCEDES BENZ | 300A/B/C | 1951 | 1957 | 15250 | 15000 | −0.0677 |
| MERCEDES BENZ | 300D | 1957 | 1962 | 22000 | 20000 | 0.0087 |
| MERCEDES BENZ | 300S CABRIO | 1952 | 1958 | 80000 | 100000 | −0.2664 |
| MERCEDES BENZ | 300S COUPE | 1952 | 1958 | 80000 | 85000 | −0.137 |
| MERCEDES BENZ | 300S ROADSTER | 1952 | 1958 | 83000 | 135000 | −0.4362 |
| MERCEDES BENZ | 300SE/SEL | 1961 | 1965 | 8833 | 10250 | −0.2098 |
| MERCEDES BENZ | 300SE/SEL | 1965 | 1967 | 6583 | 10000 | −0.3964 |
| MERCEDES BENZ | 300SEC | 1961 | 1965 | 21000 | 14750 | 0.3055 |
| MERCEDES BENZ | 300SEL | 1971 | 1972 | 7250 | 7500 | −0.1136 |
| MERCEDES BENZ | 300SEL 6.3 | 1967 | 1972 | 10331 | 12500 | −0.2422 |
| MERCEDES BENZ | 300SL GULLWING | 1954 | 1957 | 137500 | 125000 | 0.0087 |
| MERCEDES BENZ | 300SL ROADSTER | 1957 | 1963 | 108750 | 77500 | 0.2867 |
| MERCEDES BENZ | 350SL | 1970 | 1980 | 14500 | 11000 | 0.2087 |
| MERCEDES BENZ | 350SLC | 1971 | 1980 | 10000 | 8500 | 0.0787 |
| MERCEDES BENZ | 450SE/SEL | 1973 | 1980 | 10000 | 11250 | −0.1849 |
| MERCEDES BENZ | 450SL | 1971 | 1981 | 13000 | 11000 | 0.0837 |
| MERCEDES BENZ | 450SLC | 1972 | 1981 | 9500 | 9000 | −0.0321 |
| MERCEDES BENZ | 500SL ROADSTER | 1981 | 1984 | 15000 | 15000 | −0.083 |
| MERCEDES BENZ | 500SLC | 1981 | 1984 | 13000 | 13000 | −0.083 |
| MERCEDES BENZ | 600 | 1964 | 1981 | 43000 | 23500 | 0.6779 |
| MESSERSCHMITT | KR200 | 1955 | 1962 | 5500 | 5000 | 0.0086 |
| MG | 1100 | 1962 | 1965 | 2266 | 2500 | −0.1687 |
| MG | 1100 | 1966 | 1968 | 2060 | 1500 | 0.2592 |
| MG | 1300 | 1967 | 1971 | 2280 | 1750 | 0.195 |
| MG | MAGNETTE III/IV | 1959 | 1968 | 2333 | 2000 | 0.0697 |
| MG | MAGNETTE ZA/ZB | 1953 | 1958 | 4666 | 3750 | 0.1408 |
| MG | MGA 1500 fhc | 1956 | 1959 | 8333 | 8500 | −0.1011 |
| MG | MGA 1500 ROADSTER | 1955 | 1959 | 14666 | 10750 | 0.2509 |
| MG | MGA 1600 DELUXE ROADSTER | 1960 | 1961 | 14416 | 11250 | 0.175 |
| MG | MGA 1600 fhc | 1959 | 1961 | 9000 | 8000 | 0.0316 |
| MG | MGA 1600 fhc DELUXE | 1960 | 1961 | 9833 | 8000 | 0.1271 |
| MG | MGA 1600 MK11 fhc | 1961 | 1962 | 9083 | 8500 | −0.0202 |
| MG | MGA 1600 MK11 ROADSTER | 1960 | 1962 | 13339 | 10000 | 0.2231 |
| MG | MGA 1600 ROADSTER | 1959 | 1961 | 13500 | 11000 | 0.1254 |
| MG | MGA fhc TC | 1958 | 1960 | 13166 | 13500 | −0.1058 |
| MG | MGA TC ROADSTER | 1958 | 1960 | 17333 | 16250 | −0.022 |
| MG | MGB GT | 1965 | 1974 | 4977 | 5500 | −0.1702 |
| MG | MGB GT | 1975 | 1980 | 4000 | 6000 | −0.3887 |
| MG | MGB GT V8 | 1973 | 1975 | 10800 | 8250 | 0.2004 |
| MG | MGB ROADSTER | 1962 | 1974 | 8461 | 10000 | −0.2242 |
| MG | MGB ROADSTER | 1975 | 1980 | 5500 | 8000 | −0.3696 |
| MG | MGC GT | 1967 | 1969 | 6250 | 6500 | −0.1184 |
| MG | MGC ROADSTER | 1967 | 1969 | 9050 | 9500 | −0.1264 |
| MG | MIDGET 1500 | 1974 | 1979 | 4750 | 4250 | 0.0248 |
| MG | MIDGET MK1/11 | 1961 | 1966 | 4716 | 4000 | 0.0812 |
| MG | MIDGET MK111/1V | 1966 | 1974 | 4666 | 4500 | −0.0493 |
| MG | TA | 1936 | 1939 | 15000 | 15000 | −0.083 |
| MG | TB | 1939 | 1945 | 16250 | 20000 | −0.255 |
| MG | TC | 1945 | 1949 | 17000 | 17500 | −0.1092 |
| MG | TD | 1949 | 1953 | 14666 | 13000 | 0.0345 |
| MG | TF1250 | 1953 | 1954 | 17750 | 17500 | −0.07 |
| MG | TF1500 | 1954 | 1955 | 19166 | 16500 | 0.0651 |
| MG | YA/YB | 1947 | 1953 | 6166 | 5250 | 0.077 |
| MORGAN | 4/4 1600 SPORTS | 1968 | 1981 | 13250 | 9000 | 0.35 |
| MORGAN | 4/4 S1 | 1936 | 1950 | 15000 | 15000 | −0.083 |
| MORGAN | PLUS 4 PLUS | 1964 | 1966 | 16500 | 10000 | 0.5129 |
| MORGAN | PLUS 4 S11–V | 1954 | 1968 | 11833 | 9400 | 0.1543 |

| MANUFACTURER | ACTUAL CAR | YEAR FROM | YEAR TO | PRESENT VALUE | 1993 VALUE | VALUE SWING |
|---|---|---|---|---|---|---|
| MORGAN | PLUS 4 TR | 1954 | 1969 | 14000 | 11500 | 0.1163 |
| MORGAN | PLUS 4 VANGUARD | 1950 | 1958 | 10750 | 9000 | 0.0953 |
| MORGAN | PLUS 8 | 1968 | 1997 | 18500 | 15000 | 0.1309 |
| MORRIS | EIGHT SERIES E | 1939 | 1945 | 3200 | 2500 | 0.1739 |
| MORRIS | EIGHT SERIES E CONVERTIBLE | 1939 | 1945 | 5300 | 3500 | 0.3885 |
| MORRIS | 1100/1300 | 1962 | 1973 | 1450 | 700 | 0.9004 |
| MORRIS | 1800/2200 | 1966 | 1975 | 1483 | 625 | 1.1745 |
| MORRIS | COWLEY 1200 | 1954 | 1956 | 1625 | 2250 | −0.3378 |
| MORRIS | COWLEY 1500 | 1956 | 1957 | 1700 | 2250 | −0.3073 |
| MORRIS | ISIS | 1955 | 1958 | 2416 | 2250 | −0.0155 |
| MORRIS | ISIS I–II ESTATE | 1956 | 1957 | 4100 | 1300 | 1.8914 |
| MORRIS | ITAL | 1981 | 1984 | 700 | 950 | −0.3243 |
| MORRIS | MARINA 1.3/1.8 | 1971 | 1976 | 850 | 8000 | −0.9026 |
| MORRIS | MARINA 1.8TC | 1971 | 1975 | 1300 | 900 | 0.3238 |
| MORRIS | MARINA II | 1976 | 1980 | 650 | 850 | −0.2988 |
| MORRIS | MINOR 1000 | 1956 | 1970 | 2466 | 2500 | −0.0954 |
| MORRIS | MINOR 1000 CONVERTIBLE | 1956 | 1970 | 3883 | 3500 | 0.0173 |
| MORRIS | MINOR 1000 ESTATE | 1956 | 1971 | 3150 | 2750 | 0.0504 |
| MORRIS | MINOR MM | 1948 | 1952 | 3100 | 2625 | 0.0828 |
| MORRIS | MINOR MM CONVERTIBLE | 1948 | 1952 | 4466 | 3875 | 0.0568 |
| MORRIS | MINOR SII | 1952 | 1956 | 2166 | 1875 | 0.0592 |
| MORRIS | MINOR SII CONVERTIBLE | 1952 | 1956 | 3716 | 3750 | −0.0914 |
| MORRIS | MINOR SII ESTATE | 1952 | 1956 | 2883 | 2500 | 0.0576 |
| MORRIS | MORRIS MINOR 1000 | 1962 | 1970 | 2433 | 2000 | 0.1155 |
| MORRIS | MORRIS MINOR 1000 ESTATE | 1962 | 1971 | 3150 | 3000 | −0.0373 |
| MORRIS | OXFORD II–IV | 1954 | 1959 | 1466 | 2000 | −0.3278 |
| MORRIS | OXFORD MO | 1948 | 1954 | 2166 | 1500 | 0.324 |
| MORRIS | OXFORD V–VI | 1959 | 1971 | 1708 | 1517 | 0.0326 |
| MORRIS | SIX | 1949 | 1954 | 2233 | 1750 | 0.1703 |
| MORRIS | TEN SERIES M | 1939 | 1948 | 3000 | 2000 | 0.3755 |
| NSU | Ro80 | 1967 | 1977 | 3500 | 3500 | −0.083 |
| NSU | SPORT PRINZ | 1959 | 1967 | 2000 | 1600 | 0.1461 |
| NSU | TT/TTS | 1965 | 1967 | 2650 | 1500 | 0.6198 |
| NSU | WANKEL SPYDER | 1964 | 1967 | 3750 | 3500 | −0.0176 |
| OGLE | SX1000 | 1962 | 1964 | 5150 | 3700 | 0.2763 |
| OPEL | GT1900 lhd | 1968 | 1973 | 4416 | 4000 | 0.0124 |
| OPEL | KADETT RALLYE COUPE | 1966 | 1973 | 2250 | 2200 | −0.0621 |
| OPEL | MANTA SERIES A | 1970 | 1975 | 2200 | 2000 | 0.0087 |
| OPEL | MANTA SERIES B | 1975 | 1988 | 2266 | 2200 | −0.0554 |
| OPEL | MONZA | 1978 | 1987 | 2500 | 3000 | −0.2359 |
| PANHARD | 24CT | 1964 | 1967 | 4125 | 3000 | 0.2607 |
| PANHARD | DYNA 120/130 | 1950 | 1953 | 3500 | 2750 | 0.1671 |
| PANHARD | DYNA JUNIOR | 1952 | 1955 | 2800 | 2500 | 0.0271 |
| PANHARD | PL17 | 1959 | 1964 | 3800 | 3250 | 0.0722 |
| PANTHER | DEVILLE/ROYALE | 1974 | 1985 | 26000 | 7000 | 2.4058 |
| PANTHER | J72 | 1974 | 1981 | 16833 | 9000 | 0.715 |
| PANTHER | LIMA SPORTS | 1976 | 1982 | 5833 | 5000 | 0.0697 |
| PANTHER | RIO | 1975 | 1977 | 5000 | 4000 | 0.1463 |
| PEERLESS | GT | 1957 | 1960 | 7000 | 7500 | −0.1441 |
| PEUGEOT | 203 | 1948 | 1960 | 2625 | 2000 | 0.2036 |
| PEUGEOT | 204 CABRIO | 1966 | 1970 | 5000 | 2500 | 0.8342 |
| PEUGEOT | 204/304 | 1965 | 1980 | 1000 | 1000 | −0.0834 |
| PEUGEOT | 205Gti | 1983 | 1994 | 4000 | 2500 | 0.4674 |
| PEUGEOT | 304 CABRIO | 1970 | 1975 | 4333 | 3500 | 0.1352 |
| PEUGEOT | 403 | 1955 | 1967 | 1983 | 1900 | −0.043 |
| PEUGEOT | 403 CABRIO | 1956 | 1961 | 13500 | 3750 | 2.3007 |
| PEUGEOT | 404 | 1960 | 1975 | 1800 | 1500 | 0.1002 |
| PEUGEOT | 404 CABRIO | 1962 | 1969 | 7275 | 6500 | 0.0262 |
| PEUGEOT | 504 | 1969 | 1982 | 1200 | 2000 | −0.4498 |
| PEUGEOT | 504 CABRIO lhd | 1970 | 1974 | 8000 | 6250 | 0.1737 |
| PEUGEOT | 504 COUPE lhd | 1970 | 1974 | 4833 | 3000 | 0.4771 |
| PEUGEOT | 504 V6 CABRIO lhd | 1974 | 1983 | 1200 | 8000 | −0.8624 |
| PEUGEOT | 604 | 1975 | 1986 | 1500 | 700 | 0.9659 |
| PORSCHE | 356C CABRIO | 1963 | 1965 | 47500 | 20250 | 1.1509 |
| PORSCHE | 356 | 1949 | 1951 | 20000 | 20000 | −0.083 |
| PORSCHE | 356 | 1951 | 1953 | 18000 | 17500 | −0.0569 |
| PORSCHE | 356 | 1954 | 1955 | 12000 | 12250 | −0.1017 |
| PORSCHE | 356 B/C CARRERA | 1963 | 1965 | 64500 | 60000 | −0.0143 |
| PORSCHE | 356 CABRIO | 1951 | 1953 | 25000 | 27500 | −0.1664 |

| MANUFACTURER | ACTUAL CAR | YEAR FROM | YEAR TO | PRESENT VALUE | 1993 VALUE | VALUE SWING |
|---|---|---|---|---|---|---|
| PORSCHE | 356 CABRIO | 1954 | 1955 | 25000 | 15000 | 0.5283 |
| PORSCHE | 356 SPEEDSTER | 1954 | 1958 | 36000 | 39000 | −0.1536 |
| PORSCHE | 356A CARRERA | 1955 | 1959 | 38500 | 35000 | 0.0086 |
| PORSCHE | 356A/B | 1955 | 1963 | 16500 | 12250 | 0.2351 |
| PORSCHE | 356A/B CABRIO | 1955 | 1959 | 33000 | 19000 | 0.5926 |
| PORSCHE | 356C | 1963 | 1965 | 18500 | 13000 | 0.3049 |
| PORSCHE | 356C CABRIO | 1963 | 1965 | 30833 | 32250 | −0.1233 |
| PORSCHE | 911 3.0 TURBO | 1975 | 1977 | 20125 | 15500 | 0.1905 |
| PORSCHE | 911 3.3 TURBO | 1977 | 1986 | 28250 | 26000 | −0.0037 |
| PORSCHE | 911 2.0 | 1964 | 1969 | 14000 | 10750 | 0.1941 |
| PORSCHE | 911 CARRERA | 1973 | 1975 | 17000 | 15000 | 0.0392 |
| PORSCHE | 911 CARRERA 3.2 | 1983 | 1986 | 20000 | 17500 | 0.0479 |
| PORSCHE | 911 CARRERA CABRIO | 1983 | 1986 | 22000 | 25000 | −0.1931 |
| PORSCHE | 911 RSL CARRERA | 1972 | 1973 | 41500 | 35000 | 0.0872 |
| PORSCHE | 911 RST CARRERA | 1972 | 1973 | 38000 | 30000 | 0.1615 |
| PORSCHE | 911E 2.4 | 1971 | 1973 | 17000 | 16500 | −0.0552 |
| PORSCHE | 911E 2.0 | 1968 | 1969 | 13250 | 9500 | 0.279 |
| PORSCHE | 911L/T 2.0 | 1967 | 1971 | 13000 | 9000 | 0.3245 |
| PORSCHE | 911S 2.2 | 1969 | 1971 | 15500 | 13000 | 0.0933 |
| PORSCHE | 911S 2.4 | 1971 | 1973 | 18500 | 18500 | −0.083 |
| PORSCHE | 911S 2.7 | 1973 | 1975 | 11250 | 9750 | 0.058 |
| PORSCHE | 911S 2.0 | 1966 | 1969 | 17000 | 14250 | 0.094 |
| PORSCHE | 911SC 180bhp | 1977 | 1983 | 14500 | 12750 | 0.0428 |
| PORSCHE | 911SC 204bhp | 1980 | 1983 | 14000 | 15000 | −0.1441 |
| PORSCHE | 911SC CABRIO | 1982 | 1883 | 15000 | 17500 | −0.214 |
| PORSCHE | 911T 2.4 | 1971 | 1973 | 16500 | 14000 | 0.0807 |
| PORSCHE | 911T/E 2.2 | 1969 | 1971 | 14750 | 10500 | 0.2881 |
| PORSCHE | 912 | 1965 | 1969 | 6250 | 6500 | −0.1184 |
| PORSCHE | 914–4 | 1969 | 1975 | 4250 | 4750 | −0.1795 |
| PORSCHE | 914–6 | 1969 | 1971 | 7833 | 5500 | 0.3059 |
| PORSCHE | 924 | 1976 | 1985 | 5000 | 5000 | −0.0831 |
| PORSCHE | 924 CARRERA GT | 1979 | 1980 | 14160 | 17500 | −0.2581 |
| PORSCHE | 924 TURBO | 1978 | 1982 | 5666 | 5500 | −0.0554 |
| PORSCHE | 928/928S | 1977 | 1982 | 10250 | 9500 | −0.0106 |
| PORSCHE | 944 | 1981 | 1990 | 6125 | 7500 | −0.2511 |
| PORSCHE | 944 TURBO | 1985 | 1987 | 8875 | 9000 | −0.0958 |
| PORSCHE | CARRERA 3 | 1975 | 1977 | 15500 | 12500 | 0.137 |
| RELIANT | REGAL I–VI | 1952 | 1962 | 750 | 650 | 0.0578 |
| RELIANT | REGAL 3/25 3/30 | 1962 | 1973 | 700 | 600 | 0.0703 |
| RELIANT | SABRE 4 | 1961 | 1963 | 5375 | 4000 | 0.2322 |
| RELIANT | SABRE 5 | 1962 | 1964 | 6500 | 6000 | −0.0066 |
| RELIANT | SCIMITAR GTC | 1980 | 1986 | 7233 | 6250 | 0.0612 |
| RELIANT | SCIMITAR GTE SE5 ESTATE | 1968 | 1975 | 4583 | 4000 | 0.0507 |
| RELIANT | SCIMITAR GTE SE6 ESTATE | 1975 | 1982 | 5250 | 5125 | −0.0607 |
| RELIANT | SCIMITAR SE4A | 1964 | 1966 | 4350 | 4000 | −0.0028 |
| RELIANT | SCIMITAR SE4B | 1966 | 1970 | 4000 | 3625 | 0.0119 |
| RELIANT | SCIMITAR SE4C | 1967 | 1970 | 3900 | 3500 | 0.0217 |
| RENAULT | 16 | 1966 | 1978 | 1600 | 1200 | 0.2223 |
| RENAULT | 4 | 1961 | 1986 | 1100 | 1375 | −0.2667 |
| RENAULT | 4CV | 1947 | 1961 | 3000 | 3000 | −0.0831 |
| RENAULT | 4CV SPORTS | 1952 | 1956 | 4650 | 5000 | −0.1473 |
| RENAULT | 5 GORDINI | 1976 | 1981 | 2000 | 2500 | −0.2663 |
| RENAULT | 5 GT TURBO | 1985 | 1989 | 3000 | 3000 | −0.0831 |
| RENAULT | 5 TURBO I | 1980 | 1982 | 12000 | 12500 | −0.1197 |
| RENAULT | 5 TURBO 2 | 1983 | 1985 | 10500 | 8500 | 0.1327 |
| RENAULT | CARAVELLE 1100 | 1963 | 1968 | 3625 | 3000 | 0.1079 |
| RENAULT | CARAVELLE 956 | 1962 | 1968 | 2250 | 2600 | −0.2063 |
| RENAULT | CARAVELLE 956 CONVERTIBLE | 1962 | 1968 | 3916 | 4000 | −0.1022 |
| RENAULT | CARAVELLE CONVERTIBLE | 1963 | 1968 | 4333 | 4500 | −0.1172 |
| RENAULT | DAUPHINE | 1954 | 1963 | 1966 | 1625 | 0.1095 |
| RENAULT | DAUPHINE GORDINI | 1957 | 1968 | 2166 | 2125 | −0.0652 |
| RENAULT | FLORIDE | 1959 | 1962 | 3100 | 2125 | 0.3379 |
| RENAULT | FLORIDE CONVERTIBLE | 1959 | 1962 | 3750 | 3750 | −0.0831 |
| RENAULT | FUEGO | 1980 | 1988 | 1500 | 1675 | −0.179 |
| RENAULT | R10 | 1970 | 1971 | 1600 | 2000 | −0.2664 |
| RENAULT | R8 | 1962 | 1971 | 1766 | 1425 | 0.1364 |
| RENAULT | R8 GORDINI 1100 | 1964 | 1967 | 3666 | 2750 | 0.2224 |
| RENAULT | R8 GORDINI 1250 | 1967 | 1970 | 4350 | 3250 | 0.2274 |
| RENAULT | R8 1100 | 1964 | 1972 | 1875 | 2000 | −0.1403 |

| MANUFACTURER | ACTUAL CAR | YEAR FROM | YEAR TO | PRESENT VALUE | 1993 VALUE | VALUE SWING |
|---|---|---|---|---|---|---|
| RILEY | 1.5 | 1957 | 1965 | 2750 | 2875 | −0.1228 |
| RILEY | 4/68,4/72 | 1959 | 1969 | 2683 | 1900 | 0.2949 |
| RILEY | ELF 1/2/3 | 1961 | 1969 | 1866 | 2125 | −0.1946 |
| RILEY | KESTREL 1100/1300 | 1965 | 1969 | 2333 | 1425 | 0.5013 |
| RILEY | PATHFINDER/2.6 | 1953 | 1959 | 3083 | 2375 | 0.1903 |
| RILEY | RMA/RME 1.5 | 1945 | 1955 | 7800 | 5750 | 0.2438 |
| RILEY | RMB/RMF 2.5 | 1946 | 1953 | 8916 | 9500 | −0.1394 |
| RILEY | RMC ROADSTER | 1948 | 1950 | 16500 | 15750 | −0.0394 |
| RILEY | RMD dhc | 1948 | 1951 | 14500 | 14000 | −0.0503 |
| ROCHDALE | GT | 1957 | 1961 | 2200 | 2500 | −0.193 |
| ROCHDALE | OLYMPIC SERIES 1/2 | 1960 | 1968 | 3250 | 3000 | −0.0067 |
| ROLLS-ROYCE | SILVER CLOUD 11 | 1959 | 1962 | 22500 | 18000 | 0.1462 |
| ROLLS-ROYCE | SILVER CLOUD 11 dhc | 1959 | 1962 | 76125 | 50000 | 0.3961 |
| ROLLS-ROYCE | CAMARGUE | 1975 | 1985 | 48500 | 35000 | 0.2706 |
| ROLLS-ROYCE | CORNICHE | 1971 | 1977 | 22500 | 19750 | 0.0446 |
| ROLLS-ROYCE | CORNICHE dhc | 1971 | 1977 | 31500 | 33750 | −0.1442 |
| ROLLS-ROYCE | MPW CORNICHE | 1966 | 1970 | 20000 | 22500 | −0.1849 |
| ROLLS-ROYCE | MPW CORNICHE dhc | 1966 | 1970 | 30000 | 35000 | −0.214 |
| ROLLS-ROYCE | PHANTOM V JY SDV | 1960 | 1968 | 75000 | 95000 | −0.2761 |
| ROLLS-ROYCE | PHANTOM V JAMES YOUNG | 1959 | 1968 | 72500 | 50000 | 0.3296 |
| ROLLS-ROYCE | PHANTOM V MPW LIMO | 1959 | 1968 | 67500 | 65000 | −0.0478 |
| ROLLS-ROYCE | PHANTOM VI LIMO | 1968 | 1977 | 70000 | 100000 | −0.3581 |
| ROLLS-ROYCE | SC 111 MPW dhc | 1962 | 1966 | 52000 | 55000 | −0.1331 |
| ROLLS-ROYCE | SILVER 1 CLOUD dhc | 1955 | 1959 | 85000 | 70000 | 0.1135 |
| ROLLS-ROYCE | SILVER CLOUD 1 | 1955 | 1959 | 24000 | 17250 | 0.2758 |
| ROLLS-ROYCE | SILVER CLOUD 111 | 1962 | 1965 | 28750 | 22500 | 0.1717 |
| ROLLS-ROYCE | SILVER CLOUD 111 dhc | 1962 | 1966 | 52500 | 50000 | −0.0372 |
| ROLLS-ROYCE | SILVER CLOUD 111 MPW | 1962 | 1966 | 36000 | 40000 | −0.1747 |
| ROLLS-ROYCE | SILVER CLOUD 111 Flying Spur | 1962 | 1966 | 57500 | 40000 | 0.3181 |
| ROLLS-ROYCE | SILVER CLOUD 111 JY lbw | 1962 | 1966 | 45000 | 60000 | −0.3123 |
| ROLLS-ROYCE | SILVER DAWN | 1949 | 1955 | 29500 | 20000 | 0.3525 |
| ROLLS-ROYCE | SILVER DAWN dhc | 1952 | 1955 | 50000 | 55000 | −0.1664 |
| ROLLS-ROYCE | SILVER SHADOW I | 1965 | 1970 | 11750 | 11750 | −0.083 |
| ROLLS-ROYCE | SILVER SHADOW II | 1977 | 1980 | 14333 | 15750 | −0.1655 |
| ROLLS-ROYCE | SILVER WRAITH HOOPER | 1955 | 1959 | 50000 | 45000 | 0.0188 |
| ROLLS-ROYCE | SILVER WRAITH II | 1977 | 1980 | 15000 | 15000 | −0.083 |
| ROLLS-ROYCE | SILVER WRAITH MPW LIMO | 1955 | 1959 | 60000 | 85000 | −0.3527 |
| ROVER | P3 60/75 | 1948 | 1949 | 4187 | 5000 | −0.2322 |
| ROVER | P4 100 | 1959 | 1962 | 5200 | 3750 | 0.2714 |
| ROVER | P4 105R | 1956 | 1958 | 4516 | 3375 | 0.2268 |
| ROVER | P4 105S | 1956 | 1959 | 5016 | 4500 | 0.022 |
| ROVER | P4 60 | 1954 | 1959 | 5000 | 3250 | 0.4108 |
| ROVER | P4 75 | 1950 | 1954 | 4966 | 4350 | 0.0468 |
| ROVER | P4 75 | 1955 | 1959 | 4966 | 3250 | 0.4012 |
| ROVER | P4 80 | 1959 | 1962 | 3700 | 3125 | 0.0857 |
| ROVER | P4 90 | 1954 | 1959 | 4933 | 3500 | 0.2924 |
| ROVER | P4 95/110 | 1962 | 1964 | 5033 | 3625 | 0.2732 |
| ROVER | P5 3.0 | 1958 | 1967 | 4800 | 3500 | 0.2575 |
| ROVER | P5 COUPE | 1963 | 1967 | 5500 | 4000 | 0.2609 |
| ROVER | P5B 3.5 | 1967 | 1973 | 5233 | 4350 | 0.1031 |
| ROVER | P5B 3.5 COUPE | 1968 | 1975 | 6333 | 4600 | 0.2623 |
| ROVER | P6 2000/2000SC | 1963 | 1972 | 2450 | 1983 | 0.1327 |
| ROVER | P6 2000TC | 1966 | 1972 | 2975 | 2125 | 0.284 |
| ROVER | P6 2200/TC | 1973 | 1976 | 2425 | 2300 | −0.0331 |
| ROVER | P6 3500/3500S | 1968 | 1975 | 3466 | 3425 | −0.072 |
| ROVER | SDI 2000/2300/2600 | 1977 | 1986 | 900 | 900 | −0.0835 |
| ROVER | SDI 3500 | 1976 | 1986 | 1683 | 4500 | −0.6571 |
| ROVER | SDI 3500 VITESSE | 1982 | 1986 | 3433 | 4250 | −0.2593 |
| ROVER | SDI VDP | 1980 | 1986 | 2250 | 2200 | −0.0621 |
| SAAB | 95 BULLNOSE | 1960 | 1965 | 4200 | 4000 | −0.0371 |
| SAAB | 95 ESTATE | 1960 | 1968 | 4000 | 3500 | 0.0479 |
| SAAB | 95 LONGNOSE | 1965 | 1968 | 3633 | 3000 | 0.1103 |
| SAAB | 95 V4 | 1967 | 1970 | 3233 | 3750 | −0.2095 |
| SAAB | 96 TS BULLNOSE | 1960 | 1965 | 4516 | 5000 | −0.1718 |
| SAAB | 96 TS LONGNOSE | 1965 | 1968 | 3900 | 4000 | −0.1059 |
| SAAB | 96 V4 | 1967 | 1979 | 3266 | 3750 | −0.2015 |
| SAAB | 99 TURBO | 1978 | 1983 | 3233 | 2875 | 0.0313 |
| SAAB | SONNET lhd | 1966 | 1974 | 7500 | 5000 | 0.3754 |
| SAAB | SPORT/MONTE CARLO | 1962 | 1966 | 5216 | 4500 | 0.0628 |

| MANUFACTURER | ACTUAL CAR | YEAR FROM | YEAR TO | PRESENT VALUE | 1993 VALUE | VALUE SWING |
|---|---|---|---|---|---|---|
| SIMCA | 1000 | 1962 | 1968 | 1150 | 1000 | 0.0541 |
| SIMCA | 1000 BERTONE | 1962 | 1967 | 2125 | 2500 | -0.2205 |
| SIMCA | 1000 GLS/SPECIAL | 1969 | 1978 | 1650 | 1350 | 0.1209 |
| SIMCA | 1200S | 1967 | 1971 | 2000 | 1750 | 0.0482 |
| SIMCA | 1300/1500 | 1963 | 1966 | 1000 | 1000 | -0.0834 |
| SIMCA | 1301/1501 | 1967 | 1976 | 1200 | 1500 | -0.2665 |
| SIMCA | 9 ARONDE | 1951 | 1955 | 1733 | 1500 | 0.0593 |
| SIMCA | ARONDE | 1956 | 1963 | 2150 | 1250 | 0.5774 |
| SIMCA | OCEANE/PLEIN CEIL | 1957 | 1962 | 2900 | 2500 | 0.0638 |
| SINGER | 11A/111 CONVERTIBLE | 1958 | 1962 | 3700 | 3000 | 0.1308 |
| SINGER | CHAMOIS SPORT | 1966 | 1970 | 1500 | 1350 | 0.019 |
| SINGER | GAZELLE I–V | 1955 | 1965 | 2166 | 1750 | 0.1352 |
| SINGER | GAZELLE CONVERTIBLE | 1956 | 1958 | 3466 | 2500 | 0.2715 |
| SINGER | GAZELLE VI | 1966 | 1967 | 1375 | 850 | 0.4833 |
| SINGER | HUNTER | 1954 | 1956 | 2500 | 2250 | 0.0187 |
| SINGER | NEW GAZELLE | 1967 | 1970 | 1150 | 850 | 0.2406 |
| SINGER | NEW VOGUE | 1966 | 1971 | 1400 | 950 | 0.3514 |
| SINGER | ROASTER 4A/4B | 1949 | 1952 | 7500 | 7000 | -0.0176 |
| SINGER | SM ROADSTER | 1951 | 1955 | 9000 | 8000 | 0.0316 |
| SINGER | SM1500 | 1949 | 1954 | 2250 | 1750 | 0.1792 |
| STANDARD | EIGHT/TEN | 1953 | 1960 | 1266 | 1150 | 0.0096 |
| STANDARD | ENSIGN | 1957 | 1963 | 2050 | 1875 | 0.0024 |
| STANDARD | FLYING 12 | 1945 | 1948 | 3500 | 2000 | 0.6048 |
| STANDARD | FLYING 14 | 1945 | 1948 | 4000 | 2250 | 0.63 |
| STANDARD | FLYING 8 | 1945 | 1948 | 2500 | 1500 | 0.5281 |
| STANDARD | FLYING 8 TOURER | 1945 | 1948 | 4500 | 2500 | 0.6508 |
| STANDARD | LUXURY SIX | 1961 | 1963 | 2550 | 1950 | 0.1989 |
| STANDARD | PENNANT | 1957 | 1960 | 2000 | 1500 | 0.2225 |
| STANDARD | SPORTSMAN | 1956 | 1958 | 2833 | 2300 | 0.1296 |
| STANDARD | VANGUARD I | 1947 | 1952 | 3233 | 2750 | 0.078 |
| STANDARD | VANGUARD II | 1953 | 1955 | 2866 | 2000 | 0.3141 |
| STANDARD | VANGUARD III | 1956 | 1958 | 2390 | 2250 | -0.0261 |
| STANDARD | VIGNALE | 1958 | 1961 | 2250 | 2250 | -0.0831 |
| SUNBEAM | ALPINE | 1969 | 1975 | 1250 | 1000 | 0.1457 |
| SUNBEAM | ALPINE I/II/III | 1959 | 1964 | 6625 | 6000 | 0.0125 |
| SUNBEAM | ALPINE IV–V | 1964 | 1968 | 6341 | 5500 | 0.0572 |
| SUNBEAM | ALPINE ROADSTER | 1953 | 1955 | 12250 | 10250 | 0.0959 |
| SUNBEAM | HARRINGTON GT | 1961 | 1963 | 8800 | 7500 | 0.0759 |
| SUNBEAM | IMP SPORT | 1966 | 1976 | 1550 | 1250 | 0.1372 |
| SUNBEAM | IMP STILETTO | 1967 | 1972 | 1658 | 1575 | -0.0349 |
| SUNBEAM | RAPIER | 1967 | 1976 | 1500 | 1850 | -0.2567 |
| SUNBEAM | RAPIER I–V | 1955 | 1967 | 2741 | 1933 | 0.3003 |
| SUNBEAM | RAPIER II–IIIA CONVERTIBLE | 1958 | 1963 | 8266 | 4250 | 0.7834 |
| SUNBEAM | RAPIER H120 | 1969 | 1976 | 2166 | 1750 | 0.1352 |
| SUNBEAM | TIGER | 1964 | 1966 | 12500 | 10250 | 0.1183 |
| SUNBEAM | TIGER II | 1967 | 1968 | 15350 | 12500 | 0.126 |
| SUNBEAM | VENEZIA | 1963 | 1964 | 6000 | 5000 | 0.1003 |
| SUNBEAM–TALBOT/SUNBEAM | 90 MKII–IIIS | 1950 | 1957 | 5500 | 5000 | 0.0086 |
| SUNBEAM–TALBOT/SUNBEAM | 90 MKII–IIIS CONVERTIBLE | 1950 | 1957 | 8335 | 8500 | -0.1009 |
| SUNBEAM–TALBOT/SUNBEAM | TALBOT 80 | 1948 | 1950 | 3660 | 2750 | 0.2204 |
| SUNBEAM–TALBOT/SUNBEAM | TALBOT 80 dhc | 1948 | 1950 | 6650 | 5000 | 0.2195 |
| SUNBEAM–TALBOT/SUNBEAM | TALBOT 90 | 1948 | 1950 | 4166 | 3500 | 0.0914 |
| SUNBEAM–TALBOT/SUNBEAM | TALBOT 90 dhc | 1948 | 1950 | 7500 | 6500 | 0.058 |
| SWALLOW | DORETTI | 1954 | 1955 | 17000 | 9500 | 0.6409 |
| TALBOT | SUNBEAM LOTUS | 1979 | 1981 | 4500 | 4250 | -0.0291 |
| TOYOTA | CELICA | 1970 | 1977 | 2210 | 1800 | 0.1258 |
| TOYOTA | CELICA | 1977 | 1982 | 1200 | 1500 | -0.2665 |
| TOYOTA | CROWN DELUXE | 1969 | 1971 | 1500 | 2000 | -0.3122 |
| TOYOTA | MR2 | 1985 | 1988 | 4000 | 3250 | 0.1287 |
| TRABANT | P600/601 | 1963 | 1989 | 750 | 1000 | -0.3126 |
| TRIDENT | CLIPPER | 1967 | 1978 | 10000 | 10000 | -0.0831 |
| TRIUMPH | HERALD 13/60 dhc | 1967 | 1971 | 2883 | 2450 | 0.079 |
| TRIUMPH | 1300/TC/1500 | 1965 | 1973 | 1200 | 850 | 0.2945 |
| TRIUMPH | 1500TC | 1973 | 1976 | 1100 | 750 | 0.3447 |
| TRIUMPH | 1800 | 1946 | 1948 | 6000 | 5000 | 0.1003 |
| TRIUMPH | 1850HL | 1972 | 1981 | 1616 | 750 | 0.9756 |
| TRIUMPH | 2000/RENOWN | 1949 | 1954 | 6000 | 5000 | 0.1003 |
| TRIUMPH | 2000MKI/II | 1963 | 1977 | 2166 | 2125 | -0.0652 |
| TRIUMPH | 2500/2.5Pi | 1968 | 1977 | 2416 | 2375 | -0.0672 |

| MANUFACTURER | ACTUAL CAR | YEAR FROM | YEAR TO | PRESENT VALUE | 1993 VALUE | VALUE SWING |
|---|---|---|---|---|---|---|
| TRIUMPH | DOLOMITE 1300/1500 | 1976 | 1981 | 1240 | 1250 | -0.0902 |
| TRIUMPH | DOLOMITE SPRINT | 1973 | 1980 | 3383 | 2625 | 0.1816 |
| TRIUMPH | DOVE GTR4 2+2 | 1961 | 1964 | 10000 | 9000 | 0.0188 |
| TRIUMPH | GT6 MKI/II | 1966 | 1967 | 4100 | 4250 | -0.1154 |
| TRIUMPH | GT6 MKIII | 1970 | 1973 | 4800 | 4500 | -0.022 |
| TRIUMPH | HERALD 1200 & 12/50 | 1961 | 1970 | 1761 | 1500 | 0.0764 |
| TRIUMPH | HERALD 13/60 | 1967 | 1970 | 1750 | 1500 | 0.0697 |
| TRIUMPH | HERALD COUPE | 1959 | 1964 | 1883 | 1750 | -0.0131 |
| TRIUMPH | HERALD/HERALD S | 1959 | 1964 | 1583 | 1350 | 0.0754 |
| TRIUMPH | MAYFLOWER | 1950 | 1953 | 2800 | 2625 | -0.022 |
| TRIUMPH | ROADSTER | 1946 | 1949 | 16500 | 17500 | -0.1354 |
| TRIUMPH | SPITFIRE 1500 | 1974 | 1981 | 3800 | 2963 | 0.1761 |
| TRIUMPH | SPITFIRE 4 | 1962 | 1965 | 4160 | 3375 | 0.1301 |
| TRIUMPH | SPITFIRE MKII | 1965 | 1967 | 4133 | 3000 | 0.2631 |
| TRIUMPH | SPITFIRE MKIII/IV | 1967 | 1974 | 4416 | 2625 | 0.5424 |
| TRIUMPH | STAG | 1970 | 1977 | 9166 | 7500 | 0.1207 |
| TRIUMPH | TOLEDO | 1970 | 1976 | 900 | 600 | 0.3761 |
| TRIUMPH | TR2 | 1953 | 1956 | 11000 | 10500 | -0.0394 |
| TRIUMPH | TR250 | 1967 | 1968 | 9850 | 12000 | -0.2473 |
| TRIUMPH | TR3/TR3A | 1955 | 1961 | 11316 | 11000 | -0.0567 |
| TRIUMPH | TR3B | 1961 | 1962 | 11625 | 9500 | 0.1221 |
| TRIUMPH | TR4 | 1961 | 1965 | 9500 | 8500 | 0.0248 |
| TRIUMPH | TR4A | 1965 | 1967 | 9961 | 8500 | 0.0745 |
| TRIUMPH | TR5Pi | 1967 | 1968 | 11750 | 10500 | 0.0261 |
| TRIUMPH | TR6 | 1968 | 1976 | 10166 | 8500 | 0.0967 |
| TRIUMPH | TR7 | 1976 | 1981 | 2566 | 1900 | 0.2384 |
| TRIUMPH | TR7 CONVERTIBLE | 1980 | 1982 | 4066 | 2625 | 0.4202 |
| TRIUMPH | TR8 lhd | 1978 | 1980 | 7833 | 8000 | -0.1021 |
| TRIUMPH | VITESSE 1600/2.0 | 1962 | 1968 | 2533 | 2500 | -0.0708 |
| TRIUMPH | VITESSE CONVERTIBLE | 1962 | 1968 | 3733 | 3250 | 0.0533 |
| TRIUMPH | VITESSE MKII | 1968 | 1971 | 3050 | 2900 | -0.0357 |
| TRIUMPH | VITESSE MKII CONVERTIBLE | 1968 | 1971 | 4750 | 4000 | 0.089 |
| TURNER | 950 SPORTS | 1957 | 1959 | 5250 | 6250 | -0.2298 |
| TURNER | A30 SPORTS | 1955 | 1957 | 5500 | 4000 | 0.2609 |
| TURNER | CLIMAX SPORTS | 1957 | 1966 | 8000 | 7500 | -0.0219 |
| TURNER | MKII/III SPORTS | 1960 | 1966 | 5500 | 5500 | -0.083 |
| TVR | 1300 | 1971 | 1972 | 2400 | 3500 | -0.3712 |
| TVR | 3000M | 1972 | 1979 | 7340 | 6750 | -0.0029 |
| TVR | 3000S | 1978 | 1979 | 11500 | 10000 | 0.0545 |
| TVR | 350i | 1983 | 1988 | 8000 | 10000 | -0.2665 |
| TVR | GRANTURA I/II/IIA/III | 1957 | 1964 | 5000 | 6000 | -0.2358 |
| TVR | GRANTURA 1800S | 1966 | 1967 | 4700 | 5500 | -0.2164 |
| TVR | GRIFFITH 200/400 | 1963 | 1965 | 21250 | 25000 | -0.2206 |
| TVR | TAIMAR | 1976 | 1979 | 8166 | 6750 | 0.1094 |
| TVR | TASMIN | 1979 | 1983 | 5883 | 7000 | -0.2294 |
| TVR | TUSCAN V6 | 1969 | 1971 | 7416 | 6250 | 0.088 |
| TVR | TUSCAN V8 /V8 SE | 1967 | 1970 | 18500 | 15000 | 0.1309 |
| TVR | VIXEN SI-III | 1967 | 1972 | 5340 | 5750 | -0.1485 |
| TVR | VIXEN SIV/1600M | 1972 | 1977 | 5500 | 5500 | -0.083 |
| UNIPOWER | UNIPOWER GT | 1966 | 1970 | 4000 | 4000 | -0.083 |
| VANDEN PLAS | 4 LITRE | 1959 | 1968 | 4416 | 4500 | -0.1002 |
| VANDEN PLAS | 3 LITRE I–II | 1959 | 1964 | 3200 | 2250 | 0.304 |
| VANDEN PLAS | 4 LITRE R | 1964 | 1968 | 4066 | 4000 | -0.0679 |
| VANDEN PLAS | PRINCESS 1100 | 1963 | 1968 | 3583 | 1750 | 0.8779 |
| VANDEN PLAS | PRINCESS 1300 | 1967 | 1974 | 4666 | 2250 | 0.9014 |
| VANDEN PLAS | PRINCESS 1500/1750 | 1975 | 1980 | 2000 | 1750 | 0.0482 |
| VAUXHALL | 10/12/14 | 1939 | 1948 | 2800 | 2375 | 0.0811 |
| VAUXHALL | CHEVETTE HS 2300 | 1978 | 1980 | 3766 | 2850 | 0.2117 |
| VAUXHALL | CRESTA E | 1954 | 1957 | 3233 | 3000 | -0.0119 |
| VAUXHALL | CRESTA PC | 1965 | 1972 | 1650 | 1250 | 0.2106 |
| VAUXHALL | DROOPSNOOT | 1974 | 1975 | 3166 | 3750 | -0.2259 |
| VAUXHALL | FIRENZA SPORT | 1971 | 1976 | 2250 | 1575 | 0.3097 |
| VAUXHALL | MAGNUM COUPE | 1973 | 1978 | 2016 | 900 | 1.053 |
| VAUXHALL | ROYALE COUPE | 1978 | 1982 | 1900 | 1500 | 0.1614 |
| VAUXHALL | VELOX | 1948 | 1951 | 2350 | 2250 | -0.0424 |
| VAUXHALL | VELOX E | 1951 | 1957 | 2883 | 2750 | -0.0387 |
| VAUXHALL | VELOX/CRESTA PA | 1957 | 1962 | 3950 | 3250 | 0.1146 |
| VAUXHALL | VELOX/CRESTA PB | 1962 | 1965 | 1750 | 1750 | -0.0828 |
| VAUXHALL | VENTURA/VICTOR 3300 | 1968 | 1972 | 1833 | 1200 | 0.4003 |

| MANUFACTURER | ACTUAL CAR | YEAR FROM | YEAR TO | PRESENT VALUE | 1993 VALUE | VALUE SWING |
|---|---|---|---|---|---|---|
| VAUXHALL | VICTOR 101FC | 1964 | 1967 | 1966 | 1125 | 0.6023 |
| VAUXHALL | VICTOR 1600FD | 1967 | 1972 | 1125 | 500 | 1.0642 |
| VAUXHALL | VICTOR F | 1957 | 1961 | 2066 | 2150 | −0.119 |
| VAUXHALL | VICTOR FB | 1961 | 1964 | 950 | 1450 | −0.3991 |
| VAUXHALL | VICTOR/VENTURA FE | 1972 | 1976 | 1733 | 1400 | 0.1349 |
| VAUXHALL | VISCOUNT | 1966 | 1972 | 1650 | 1500 | 0.0086 |
| VAUXHALL | VIVA BRABHAM | 1967 | 1968 | 3633 | 2000 | 0.6657 |
| VAUXHALL | VIVA GT | 1968 | 1970 | 2345 | 1500 | 0.4334 |
| VAUXHALL | VIVA HA | 1963 | 1966 | 1133 | 925 | 0.1229 |
| VAUXHALL | VIVA HB | 1966 | 1970 | 1075 | 750 | 0.3142 |
| VAUXHALL | VX 4/90FD | 1967 | 1972 | 1466 | 750 | 0.7922 |
| VAUXHALL | VX4/90FB | 1961 | 1964 | 1766 | 2250 | −0.2804 |
| VAUXHALL | VX4/90FC | 1964 | 1967 | 1800 | 1500 | 0.1002 |
| VAUXHALL | WYVERN | 1948 | 1951 | 2033 | 2000 | −0.0679 |
| VAUXHALL | WYVERN E | 1951 | 1957 | 2260 | 2250 | −0.0791 |
| VOLKSWAGEN | 1302/1302S | 1970 | 1972 | 3237 | 2450 | 0.2115 |
| VOLKSWAGEN | 1303/1303S | 1972 | 1975 | 2875 | 2717 | −0.0297 |
| VOLKSWAGEN | BEETLE | 1954 | 1960 | 5500 | 3625 | 0.3913 |
| VOLKSWAGEN | BEETLE | 1960 | 1965 | 3700 | 3250 | 0.044 |
| VOLKSWAGEN | BEETLE 1100 | 1945 | 1954 | 6583 | 4500 | 0.3413 |
| VOLKSWAGEN | BEETLE 1200 | 1966 | 1978 | 3200 | 2750 | 0.067 |
| VOLKSWAGEN | BEETLE 1200L | 1979 | 1985 | 3550 | 3500 | −0.07 |
| VOLKSWAGEN | BEETLE 1300 | 1965 | 1973 | 3250 | 2750 | 0.0837 |
| VOLKSWAGEN | BEETLE 1500 | 1966 | 1973 | 3450 | 3000 | 0.0544 |
| VOLKSWAGEN | CABRIO | 1949 | 1954 | 8250 | 8500 | −0.11 |
| VOLKSWAGEN | CABRIO | 1954 | 1960 | 7625 | 7000 | −0.0012 |
| VOLKSWAGEN | CABRIO 1302/1303 L/S | 1970 | 1972 | 8125 | 10125 | −0.2642 |
| VOLKSWAGEN | CABRIO 1500 | 1966 | 1973 | 7750 | 8250 | −0.1386 |
| VOLKSWAGEN | GOLF MK1 GTi | 1978 | 1984 | 2583 | 3250 | −0.2712 |
| VOLKSWAGEN | KARMANN GHIA | 1955 | 1974 | 6500 | 7500 | −0.2053 |
| VOLKSWAGEN | KARMANN GHIA dhc | 1958 | 1974 | 8416 | 9500 | −0.1876 |
| VOLKSWAGEN | SCIROCCO | 1974 | 1992 | 1750 | 2000 | −0.1976 |
| VOLVO | 121/122 | 1956 | 1967 | 3066 | 2500 | 0.1247 |
| VOLVO | 122S/B18 | 1961 | 1967 | 3233 | 4000 | −0.2588 |
| VOLVO | 123GT | 1966 | 1967 | 3800 | 4000 | −0.1288 |
| VOLVO | 144 | 1967 | 1974 | 1100 | 900 | 0.1202 |
| VOLVO | 164 | 1968 | 1973 | 2250 | 4000 | −0.4842 |
| VOLVO | 244 | 1974 | 1980 | 1625 | 1800 | −0.1722 |
| VOLVO | P1800/P1800S | 1961 | 1969 | 4950 | 6750 | −0.3275 |
| VOLVO | P1800E | 1967 | 1972 | 4450 | 4750 | −0.1409 |
| VOLVO | P1800ES ESTATE | 1971 | 1973 | 4850 | 5050 | −0.1193 |
| VOLVO | PV544 | 1958 | 1965 | 4500 | 4000 | 0.0316 |
| WOLSELEY | 1100 | 1962 | 1968 | 2416 | 1500 | 0.4768 |
| WOLSELEY | 12/48 | 1938 | 1948 | 3000 | 2000 | 0.3755 |
| WOLSELEY | 1300 | 1967 | 1971 | 2450 | 1375 | 0.6333 |
| WOLSELEY | 14/60 | 1939 | 1948 | 3500 | 2500 | 0.2839 |
| WOLSELEY | 15/50 | 1956 | 1958 | 2825 | 2750 | −0.058 |
| WOLSELEY | 15/60 16/60 | 1958 | 1971 | 2716 | 1625 | 0.5327 |
| WOLSELEY | 1500 | 1957 | 1965 | 2800 | 2500 | 0.0271 |
| WOLSELEY | 18/85 | 1967 | 1972 | 1833 | 1200 | 0.4003 |
| WOLSELEY | 2200 WEDGE/SIX | 1975 | 1972 | 1933 | 1400 | 0.2659 |
| WOLSELEY | 4/44 | 1952 | 1956 | 2866 | 2500 | 0.0514 |
| WOLSELEY | 4/50 | 1952 | 1954 | 2766 | 1350 | 0.8791 |
| WOLSELEY | 6/80 | 1948 | 1954 | 3638 | 2500 | 0.3346 |
| WOLSELEY | 6/90 | 1954 | 1956 | 3300 | 2000 | 0.5131 |
| WOLSELEY | 6/90 | 1956 | 1959 | 3100 | 2500 | 0.1372 |
| WOLSELEY | 6/99 6/110 | 1959 | 1968 | 2833 | 1925 | 0.3497 |
| WOLSELEY | HORNET | 1963 | 1969 | 2533 | 1900 | 0.2225 |

# MODEL CAR OF THE YEAR

Last year's winner – the evocative Morgan sports car – was a fine example of the new breed of affordable mass production miniatures which are emerging from companies such as Vitesse and Minichamps. Such competition is good news for collectors, but inevitably the choice of subjects has to have mass appeal to warrant the tooling up costs. However, alongside these giants are a number of dedicated manufacturers specialising in smaller productions of hand crafted examples featuring the rare, the humble, and the specialist motor

cars from our past. This year's Model of the Year is from one of the leading companies in this field, Somerville Models from Lincolnshire. The honoured model is their new range of the Austin Allegro Series III, which is available in five colours (including an Avon & Somerset police version) all costing around £70.00 via the established model shops.

Loved or hated, the Allegro (see Stanley 100 page 99) was an instantly recognizable design and therefore makes a distinctive model. The original BL Series III brochures boasted 30 body colours and 15 model variations, the most conspicuous alteration being the rectangular or twin headlamp designs. Somerville have finished each car in the most beautiful detail. Looking at these pictures you might imagine them to be just the same as an old Dinky or Corgi model but in your hands you can feel real quality. They are considerably heavier and with a glazed paint finish that

just feels like a real car. Under the guiding hand of Doug McHard and his wife Roly, a small team of skilled craftsmen and women manufacture every part. Perfectly scaled and detailed road tyres, clear glass windows which fit perfectly and tiny etched wipers with the correct satin finish. Care is taken to recreate the particular BL interior trim of the time, chrome that doesn't appear over-bright, even the minute BL boot logo. This may not be a crowd pleasing Shelby Cobra in full racing colours, but it is a brilliant example of Somerville's mastery of ⅓rd scale model engineering.

Started 18 years ago by Doug with a model London Taxi, the company has grown, moved and built up a reputation for creating interesting models, including Ford Anglias, Rovers and Rileys through to Sunbeam Talbots and ranges of early Saabs and Volvos. Doug's own background embraces art design, engineering, plus 10 years at Meccano. As their Marketing Director he saw the potential for limited quality production runs of collectors' cars which Meccano's Dinky Cars would see as commercially impractical. Part of the fun, of course, is in choosing the cars.

Now with Roly undertaking much of the revered Somerville paintwork, the McHard's sell out everything they produce and waiting lists exist for most of their models. There is even a Somerville Society which unites collectors and offers them rare, limited edition cars: These models all appreciate in value and it's easy to see why.

# INDEX

# Miller's Collectors Cars Price Guide 1998-1999

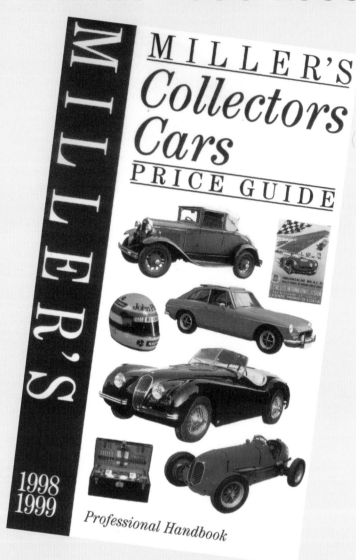

**£19.99**

## For anyone interested in collectors cars, this is a must!

With over 2,000 new photographs the guide reviews all aspects of collecting from veteran and vintage to today's collectable cars. Special attention is given to Formula 1 automobilia and American cars, with an exciting in-depth feature on the desirable Jaguar. For the first time Miller's presents "Miller's Starter Classics", an invaluable feature full of helpful tips on selected marques for the enthusiast on a budget. A wide range of choices are included that offer affordable, reliable and interesting classic motoring. Marques are presented alphabetically and each picture is accompanied by a detailed caption listing year of manufacture, condition, degree of originality and a price range. An indispensable authority among car experts, dealers and enthusiasts Miller's Collectors Cars Price Guide is the only illustrated collectors car price guide available.

New edition available from October 1997

## Available from all good bookshops and specialist wholesalers. In case of difficulty please phone 01933 443863

Miller's Publications is part of Reed Books Limited
Registered Office: Michelin House, 81 Fulham Road, London, SW3 6RB
Registered in England No: 1527729